M000080706

ORIGINAL JOURNALS

OF THE

LEWIS AND CLARK EXPEDITION

1804-1806

WITH FACSIMILES, MAPS, PLANS, VIEWS, PORTRAITS, AND A BIBLIOGRAPHY

VOLUME SIX

PART I

*Scientific Data accompanying the Journals of Lewis and Clark;
Geography, Ethnology, Zoölogy*

*Of this Edition on Van Gelder Hand-made Paper
two hundred copies only have been printed
of which this is*

No.

The Southern History Co.   Eng by Williams N.Y.

ORIGINAL JOURNALS

OF THE

LEWIS AND CLARK EXPEDITION

1804-1806

PRINTED FROM THE ORIGINAL MANUSCRIPTS
in the Library of the American Philosophical Society and
by direction of its Committee on Historical Documents

TOGETHER WITH

MANUSCRIPT MATERIAL OF LEWIS AND CLARK
from other sources, including Note-Books, Letters, Maps, etc.,
and the Journals of Charles Floyd and Joseph Whitehouse

NOW FOR THE FIRST TIME PUBLISHED IN FULL
AND EXACTLY AS WRITTEN

Edited, with Introduction, Notes, and Index, by

REUBEN GOLD THWAITES, LL.D.

Editor of " The Jesuit Relations and Allied Documents," etc.

VOLUME SIX

Part I

NEW YORK

DODD, MEAD & COMPANY

1905

Copyright, 1905
BY THE STATE HISTORICAL SOCIETY OF WISCONSIN

Copyright, 1905
BY JULIA CLARK VOORHIS
ELEANOR GLASGOW VOORHIS

Copyright, 1905
BY THE AMERICAN PHILOSOPHICAL SOCIETY

Copyright, 1905
BY DODD, MEAD & COMPANY

Published July, 1905

THE UNIVERSITY PRESS
CAMBRIDGE, U. S. A.

To

THEODORE ROOSEVELT, LL.D.

PRESIDENT OF THE UNITED STATES

Upon the Hundredth Anniversary of the Departure of the
Trans-Mississippi Expedition of Lewis and Clark, this
first publication of the Original Records of
their "Winning of the West" is most
respectfully dedicated

MADISON, WISCONSIN
May 14, 1904

Original Journals of the
Lewis & Clark Expedition

Edited, with Introduction, Notes, and Index by
Reuben Gold Thwaites

As Published in 1904

Volume VI, Parts 1 & 2

Vol. VI, Parts 1 & 2 Trade Paperback ISBN: 1-58218-657-X
Vol. VI, Parts 1 & 2 Hardcover ISBN: 1-58218-666-9

All rights reserved, which includes the right to reproduce this book
or portions thereof in any form whatsoever except as provided by the
U. S. Copyright Law. For information address Digital Scanning, Inc.

Digital Scanning and Publishing is a leader in the electronic republication
of historical books and documents. We publish many of our titles as
eBooks, as well as traditional hardcover and trade paper editions. DSI is
commited to bringing many traditional and little known books back to
life, retaining the look and feel of the original work.

©2001 DSI Digital Reproduction
First DSI Printing: February 2001

Published by DIGITAL SCANNING, INC.
Scituate, MA 02066
www.digitalscanning.com

Original Journals of the Lewis and Clark Expedition
Four Photographs supplied with permission by
Ernst Mayr Library of the Museum of Comparative Zoology
Harvard University, Cambridge, MA 02138
"Snags On the Missouri River" (Vol. 1 part 1)
"Winter Village of the Minatarres" Vol. 1 Part II)
"Fort Mackenzie" (Vol. II Part 1)
"Indians Hunting the Bison" (Vol. III, Part 1)

CONTENTS TO VOL. VI

PART I

THE ORIGINAL JOURNALS OF CAPTAINS MERI-
WETHER LEWIS AND WILLIAM CLARK. *Scientific
Data*

LIST OF ILLUSTRATIONS

Vol. VI — Part I

The Original Journals of Captains Meriwether Lewis and William Clark

---

SCIENTIFIC DATA ACCOMPANYING THE SAME

SCIENTIFIC DATA ACCOMPANYING
The ORIGINAL JOURNALS OF
LEWIS AND CLARK

I.   GEOGRAPHY

A.   COURSES AND DISTANCES

THE courses and distances were usually inserted in the journals at the close of each day's record; when so given, they have been allowed to stand in the text. In other places, they were grouped consecutively for a number of days, or for some stretch of the route.   In such cases, we have transferred them from the text to this division of the record, indicating the writer of each section and the codex wherein found. — ED.]

Distances of the Missouri and each days assending,[1] from the mouth

		21	miles to St Charles

miles, 83
$$\begin{cases} 3\frac{1}{4} \\ 18 \\ 9 \\ 10 \\ 10 \\ 18 \\ 15\frac{1}{2} \end{cases}$$

104¾   To the *Gasconnade* River S. S.

34
$$\begin{cases} 4 \\ 17 \\ 13 \end{cases}$$

138¾   Great *Osarge* River S. S.

[1] The following is found in Codex A, pp. 134, 135, and is in Clark's hand.

[3]

$63\frac{1}{2}$ { 5 / $17\frac{1}{2}$ / 12 / 14 / 14

$201\frac{1}{4}$ *Mine* River South Side

25 { 12 / 13

$226\frac{1}{4}$ the two Rivers of *Charlton* N. S.

19 { 10 / 9

$245\frac{1}{4}$ Old *Missouri* village N. S.

9 { 9

$254\frac{1}{4}$ *Grand* River North Side

110 { 8 / 12 / 10 / $17\frac{1}{2}$ / $6\frac{3}{4}$ / $7\frac{1}{2}$ / $10\frac{1}{2}$ / $3\frac{1}{2}$ / $11\frac{1}{2}$ / 13 / $9\frac{3}{4}$

$364\frac{1}{4}$ To the *Kanzas* River South S.^{d}

67 { 7 / 10 / 12 / $11\frac{1}{2}$ / $11\frac{1}{4}$ / 15

431   To upper or 2nd old Village of the *Kanzas*. S. S.

49 { $10\frac{3}{4}$ / 12 / 14 / $12\frac{1}{4}$

480   To the *Nordaway* River N. S.

[4]

30 $\left\{\begin{array}{l} 14 \\ 10 \\ 6 \end{array}\right.$

510 To the Grand *Nemahar* River S. S.

60 $\left\{\begin{array}{l} 20\frac{1}{2} \\ 9\frac{1}{2} \\ 9\frac{3}{4} \\ 20\frac{1}{4} \end{array}\right.$

570 *Baldpated Prarie* North Side

60 $\left\{\begin{array}{l} 18 \\ 10 \\ 18 \\ 14 \end{array}\right.$

630 Mile = 210 Leagues to the Great *River Platt* on the South Side.

12   12

642 To Camp [White Catfish July 22–28, 1804.]

[Field notes and survey of the Great Falls of the Missouri, made by Clark, June 17–19, 1805. — ED.[1]]

Courses of the Missouri from the commencement of the portage below Portage River to the most South-Eastwardly bend above the Medicine River, noting the particular Cataracts cascades and the hight they fall as measured; together with an estimate of the decline of the water in rapids &c &c. Sept. [June] 17 & 18th 1805. (S. E. Side)

S. 9° E 286 poles to the enterence of portage river 55 feet
yd² wide at 80 poles a rapid of 4 feet,
the computed decent of the water above
is 4 feet together makes   8

S 10° W. 280 Po: from the enterence of portage River up
the Lar⁴ Side of the Missouri. the com-
puted distance the water [falls] in this distance is about 10 feet 10

[1] The following survey notes are found in the Clark-Voorhis note-book, No. 1. They were copied by Lewis in Codex E, pp. 103–106, with some variations, chiefly due to mistranscription. Lewis, however, makes the final estimate 352 feet, 2¾ inches, instead of Clark's 360 feet, 2¾ inches. See map in our vol. ii, pp. 176, 178, under date of June 20, 1805. — ED.

S 10° E 160 Po. d° . . d° . . d° . . d° Decent of 6

South 240 Po. d° . . d° . . d° . . d° computed decent of 18

S. 81° W. 400 Po. d° . . d° . . d° . . d° computed decent of 13
passing a deep small rivene in this course.

S. 15° W. 160. Poles. the decent of the water within which
distance is about five feet river inclosed in
rocks 5

S 75° W. 80. Poles. to the enterance of a Steep rivene
at which there is a fall of 3 feet which
aded to the probable decent of the water
in that distance 2 feet makes 5

N. 82° W. 340. Poles. to the Grand Cataract of *87 feet* $^3/_4$
of an inch. Computed decent of water in
this distance 6 feet. The river at this
Cataract 280 yards wide and just below 93
yards wide total. . . . . 93 ¾

S 24° W. 90 Poles. passing a fall of 2 feet purpinducular
which added to the estimated decent of 13
feet within the first 200 yd^s next above the
Cataract makes a decent in this distance
rather more than 15

S 19° W. 80. Poles. passing a rivene and cascade decent
about 3

S 11° W. 80 Poles passing a Cascade of 4 feet, which together with the probable decent of the
water 2 feet is 6

S 31° W 320 Poles. opposit to a rapid of 3 feet 6 inch fall
which added to the probable decent of the
water within this distance of 5 feet 6 inches is 9

2616 river inclosed in rocks of a Dark colour 191 ¾

S 52° W. 178 Poles. through a handsom leavel plain, the
river makeing a bend to the right decent
of the water probably about three feet 3

S 40° W. 970 Poles. to a fall of 19 feet, below which
there is a deep rivene at the enterance of
which a fall of 5 feet which added to the
probable decent in this distance of 10 feet
makes 34

REMARKABLE HILLS ON THE UPPER MISSOURI

N. 84° W.	102	Poles to the 2nd Great Cataract of *47 feet 8 inches* the river at this Cataract is 473 yards wide and confined clifts of rocks	47.8
N. 86° W.	135	Poles. passing a fall of 6 feet 7 inches which added to the probable decent of the water above the pitch of 47 feet 8 inches makes a fall of	14.7
S 49° W.	58	Poles along the river water verry rapid a probable decline of 2 feet	2
S 78° W.	156	Poles. to a large fountain near the river probable decent of the water in this distance may be 3 feet	3
S 25° W.	124	Poles. on the river passing several small rapids and swift water the probable decent in this instance four feet	4
S 35° W.	240	Poles. passing a rock in the river an three trees on the Lar^d Bank the fall of the water within this distance at least 8 feet . .	8
S 58° W.	88	Poles. up the river, the probable decent in this distance Eighteen inches	1.6
S 40° W.	80	Poles. to the upper pitch of *26 feet 5 inches* river is here 580 yards wide. to this fall add the probable decent in this distance of *2 feet,* also [o]ne pitch above of *5 feet,* and the decent from the head of the rapids of *18 feet* exclusive of the 5 feet pitch makeing in all *38 feet 5 inches* fall	51.5

4747 poles	Total Falls	360.2 ¾

= 14 miles ¾ and 27 poles

S. 81° W.	320	Poles to the head of the rapids passed a rivene
S. 55° W.	130	Poles along the river. low banks
S 36° W.	278	Poles to a tree on the edge of the water pass^d a grove at 120 poles opposit to which the river is 1400 yards wide
S 6° W.	140	Poles. to á small grove at a rapid on Ld Side.
S 64° E.	78	Poles to the lower point of a timber in a deep bend.
S 14° E.	90	Poles to a tree in the bend opposit to some low timber.
S 17° W.	160	Poles to the river opposit to the enterance of Medicine River which is 137 yards wide, and the Missouri just above it is 300 yards wide.
S 1° W.	88	Poles opposit to the lower point of a Small Island.

S. 45° E   170 Poles.   to some low timber near some old Lodges.

S. 13° E.   380 Poles.   to the river opposit the lower point of *White Bear* Island

N. 88° E.   70 Poles.   opposit to the lower point of a Second Island which is small.

N. 71° E.   120 Poles.   to a rockey hill side opposit to a third Island which is seperated from the Lar^d Shore by a very narrow chanel.

S 25° E   664 poles to a bend of the river, passing the upper points of the 1st & 3rd Islands (at our camp) at 144 poles, and flattery run at 284 further river wide still low banks.

S 70° E.   160 Poles to the top of a high hill near the moste extreme S Easterly bend of the river. from this point the Missouri bears S 85° W. for about 10 miles. the gap of the Mt^s where the Missouri enters bears S. 25° W. [blank space in MS.] miles and the Pinical of the South Mt^s bears N 84° E.

☞ from this Survey and estimate it results, that the Missouri experiences a decent of 360 feet 2 inches and ¾ in the distance of [14¾] Miles and [27] Poles.

Portage N° 1

The course from the White Bear Islands above the portage N. 42° E 4 miles leaveing the riveens of flattery run to the right. thence a course to the South Extremity of a ridge North of the South Mountains for 8 miles & a half passing three riveens, the 2^d is willow run. 11 miles from the Islands. Thence a course to the highest pinical of the North Mountain, leaveing the riveens of Portage or red Creek to the right, & the riveens of the river to the left to the mouth of Portage Creek 4 miles & a half, to the perogue which is on the river North Side & nearly opposit the place we buried Sundery articles is 1 mile down the river, The Swivel we hid under the rocks in a clift near the river a little above our lower camp

Courses & Distance from White Bear Islands to the mouth of Portage Creek

N 42° E   4 miles to a ellevated part of the Plain
N 66° E   3 miles passed the head of a Drean
N 45° E   4 miles to willow run
N. 18 E.   4 miles passed the head of a Drean
N. 10° W.   2 miles to the mouth of Portage Creek
N. 9. W.   ¾ & 46 P. to the perogue on South side of the R.
_____
17 ¾ & 46 P.   Portage through an open butifull plain

Course of the Missouri through the 1ʂᵗ Rocky Mountain and distance estimated.[1]

S. 20° W.   ³⁄₄ to a high clift   the mountain on L.S.   passed the Pine Island at ¼   a Small run above on L.S. & the Lᵈ & Stᵈ points.

West   ¼ to a bend on the Starᵈ Side   High Clifts
South   ¼ to a bend on the Larboard Side   dᵒ
N. 60° E   ½ to a bend on the Starboard Side   dᵒ
            passed an Island
S. 20° W.   ½ to a bend on the Larboard Side   dᵒ
West   ½ to a bend on the Starboard Side   dᵒ
S. 30° E   1 to a bend on the Larᵈ Side   passᵈ an Island L.
West   1¼ to a bend on the Starboard Side
S. 5° W   ½ to a point of rocks in a Larᵈ bend
N. 75° W   ³⁄₄ to a bend on the Starᵈ Side (Campᵈ 17 July)   Clifts
S. 15 W   1¼ to a Larᵈ bend   a high Clift of M :
West   1¼ to the mouth of Dearbourn's River Stᵈ Side 80 yds. wide & furnishes a considerable qtʸ of water & has a gravelery bottom
S. 45. W   2½ to a Starboard bend
S. 8° E   6½ to the Center of a bend on the Larᵈ Side passing Several Small bends   passed a Small Creek on Larᵈ at 1 mile   an Island on Stᵈ
S. 80° W.   ½ to a tree in the center of the Starᵈ bend
S. 20° W.   1½ to the center of the Starᵈ bend   psᵈ an Isᵈ
S. 70° E   ¼ to a bluff in the Starᵈ bend
S. 75 W.   1½ to the Center of the Stᵈ bend passing a Small Creek at ½ M on Stᵈ Side
S. 5° W   ½ to the enterence of a large Creek 30 yards wide in the Starᵈ bend ordways creek
S. 30° E   2½ to the center of a bend on the Larᵈ Side   the vallie now widens
S. 40° W.   ³⁄₄ to the center of a Starᵈ Bend
S. 85° E   2 to the center of a Larᵈ bend passing three short bends. (campᵈ 18ᵗʰ July)
South   ¼ to a pine tree on the Starᵈ Side bend
S. 85° E   2 to the center of a Larᵈ bend
S 38° W   1 to a pine in the Stᵈ bend

[1] The following matter is found in Codex G, pp. 26, 27, in Clark's handwriting, and describes the route from July 17 to 20, 1805, inclusive. — ED.

South   1½ to the Center of the Star.ᵈ bend
N. 10° W. 2½ to the Center of the Lar.ᵈ bend
S. 30 E 1¼ to the Center of the Star.ᵈ Bend
S. 25° E 4½ to the Center of the Lar.ᵈ Bend
S. 28° W 1 to the Center of the Starᵈ bend passing two Islands near the commencement
S. 60° E 1¼ to the Center of a Starᵈ Bend
N. 70° E 1½ to the enterence of a Small Creek in a Larᵈ bend passing an Island near Starᵈ Side
S. 25° E 1½ to a point of rocks in a bend on the St.ᵈ side those rock[s] put in to the river on both Sides, are purpendicular and about 1200 feet high, this place has So Singular appearance that I call it the gate, the water appears to have forced its way through this emence body of Solid rock, and thrown on either Side below Collums of rock mountains high
S. 55° E ¼ to the Center of a Larᵈ Bend
S 10° W 3½ to a bend on the Larᵈ Side passing an Islᵈ at 1¼ in Center of the river (campᵈ 19ᵗʰ July.)
S. 40° W ½ to a high rock in a Larᵈ Bend here the high and perpundicular rocks Cease and the Vallies widen to more than their usial extent Since we have entered the mountains
S. 55° W. 1 to the center of the Starᵈ Bend at which place a large Creek falls in behind Some Islands on the Starᵈ Side Potts Creek Indians set the Prarie on fire up this Crᵏ

50¼

Course of the Missouri from the Gate to the three forks.[1]

S. 64° E 2½ to the center of the Larᵈ Bend, passing two Islands, the hills again the banks of the river at 1¾ miles
S. 15° E ¼ to the center of a Starboard bend
East 1½ to the center of a Larᵈ Bend passed Some Islands on the Larᵈ Side
S. 12° E 1½ to the Center of a Starᵈ Bend passing a Small Creek on Larᵈ Side at ¾ of a M.

[1] The following is found in Codex G, pp. 34–37, in Clark's handwriting, and describes the route from July 20 to 27, 1805, inclusive. — Ed.

S.	50° E	1¼	to the Center of a Lar^d Bend
S.	20° E	2½	to the Center of a Star^d Bend
S.	65 E	2	to a point in the Star^d Bend, passed three Islands at 1 m
N.	75° E	2	to the Center of a Lar^d Bend passing an Island. (*Camped 20th July*)
S.	5° W.	½	to a Lar^d Point ops^d an Island
S.	30° E	1	to the center of a Lar^d Bend the hills now become low and the Countrey opens on either Side.
S.	25° W.	3	to the center of a Star^d bend passing a large Island on the Lar^d Side 1 m
S.	80° E.	3½	to a p^t in the Star^d Bend passing a large Creek on Star^d Side at 2½ M Pryors vally Creek 28 yds wide
N.	40° E	1	to the Center of a Lar^d Bend
S	65° E	3	to the Center of a Star^d Bend
S.	60° E	3½	to the Center of a Star^d Bend, throughout this the river is divided by a number of Small Islands near the Star^d Side wide bottoms on the Lar^d (*Camp^d 21st July*)
N.	75° E.	2¼	to a Lar^d Bend 1 m above a large Island
S	34° E	3	to the center of a Star^d bend at the upper point of an Island called onion Island
S.	80° E	1½	to a Star^d bend passing Several Islands
N.	45° E	1	to a Lar^d bend passing Several Islands
S	25° E	6	passing four long Circular bends, and Several large Islands to a point of the Bluff Star^d Side a large Creek Well timbered falls in on the Star. Side ¾ of a mile below the extremity, I call White paint Creek.
S.	12° E	6	to a Bluff point on the Star^d Side passing on a direct line thro' a General bend the debth of which is 3 miles : within this general bend there are four Smaller circular bends, bottoms continue wide the river Crooked and full of Islands &c. Encamped 22 July 4 m Short of the distance of this course by water.
S.	20° E	2	to a point of the Star^d Bluff
N.	60° E	1½	to a Lar^d Bend passing a large Island on Star^d
S	30 E	1½	to a Star^d Bend passing the upper point of the Island at ½ a mile.

S 70° E 1¾ to the Center of the Lar.ᵈ Bend passing two out lets to the river on the Starᵈ

S 5° E 1½ to the lower point of an Island, the river 300 yards wide at this place

S 20° E 2 to the center of a Larᵈ bend passed an Islᵈ

S. 10° W 1½ to the center of a Starᵈ bend

S. 80° E 1 to a point in Starᵈ bend

N. 85° E 3 to a tree in the Center of the Larᵈ Bend

S. 20° W. 3 to a Star.ᵈ Bend passing over a large Island comencing at 2 miles, a Creek

N 70° E 1½ to a point of high timber on Starᵈ Side

S. 20° W. 2 to Some dead timber in the Center of a Star.ᵈ bend. (*encamped 23ᵈ July*)

S. 40° E 1 to a Lar.ᵈ bend passing between 2 large Islands

S 50° W. ½ to the Center of Starᵈ bend opposit an Island

S. 15° E 1½ to a point of high timber in a bend on the Lar.ᵈ Side.

S. 40° W 1¼ to the Center of a Starᵈ Bend low Bluffs touching the river at this point.

South 3½ to a Bluff Point in a Star.ᵈ bend, passing an Island on Star.ᵈ Side

S. 85° E ½ to a Lar.ᵈ Bend opposit ops.ᵈ a large Plain

S. 30° E 1 to a Bluff point in Starᵈ Bend

East ¾ to a point in the Lar.ᵈ bend passing a Small Island.

S 30° E 3 to the lower point of a large Island

S. 85° E 1½ to a tree in the Lar.ᵈ Bend

South ½ to a tree on the Star.ᵈ Shore opposit the upper point of an Island

S. 80· E 1 to the Center of a Lar.ᵈ Bend passing the upper point of an Island on Larᵈ

S. 10° W. 1½ to the Center of a Starᵈ Bend passᵍ an Island at ¾ of a mile

East 2 to the Center of a Lar.ᵈ bend passing two Small Islands (*Campᵈ 24ᵗʰ July*)

S. 25° W. 1 to the Center of a Star.ᵈ Bend

S. 10° W. 1¼ to a point in a Starᵈ Bend passing a Small Island on Lar.ᵈ Side

S. 5° W. 3½ to a point in a Starᵈ Bend

S. 40° E. 1¼ to a tree in the Star.ᵈ bend passing a point on Larᵈ at ½ a mile

N. 80° E 2½ to the a Starᵈ Bend passing a Small Island at ½ a mile *Gass's Crick*

South	3	to the center of a Star.^d Bend

South   3   to the center of a Star.ᵈ Bend

S. 75.° E 1½ to a Bluff Point on Star.ᵈ here the river again enters the mountains I believe it to be the 2ᵈ Chain of Rocky Mᵗˢ

S. 55.° E 1 to a point in a Lar.ᵈ Bend

S 30.° E ½ to a point in a Lar.ᵈ Bend

South ½ to a Clift of rocks in the Lar.ᵈ Bend. (*Camped 25ᵗʰ of July*)

N. 45.° W ¼ to a object in the Star.ᵈ bend.

S. 60.° W 1 to a point in Lar.ᵈ bend passed four Small Islands.

S 55.° W. ½ to the Center of a Star.ᵈ Bend

S. 65.° E 1 to a Clift of rocks in a Star.ᵈ Bend passing 2 Small Islands.

N. 65.° E 1 to the enterence of a Creek in Lar.ᵈ bend

S. 15. E 1 to the enterence of a Small run in the Lar.ᵈ bend the hills here recede from R. call it Howards Creek

S. 55.° W. 1½ to the center of a Star.ᵈ bend

S. 12 W. 2½ to a point in the Star.ᵈ bend

S. 15.° E 3½ to a point of high timber on the Lar.ᵈ passing 3 Islands und.ʳ Lar.ᵈ Shore

S. 25.° W. 1 to the Center of a Star.ᵈ Bend

East 1¼ to the Center of a Lar.ᵈ bend ps.ᵈ Sd.ʸ Isd.ˢ

S. 20.° E 2½ to the Cent.ʳ of Lar.ᵈ bend ps.ᵈ Sev.ʳˡ Sm. Isld.ˢ L.S.

S. 48.° W. 1½ to a rock in the Center of Lar.ᵈ bend (*Encamped 26ᵗʰ July*)

N. 65.° W. ½ to the Center of Star.ᵈ bend passed an Isl'ᵈ St.ᵈ

South 1¼ to a Clift of high rock on Star.ᵈ here the river is again confined between high hills

S. 2.° E. 2½ to the Center of a Lar.ᵈ bend pass.ᵈ Sm.ˡ Is.ᵈ

S. 45.° W. 1¼ to the upper part of a high Clift of rocks in a Star.ᵈ bend. opposit to the *Mouth* or enterence of the *East fork* of the *Missouri* we call *Gallitins River* 70 yds.

S. 45.° W. ¼ to the junction of the *North & Middle fork* of of the *Missouri* each of these streams is from 90 to 90 [originally written 40 to 60. — ED.] yards wide a Strong Current dischargeing much water. Middle fork Maddisons River & the North fork Jeffersons River we assended it (*Encamped on N. fork the 27ᵗʰ 28ᵗʰ & 29ᵗʰ July*)

130¼

Course and Distance up the Main North fork of the Missouri.[1]
(July 30th)

	miles	
N. 45° W.	1/4	to a small Bayou in the Star^d Bend
S 30 W.	1/2	to a Starboard bend
S 20° E	1/4	to a Larboard bend. encamped 27th 28th & 29th on Lar^d in an island.
N. 70° W.	1/4	to a Starboard bend
S. 20 W	1/2	to a St^d bend passing an Island on St^d Side.
S. 80° E	1/4	to a Larboard bend
S. 50° W	1/2	to the lower point of an Island
South	1/2	to a Lar^d Bend
S. 45° W.	1/8	to a tree in the Lar^d Bend
N. 45° W	1/4	to the upper point of an Island
West	1/2	to bend on Lar^d opposit an Island
N. 60° W	1/8	to a Chanel passing thro' the Island
South	1/4	to a Lar^d bend ops^d an Island passed several Small Bayoes Lar^d Side
West	1/2	to the upper point of an Island passing a Bayou on the Lar^d Side
S. 70° W	1/4	to a Bayou on the Lar^d Side
West	1	to the upper point of an Island passing the upper point one other at 1/4, one at 3/4 of a mile & two Bayous on the L.S.
S. 60° W	1	to a high band on Star^d bend
S. 35° W	3/4	to the upper point of a Bluff in a Star^d bend opposit an Island
S. 45° E	3/4	to the Lar^d bend pass^d the p^t of an Island & a Bayou
S. 35° W.	1/4	to the Lar^d bend opposit an Island
West	1/4	to the Star^d bend opposit an Island ps^d 1
S. 30° W	3/4	to an Island in the Star^d bend opposit a high plain
S. 20° W. s1	1/4	to a Clift of rocks under a Mountain S.S. passed an Island
South	1/2	to a point on the Star^d Side
S. 30. W.	1/4	to a high Clift of uneaven rock on the Star^d Side ops^d an Island
S 45° W.	1/8	to the Star^d bend under a Clift
S. 45° E	1/4	to a Bayou in the Lar^d Bend passing an Island
S 60° W	1/8	to Bayou in the Star^d bend above an Isl^d

[1] The following is found in Codex G, pp. 39-41, in Clark's handwriting, and describes the route from July 30 to Aug. 1, 1805, inclusive. — ED.

COURSES AND DISTANCES

S. 50° E	¼	to a Bayou Lar^d bend opposit Several Small Islands
S. 45° W.	¼	to the Mouth of a Bayou L^d bend
S. 20° W	¼	to a Bayou in the Lar^d bend passing the upper point of an Island Lar^d
S. 70° W	¼	to the St^d bend. *(Encamped 30th July)*
West	⅛	to a Bayou in the Star^d bend
South	1	to a Bayou on the Lar^d Side at the mouth of a [*Pholosiphy*] *river* Damed by the Beaver 8 feet
West	¾	to the Star^d Bend at the mouth of a Bayou passed 2 Small Islands one on each Side
South	½	to the Lar^d Bend opposit 2 Islands
SW.	½	to the Lar^d Side passed a Bayou L.S.
West	½	to a tree in the Star^d Bend
South	⅛	in the Star^d Bend
S. 60° E	¼	to a Prarie above willows on Lar^d Side
S. 25° W	¼	to the lower point of an Island
East	⅛	to the 2nd mouth of the little river L.S^d
S 20° W	1¼	to a bend on the Star^d Side pass^d 2 Small Is^ds
S. 25° E	¼	to a Lar^d bend passed the place I crossed the 26 inst: river 100 yds wide 3 feet deep.
SW	⅛	to a Star^d Bend
South	¼	to a Lar^d bend
S 20° W	¾	to the Lar^d bend ops^d an Island
West	½	to a Small Bayou in Lar^d bend
S 60° W	1	to the head of the Island
S 45° W.	1¼	to a Clift of a mountain on the Lar^d Side passed the (Island on Star^d)
S 80° W	½	to a Clift of a Knob on the St^d S^d Here the Clifts jut in on both sides leaveing a narrow bottoms.
SW.	¾	to a Low Bluff above the Lar^d Clift in a Lar^d Bend
NW.	1	to a point of rocks on the Star^d Side upper part of the Clift.
S 80° W	¼	to a Lar^d Bend, an Island Lar^d Side
N. 80 W	1	to the Star^d Bend passed an Isl^d
S. 60° W	¾	to a Small Island in the Star^d Bend
South	⅛	to a tree in the Lar^d Side
S 70° W	¾	to a Star^d Bend passed an Isl^d
S 20° W.	1¾	to the foot of a mountain in a bend to the Lar^d Side
N. 70° W.	¾	to a Starboard bend
S. 70° W.	½	to Some bushes in a Lar^d bend passed the mouth of a Small run L^d *(Encamped 31st July)*

[15]

N. 30° W. 1   to a Point of rocks on the Lar^d Side,   at this place the river passes thro a Spur of the Mountain of Perpendicul^r Clifts

N. 60.° W   3/4   to the uppar part of a rock in St.^d bend

S. 70° W   1 1/2   to a Clift on the Lar^d Side

S. W.   1/2   to a Star^d Bend

S. 26 W.   1 3/4   to a Bluff on Star^d Side.

South   1/2   to the Lar^d bend,   at this place the river enter a high mount.^n of Steep uneaven Clifts

Miles   37

Continued August 1st 1805 [1]

N. 30° W   1 1/4   to a Star.^d Bend under a high Clift

N. 80.° W   1/4   to a Clift of high rocks in St^d bend a Small bottom on the Lar^d Side

S. 60° W.   1/2   to a Lar.^d Bend, under a pine hill

N. 25.° W.   1/4   to a Small Island on the Lar^d Side

N. 30 E   1/4   to the Star^d Bend high Clifts both Sd^s

N. 80° W   3/4   to the Mouth of a bold Creek on the Lar^d Side passing an Isl^d and riffle of 6 feet fall [*Frasures fall & Creek*] here the river again enters a vallie

North   1/2   to the Star^d bend under a hill

NW.   1/2   to a Lar^d bend

N. 70° W   1 1/2   to the point of an Island passed Several Small Islands

North   1/4   to a Star^d bend

West   3/4   to the lower point of an Island

NW   1/4   to the mouth of a large Creek St^d [*R. Fields Creek & Vally*] 28 y^d w^d   (*Encamped the 1st of aug^t*)

S. 80° W.   3/4   to a Star.^d Bend

S. 30° W   1/4   to a Lar.^d Bend

West   1/4   to a Bayou in the Lar^d Bend

North   1/2   to a Star.^d bend passing a riffle and 2 Small Islands

S. 30.° W   3/4   to a Lar^d bend passed an Island

N. 45.° W.   1/2   to a St^d bend passed a Bayoe L^d

West   2   to an Island passing two points on the Lar^d Side two Islands and Several Bayous on the Lar^d Side th[e] Vallie from 6 to 10 mile wide

South   1 1/8   to a Lar^d Bend

NW   1/4   to a Star^d bend of the Island

---

[1] The following continuation is found in Codex G, pp. 46–49, in Clark's handwriting, and describes the route from Aug. 1 to Aug. 5, 1805, inclusive. — ED.

S 40° W	⅛	in the Star.ᵈ bend of the Islᵈ
S. 60 E.	¼	to a Lar.ᵈ bend passing the point of the Island on the Star.ᵈ Side
SW	½	in the Larᵈ bend
N. 10° W.	¾	in the Star.ᵈ bend passed a Bayou
N. 80.° W	¼	in the Star.ᵈ Bend of an Island
S. 30.° W	¾	to a Lar.ᵈ Bend passed the Island
North	¼	to a Starᵈ Bend
S.W.	1	to the mouth of 3 Bayoes in a Stᵈ bend
S. 30.° E	½	in a Lar.ᵈ Bend
S. 50° W	⅛	in the Larᵈ Bend
N. 20° W	½	to a Bayoe in the Starᵈ Bend
S. 20.° W	½	to a Larᵈ Bend
N.W.	¼	to a low Bluff in a Star.ᵈ Bend
S.W.	⅛	in a Star.ᵈ Bend pass.ᵈ a Bayou Stᵈ Side
S. 20° E	½	to a Larᵈ Bend
S. 50.° W	¼	to a lower point of an Island
West	¼	to a Star.ᵈ Bend passing a Bayoe on the Stᵈ. Side and the Isᵈ to a Bayoe Stᵈ
S. 60° E	½	to a Lar.ᵈ Bend passed an Isl.ᵈ
S 45° W	¼	to a Bayou in the Star.ᵈ bend
South	¼	to a Larᵈ Bend
S. 60.° W.	½	to a Star.ᵈ Bend at the mouth of a Bayoe rapid & 30 yds wide
S.E.	⅛	in the Star.ᵈ Bend
East	⅛	to the Larᵈ Bend
South	½	to the Mo: of a Bayoe in Star.ᵈ Bend
S. 70.° W	¾	to a Star.ᵈ Bend
South	¼	to a high bottom in a Starᵈ Bend
S. 70° E	½	to a Lar.ᵈ Bend (*Campᵈ 2ᵈ August*)

3ᵈ Augᵗ

South	½	in a Larᵈ Bend
West	1¼	to a Star.ᵈ Bend
S. W.	½	to the Star.ᵈ Bend a Small Creek [*called panther C.*]
S. 20° W.	½	in the Starᵈ Bend
S. 80.° E.	1¼	to the Lower point of an Island
South	¼	to a Stᵈ point of the Island
S. 30° E	¼	to a Bayoe in the Island
South	1½	to the upper point of the Island haveing passed 3 points undʳ a Cliff
S. 10° W.	4	on a Direct line to the mouth of a Creek Small the

Dreans of a mountain in which, there is *Snow* in view,
river passed under this Mountain on the Lar^d Side &
has Several Short bends in this Course   Vallie wide
& to the Stard Side

S 25° W.	1	to a Small run in a Lar^a bend
S. 60° W.	1	to a low Stoney Bluff in a Star^d bend. opposit an Island, pass^d 1
S. 20° W	1	to the lower point of a Island L^d passed one and thro a narrow rockey Channel under the bluff (*Encamped the 3 of Aug^t.*)
S. 45° W.	5	on a Direct Course to a Lar^d bend passed 4 bends to the Lar^d Side & several Bayoes on either Side
S. 20° W.	4	with the river to a Bluff on the Lar^d side, passed three bends on the Star^d and two Small Islands & 2 Bayoes S^d
S. 60° W.	6	with the river to an Island passed Six round bends on the Star^d and several Small Bayoes. (*Camp^d 4th Aug^t.*)
S. 45° E	½	to a Lar^d bend. a Bayou Ld Side
S. 15 W	½	to a Star^d bend passed an Island
South	1	to a Lar^d bend ps^d a Small Island and a Bayou on the Star^d Side
S. 45° W.	¼	to a Star^d Bend passed an Island
S. 30° W	2	to a low Clift at the mouth of a Bayoe on the Star^d Side passed 3 rapids in this course
S. 60° E	½	to a Lar^d bend passed an Island St^d Side
S. 30° W.	½	to a Bluff in the Star^d bend
South	¼	in the Star^d bend passed a bad rapid
S 45° E	¼	to a Lar^d bend
South	½	to a Bluff in a Star^d bend
S 45° E.	½	to a Lar^d bend
S. 15. W.	¼	to a Star^d bend under a Bluff
East	½	to a Lar^d Bend passed a Bayoe on St^d Side
S 5° W	¼	to a Bayoe in the Lar^d Bend
S. 45° W	½	to a Star^d bend passed an Island
West	¼	to a Bayoe in the Star^d Bend
S. 45° E	¼	to a Lar^d Bend passed an Island
South	½	to the forks, passed an Island. Those forks is nearly of the Same Size the NW. fork the most rapid & clear and the one most in our course, the S.E. fork is Still of a Greenish Colour and appears to come from the S.E. between two mountains

98   up the North fork

VIEW OF THE STONE WALLS, on the Upper Missouri

assended the N.W. Fork 9 Miles on a Course S. 30° W. to a Bluff
on the Star.ᵈ Side passed Several Bayoes & Islands

Course Distance &c. above Wisdom River

August 7ᵗʰ ¹

S 45°. E   7   miles by water 3 miles by land to the mouth of a Creek
12 ydˢ wide on the Larᵈ Side   passed Seven bends
to the Starᵈ side and Several Small Bayoes on each
side.

Courses of August 8ᵗʰ

South   5   miles by water 2 m. by land passing seven bends on the
Larᵈ Side two Isldˢ. & several Bayoes to the mouth
of *Philanthophy* river on the Larᵈ Side 30 yds. wide
& navagable

S. 20° W.   14   miles by water & 6 by land on a Direct Course to a
fiew high trees on the Starᵈ Side   the river bending
round to the East 2 miles from this course.   passed
an Island at 1 mile, another at 7 miles, Several small
Bayoes & 35 bends to the Starᵈ   most of those
bends are Short & round.

August 9ᵗʰ

S. 12°. W.   11   miles by water 4 miles derect to a Starbᵈ bend passᵈ two
Small islands, 16 short round bends on the Starᵈ Side.
we *Dined*

S. 10° E   3   miles by water 1 m. direct to a high bottom on the
Larᵈ Side passed an Island, a Bayoe on the Larᵈ Side.
four Short bends on the Starᵈ Side.

August 10ᵗʰ

S. 30°. W.   6½   miles by water 2 miles Direct to a Clift of rocks 150
feet high Stᵈ Side Called by the Snake Indians the
Beavers head, a Clift 300 distant from the Beavers
head about 50 feet high   passed 8 bends on the
Starᵈ Side two Small bayoes on the Larᵈ Side

S. 60° W.   6½   miles by water (2 miles on the course) to a low bluff
on the Larᵈ Side, passed four Island[s] & 18 bends
on the Starᵈ Side passing near a low bluff on Starᵈ
Sᵈ   passed Several Small Bayoes.

---

¹ The following is found in Codex G, pp. 60–62, in Clark's handwriting, and
describes the route from Aug. 7 to 14, 1805, inclusive. — Eᴅ.

S. 20° W.   3   miles by water 1 m. by land to the lower point of 3000 mile Island passed three Small Islands, 6 bends on the Star.^d Side, 6 Bayoes on either Side

S. 25° W.   3½ miles by water 1½ m. by land to the head of the Island Passed Sevin bends on the Lar.^d Side of the Islands & 2 Bayoes on the Lar.^d Side. The Star.^d Channel passes near the Bluffs

South   7½ miles by water 2½ m. by land to the head of a large Island, the main Chanel on the Lar.^d Side, passed 3 Small Islands and Several Small Bayoes and 15 bends on the Star.^d Side

S. 8° W.   5½ Miles by water 2 miles direct to the head of a large Island, main Chanel on the Star.^d Side   passed maney Bayoes, 3 Islands, & 9 bends on the Star.^d Side

S. 10° W.   6½ miles by water 2 m^s by land to a Star.^d bend passed four Small Islands and 2 large Island[s] Several Bayoes and a number of Short bends. passed a run on the Star. Side

_____

79

South   4   miles by water 1 [m. by land] to a point of ruged rocks about 70 feet high on the Star.^d S^d Passed the head of the Island ops^d to which we Encamped at 2½ M^s the mouth of a Creek bold running Stream 7 yards wide back of an Island on the Lar.^d Side Mc Neal Creek

S. 30° W.   6   miles by water 3 m by land to the Clift of high rocks on the Star.^d Side passed Several Islands and Bayoes on either Side, the river verry Crooked & bends Short

S. 14° W. 22   miles by water the river makeing a Gen! Bend to the East 8 miles by land to a place the river Passes a mountain high Clifts on either side, river crooked Cold rapid & Sholey, almost one continued rapid passed a number of *bayoes* & Small Islands   passed a bold running Stream on the Star.^d Side 4 yards wide & 3 feet deep at 7 miles, passed a bold running

Stream from a Spring on the Lar^d Side at 15 Miles.
Encamped the 13th of august at 6 miles on Ld Side
Encamped 14th of august at 20 miles on the Lar
Side, a high Clift on the Course 3 miles near the
upper part of which the Creek passes

III

Course and distance of the River Jefferson Continued[1]

Augt 15th

S. 25° W.   6 Miles by water (4 by land) to the Mo: of a Creek 10
yards wide bold current I call Willards Creek   Passed a
point of rocks on the Star^d Side at 2 miles, one on the
Lar^d   at 5 miles passed a bold running Stream at 4 miles
on the Lar^d Side & an Isl^d

S. 22° E   3 miles by water (1 mile by land) to a Small bottom on the
Lar^d Side   passed a high Clift on the Star.^d   opposit is
a high slopeing hill

S. 20° W   6 Miles by water (2 by land) to a Small branch on the
Lar^d Side passed no wood except Srub.   Clear bottom

(16th August)

S. 18° W   7 miles by water (3 by land) to a Lar^d bend under a low
bluff, the river bending to the St.^d under Some high land
verry crooked Shallow rapid & Small, passed Several
Island[s] 4 of them opposit each other. *Service berry
Vallie*

S. 12° W   4 Miles by water (2 by land) to a high Clift on the Star^d
Side pass Several Small Is^ds & Bayoes

S. 50° E.   1½ m. by water (1 by land) to the mouth of a bold running Stream on the Lar^d Side opposit a Considerable rapid
Clifts on both Sides below high St^d above

S. 45° W   ½ mile to the lower point of an Isl^d in the middle

(17th August)

S. 30° W.   10 Miles by water 4 by land to a high Knob in the forks of
the river.   river bending to the Star^d Side.   met Indians
& Encamped to make a Portage

mils 39

---

[1] The following is found in Codex G, p. 67, in Clark's handwriting, and describes
the route from August 15 to 17, inclusive. — ED.

[Distances from the Narrows to mouth of Columbia].[1]

From Timm or long narrows to the first village St.d Side	14	14
To friendly village	6	
To Pilgrim rocks	7	13
To Catterract River & vilg.	11	
To a village on St.d 3 houses Comsm.t of Mountain	9	
To [blank space in MS.] River 60 y.ds St.d S.d	12	
To the Great Shute	6	38
To the last rapid	6	44
To Quick Sand River on the West side of Mountain	26	26
To Tomahawk village S.	16	
To a vilg on Lar.d Side at which place M.t Ranier may be seen	20	
To p.t ops.d a large village beh.d an Island	12	
To the narrows of a low mountain	11	59
To a village or 2 Houses Lar.d side	16	
To a village North of some low marshey Islands St.d	33	
To 4 houses under a St.d Hill	15	
To Shallow Bay	16	
To [blank space in MS.] Inlet	8	88
To Point open Slope below the Station Camp 1805	3	
To Chinnook R. Haley's bay	12	
To Point Disap.t	13	28
	147	

From the M. of the Creek N.o 1 to a point up the River on the opposite Side N.o 1 is S. 88.o E.[2]

To the nearest pinical of the mountain is S. 44.o E.
To point N.o 2, is S. 30° E.
To Lower point N.o 3 is S. 50.o W.
To a stake is S. 71° W. 82 poles to a 2.d stake is S. 75.o W. 112 poles at a vilg. of 26 Houses, thence to a stake is S. 84 W. 88 poles at a run To the Stake at Camp N. 89° West 94 Poles

From Camp

To the p.t N.o 1 is East
To the Mountain is S. 49. E
To point N.o 2. S. 47.o E.

---

[1] This list of distances is found on a separate leaf towards the end of the Clark-Voorhis field-book. — ED.

[2] These bearings in and about the mouth of the Columbia were found entered on a separate leaf towards the end of the Clark-Voorhis field-book. — ED.

To point N° 3. S. 41.° W.
To Cape Disap^t S. 88 West
Down the river N. 77.° W
134 Poles to a Creek and (N. 5 West in a bend)
To the mountain & Point N° 2 in same course S. 49.° E.
To Point N° 3. S. 35.° W.
To Cape Disap^t is S. 87.° W.
To a Point between N. 80 West about 1 mile
To point Addams is S. S. E. from Camp

Courses and estimated distances from the Quawmash Flats on the West side of Rocky Mountains to Travellers rest.[1]

East.— 11 m^s to Collins's Creek 25 y^ds wide, passing a small prarie at 9 m^s road hilly, thickly timbered.

N. 45.° E. 13 to the crossing of Fish Creek 10 y^ds wide passing a small creek at 6 m^s

N. 75.° E. 9. to a small branch of hungry Creek. the road passing along a ridge with much fallen timber. some snow at the extremity of this course.

N. 22½ E. 5. to the heads of the main branch of hungry Creek. road hilly, some snow.

N. 75.° E. 3. down hungry Creek on its No[r]th side, passing 2 small branches on it's N. side, the 1st at ½ M and the 2nd at 1½ m^s further.

N. 75.° E. 6. still continuing on the N. side of the creek to the foot of the mountain, passing 3 north branches and 1 South branch of the Crek.

N. 45.° E. 3. to the summit of the mountain where we deposited our baggage on the 17th ins^t

N. 45.° E. 15. to an open prarie on the side of a mountain having kept the dividing ridge between the Waters of the Kooskooske and Chopunnish rivers.

N. 45.° E. 28. to an open prarie on the South side of a mountain, having still kept the same dividing ridge mentioned in the last Course, though you ascend many steep mountains and decend into many deep hollows.

---

[1] The following is found in Codex L, pp. 70, 71, in Lewis's handwriting, and describes the route from June 24 to June 30, 1806, inclusive. — Ed.

East —   3. to the extremity of a ridge where we decend to a deep
              hollow. much fallen timber caused in the first in-
              stance by fire and more recently by a storm from
              S. W.

N. 45° E. 10. along a high snowey ridge to an open hillside of con-
              siderable Extent passing the road at 4½ m̥ˢ which
              turns off to the right and leads by the fishery at the
              entrance of Colt Creek.

N. 45° E. 12. To the quawmash flatts at the head of a branch of the
              Kooskooske, passing the Kooskoske 35 yᵈ wide at
              5 miles. from hungry Creek to this river the road
              may be said to be over snow as so small a propor-
              tion of it is distitute of it. after passing this river
              the road dose not agin ascend to the snowy hights.
              at 7 m̥ˢ on this course again fell into the road which
              leads by the fishery about 4 mˢ above the mouth of
              Quawmash Creek.

North —   4 to the Hotspring Creek on the main branch of trav-
              ellers rest.

N. 20° E. 3. to the warm or hot Springs down the N. side of the
              creek.

N. 20° E. 3. down the creek passing a Northern branch 3 yᵈˢ wide
              at 1. M. also the Creek itself twice a short distance
              below the Northern bran[ch]

N. 45° E. 10. along the North side of the creek to the entrance of
              a N. branch of the same 8 yᵈˢ wide. a road leads
              up this branch.

N. 60° E. 9. down the N. side of travellers rest creek to the prarie
              of the Creek and the Vally of Clark's R.

East —   9 to our encampment on the S. side of travellers rest,
              passing the creek 1 M. above and 2 from its mouth

Total   156

Courses and Computed Distances from the Enterance of Travellers
rest Creek into Clarks River to the Falls of Missouri [1]

North   7 Miles to the crossing of Clarks river, vally wide the
              top of the hills covered with long leafed pine. bot-
              toms pine & Cotton wood passed a Small branch

---

[1] The following is found in Codex N, pp. 144–148, in Clark's handwriting, and
describes Lewis's route from July 3 to 10, 1806, inclusive, over what is known as
Lewis and Clark's Pass. Cf. Clark's Summary Statement, *post.* — Ed.

		at 3 miles on W Side and at 1 M. further a Small Creek on the E. Side. at 5 miles Clarks river is joined by an Easterly fork 120 yards wide.
N 75° E.	7.	Miles through a handsom leavel plain to the point where the East fork enters the mountains, or where the hills close it in on both Sides. passed a large Creek 15 y.ᵈ wide at 6 miles also one at 3 miles.

July 4

S 75° E.	3	miles allong the North Side of the river, the bottoms widen. a prarie.
N. 45° E.	1	M. passing a small branch at the extremity of this course.
S. 45° E	1	M. to the forks of the East fork of Clarks river a handsom wide plain below on the South Side.
East	8	Miles on a Buffalow road up Co-kah-lah-ish-kit river through a timbered Country Mountains high rocky and but little bottom land pore.

July 5ᵗʰ

N. 75° E	3½	Miles passed a Stout Creek on N. Side at 2½ miles. another just above.
N. 25° E	12	Miles passed a Small creek at 1 mile on the S. Side on which there is a handsome and extencive vally and plain for 10 or 12 miles also another Creek 12 yds wide at ½ a mile on the N. Side, and another 8 yds wide on the N. Side at 5 miles. and one ½ mile Short of the extremity of the course arrived at a high prarie on the S. Side from one to 3. miles in width, extending up the river. great number of wild horses on Clarks river about the place Cap.ᵗ L. crossed it. we saw several.
East	6	Miles to the enterance of Warners Creek 35. yards wide through a high extencive prarie on the N. Side. hills low and timbered with the long leafed pine, larch and Some fir. the road passes at some distance to the left of the river and these courses is with the river.
N. 22° W.	4	Miles to a high insulated Knob just above the enterance of a Creek 8 yards wide which discharges itself into Werners Creek.
N. 75° E	2½	Miles to the river passing through a handsom plain

on Werners Creek crossing that Creek at one mile and leaveing a high prarie hill to the right seperateing the plain from the river. Saw 2 swan in this butifull creek.

East 3 Miles to the enterance of a large Creek 20 yards wide called Seamons Creak, passed a creek at 1 mile 8 yds wide, (this course is with the river) the road passing through a high extencive prarie, a vast number of little hillocks and Sink holes. at the head of those 2 Creeks is high broken mountains Standing at the distance of 10 m. forming a kind of cove Generaly of open untimbered country.

July 6th

East 14 Miles to the point at which the river leaves the extencive plains and enters the mountains these plains is called the prarie of the Knobs, passed the North fork of Cokah-lar, ishket river at 7 miles, it is 45 yards wide deep & rapid. passed a large crooked pond at 4 miles further. Great number of burrowing Squirels of the Species common to the Columbian plains. the main branch is 50 yards wide and turbid the other Streams are clear, these plains continue their course S. 75° E and are wide where the river leaves them. up this vally and Creek a road passes to the Missouri.

N. 60° E. 1½ miles up the river. bottoms narrow and and country thickly timbered. Cotton wood and pine grow interm[i]xed in the river bottoms passed Several old indian encampments.

N. 80° E. 2 Miles to two nearly equal forks of the river. here the road forks also one leading up each river. passed a Creek on N. side 12 yd. wide.

N. 75° E. 8 Miles over a Steep high bald toped hill for 2 miles thence 3 M. through a thick woods along the hill Side. bottoms narrow. crossed a large Creek in a butifull plain much beaver Sign.

July 7th

N. 75° E. 6 M. through a leavel butifull plain on the N. side of the river much timber in the bottoms, hills also timbered with pitch pine crossed a branch of the

		Creek 8 yds. wide at ¼ M. also passed a creek 15 yds. wide at ¼ further.
North	6	M⁣ passed the main Creek at 1 M¹ and kept up it on the right hand Side through a handsom plain. the main Stream bore N W. & W as far as I could See it, a right hand fork falls into this creek at 1 m¹ above the Commcm⁣ of this course.

North 6 M⁣ passed the main Creek at 1 M¹ and kept up it on the right hand Side through a handsom plain. the main Stream bore N W. & W as far as I could See it, a right hand fork falls into this creek at 1 m¹ above the Commcm⁣ of this course.

N. 15° E   8 M⁣ over two ridges one [on] again Strikeing the right hand fork at 4 M⁣ then continuing up it on the left hand Side. much apperance of beaver maney dams. bottoms not wide and covered with willow and grass.

N. 10° E.   3 M⁣ up the Same creek on the E Side through a handsom narrow plain.

N. 45° E.   2 M⁣ passing the dividing ridge between the waters of
——— the Columbia from those of the Missouri at ¼ of a
106¾ mile. from this gap which is low and an easy asent, the road decends and continues down a creek.

N. 20° W.   7 M⁣ over Several hills and hollows along the foot of the mountain, passed 5 small riverlets running to the right.

July 8ᵗʰ 1806.

N. 25° W.   3 M⁣ to the top of a hill from whence we saw the Shishequaw Mountain about 8 M⁣ distant imediately before us, passed torrent river at 3 M⁣ this Stream comes from the S. W. out of the Mountains which are about 5 miles to our left the bead of the river is 100 ydˢ wide tho' the water only occupies about 30 yᵈˢ it runs a mear torrent tareing the trees up by the roots which Stand in it's bottoms, we discover this to be Dearborns River. "The Shishequaw Mountain is a high insulated conic mountain Standing Several miles in advance of the Eastern range of the rocky Mountains" near the Meadecine River.

North   14½ Miles through an open plain to Sishequaw Creek 20 yards wide about 10 M⁣ below the Mᵗⁿ which bears S. 32° W. from us, haveing left the road to our left which keeps near the Mtˢ

[27]

N. 50° E. 2 M^s to the discharge of Sishequaw Creek into Medecine River through an extencive leavel and butifull
bottom.

N. 85° E. 8 M^s down the Medecine river to a large Island. the
$\overline{28\frac{1}{4}}$ bottoms are extensive low and leavel. the lands
of neither the Plain or bottom are fertile it is of a
light colour intermixed with a considerable portion
of gravel. the grass Generaly about 9 inches high.

July 9th

N. 80° E. 4 M^s through a handsom leavel wide bottom in which
there is a considerable quantity of the narrow leafed
cotton wood timber. The river is generally about
80 yd^s wide rapid it's bed is loose Gravel and pebbles its banks low but seldom overflow. water
clear.

S. 85° E. 4 M^s down on the S. W. Side of Medecine river through
wide and leavel bottoms Some timber.

July 10th

N. 75° E. 24 Miles down the river. 7 M^s of the latter part of the
course no timber. passed a rapid bottom wide
and extensive a great number of small islands in
the river.

S. 75° E 8 Miles to the Missouri at the White Bear Islands at
the head of the portage above the falls, passed
through the plains. at which place Capt Lewis
$\overline{183}$ continued untill the 15th July 1806. and left 6
men and proceeded towards the head of Marias
river with the other 3 men as before mentioned.

The most derect and best course from the dividing ridge which
divides the waters of the Columbia from those of the Missouri at the
Gap where Capt Lewis crossed it is to leave a Short range of mountains
which pass the Missouri at the Pine Island rapid to the right passing
at it's basse and through the plains pass fort mountain to the White
bear Is^{ds} or Medecine river, a fine road and about 45 miles, reducing
the distance from Clarks river to 145 miles one other road passes
from the enterance of Dearborns River over to a *South branch* of the
Cohahlariskkit river and down that river to the main fork and down
on the N. Side of the main fork to Clarks river &c.

B. LEWIS'S SUMMARY VIEW OF RIVERS AND CREEKS, ETC.[1]

A SUMMARY VIEW OF THE RIVERS AND CREEKS, which discharge thems[elves] into the Missouri; containing a discription of their characters and peculiarities, their sources and connection with other rivers and Creeks, the quality of the lands, and the apparent face of the country through which they pass, and the width, and distance of their entrances from each other; to which is also added a short discription of some of the most remarkable points and places on the Missouri; taken from the information of Traders, Indians & others; together with our own observations, from the junction of that river with the Mississippi, to Fort Mandan.

The confluence of the Mississippi and Missouri Rivers is situated in 89°. 57′. 45″ Longitude West from Greenwich, and 38°. 55′. 19″. 6. North Latitude. Ascending the Missouri from hence, at the distance of 21 miles, you arrive at the Village of S. Charles, situated on the North bank of the river, in a narrow tho' elevated plain, which is bounded in the rear by a range of small hills; hence the appellation of *Petit cote*, a name by which, this village is better known to the inhabitants of the Illinois, than that of S. Charles. The village is bisected or divided into two equal parts by one prinsipal street about a mile in length, runing nearly parallel with the river. It contains a Chapple, one hundred dwelling houses and about 450 inhabitants. the houses are generally small and but illy constructed. a great majority of the inhabitants are miserably poor, illiterate, and when at home, excessively lazy; tho' they are polite, hospitable and by no means deficient in point of natural genious. they live in great harmony among themselves, and place as implicit confidence in the doctrines of their spiritual pastor, (the Roman Catholic priest) as they yeald passive obedience to the will of their temporal master, the Commandant. A small garden of vegetables is the usual extent of their cultivation. this labour is commonly imposed on the old men and boys; those in the

[1] Found in Codex O, pp. 19–128, and apparently written at Fort Mandan during the winter of 1804–05. — ED.

vigor of life view the cultivation of the soil as a degrading employment, and in order to gain the necessary subsistence for themselves and families, either undertake hunting voyages on their own account, or engage themselves as hirelings to such as possess sufficient capital to extend their traffic to the natives to the interior parts of the country. on those voyages in either case, they are frequently absent from their families or homes, the term of six, twelve, or eighteen months, during which time they are always subjected to severe and incessant labour, exposed to the ferosity of the lawless savages, the vicissitudes of the weather and climate, and dependant on chance and accedent alone, for food, raiment, or relief in the event of malady; yet they undertake those voyages with cheerfullness, and prefer the occupation of the hunter, or engage, to that of the domestic, and independent farmer.

Ascending the Missoury at the distance of 12 miles, *Bonhomme* Creek discharges itself on the S. side. it is 23 yards wide at it's entrance is of no great length, & passes through a fertile well timbered country, inhabited by American emigrants principally.

At the distance of 9 miles higher up we pass the mouth of the *Osage woman's* river, which discharges itself on the N. side; it is 30 yards wide at it's entrance, heads with two small streams which discharge themselves into the Mississippi a small distance above the mouth of the Illinois River, is navigable for perogues some miles during the spring season, and waters a fertile well timbered country inhabited by about fifty American families. this part of the country is generally called Boon's settlement, having derived it's name from it's first inhabitant Colo Daniel Boon, a gentleman well known in the early settlement of the state of Kentucky.

About 9 miles higher up, and 69, from the Mississippi, Chaurette Creek falls in on the N. side. it is 20 yards wide at it's mouth, waters a tolerable country well covered with timber, but is of no great extent. it heads with the waters of the River Ocuivre [1] a branch of the Mississippi. immediately below the mouth of this creek five French families reside, who subsist by hunting and a partial trade w[h]ich they mantain with a few detached Kickapoos who hunt in the neighbourhood. this is the last settlement of white persons which we meet with in ascending the Missouri.

At the distance of 34 miles higher up the *Gasconade* disembogues on the S. side behind a small Island covered with willow. at it's entrance it is 157 yards wide, but is much narrower a little distance up, and

---

[1] The Cuivre River, which falls into the Mississippi a little below Hastings, Ill. — ED.

is not navigable, (hence the name *gasconade*) this river is of no great length, heads with the Marameg & S: Francis rivers. the country watered by this river, is generally broken, thickly covered with timber and tolerably fertile. the hills which border on the Missouri near the mo[u]th of this river are about 300 feet high, containing excellent limestone in great abundance. I have observed in ascending the Missouri to this place, that whenever the river washes the base of the hills on either side, it discloses large quarries of this stone, lying in horizontal stratas, from 10 to 40 feet in thickness. this stone is of light brown colour, with a smal tint of blue; fracture imperfect conchoidal; when broken it presents the appearance of a variety of small shells and other marine substances, of which it seems to be entirely composed. in this solid and massive rock, are inclosed stones of yellowish bro[w]n flint, of bulbous and indeterminate shapes, from an ounce, to ten or twelve pounds weight. these stratas of limestone are not unusually found overlaying a strata of freestone, or soft sandstone, from two to twenty feet in thickness. this stone produces lime of an excellent quality, and is the same with that, which makes it's appearance on the Mississippi from Cape Gerrardeau, to the entrance of the Missouri.

F[i]fteen miles up we pass *Muddy River* which falls in on the N side. this river waters a most delightfull country; the land lies well for cultivation, and is fertile in the extreem, particularly on the Missouri, both above and below this river for many miles; it is covered with lofty and excellent timber, and supplyed with an abundance of fine bould springs of limestone water. this river is 50 yards wide several miles above it's mouth.

2 miles higher up *Muddy creek* discharges itself; it is 20 yards wide at it's mouth, heads with cedar Creek, and the branches of Muddy river. the country through which it passes is similar to that last mentioned.

At the distance of 19 miles higher up, you arrive at the mouth of the *Osage River;* being 137 miles from the junction of the Missouri and Mississippi. it is 397 yards wide at it's mouth, opposite to which, the Missouri is 875 yards wide. it disembogues on the S. side just above a cluster of small Islands. it takes it's rise in an open country of Plains and Praries, with some of the Northern branches of the Arkansas; some of it's tributary streams on it's North side, also have their sou[r]ces in a similar country, with the Southern branches of the Kanzas river. The rivers Arkansas and Kanzas circumscribe the length of this river, and interlock their branches to the West of it. The country watered by this river, is generally level & fertile, tho' it is more broken on the lower portion of the river; the bottom lands are wide, well timbered, and but partially liable to inundation; the soil consists of a black rich loam many feet in debth. the uplands also consist of a dark loam overlaying a yellow or red clay ; a majority of the country consists of plains intersperced with groves of timber. the timber still diminishes in quantity as you proceed Westwardly with the river. on the South side of this river 30 leagues below the Osage Village, there is a large lick, at which some specimenes of the bones of the Mammoth have been found; these bones ar[e] said to be in considerable quantities, but those which have been obtained as yet, were in an imperfect state. M: Peter Chouteau, a gentleman of S: Louis, made an attempt some years since to explore this lick, but was compelled to desist from his labour, in consequence of the quantity of water discharged into the lick from a neighbouring spring, which he had not the means or the leasure to divert; since which time, no further attempt has been made. The specimens obtained by M: Couteau were large; but much mutilated. the Osage river is navigable 120 leages for boats and perogues of eight or ten tons burthen, during the fall and spring seasons ; in winter it's navigation is obstructed by ice, and during the Summer months it experiences an unusual depression of it's waters, a characteristic of most streams, which have their sources in an open plain country, or which, in their courses pass through a majority of that discription of lands. the bed of the river is generally composed of mud, gravel and sand, and is but little obstructed by rocks or driftwood.

At the distance of five miles above the mouth of the Osage river, *Murrow* [Moreau] Creek falls in on the S. side, 20 yards wide at it's mouth and navigable for perogues a few miles. it takes it's rise with the waters of the Osage river and those of Salt river (branch of the Missouri) it traverses in it's course to the Missouri, a tolerable country, well timbered and water[e]d. the mouth of this creek is the point at which the Saukes, Foxes, and Ayouways usually pass this river [to] wars with the Osages.

7 miles higher up, *Cedar Creek* falls in on the N. side, above an Island, on which there is Cedar, hence the name of the creek. it heads with muddy creek, and passes though a delightfull country in it's course to the Missouri. it is well timbered and abounds in springs of excellent water.

at the distance of ten miles further you pass the mouth of *Good-woman's* Creek, about 20 yards wide. opposite to the entrance of this creek the Missouri washes the base of a high hill which is said to contain lead ore, our surch for this ore however pruved unsuccessfull and if it dose contain ore of any kind, it must be concealed. this Creek takes it['s] rise in the highlands with Split rock Creek and passes through a fertile country well timbered and watered. in the last nine miles of it's course it passes through an extensive fertile bottom nearly parallel with the Missouri.

Nine miles higher you pass the mouth of *Manitou* Creek on the S. Side. it is but a small creek head[ing] a few miles back in an open country; the land ab[o]ut it's entrance on the Missouri are of an excellent quality and covered with good timber.

Nine miles further *Split rock* Creek discharges itself on the N. side, twenty yards wide and navigable for perogues some miles. it waters a well timbered country; the land about the mouth, appears to be of the second quality, or at least inferior to that heretofore seen in ascending the Missouri.

At the distance of 3 miles, still ascending, *Salt* river disembogues on the S. side; being 180 miles from the entrance of the Missouri. it is 30 yards wide and navigable for perogues 40 or 50 miles; passes through a delightfull country, intersperced with praries. so great is the quantity of salt licks and springs on this river that it's waters are said to be brackish at certain seasons of the year. one large lick and spring are situated on it's S. E. bank about nine miles from the Missouri. this river heads with the waters of the Osage river, Murrow Creek, and Mine river.

Ascending the Missouri ten miles further we arrive at the entrance of Manitou river, which disembogues on the N. side, just below a high clift of limestone rock, in which we found a number of rattle-snakes of large size. this stream is about 30 yards wide, and is navigable for perogues some miles. about three miles from the Missouri on the lower side of this river there are three small springs of salt water which do not appear to be of the best quality. the country about the mouth of this river, particularly on it's lower side, is a charming one; the soil fertile in the extreme, and well covered with excellent timber. the country on the upper portion of this river is but little known.

At the distance of nine miles further, *Good-woman's* river falls in on the N. side; it is 35 yards wide at it's entrance; meanders through an extensive rich bottom nearly parallel with the Missouri for some miles befor it discharges itself. it is navigable for perogues 15 or 20 miles, waters a fine farming country intersperced with open plains and praries, and heads with the little Shariton river.

At the distance of nine miles *Mine river* discharges discharges itself on the S. side. it derives it's name from some lead mines which are said to have been discov [er] ed on it, tho' the local situation, quality, or quantity of this ore, I could never learn. this river is 70 yards wide at it's entrance, navigable for perogues 80 or 90 miles, and through the greater part of it's course runs parellel with the Missouri; at the distance of 70 miles up this river it is only 5 leagues distant from the Missouri. it takes it's rise in an open hilly country with Bluewater river and some of the Northern branches of the Osage river. the courant of this river is even and gentle. The country through which it passes is generally fertile, and consists of open plains and praries intersperced with groves of timber. near it's entrance the country is well timbered and watered, and the lands are of a superior quality.

Twenty two miles higher up the two Shariton rivers discharge themselves on the N. side, the smaller falling into the larger on it's lower side at a small distance from the Missouri. the little Shariton river heads with Good-woman's river, and is 30 yards wide at it's entrance; this country has not been much explored, the portion of it which is known is fertile, and consists of a mixture of praries and woodlands. The larger Shariton is 70 yards wide above the entrance of the smaller, and is navigable for perogues nearly to it's source. it takes it's rise near the Red Cedar river a Western brance of the river Demoin. the country through which it passes is level, and fertile consisting of an irregular mixture of woodlands and praries, each alternately predominating in different parts.

Twenty two miles higher up, the *Grand river* disembogues on the N. side just above a beatifull and extensive prarie in which the ancient village of the Missouris was situated. Old Fort Orleans is said to have stood on the lower point of an Island a few miles below this place, no traces of that work are to be seen. this river is 90 yards wide at it's entrance and is said to be navigable for boats and perogues a considerable distance. it heads with the Rackoon river a branch of the Demoin. The country through which it passes is similar to that discribed on the larger Shariton river. about the entrance of this river the lands are extreemly fertile; consisting of a happy mixture of praries and groves, exhibiting one of the most beatifull and picteresk seens that I ever beheld.

At the distance of eight miles *Snake creek* falls in on the N. side. 18 yards wide at it's entrance. it runs parallel with the Missouri nearly it's whole extent, passing through a delightfull country, well timbered and watered.

Thirty seven miles higher up Tigers Creek falls in on the N. side, opposite to the upper point of a large island. some excellent bottom lands in the neighbourhood of it's mouth; interior country not known.

Fifteen miles higher up *Eubert's* river and Creek fall in on the S. side, opposite to an island, which concealed their entrances from our view. they are but small streams, head with the Mine river, and water an excellent country, consisting of a mixture of praries and woodlands.

Twenty six miles further, *Hay Cabbin* Creek falls in on the S. side. it heads near the Bluewater river and passes through a good country. the land is very fine and well timbered near it's mouth.

Seventeen miles above, *Bluewater river* falls in on the S. side; 36 yards wide at it's entrance; and navigable but a short distance. it has one considerable fall, and several rappids well situated for waterworks. it heads in an open country with Mine river, and passes through a roling country. the lands are tolerably good; it's bottom lands are wide, fertile and sufficiently covered with good timber; some beatifull natural meadows are also seen on it's borders.

Still ascending the Missouri, at the distance of 9 miles the Kanzas river disembogues itself on the South side; being 364 miles from the junction of the Missouri and Mississippi. This river takes it's rise not very distant from the principal branch of the Arkansas in a high broken sandy country, forming the Southern extremity of the *black hills*. from hence it takes it's course nearly East about 300 leagues through fertile and leavel, plains & praries, intersperced with groves of timbered land; it then enters a country equally fertile and well timbered, through which it meanders about 20 leagues further and discharges itself into the Missouri. it has been navigated 200 leagues and there is good reason to believe from the appearance of the river and country at that point that it is navigable for perogues much further perhaps nearly to it's source. The rivers Platte and Arkansas interlock their branches West of this stream. there are no obstructions to the navigation of the Kanzas, it's current is gentle, and the bed of the river composed of soft loam, gravel and sand; in the summer and autumn it's waters are transparent. about ¾ of a mile from the entrance of this river on it's North side there is a handsome bluff about 100 feet high, which furnishes an excellent situation for a fortification; there is an abundance of excellent timber for the purpose immediately at the place. The Colateral branches of this river, and the most remarkable places on the same so far as we have been enabled to inform ourselves are as follow —

Names of Creeks rivers & remarkable places	distances from each other	distances of each from the Mouth of the Kanzas	width in yards	the side of the Kanzas into which they fall
The three rivers, near each other and about the same size	—	10	20	N.
The St [r]anger's wife river	5	15	35	N.
Bealette's Creek.	3	18	22	N.
Wor-rah-ru za river	1	19	40	S.
Grasshopper Creek.	2	21	25	N.
Heart river	10	31	30	N.
The old Kanzas Village	9	40	—	N.
Full river	5	45	50	S.
Black-paint river	27	72	38	N.
Bluewater river and the present village of the Kanzas just below	8	80	60	N.
Me-war-ton-nen-gar Creek	5	85	18	N.
War-ho-ba Creek	3	88	15	S.
Republican river	15	103	200	N.
Solomon's Creek	12	115	30	N.
Little salt Creek	10	125	30	N.

On the West side of the Republican river, about sixty leagues above it's junction with the Kanzas, a small creek falls in on the S. W. side, called *Salt creek*, the water of this creek is excessively salt, salt in it's dry and granulated state, is to be found in large quantities on the borders of this stream throughout it's whole extent; the earth on which it forms, is remarkably furm, and the salt can be readily collected, free from any extranious substance, by sweeping with a brush of feathers.

Ten miles higher up the Little river Platte falls in on the N. side, 60 yards wide at it's entrance.   it heads in open plains between the Nadawa and grand rivers, and through the principal part of it's course passes through high open plains interspersed with groves of timber. 6 or seven leagues before it discharges itself into the Missouri, it meanders through a high fertile well timbered bottom nearly parallel with that river, and receives in it's course severall handsom creeks, which discharge themselves into it from the hills.   at the distance of 12 leagues it's navigation is obstructed by a considerable fall, above which, it is shallow and interrupted by such a number of rappids, that it is no further practicable. This fall, and many of the rapids afford excellent situations for gristmills, and other water-works.

Twenty five miles further *Turkey Creek* falls in on the S. side.   this creek is but small, passes through open bottoms nearly parallel with the Missouri, and in rear of an Old Kanzas Village.   this creek once furnished water to an old French garrison situated near it's mouth.

Thirty three miles further *Independance* creek falls in on the S. side, a little below the second old village of the Kansas; is 22 yards wide at it's mouth; it possesses some excellent bottom lands, and waters a beatifull and fertile country consisting of high open plains and praries principally; on it's borders, and about it's entrance there is a sufficient quantity of timber. it takes it's rise with the *Stranger's wife* river, and the waters of Woolf river. we knew of no name by which this creek was called, and therefore gave it that of *Independance*, from the circumstance of our having arrived at it's mouth on the 4th of July 1804.

At the distance of 48 miles higher up *Nadaway* river discharges itself on the N. side nearly opposite to the upper point of a large Island, which bears it's name. it is 70 yards wide some miles above it's mouth, and is navigable for perogues a very considerable distance. it takes it's rise with grand River, Nish-nah-ba-to-na, and the waters of the river Demoin; and passes in it's course to the Missouri through a fine fertile country, consisting of a mixture of woodlands and plains; the lands about it's mouth are well timbered and water[e]d.

Fourteen miles [further] up the Missouri, Woolf river discharges itself on the S. side. it is 60 yards wide at it's entrance and navigable for perogues a considerable distance; takes it's rise with the waters of the Kanzas and Ne-ma-haw rivers, and in it's course to the Missouri passes through a level fertile country principally open plains and praries, tho' generally well watered and possesses a sufficient quantity of timber on it's borders and near it's mouth. great quantities of grapes, plumbs & raspberries are found in the neighbourhood of this stream.

Sixteen miles higher up, *Big Ne-ma-har* falls in on the S. side, opposite to an Island covered with willows; it is 80 yards wide, and navigable for large boats some distance, and for perogues nearly to it's source. it heads with Blue-water river, branch of the Kanzas, and throughout it's whole course, passes through rich, and level plains, and praries. there is some timber on it's borders, and about it's entrance; it's tributary streams are also furnished with some timber. the country is well watered.

Three miles further the *Tarkio Creek* falls in on the N. side, twenty three yards wide at it's entrance; it is navigable for perogues a short distance. it heads with the Nadiway and passes through a tolerable country of plains and woodland.

Twenty five miles higher up The *Nish-nah-ba-to-na* River discharges itself opposite to the lower point of an Island on the N. Side, and is 50 yards in width at it's entrance. it heads with the Nadawa river and passes through a fertile country deversifyed with plains meadows and woodlands; considerable bodys of the latter appear in some parts of this country. at the *Bald-pated prarie*, it enters the Missouri bottom and approaches that river within 300 paces, when it returns again to the highlands, and continues it's course along the foot of the same about 30 miles before it discharges itself. at the Bald pated prarie it is 40 yards wide, possesses considerable debth of water, and is navigable many miles; the country lying between the Missouri and this river, from the Balld pated prarie nearly to it's mouth, is one of the most beautiful, level and fertile praries that I ever beheld; it is from one to three miles in width. there is a considerable quantity of timber on the banks of the Missouri, and but little on the Nishnabatona.

At the distance of eight miles higher up, the Little Ne-ma-har River falls in on the S. side. 40 yards wide. it heads with salt River branch of the River Platte, and passes through an open fertile country in[t]ersperced with groves of timber. it is navigable some miles for large perogues. there are several handsome streams of fine water, which fall into the Missouri both above and below the mouth of this river in it's neighbourhood.

Fifty two miles higher up, *Weeping water* Creek falls in on the S. side. it is 25 yards wide at it's entrance, heads in high broken plains near Salt River, and passes through a roling country, mostly uncovered with timber and not very fertile there is a scant proportion of timber on it[s] banks and some clumps of trees are scattered over the face of the country. there is some handsom bottom lands on this stream, and the country is generally well wartered.

Thirty two miles higher up, and distant 630 from the confluence of the Missouri and Mississippi, the great river *Platte* disembogues on the S. side. The steady, regular, and incessant velocity of this stream, is perhaps unequaled by any on ea[r]th; notwithstanding it's great rapidity the surface of the water continues smooth, except when occasionally interruped by a boiling motion, or ebullition of it's waters. this motion of the water is also common to the Missouri, and Mississippi, below the mouth of that river, and always takes place in the most rappid part of the current; in this manner the water is seen to rise suddenly many inches higher than the common surface, then breaking with a rappid and roling motion, extends itself in a circular manner in every direction arround, interrupting the smooth, tho' rappid surface of the water for many yards. this ebullition of the water of those rivers, is a singular phenomenon, nor do I know to what cause to attribute it, unless it be, the irregular motion of large masses of sand and mud at their bottoms, which are constantly changing their positions. The bed

of the river Platte is composes[d] almost entirely of white sand, the
particles of which, are remarkably small and light; these collecting,
form large masses, which being partially buoyed up, are hurryed along
at the bottom by this impetuous torrent, with irresistible force; sometimes obstructed by each other, suddenly stop; and form large sand
bars in the course of a few hours, which are again as suddonly dissi-
pated to form others, and to give place perhaps to the deepest channel
of the river. From the experiments and observations we are enabled
to make, with rispect to the comparitive velocity of the currents of the
Mississippi, Missouri and Platte rivers, it results, that a vessel will
float in the Mississippi below the mouth of the Missouri, at the rate of
four miles an hour; in the Missouri from it's junction with the Mississippi to the entrance of Osage river at the rate of 5½ to 6 miles
an hour; from thence to the Kanzas from 6½ to 7; from thence
to the Platte, from 5½ to 6 miles an hour, while that of the Platte
is at least 8. The current of the Missouri above the entrance of the
Platte is equal to about 3½ miles an hour as far as the mouth of the
Chyenne river, when it abates to about 3 miles an hour, with which
it continues as far as we have yet ascended it; and if we can rely on
the information of the Indians, it's current continues about the same
to the falls of the Missouri, situated five hundred miles above Fort
Mandan. The river Platte dose not furnish the Missouri with it's
colouring matter, as has been asserted by some; but it throws into it
immence quant[it]ies of sand, and gives a celerity to it's current, of
which it dose not abate untill it joins the Mississippi. The water of
the Platte is turbid at all seasons of the year, but it is by no means as
much so, as that of the Missouri; the sediment it deposits consists of
small particals of white sand, while that of the Missouri is composed
principally of a dark rich loam in much greater quantity. This river
has in some few instances been navigated as high as the Pania Village
with perogues, but it is attended with infinate labour and risk. Hunters
have also ascended this river in small canoes as high as the Woolf river,
a distance of 35 leagues; and the savages sometimes descend in small
leather canoes made of a Buffaloe's skin. When the Plat enters the
Missouri it's superior force changes and directs the current of the latter
ag[a]inst it's Northern bank, compressing it within a channel of not
more than one fifth of the width it had just before occupyed. this
river is 600 yards wide at it's entrance; and when we passed it, on
the 21[st] of July, it's greatest debth of water was five feet. we were
informed by one of our engages, who is well acquainted with this river
for a considerable distance, that in many places it was from two to

three miles wide, containing great numbers of small islands and sand bars, and that the navigation became wo[r]se, the higher he ascended. the banks of this river are very low, yet it is said, that it very seldom overflows them, or rises more than about 6 feet perpendicular above it's lowest tide. The position of the head of the Southern, or main branch of this river is not well asscertained; on connecting the sources of the rivers better known, it appears most probable, that it takes it's rise in the Rockey, or shineing Mountains with the Bravo or North river, and the Yellow stone river, branch of the Missouri; from whence it takes it's course nearly East, passing the heads of the Arkansas at no great distance from Santa Fee, continues it's rout to the Missouri, through immence level and fertile plains and meadows, in which, no timber is to be seen except on it's own borders and those of it's tributary streams. commencing at the Missouri and ascending this river, it's principal subsidiary streams are first the *Salt river*, seven leagues distant, falls in on the S. side, and is 50 yards in width. this stream is however more remarkable for the excellency of it's salt licks and springs than for it's magnitude. the whole courant of this river is brackis[h] in the Summer season quite to it's mouth. There are three principal salines on this stream; the first at the distance of 50 miles from it's mouth, and the others at no great distance above; two of these furnis[h] considerable quantities of salt in it's dry and granulated state, the other furnishes salt both granulated, and in compact masses. the granulated salt is found on the surface of a compact and hard earth composed of fine sand with a small proportion of clay producing no vegitable substance of any kind and is easily collected by sweeping it together with a soft broom or brush of feathers. the massive salt is formed by concretion, and is found either on the surface of the earth over which the water passes, or adhering to stones sticks or other furm substances washed by the salt water in it's passage. I have obtained no satisfactory account of any fossil salt being found in Louisiana, altho' repeated enquiries have been made off such as possess the best information of the interior parts of the country; I am therefore disposed to believe, that those travellers who have reported it's exhistance, must have mistaken this massive salt, formed by concretion, for that substance. saltpetre has been found in it's crystallized state in some limestone caverns near the head of this river.

Thre[e] leagues above the salt river a beatifull clear and gentle stream called *Corne des Cerfe*, or *hart's horn* river discharges itself on the N. side. it is about sixty yards wide. it takes it's rise in some sandy plains between the Wolf River and the Quecurre; thence runing East-

HERD OF BISONS, on the Upper Missouri

wardly approaches the Missouri within a few leagues opposite to the entrance of the Sioux river, thence veering about to the S. E. passes through a fertile level country, parallel with the Missouri to the River Platte. it is navigable a considerable distance for canoes and light perogues. there is but little timber in the country through which it passes.

Ascending the Platte five leagues further you pass the village of the Ottoes and Missouris situated on the S. side. 15 leagues higher up and on the same side, the Panias Proper, and Republican Panias reside in one large village. five leagues further still ascending, the Wolf river falls in on the N. side. 400 hundred yards wide, and is navigable for Perogues between 4 and 500 miles, and for large boats a very considerable distance. This stream takes it's rise in a remarkable large fountain, situated in a level plain, equadistant betwen the rivers Quicurre and Plat, at some little distance below the *Cote noir* or Black Hills; from whence it passes through level and fertile plains and meadows in which there is scarcely a tree to be seen except on it's own borders, and those of it's tributary streams. the current of this river is gentle and sufficiently deep; it's bed is composed principally of a brown sand, unbroken by rocks or drift wood, and has no rappids worthy of notice from it's source to it's mouth.

At the distance of seventy five leagues higher up, *Ringing Water* river falls in on the S. side, about 300 yards wide. heads in the Black hills near the source of the Kanzas, and passes through an open tho' broken country about half it's course; it then decends into a level and fertile country composed almost entirely of open plains and meadows through which it passes to the Platte.

Just above the black hills, th[r]ough which the Platte passes, a large river said to be nearly as large as the South fork, falls in on the N. side, after haveing continued it's rout along the Western side of the Black hills for a very considerable distance. the distance from the entrance of this river to the mouth of the Platte is not well asscertained. This is usually called the Paducas fork; it heads with the Bighorn river, branch of the Yellow Stone, in some broken ranges of the Rockey mountains. it's upper portion passes through a hilly, broken and Mountanous country, possessing considerable quantities of timber; it then descends to a plain open and level country lying between the Rockey Mounts and the black hills, through which it passes to join the Platte. there are some considerable bodies of woodland on and near this stream.

The smaller branches of the rivers Platte & Wolf so far as they are known to us are as follows; they uniformly water a level open country generally fertile.

Names of streams falling into the Platte	Distances from the Missouri in leagues	width in yards	side of the river on which they discharge
Shell river	27	30	N.
Short Leg river	40	30	S.
Deer Creek	52	28	S.
The Falling Creek	70	20	S.
T[h]ose of the Loups, or Wolf River			
Little willow Creek	42	25	N.
Mustle shell Creek	45	20	N.
Elk Creek	49	26	S.
Gravley Creek	54	20	S.
White Bluff creek	64	20	S.
Deepwater Creek	79	25	S.

Three miles above the entrance of the river Platte Butterfly Creek falls in on the S. side, 18 yards wide, heads in the plains between the Hart's Horn river and the Missouri; the courntry fertile with but little timber.

7 miles higher Musquetoe Creek falls in on the N. side; it is 22 yards wide and heads with the Nishnahbatona river in an open country. the Missouri bottom through which it passes is about 6 miles wide, level, extreemly fertile and about one half well covered with timber.

20 miles further *Indian Creek* falls in opposite to the lower point of an Island on the N. side, three miles above an old Ayouway's village. it heads in the highlands a few miles back; passes through the Missouri bottom and approaches the river within 20 feet, 6 miles above it's entrance; at this point it is 5 feet higher than the water of the Missouri. it is 15 yards wide.

8 miles higher up Bowyer's river falls in on the N. side. it is 25 yards wide, and navigable for perogues some distance; passes through a country tolerably fertile, with but little timber.

Twelve miles above the mouth of Bowyer's river we arrive at the *Council Bluff* on the S. side. this is one of the points, which in our statistical view of the Indian Nations of Louisiana, we have recommended as an eligible position for a trading establishment. it is a delightfull situation for a fortification, & commands a view of the river both above and below for a considerable distance. the base of the Bluff is washed by the river about a mile; it is about 60 feet high & nearly perpendicular; at it's lower extremity it leaves the river nearly at right angles, decending with a handsome and regular declivity on it's lower side about 40 feet to a high, level, fertile and extensive bottom, lying betwen itself and the river. the top of the bluff is a level plain from one to two miles in width, and about five miles in length. This place would be sufficiently convenient for the Ottoes, Missouris, Panias Proper, Panias, Loups, Panias Republican, Poncaras, Mahas, & the Yanktons Ahnah. if peace is established between the various tribes of Indians inhabiting this immence country, it is more than probable, that this post would also be visited by many of those wandering bands, who inhabit the country west of the black hills. The principal difficulty which will attend the erection of a fortification at this place is the want of proper timber with which to build. there is a sufficient quantity of a species of poplar common to all the bottom lands of the Missouri, called by the French inhabitants of the Illinois — Liard, and by the Americans Cotton-wood. it is a soft white wood, by no means dureable, and of which it is extreemly difficult to make plank or scantling. there is some oak in the neighbourhood but it is of an inferior quality. I concieve that the cheepest and best method would be to build of brick, the ea[r]th appears to be of an excellent quality for brick, and both lime and sand are convenient. The drift wood of the Missouri will always supply a sufficient quantity of fuell independant of that in the neighbourhood. with rispect to quality and quantity of timber, this bluff is better situated than any other for upwards of a thousand miles above it, and equal to any below it for many miles.

Leaving the council Bluff and ascending the Missouri 39 miles we arrive at the mouth of Soldier's river 30 yards wide. it heads with the river Demoin, and passes to the Missouri through an open, level and fertile country. is navigable for perogues a considerable distance.

44 miles further up *Ye-yeau War da-pon* or *stone river* falls in on the N. side. this river is known to the traders of the Illinois by the name of little *Sioux river*, but as they have given the appellation of Sioux to four distinct streams we thought it best to adopt the name given it by the Siouxs, to whos[e] country it's entrance forms the lower boundary on the Missouri. this stream is 80 yards wide at it's entrance; takes it's rise in a small lake nine miles distant from the River demoin, with which, it communicates in high water through a small channel; the river demoin is but shallow at this point tho' it is 70 or 80 yards wide, and said to be navigable. this stream is navigable from it's sou[r]ce to the Missouri for perogues or canoes, passes through a broken country with but little timber. the land is tolerably fertile. an Easterly and most navigable fork of this river is formed by the discharge of Lake Dispree [d'Esprit or Spirit Lake] 22 leagues in circumference; this

lake is long not very wide and approaches the river demoin within 15 miles. the country between the Demoin and Lake Dispree is level with but little timber, and interrupted with a number of small lakes or ponds.

From the entrance of the *Ye-yeau War-da-pon*, to the Old Maha Village, a distance of 100 miles, there is not a single stream which discharges itself into the Missouri, that is worthy of notice. The *Maha creek*, on which the last village occupyed by that nation was situated at some little distance from the Missouri, discharges itself on the S. side through several channels. this creek is but small, takes it's rise in some level and fertile praries near the Hart's Horn river and passes through a delightfull country in it's course to the Missouri. the distance from the old Maha village to the Council Bluff is 90 miles by land.

16 miles higher up Floyds river falls in on the N. side 38 yards wide. This river is the smallest of those called by the trade[r]s of the Illinois the *two rivers of the Sioux*, but which with a view to discrimination, we have thought proper to call Floyd's river in honor of Serg^t Charles Floyd, a worthy and promising young man, one of our party who unfortunately died on the 20th of August 1804, and was buried on a high bluff just below the entrance of this stream. This river takes it's rise with the waters of the rivers Sioux and Demoin; from whence it takes it's course nearly S. W. to the Missouri, meandering through level and fertile, plains and meadows, intersperced with groves of timber. it is navigable for perogues nearly to it's source.

3 miles above Floyds river, The river Sioux disembogues on the N. side above a bluff; it is one hundred and ten yards wide at it's entrance, and navigable nearly to it's source; with the exception of one fall of about twenty feet high, situated 70 leages from it's mouth. it takes it's rise with the St Peter's and Vulter rivers, in a high broken and woody country called the *Hills of the prarie*. it waters a deversifyed country, generally level fertile and uncovered with timber; in some parts particularly, near the falls, it is broken & stoney, and in others, intersected by a great number of small lakes which possess some timber generally on their borders. at no great distances below the falls and in a remarkable bend of the river, three handsom streams fall in on it's East Side at no great distance from each other; the 1st ascending is the *Prickley Pear river*, which takes it's rise in some small lakes near the Demoin. the 2^{ed} *The River of the Rock*, passes the head of the River Demoin, and takes it's rise in small lakes. the third is called *red pipe stone river*, which heads with the waters of the River St Peters. the country watered by this last river is remarkable for furnishing a red stone, of which the savages make

their most esteemed pipes. the Indians of many nations travel vast distances to obtain this stone, and it is ascerted, tho' with what justice I will not pretend to determine, that all nations are at peace with each other while in this district of country, or on the waters of this river.

Sixty miles above the Sioux river the *White Stone river* discharges itself on the N. side. it is 30 yards wide at it's entrance, heads in a chain of Nobs West of the bend of the Sioux river, and passes in it's whole course through level — beautifull and fertile plains and meadows entirely destitute of timber. it is not navigable.

20 miles higher up *little* bow creek falls in on the S side, below an old Maha village. it is 20 yards wide and waters a beautifull, fertile, plain, and open country. the remains of two small ancient fortifications, are found on this creek at a short distance from it's entrance.

12 Miles higher up, and distant 974 from the junction of the Missouri and Mississippi, the *river James* discharges itself; it is 90 yards wide, and navigable for perogues a very considerable distance; it's current is gentle and it's bed composed of mud and sand. it takes it's rise with Chyinne river, branch of Red river which discharges itself into Lake Winipic. This st[r]eam pases through an open country of plains and meadows through it's whole course. the land is generally fertile, and a scant proportion of timber is found on the banks of the river. The Siouxs annually hold a fair on some part of this river, in the latter end of May. thither the Yanktons of the North, and the Sissitons, who trade with a M! Cammaron on the head of the S! Peters river, bring guns, pouder & balls, kettles, axes, knives, and a variety of European manufactures, which they barter to the 4 bands of *Tetons* and the *Yanktons Ahnah*, who inhabit the borders of the Missouri & upper part of the River Demoin, and receive in exchange horses, leather lodges, and buffaloe robes, which they have either manufactured, or plundered from other Indian nations on the Missouri and west of it. This traffic is sufficient to keep the Siouxs of the Missouri tolerably well supplied with arms and amunition, thus rendering them independant of the trade of the Missouri, and enableing them to continue their piratical aggressions on all who attempt to ascend that river, as well as to disturb perpetually the tranquility of all their Indian neighbours. I am perfectly convinced that untill such measures are taken by our government as will effectually prohibit all intercourse or traffic with the Siouxs by means of the rivers Demoin and S! Peters, that the Citizens of the United States can never enjoy, but partially, those important advantages which the navigation of the Missouri now presents. it appears to me that with the assistance of the garrisons of S! Louis, and Chicargoo,

with the establishment of two others, the one at or near the entrance of the Oisconsin and the other on the Mississippi at Sand lake, that the passages of the trade[r]s to the rivers Demoin and Sᵗ Peters would be sufficiently guarded. by prohibiting the trade with the Siouxs through the Sᵗ Peters and Demoin for a few years, they will be made to feel their dependance on the will of our government for their supplies of merchandize, and in the course of two or three years, they may most probably be reduced to order without the necessity of bloodshed. in the mean time the trade of the Missouri will be acquiring a strength, and regularity within itself, and an influence among other indian nations, which could not be easily interrupted by the Siouxs, when the government should hereafter t[h]ink proper to reestablish an intercourse with them, through the channels of the Sᵗ Peter's and Demoin rivers.

At the distance of 38 miles higher up *Plumb Creek* falls in on the N. side. this creek is but small, heads in the highlands a few miles back, and passes through beatifull level and fertile praries in it's course to the Missouri.

8 miles higher up *white Paint Creek* falls in on the S. side, 28 yards in width. it takes it's rise in a broken Hilly and open country between the Quicurre and Hart's horn rivers. passes through a broken country with some handsome plains an[d] praries, it is not navigable. but possesses many excellent situations for grist mills and other waterworks.

6 miles above this creek and at the distance of 1026 from the entrance of the Missouri, the *River Quiccurre (Qui-court.)* or *rappid river*, discharges itself on the S. side; where it is one hundred and fifty two yards wide. this river takes it's rise in the Black hills, about one hundred leages West of it's mouth, and passes through a variagated country. at it's source and for seventy five leagues below the country is mountanous rockey and thickly covered with timber, principally pine; the bed of the river is interrupted by immence quant[it]ies of loose and broken rocks, many ledges of rocks also lie ac[r]oss this stream over which it tumbles perpendicularly from 6 to 15 feet. in this country the Indians as well as some of the French hunters report the existence [of] many mines. some of lead, others of a metal resembleing lead, but of a lighter colour more dense & equally malleable; it is not stated to be silver. this metal is said to be readily extracted from it's ore which is a loose earth, with the heat of a common fire of wood. there are said to be some sand plains of considerable extent lying between the upper portion of this river and the Hart's Horn river. the country on it's lower portion for 25 leagues consists of open plains and meadows, with but a very small proportion of timber; the bed of the river here

consists entirely of a coarse brown sand. the velocity of it's current is nearly or quite equal to that of Platte. it is not navigable a single mile.

8 mile above the rappid rive[r] the *Poncar* river disembogues on the S side, 30 yards wide. Three miles from the mo[u]th of this river on it[s] S. side the Poncars resided a few years since in a fortifyed village, but have now joined the Mahas and become a wandering people. Poncar river heads in the open plains not far from the mouth of White river, and runs nearly parallel with the Missouri passing through some tolerably fertile plains and meadows.

At the distance of 114 miles higher up, White river discharges itself on the S. side. it is 300 yards wide at it's entrance, and is navigable for boats and perogues for many leagues. this river is perfectly the Missouri in miniture, resembleing it in every particular. it takes it's rise short of the black hills, with the waters of the C[he]yenne and rappid rivers, in an open country; from whence it passes through level and fertile plains & meadows, in which there is scarsely any timber to be seen. some pine most probably grows on it's borders, I discovered several sticks of that timber among the driftwood at it's entrance.

22 Miles higher up, the Three rivers of the Siouxs pass discharge themselves, on the N. side, opposite to a large Island well covered with timber. the 1st of these streams which we meet with as we ascend is 35 yards wide, and is navigable for perogues some distance, with a few obstructions of rappids or shoals. it heads with James's river, and possesses but little timber on it's borders. the country on the upper side of this river is a high level and fertile plain of many leagues in exten[t] the lower side generally broken Praries, neither possessing any timber worthy of mention. the other two streams are small, extending only about 8 miles back, and water a country of high handsome and fertile plains, with but little timber.

From hence to the commencement of the *big bend* is twenty miles; in this distance you pass four small Creeks, which discharge themselves on the S. side, and one on the N. side; these creeks take their rise at the distance of 6 or 7 miles in the open plains, and possess but little timber. the bottoms of the Missouri are generally wide and but badly timbered. the big bend of the Missouri lies in a circular form, and is 30 miles around, while it is only one mile and a quarter across the gorge.

5 miles above the uper extremity of this bend *Tylor's river* falls in, on the S. side. this river is about 35 yards wide, and is navigable some miles for perogues. it takes it's rise in an open country between the White

river and river Teton, and passes through a level fertile and open country. below the mouth of this river on the Missouri there is an extensive bottom well covered with timber, consisting principally of red cedar.

55 miles higher up, the Teton River discharges itself on the S. side. this river is seventy yards wide, and is navigable for perogues many leagues. it heads with the waters of the Chyenne and White rivers, and passes through open and fertile plains and meadows. possesses some timber on it's borders, as do also it's tributary streams. in these plains there is rarely an instance of a tree to be seen.

47. miles above the entrance of the Teton river and 1327 from the Mouth of the Missouri, the rive[r] Chyenne disembogues on the S. side, and is abot 400 yards wide at it's entrance, and is navigable for perogues to it's forks near the black hills, a distance of 200 miles by land, nearly due west from it's entrance. The Northern branch of this river penetrates the Black hills, and passes through a high broken well timbered country to it's source, the Southern fork takes it's rise in the Black hills, on their E side, and passes through a broken country covered with timber, to it's junction with the N fork; from whence united, they take their course through a woody and broken country fror some few leagu[e]s, then entering an open fertile and level country it continues it's rout to the Missouri the timber of the Black hills, and on this river near them, consists of pine and Cedar principally; on it's lower portion Cottonwood and Cedar, of which however there is but a scant proportion and that confined immediately to the river hills and bottoms. about the entrance of this river we have recommended an establishment for the purpose of trading with the Indians. it's position is central and sufficiently convenient for a number of Nations and tribes; but the difficulty of procuring timber for the purpose of building is very considerable, tho' in this particular it is equal to any other for an emence distance both above and below it. a difficulty also arises with rispect to lime of which there is none in it's neighbourhood. large quantities of tar may be procured on the river near the Black hills, and may be readily brought down the river. tar and sand in the proportion of one gallon to the Bushel, make a furm and strong cement. if an establishment is made at this place, the work must of necessity be principally formed of brick; there being no stone and but little timber. the drift-wood of the Missouri will supply an ample quantity of fuell.

78 miles higher up, *Otter Creek* falls in on the N. side, 22 yards wide, navigable a few miles in high water. it takes it's rise in open plains nearly E. of it's entrance, and passes through a similar country; very little timber in it's vicinity.

3 miles higher up, and on the S. side, the *Sar-war-car-na* river discharges itself, 90 yards wide. it is navigable for perogues 40 or 50 leagues; takes it's rise short of the Black Hills with the waters of the Chyenne; from whence it meanders through fertile and level plains and meadows, almost entirely destitute of timber.

22 miles above, *We-ter-hoo* river discharges itself on the S. side. this stream is 120 yards wide; and may be navigated nearly to it's source in the Black Hills. It passes through a country similar to that discribed on the *Sar-war-kar-na*.

2 miles higher up, and the same distance below an island on which [is] the lower village of the Ricaras, the river *Ma-ro-pa* falls in, on the the S. side; it is 25 yards wide at it's entrance; takes it's rise about 5 leagues west of the the entrance of the *war-re-con-ne* river, in open plains. it passes through an uneven roling country, without timber, and but badly watered, for the distance of about 50 miles, nearly parallel to the Missouri, before it discharges itself. The Ricaras obtain a red and black earth on the borders of this stream, which they use for the purpose of painting their skins, or ornamenting their Buffaloe robes, which at all seasons of the year constitutes a principal article of their dress.

Leaving the mouth of this river and ascending the Missouri, at the distance of 2½ miles you pass the 1st Ricara village, from 3½ to 4 miles further, you pass two others situated on the South side near the river. still ascending at the distance of 24 miles above the entrance of *Ma-ro-pa* river, the *Stone Idol Creek* falls in on the N. side; 18 yards wide. it heads in a small lake a few leagues distant and passes through a rich level plain; the land is fertile but without timber. a canoe can pass from the river to this lake.

37 miles higher up, *Sar-kar-nak or Beaver Creek* falls in on the N. side, at the lower point of an Island. about 20 yards wide, heads in some small lakes a few miles from the river, and passes through a level fertile and open country.

3 Miles further still ascending, and at the distance of 1498 miles from the entrance of the Missouri, *War-re-con-ne* river falls in on the N. side just above an island. it is 35 yards wide at it's entrance, and is navigable in high water to it's source. takes it's rise in an assemblage of small lakes, in level and open plains, not very distant from the head of James's river. in it's course to the Missouri it passes through extensive, level and fertile, plains and meadows, in which scarsely a tree is to be seen.

13 miles higher up the *Cannon Ball* river falls in on the S. side, and

is 140 yards wide. it is navigable for boats a considerable distance, with a few interruptions of rappids, and for perogues and Canoes nearly to it's source. it takes it's rise in a level country with the Chesschetar and the waters of the Wetarhoo rivers, from whence in it's course to the Missouri it passes through a variety of country, some broken & partially timbered, near it's source; other parts broken, hilly and bare of timber, and in others beautifull and extensive plains and meadows, with but little timber, all sufficiently fertile, and some extreemly so. there is some Cottonwood, Ash and Elm on it's borders.

5 miles higher up the *Fish Creek* discharges itself on the N. Side; 28 yards wide. it takes it's rise in small lakes, in the open plains, and passes through handsome plains and meadows, in it's course to the Missouri; but little timber on it's borders.

35 miles higher up, *Chess-che-tar*, or heart river falls in on the S. W. side; 38 yards wide; not navigable except in high water, and then but a short distance. it heads with the waters of the Knife river in open plains S. W. of the turtle mountain. in it's course to the Missouri it passes through open plains and meadows, generally fertile, and always untimbered. there is some Ash, Cottonwood, and Elm on it's borders.

14 miles higher up, Hunting creek discharges itself on the S. side. it's bottom lands are wide and fertile with but little timber, takes it's rise in, and passes through an open country of high plains.

50 miles higher up at the distance of 1,615 miles from the junction of the Missouri and Mississippi, the Knife river falls in near the Village of the Ahwahharways on the S. side a little above the Mandans. this river is about 80 yards wide, but is not navigable, except for a few days in the spring of the year. It takes it's rise in the turtle Mountains about 90 Miles N. W. of it's mouth, and passes through an open fertile country. there is a considerable quantity of timber on the upper part of this river, and much more on it's borders generally than is met with on streams of the same size in this open country. The Mine-tares, Ahwahharways, and Mandans hunt principally on this river, and many of [the] Minetares pass the winter on it, in small parties, of 5 or six families.

As we have only ascended the Missouri, a few miles above the Mouth of Knife river, the subsequent discription of this river, and it's subsidiary streams are taken altogether from Indian Information. the existence of these rivers, their connection with each other, and their relative positions with rispect to the Missouri, I conceive are entitled to some confidence. information has been obtained on this subject, in the course of the winter, from a number of individuals, questioned

seperately and at different times. the information thus obtained has
been carefully compared, and those points only in which they generally
agreed, have been retained, their distances they give, by days travel,
which we have estimated at 25 miles p^r day.

About fifteen miles above the mouth of Knife river, the *E-pe,-âh-zhah*,
or *Miry river* discharges itself on the N. Side. it is but an inconsiderable stream as to width, but extends itself through level and open plains
about 30 miles N. E. of it's entrance, taking it's rise in some small
lakes, strongly impregnated with Glauber Salts. not navigable.

Ascending the Missouri about one hundred miles further, the *E-mâh-
tark',-Ah'-zhah.* or Little Missouri discharges itself on the S. side. about
the width of Knife river. takes it's rise in the No[r]thern extremity of
the Blackhills. and passes through a broken country with but little
timber. it passes near the turtle mountain in it's course to the Missouri.
it is said not to be navigable in consequence of it's rappidity and shoals.

About 117 miles higher up, the *Ok-hâh-,Ah-zhah*, or *White earth
river*, discharges itself on the N. side. it is said to be about the size
of the Cannonball river; takes it's rise N. Westwardly from it's mouth
in level open plains with the waters of the S. fork of the Saskashawin
river, and passes through an open and level country generally without
timber some timber on the borders of this stream. it is navigable nearly
to it's source, which is said not to be very distant, from the establishment
of the N. West Company on the S. branch of the Saskashawin. if
this information be correct it is highly probable that a line drawn due
West from the lake of the Woods, in conformity to our treaty with
Great Britain, would intersect the waters of this river, if so the boundary of the United States would pass Red river betwen the entrance of
the Assinniboin and Lake Winnipic, including those rivers almost entirely, and with them the whole of the British trading establishments
on the red Lake, Red river and the Assinniboin should the portage
between the Saskashawin and *White earth* river, prove not to be very
distant or difficult, it is easy to conceive the superior advantages, which
the Missouri offers as a rout to the Athabasca country, compared with
that commonly traveled by the traders of Canada.

About 3 miles above the mouth of *White Earth* river the *Mee'-ah'-
zah*, or *Yellowstone river* discharges itself on the S. side. this river is
said to be nearly as large as the Missouri, but is more rappid. it takes
it's rise in the Rocky mountains, with the waters of a river on which
the Spaniards reside; but whether this stream be the *N. river*, or the
waters of the Gulph of California, our information dose not enable
us to determine. from it's source it takes it's course for many miles

through broken ranges of the Rocky mountains, principally broken, and stoney, and thickly timbered. the vallies said to be wide in many places and the lands fertile. after leaving the Rocky mountains it decends into a country more level, tho' still broken, fertile and well timbered. this discription of country continues as far down as the *Oke-tar-pas-ah--ha*, where the river enters an open level and fertile country through which it continues it's rout to the Missouri; even in this open country it possesses considerable bodies of well timbered land. there are no stream[s] worthy of notice which discharge themselves into this river on the N. side, the country between this river and the Missouri being watered by the *Mussle shell* river. the yellow Stone river is navigable at all seasons of the year, for boats or perogues to the foot of the Rocky Mountains, near which place, it is said to be not more than 20 miles distant from the most southernly of the three forks of the Missouri, which last is also navigable to this point. if Indian information can be relied on, this river waters one of the fairest portions of Louisiana, a country not yet hunted, and abounding in animals of the fur kind. The bed of this river is formed of sand gravel and yellow rock. from the great rapidity of this stream after it enters the rocky mountains, it is said not to be navigable. we are informed that there is a sufficiency of timber near the mouth of this river for the purpose of erecting a fortification, and the necessary buildings. in point of position, we have no hesitation in declaring our belief, of it's being one of the most eligible and necessary, that can be chosen on the Missouri, as well in a governmental point of view, as that of affording to our citizens the benefit of a most lucrative fur trade. this establishment might be made to hold in check the views of the British N. West Company on the fur-trade of the upper part of the Missouri, which we believe it is their intention to monopolize if in their power. They have for several years maintained a partial trade with the Indian nations on the Missouri near this place, over land from their establishment at the entrance of Mouse river on the Assinniboin, unlicenced by the Spanish government, then the sovereigns of the country. But since the U'States have acquired Louisiana, we are informed, that relying on the privilege extended to them by our treaty with Great Britain, they intend fixing a permanent establishment on the Missouri near the mouth of Knife river, in the course of the present summer. if this powerfull and ambitious company, are suffered uninterruptedly to prosecute their trade with the nations inhabiting the upper portion of the Missouri, and thus acquire an influence with those people; it is not difficult to conceive the obstructions, which they might hereafter through the medium of that influence, oppose to the will of our government, or the navigation of the Missouri. whether the privileges extended to British subjects, under existing treaties with that power, will equally effect a territory not in our possession at the time those treaties were entered into, is not for me to determine; but it appears to me, that in this rispect Liouisiana is differently situated, from the other territory of the United States.

The tributary streams of the Yellow stone river so far as we have been enabled to inform ourselves are as follow.

Names of the subsidiary streams of the Yellow Stone river, ascending from it's entrance	distance from each other & of the 1st from the mouth of the river	side on which they discharge.
	Miles	
Oke--tar-pas-ah-ha	75	S.
War-rah-sash, or powder river	75	S.
Le-ze-ka, or tongue river	50	S.
Mar-shas-kap river	100	S.
Ark-tar-ha river	125	S.
Ar-sar-ta, or big-horn	75	S.
Stinking Cabbin creek	175	S.

About one hundred fifty miles on a direct line, a little to the N. of West, a river falls in on the N. side called by the Minetares *Ah-mâh-tâh*, ru-shush-sher or the river which scolds at all others. this river they state to be of considerable size, and from it's position and the direction which they give it, we believe it to be the channel through which, those small streams, on the E side of the Rocky mountains laid down by M\. Fidler, pas to the Missouri. it takes it's source in the Rocky mountains S. of the waters of the Askow or bad river. and passes through a broken country in which, there is a mixture of woodlands and praries. it is worthy of remark that, the Missouri in it's course from the mouth of the yellow stone river to the entrance of this riv\. passes considerably further to the North than the mouths of either of these rivers; this information we have received since our map has been completed. it will be observed by reference to the map, that there are no streams falling in-to the Askow on it's S. side, from which, it is probable, that the country nearly to it's borders, is watered by the streams of some other river, and as the Missouri runs considerably N. above the Mouth of the Yellow stone river, and that on it's nothern border no stream of any magnitude discharges itself except the scolding river, the probability is that the country very near to the Askow is watered by the little rivulets of the Missouri, and the branches of the s[c]olding river. I have scarsely a doubt, but that a line drawn due West from the Lake of the Woods, in conformity to our treaty with Great Britain, will intersect the waters of the Missouri, if not the main body of that river itself.

About 120 miles on a direct line, nearly S. W. the Mah-tush,-ah-zhah, or Muscle shell river falls in on the S. side. this river is about the size of the Cannonball river, heads in a range of mountains which commence about the falls of the Missouri, and extending themselves nearly South terminate near the yellow stone river. this stream passes through a broken and woody country. The woody country commences on the Missouri just above the mouth of this river.

About 120 miles further a little to the S. of West, on a direct line, the great falls of the Missouri are situated. this is discribed by the Indians as a most tremendious Cataract. they state that the nois it makes can be heard at a great distance. that the whole body of the river tumbles over a precipice of solid and even rock, many feet high; that such is the velocity of the water before it arrives at the precipice, that it projects itself many feet beyond the base of the rock, between which, and itself, it leaves a vacancy sufficiently wide for several persons to pass abrest underneath the torrent, from bank to bank, without weting their feet. they also state that there is a fine open plain on the N. side of the falls, through which, canoes and baggage may be readily transported. this portage they assert is not greater than half a mile, and that the river then assumes it's usual appearance, being perfectly navigable.

About 15 miles further on a direct line a little to the S. of W. a large stream called Mah-pah-pah,-ah-zhah, or *Medicine river* falls in on the N. side. this river heads in the rocky Mountains opposite to a river which also takes it's rise in the same mountains and which runing West discharges itself into a large river, which passes at no great distance from the Rocky mountains, runing from N. to South. it passes through a mountanous, broken and woody country. not navigable in consequence of it's rapidity and shoals.

About 60 miles further on a direct line nearly S. W. the Missouri passes through the first connected chain of the Rocky mountains. and is said to be rapid and shoaly from hence to the second chain of the rocky Mountains a distance of 75 miles further, about the same course last mentioned. above this second range of mountains the current of the Missouri is said to be smoth even and gentle; here two small rivers fall in on the S. side, receiving their waters from the west side [of] these mountains between the Missouri and the Yellow stone river.

Still proceeding S. W. about 75 miles further the Missouri divides itself into three nearly equal branches just above a third chain of very high mountains, all these streams are navigable for some distance. the most No[r]thern is the largest, and is navigable to [the] foot of [a] chain of high mountains, being the ridge which divides the the waters of the Atlantic from those of the Pacific ocean. the Indians assert that they can pass in half a day from the foot of this mountain on it's East side to a large river which washes it's Western base, runing from S. to N. at no great distance below the *Flat-head* Indians live in one considerable village on the western border of this river. this is the utmost extent of the war exurtions of the Minetares and we have therefore been unable to acquire any information further West than the view from the top of thes[e] mountains extend. The Indians inform us that the country on the Western side of this river consists of open & level plains like those they themselves inhabit, with a number of barren sandy nobs irregularly scattered over the face of the country; the E. side of the river, betwen it and the mountains is broken, and thickly covered with pine. they state that there are no buffaloe west of the second range of the Rockey mountains, and that the Flat-heads live principally on a large fish, which they take in the river on which they reside. The Snake Indians also frequently visit this Western river at certain seasons of the year, for the purpose of taking fish which they dry in the sun and transport on horses to their villages on the three forks of the Missouri. This river we suppose to be the S. fork of the Columbia, and the fish the Salmon, with which we are informed the Columbia river abounds. this river is said to be rapid but as far as the Indian informants are acquainted with it is not intercepted with shoals. it's bed consists principally of sand and gravel.

The waters of the Missouri are transparent at all seasons of the year above the falls.

With rispect to other rivers, their Subsidiary streams, and their connection with other rivers and streams, the map which is herewith forwarded, will give you a more perfict idea, than a detaled discription of them would do. the mountains, salines, trading establishments, and all the other remarkable places, so far as known to us, are also laid down on this map.

MERIWETHER LEWIS Cap.ᵗ
1ˢᵗ U'S Regᵗ Infty.

C. CLARK'S SUMMARY STATEMENT OF RIVERS, CREEKS, AND MOST REMARKABLE PLACES.

CLARK made three tabulations of this character: (1) That found in Codex C, pp. 242–253, having been drawn up at Fort Mandan; (2) another in Codex I, pp. 2–12 (also, substantially the same, in Clark-Voorhis note-book No. 4), made at Fort Clatsop, and giving the route out; and (3) a final draft, both in Codex N, pp. 128–142, and in Clark-Voorhis note-book No. 4, prepared apparently after the return home. The third tabulation seeks to give the best route from the mouth of the Missouri to the Pacific Ocean, and includes Lewis's short-cut path homeward, between Travellers' Rest Creek and the Falls of the Missouri —given, however, in the reverse order. We have, for convenience of consultation, herein amalgamated these several statements. — ED.]

A Summary Statement of the Rivers Creeks and most remarkable places, their distances from each other &c. their distances from the Mississippi assending the Missouri, across the Rocky mountains and down the Columbia to the Pacific Ocian as was explored in the year 1804, 5, and 6, by Cap.^{ts} Lewis & Clark &c

Names of remarkable places	The width of rivers and creeks in y^{ds}	Side on which they are Situated	Distance from one place to another	Distances up the Missouri from the Mississippi	Latitude North of important places
	yards		Ms	Ms	
River Dubois { Latitude 38° 55' 19 6″ { Long^{td} 89° 57' 45″					
To the Village of St Charles		N.E.	21	21	38° 54' 39″
" Bon-homme Creek	—	S. W	12	33	
" the Osage Womans River	30	N.E.	20	41	
" a Cave Called the Tavern	—	S. W	5	47	
" " Chauretts Village & Creek	20	N.E.	27	68	
" " Shepherds Creek		S. W.	15	83	
" " Gasconnade River	157	S. W.	17	100	38° 44' 35.3″
" " Muddy River	50	N.E.	15	115	
" Grand Osage River	397	S. W.	18	133	38° 31'16.9″
" the Murrow Creek	20	S. W.	5	138	

THE ELKHORN PYRAMID, on the Upper Missouri

Names of remarkable places	The width of rivers and creeks in yds	Side on which they are Situated	Distance from one place to another	Distances up the Missouri from the Mississippi	Latitude North of important places
	yards		Ms	Ms	
To the Cedar Island & Creek	20	N.E.	7	145	
" " Lead Mine Hill		S.W.	9	154	
" " Manitou Creek	20	S W.	8	162	
" " Split rock Creek	20	N E.	8	170	
" " Saline or Salt River	30	S.W.	3	173	
" " Manitou River	30	N.E.	9	182	
" " Good Womans River	35	N.E.	9	191	
" " Mine River	70	S.W.	9	200	
" " Arrow Prarie		S.W.	6	206	
" Two Charliton Rivers	{30 {70	N.E.	14	220	
" " antient village of the Missouri Nation near which place Fort Orleans stood		N E.	16	236	
" Grand River	90	N.E.	4	240	38° 47' 34"
" " Snake Creek	18	N.E.	6	246	
" " antient village of the little Osarge		S.W.	10	256	
" " Tiger's Island and Creek	25	N.E.	20	276	
" " Eueberts 1 Island Creek		S.W.	12	388	
" " Fire prarie Creek		S.W.	12	300	
" " Fort point		S.W.	6	306	
" " Hay Cabin Creek	20	S.W.	6	312	
" " Coal Bank		S.W.	9	321	
" " Blue water River	30	S.W.	10	331	
" Kanzas River	230	S.W.	9	340	39° 5' 25.7"
" the Little River Platt	60	N.E.	9	349	
" [point] 1½ Ms above Dimond Island		S.W.	—	—	39° 9' 38.6"
" the Waucarba, Warconda Island opposite the 1st Old Kanzas Village	—	S.W.	26	377	
" 3 Ms below the 2d old village of the Kances	—	S.W.	—	—	39° 25' 47.5"
" " Independance Creek a mile below the 2nd old Kanzas Village		S.W.	28	405	
" " St Michaels prarie		N.E.	25	430	
" " Nadawa River	70	N.E.	20	450	39° 39' 22.4"
" " Wolf or Loup River	60	S.W.	14	464	
" Big Ne-me-har River	80	S.W.	16	480	39° 55' 56"
" the Tar-ki-o Creek	23	N.E.	3	483	
opposit the center of Good Island	—	S.W.	—	—	40° 20' 12"
" " Neesh-nah-ba-to-no River	50	N E.	25	508	
" " Little Ne-ma-har River	48	S.W.	8	516	40° 8' 31.8"2

1 Biddle renders this (ii, p. 422) as " Hubert's ;" but in the text of this journal (i, p. 16) he makes it " Eau Beau, or Clear Water." — ED.

2 This latitude is given, Codex A, p. 180, as that " opsd a Island mentioned in the 2d & 3d Course of the 15th of July on L. S." This is so near the Little Nemahar River that it is given as the latitude of that stream. — ED.

Names of remarkable places.	The width of rivers and creeks in yᵈˢ	Side on which they are Situated	Distance from one place to another	Distances up the Missouri from the Mississippi	Latitude North of important places
	yards		Ms	Ms	
To the *Bald pated prarie* the Neesh-nahbatona within 150 yards of the Missouri	—	N.E.	23	539	40° 27′ 6.4″
P^t opposit to a Island being the extremity of the 4th course of July 19th on L. S.	—	S. W	—	—	40° 29′ 38″
" " Weeping Water Creek	25	S. W.	29	568	
" " *River Platt* (or Shoal river	600	S. W.	32	600	40° 54′ 35″
" " Butterfly or papelion Creek	18	S. W.	3		
" " Musquetor Creek	22	N.E.	7	610	
" " Camp p^t of observ^n 10 m^s N. 15° W of Platt R *White Catfish Camp*	—	S. W.	—	—	41° 3′ 19.4″
" " antiant Village of the Ottoes		S. W.	11		
" " antient Ayauways Village below a Bluff on the N. E. Side		N.E.	6		
" " Bowyers river	25	N.E.	11		
" Councill Bluffs (establishm^t)		S. W.	12	650	41° 17′ 0″
opposit pond Inlet August 4th	—	S. W.	—	—	41° 25′ 3″
on the Side of a Sand Island August 5th	—	—	—	—	41° 30′ 6″
" Soldiers River	40	N.E.	39	689	
" *Ea-neah, Wau-de-pon* or Stone River Little Sieux R.	80	N.E.	44	733	41° 42′ 34.3″
" the hill where the Late King of the Mahars was buried on a high hill		S. W.			42° 1′ 3.8″
" the *Wau-can-de* or bad Sperit Creek		S. W.	55	788	
around a bend of the river to the N. E. the Gorge of which is only 974 Yds			21	809	
To an Island 3 miles N E of the Mahar vil^g Camp *Fish* aug^t 14th			27	836	42° 13′ 41″
" Floyds Bluff and River	35	N.E.	14	850	
" the Big Sieoux River	110	N.E.	3	853	42° 23′ 49″
" " commencement of the Copperas cobalt, pirites and alum bluffs		S. W.	27	880	
To the Hot or burning Bluffs		S. W.	30	910	
" " White Stone River	30	N.E.	8	918	
" " Petite Arc an old Mahar Village. at the mouth of little bow Creek	15	S. W.	20	938	
" *River Jacque* or James River	90	N.E.	12	950	42° 53′ 13″
" the Calumet Bluffs (of mineral)		S. W.	10	960	
" Antient fortification Good mans Is^d		S. W.	16	976	
" Plumb Creek	12	N.E.	10	986	
" White paint Creek	28	S. W.	8	994	
" Quicurre or rapid river	152	S. W.	6	1000	

Names of remarkable places	The width of rivers and creeks in yds	Side on which they are Situated	Distance from one place to another	Distances up the Missouri from the Mississippi	Latitude North of important places
	yards		Ms	Ms	
To the Poncar River & Village	30	S.W.	10	1010	
" " Dome and village of Burrowing or barking Squirels		S.W.	20	1030	
" " Island of Cedar			45	1075	
" White River (handsom Spot)	300	S.W.	55	1130	
" the three Rivers of the Seioux pass opposit an Island	35 &c.	N.E.	22	1152	
" an Island in the comencmt. of the big bend		N.E.	20	1172	
" upper part of the big bend, or " Grand de Tourte" the gorge of which is 1¼ Ms		S.W.	30	1202	
" Tylors River	35	S.W.	6	1208	
" Louisells [*Loisel's*] Fort on Cedar Island			18	1226	44° 11' 33"
" Teton River	70	S.W.	37	1263	
" the upper of five old Ricara Villages reduced by the Sieoux & abandoned		S.W.	42	1305	
" Chyenne River (place for an Estmt)	400	S.W.	5	1310	44° 19' 36"
" an old ricara village on *La-hoo-catts* Island			47	1357	
" Otter Creek	22	S.W.	35	—	
" *Sar-war-kar-na* River	90	S.W.	40	1397	45° 35' 5"
" *We-tar-hoo* River	120	S.W.	25	1422	
" Maropa River	25	S.W.	2	—	
To 1st Ricaras Village on an Island		S.W.	4		
" 2d *Ricaras* 3 Villages		S.W.	4	1430	
" the Stone Idol Creek	18	N.E.	18		
" " *War-re-con-ne* River	35	N.E.	40	1488	
" Cannon Ball River	140	S W.	12	1500	46° 29' 0"
" *Shy-wish* or Fish Crek	28	N.E.	5		
" Chesschetar River near 6 old Mandan Vgs	38	S.W.	40	1540	
" Hunting Creek	25	S.W	14		
" the Old Ricara & Mandan Villages		S.W.	40	1580	
" Fort Mandan (wintering post of 1804)		N.E.	20	1600	47° 21' 47"

[Here, in the journal written at Fort Mandan (Codex C), Clark inserted the following table based upon Indian information. — ED.]

The Missouri and it's Subsidiary Streams higher up; are taken altogether from information collected dureing the Winter 1804, 5 of Indians &c.

	near yds		about miles	miles
To the Mouth of the little Missouri or *E- mâh-tark, Ah-Zhah*	100	S. W.	100	1730
To Ok-hah, Âh-zhah, or the White Earth River	100	N. W.	117	1847
To the Mouth of *Mee, Ah-zhah* or *Yellow Stone* River	400	S. W.	3	1850
To the mouth of *Ah-mâh-tâh, ru-shush-sher,* or the Rivet which Scolds at all others	abt. 100	North	150	2000
To the Mouth of the *Mah-tush; ah-zhah* or the Muscle Shell River	140	South	120	2120
" the Great Falls	—	—	120	2240
" *Mah-pat-puh, Ah-zhah* or Medison River	150	N. W.	15	2255
To the 1st Chain of Rockey mountains about	—	—	60	2315
To the 2nd Chain of Rockey mountains about	—	—	75	2390
To the *three* forks of the Missouri above the 3rd Chain of mountains	—	—	75	2465
To the foot of the next mountain nearly West	—	N. W.	50	2515
To a large River on the West of the mountain	—	—	15	2530

The Yellow Stone River and it's Subsidiary Streams &c.

	yards		miles	miles
To the mouth of *Oke-tar-pas-ah-ha*	abt. 30	S. E.	75	1705
" *War-rah-sash* or Powder R	" 40	S. E.	75	1780
" *Le-ze-ka* or Tongu[e] River	" 100	S. E.	50	1830
" *Mar-shas-kap* River	" 40	S. E.	100	1930
" Little Wolf mountain Creek	" 20	N. W.	55	1985
" *Ark tar-ha* River	" 30	S. E.	70	2055
" *Ar-sar-ta* or Bighorn R	" 150	S. E.	75	2130
" To the Rockey or Shineing Mountains	—	N. W.	200	2330

[From Fort Mandan]	Width in Yards	Side on which they are situated	Distance from one place to another	Distances up the Missouri from the Mississippi	Latitudes & remarks &c
To Mandan Villages 1 on each Side			4	1604	
" Knife river on which the two Minetarre and the Mahar has villages are Situated near the mouth	80	S.W.	2	1606	
" the Island			11	1617	small
" Menatarras Wintering Village St^d	—		13½	—	abandoned
" " Miry River on Star^d side	10	N.E.	15	1633	bold stream
" an Island in the little bason			28		small
" Little Missouri River	134	S W.	29	1690	47° 31'. 26".2. N.
" the Wild onion Creek	16	N.E.	12	1702	a little water
" " Goose egg Lake	300	N.E.	9	1711	Small
" " Shabonos Creek	20	S.W.	16	1727	47° 47' 16"$\frac{3}{10}$ N.
" " Goat pen Creek	20	N.E.	16	1743	{ at this place Mouse river approaches near the Missouri
" " Halls Strand Lake & Creek		N.E.	47	1790	extream N. point
" " *White earth* River	60	N.E.	50	1840	Still & deep
Rochejhone or Yellow Stone River	858	S.W.	40	*1880*	48° –00'–00" N.
to Marthys River	50	N.E.	60	1940	High Coloured
" Porcupine River	112	N.E.	50	1990	Some timber on it
To 2000 Mile Creek	30	S.W.		1993	no water at pes^t
To Indian Fort Creek dry	—	S.W.	10	2003	a fort of logs
" the little Dry Creek	25	S.W.	27	2030	no water in it
" Lack water Creek	25	N E.	1½	2031½	d? d? d? d?
" the Big Dry Creek	100	S.W.	7½	2039	d? d? d? d?
" " Little Dry River	200	S.W.	6	2045	d? d? d? d?
" " Gulf in a Star^d Bend			32	2077	47° 36' 11"
to *Milk River*	150	N.E.	13	2090	Color of tea
" Big Dry River	400	S.W.	25	2115	no water runing
" Werners Run	10	N.E.	9	2124	47° 25' –33"$\frac{1}{10}$.
" Pine Creek	20	N.E.	36	2160	Saw 1st pine
" Gibsons River	35	N.E.	17	2177	a little running wat^r.
" Brown Bear defeated Creek	40	S.W.	12	2189	d° d° d°
" Brattens River	100	N.E.	24	2213	47° 13' 51" N.
" Burnt Lodge Creek	50	S.W.	6	2219	no water running
" Wisers Creek	40	N.E	14	2233	a little running W.
" Blowingfly Creek	25	S.W.	32	2265	d° d° d°
" Muscle Shell River	110	S.W.	5	2270	47° 0' 24.6"
" Grouse Creek	20	N.E.	30	2300	no running water
" Teapot Creek	15	N.E.	8	2308	d° d? d?
" North Mountain Creek	30	N.E.	28	2336	running water
" South Mountain Creek	30	S.W.	18	2354	d? d?
" Ibex Island			15	2369	{ Killed the 1st big horn
" Goodriches Island			9	2378	

[From Fort Mandan]	Width in Yards	Side on which they are situated	Distance from one place to another	Distances up the Missouri from the Mississippi	Latitudes & remarks &c
To Windsers Creek	30	N.E.	7	2385	some water runs
" Softshell turtle Creek	25	N.E.	6	2391	d° d° d°
" Elk rapid (Swift water)			9	2400	{ Doe Elk & fawn swam over
" Thompsons Creek	28	N.E.	27½	2427½	{ vally above M^{ts} bold stream
" Bull Creek	25	S.W.	8½	2436	{ a Buffalow crossed a canoe & then charged through camp
" Judieths River Big horn	100	S.W.	3	2439	killed 3 big horns
" Vally Creek	20	N.E	1	2440	thro a vally N.
" Ash rapid (swift water)			3	2443	Some Ash trees.
" Slaughter River	40	S.W.	11	2454	{ a great n° of buffalow drove down a clift and dashed to pieces on St^{d} I speared a wolf.
" the Stone Wall Creek above those emence nateral walls	30	N.E.	26	2480	{ curious appearance of walls below
" Maria's River	186	N.E.	41	2521	47° 25' 17.2 N.
" Snow River	50	S.W.	19	2540	{ M^{ts} Cov^{d} with Snow head of this river
" Shields River	35	S.W.	28	2568	bold Stream
" the foot of the enterance of portage *River* 5 Miles below the Great falls	45	S.W.	7	2575	47° 8' 4" 9/10 N.

[From this point the final draft follows the land route — Lewis and Clark's pass to the Kooskooskee. The table here inserted follows the actual route going out and is taken from both Codex I and Clark-Voorhis note-book No. 4. — ED.]

Names of remarkable places.		[Distance] from one place to another	Distance to the mouth of Missouri	Latitudes & remarks, &^{c}
to Portage River Lar^{d} Side	55	1	2576	rapid & Sholey
to the first great fall of 87 feet pitch		6	2582	Continual Spray
to the Second fall of 19 feet pitch		3½	—	or 1718 poles
to the Grand Cascade of 47 feet 8 In. pitch		½	—	= 102 poles
to the upper fall of 26.5 pitch total fall above port^{g} about 362 feet		2¾	2590½	= 881 poles
to Medicine River St^{d}	137	3¾	2594¼	1196 poles

Names of remarkable places	[Distance] from one place to another	Distance to the mouth of Missouri	Latitudes & remarks, &c
to the head of the Portage on the Ld at the White Bear Islands, the land portage 18 miles thro. a plain	3	2597¼	{ 972 poles / 47° 3′ 33″ N.
to Smith's River Lard 80	30¾	2628	bold current & Vally.
to the Rockey Mountains at Pine Island rapid 40¼		2668¼	46° 42′ 14″ 7/10
to Dearbourne's River Std 80	8¾	2676	bold current & in Mtn
to Gun brook Ld 10	2	2678	found a fusee
to Ordways Creek Std 25	10	2688	bold Current V [al]ly
to the Great gate of the rocky Mounts river confined in a narrow Chanel between clifts 10 or 1200 feet high	24	2712	{ W. Clark crossed Sd / Mt.
to Potts's Vally Creek Std bold	6	2718	Wide Vally N.
to Pryors Vally River Std 28	20	2738	Latd 46° 10′ 32″ 9/10 N bold Current and wide extensive Vally saw a smoke N.W.
to White Earth Creek Std 15	30	2768	bold
to WhiteHouse Creek Lard bold	11	2779	Some timber on it
to Yorks 8 Islands	23	2802	{ W.C. on land York / tired
to Gass's Vally Creek Std 25	14	2816	bold & 3 forks
to the Little Gate of the Mountain	5	2821	we saw a horse
to Howards Creek Lard bold	6	2827	{ Mistook the opening / of the creek for the [1]
to the Three Forks of Missouri at Jefferson, Maddison & Gallitins rivers. Gallitins on Ld and 70 Yds wide Maddeson 90 yds wide & Jeffersons 90 yds wide and is the Std fork	21	2848	{ W. C. return to the / party very sick. 45° 22′ 34″. N
Up Jeffersons River			
to Philosophy River on Ld side 30	15	2863	*bold rapid* full of beaver
to the Narrows of the 3d Mountn	17	2880	M. L. go a head
to Frasures Creek & rapid Ld bold	8	2888	*bad rapid*
to R. Field's Vally Creek Sd 28	4	2892	R. F. killed 4 deer
to Wisdom River Std 40	55	2947	45° 2′ 21″ 6/10 N
to Philanthrophy River Ld 30	12	2959	river crooked
to Beaver head Clift Stad	34	2993	do do
to McNeals Creek Ld 17	37	3030	bold stream
to the 4th Gap of the Mountain	28	3058	{ Saw Several rattle / snakes
to Willards Creek Std bold	6	3064	{ Willard discovered this the day before we got to it.
to a rapid at the Narrows of 5th Mtn	21	3085	{ a bad rapid for half / a mile

[1] MS. illegible. — ED.

Names of remarkable places	[Distance] from one place to another	Distance to the mouth of Missouri	Latitudes & remarks &c
to the East Fork of *Jeffersons* river at which place left the canoes and commen[c]ed a portage	11	3096	44º 35′ 28″ $\frac{1}{10}$
to the 3 forks in Snake Indian cove	15	3111	W. C. Camp with Inds
to the head Spring of *Jeffersons* river in a Dividing ridge of the rock[y] M.	13	3124	meet an Ind on a Mule
to East fork of Lewis's river the S.E. branch of the Columbia at the *So so nee* or Snake indian incampment in Lodges made of bushes at which place the river is 36 yds	10	3134	*44º 23′ 22″ $\frac{7}{10}$*
to the main fork of Lewis'es River Ld 90	18	3152	from the South East
to Salmon Creek Std Side bold	9	3161	Shields killed a salmon
to Tower run Std small	14	3175	leave Lewis's river
Up tower run to the forks of the road	4	3179	road leaves the river to the right
Across the hills. To fish Creek six miles north of it's mouth 25	20	3199	hilly road
Up Fish creek to the forks of the road & Creek	7½	3206½	leave the road to the right
to the Top of a Snow Mountain at the head of the west fork of fish creek	21½	3228	pilot lost his way
to Clark's River at a Village of 33 tents of Flathead	12	3240	River from right
Down Clark's River			
to flour Camp Creek Ld bold	7	3247	over a mountn
to Horse Vally Creek from the right	26	3273	bold stream
to Scattered Creek from the right passing through Hors[e] Vally	22	3295	*46º 41′ −38″.9*
to Travellers rest Creek Ld 30	21	3316	*46º 48′.28″.$\frac{8}{10}$*
passing up Travellers rest Creek to the forks of the road and Creek Sd	11	3327	Here we fall into the Portage from the Falls of the Missouri across the Mountains road to our right
to the Hot Springs on the right	14	3341	nearly boiling
to the Glades on the Dividing Mt	10	3351	
to the forks of Glade Creek	6	3357	a fork from the North we crossed to S.E. side
to Koos-koos-ke river at the enterance of Glade Creek	9	3366	*Killed and eate a Coalt*
to the foot of the Great Mountains	6	3372	open Hilly pine country
Across the Great *Rocky Mountains*			
to the top of a Mountain Covered with Snow the 15th of Septr a road comes in from the right on the mountain	8	3380	Snow high ruged

Names of remarkable places	[Distance] from one place to another	Distance to the mouth of Missouri	Latitudes & remarks, &c.
to a branch running to the right on M	13	3393	Snowed all day / Eate a coalt
to a branch running to the left	10	3403	Eat a Coalt
to Hungary Creek from the right	32		Hills covered with snow
to the forks of Collins's Creek from the right	26		Killed a Horse
to the foot of the Rocky Mountains on the West side	8	3469	open pine country
to the *Cho-pun-nish* Village	6		seat^d in a small prarie
to Koos-koos-ke River at the Mouth of Village Creek from the right	17		about 120 y^{ds} wide
to Rock dam Creek Star^d 20 yds	3	[3495]	damed by rocks

[At this point the navigation by water was again resumed, and our table hereafter follows the final draft. The two tables of distances from the Mississippi differ according to the varying length of the routes — direct and actual. — ED.]

Remarkable places decending the Columbia &c &c	width of the rivers and Creeks	the Side on which they are Situated	Distance from one place to another	Distance Decending the Columbia	Distance from the Mississippi [direct route]	Distance from the Mississippi [actual route]	Latitude Remarks &c
	yds		M^s.	M^s	Miles		
To the enterance of Rock dam Creek	20	N.	8	8	2923	3495	
" " Chopunnish River	120	N.	5	13	2928	3500	46° 34' 56.2"
" Canister run	—	—	19	—	—	—	passed 16 rapids
" " Colters Creek	35	N.	18	50	2978	3537	passed 14 rapids
" Lewis's River at the enterance of the Kooskooske river	200	S.	23	73	2988	3560	46° 29' 21.7"
" the Swet house Village & run		S.	7	80		3567	Passed 1 rapid
" " Pilots Village		N.	11	91	3006	3578	passed 4 rapids
" a Village of Mat Lodges		N	13	—		3591	" 3 "
" " *Ki-moo-e-nimm* Creek	20	S	35	139		3626	" 8 "
" Drewyers river below the Narrows of Lewis's R 2½ miles & 30 yds wide	30	N.	5	144	3059	3631	" 1 "
" the Cave rapid (Canoe Sunk)			28	172		3659	passed 5 rapids
" the Bason rapid. (bad)			34	206	3121	3693	" 8 "
" " Discharge Rapid (bad)			14	220	3135	3707	" 4 "

Remarkable places decending the Columbia &c &c	width of the rivers and Creeks	the Side on which they are Situated	Distance from one place to another	Distance Decending the Columbia	Distance from the Mississippi [direct route]	Distance from the Mississippi [actual route]	Latitude Remarks &c
	yds		Ms.	Ms.	Miles		
To Columbia at the mouth of Lewis's river from the East		S.E.	7	227	3142	3714	46° 15′ 13.9″
" Wallarwallars River passd 11 large mat Lodges of that nation	40	S.E	16	243	3158	3730	passed 2 rapids one bad. hills about 200 feet.
" Muscleshell Rapid (bad) passed 33 mat lodges of the Wallarwallars			25	268	3183	3755	passed 2 rapids Low Cty C[om]. m[ences on] Ld
" Pillacon Rapid. passed 48 lodges of the Pishquitpahs nation		N.	22	290	3205	3777	low country on both sides of R
" 21 lodges of the wahhowpum nation residing on three Islands at the commencement of the high country		N.	18	308	3223	3795	passed 2 rapids (horse secrfised to the dead)
" 8 Lodges of the wahhowpums at short rapid		N.	27	335	3250	3820	passed 2 rapids
" the Short Rapid	—	—	6	—	—	3826	" 1 "
" Rocky Rapid. 9 lodges of the Same nation		N.	7	348	3263	3833	" 1 "
" River La Page, bad rapid	40	S.	9	357	3272	3842	" 2 "
" 27 lodges of the Enesher nation at fish tack rapid		N.	10	367	3282	3852	Campd passed 1 rapid
" Towannahiooks River	180	S	8	375	3290	3860	we all viewed it above its mouth
" The Great Falls or the Columbia river of 37 ft 8 Ins near which there are 40 Mat lodges of the Enesher Nation		N.	4	379	3294	3864	45° 42′ 57.3″
The Short narrows 45 yds wide			2	381	3296		passed 1 rapid
" Skillute Village of 21 large wood houses at the long narrows from 50 to 100 yds wide		N.	4	385	3300	3870	45° 1′ ″1
" Chilluckitequaw Village of 8 large wood houses		N.	14	399	3314	3884	bought Dogs

[1] The latitude here given is imperfect. — ED.

Remarkable places decending the Columbia &c &c	width of the rivers and Creeks	the Side on which they are situated	Distance from one place to another	Distance Decending the Columbia	Distance from the Mississippi [direct route]	Distance from the Mississippi [actual route]	Latitude Remarks &c
	yds		M^s	M^s	Miles		
To Cataract river a few miles below a Village of 7 houses and immediately above one of 11 Houses of the Chilluckittequaw nation	60	N.	10	409	3324	3894	10 nations live up this river. no fish
" Sepulchre Rock, opposite to a Village of H^s of Chilluckitteq^s		N.	4	413	3328		
" River Labeich opposite to 26 houses of the Smackshop Nation, Houses scattered on the N. Side each side	46	S	9	422	3337	3907	the first houses we have seen on the south side
" Little Lake Canoe Creek 3 houses of the Smackshop nation	28	N.	10	432	3347	3917	saw Several Canoes encamped
" Cruzatts River	60	N.	12	444	3359	3929	stumps out from shore some dist^s
" The Grand Rapid just below the village of the Yehuh tribe of the Shahala Nation of 14 wood houses		[*]N	6	450	3365	3935	45° 44' 3.8"
" Clahcellah Village of the Shahala nation, near the foot of the rapids. 7 Houses		N.	6	456	3371		
" Wahclellar Village of the Shahala Nation 23 houses just below the entrance of the beacon rock creek [1]		N.	6	462	3377		This Beaten rock rises from a leavel bottom near the R
Tide Water. " Phoca Rock in the river 60 feet above water 100 foot high			11	473	3388	3958	This rock is near the middle of the river Saw Seal's

[1] The Indian habitations in this region shifted periodically, as is evident from the journal entry April 9, 1806. On the downward journey they differed from those of the return, as given here. The entries, therefore, in Codex I (compiled at Fort Clatsop), and depicted on the map of the Great Rapids, are as follows: "to a Village below the great rapids of 4 houses abandoned ops^d a. 2^d bad rapid, one mile not inhabited; to 4 houses of the *Sha-ha-lah* Nation at the lower rapids of the Columbia river at *tide water*, 6 miles, not inhabited; to a Village of 9 houses of the Shahalah Nation on the Star^d Side near the beaten rock 800 feet hi[gh] 5 miles, a man with a brass barrel gun." These three entries take the place of the two in the text,

Remarkable places decending the Columbia &c &c	width of the rivers and Creeks	the Side on which they are Situated	Distance from one place to another	Distance Decending the Columbia	Distance from the Mississippi [direct route]	Distance from the Mississippi [actual route]	Latitude Remarks &c
	yds		M^s	M^s	Miles		
To the Commencement of the Columbian Vally, wide & beautiful	—	—	6	—	—	3964	rich & extensive
" Quicksand River	120	S.	3	482	3397	3967	shallow & Spreads over a wide bar
" Seal River ops^d upper p^t of white brant Isl^d	80	N.	3	485		3970	emence N^o of brant
" Nechacokee village opposite to the dimond Island		S.	4	489		3974	2 large Ponds on this Island.
" White goose Isl^d ops^d Low^r p^t	—	—	6	—	—	3980	I sho[t] white gees
" Shahala Village of 25 temperary houses		S.	6	501	3416	3986	grass houses &c^s
" the head of image Canoe Isl^d	—	—	4	—	—	3990	met 2 canoes on which was images
" Multnomah River	500	S.	10	515	3430	4000	Ind^d stol^d Tomh^k
" Multnomah Village [*]at narrow part of the Columbia		S.	6	521	—	4006	Camp^d op^s a N^o of noisey fowls
" Quathlahpohtle Village at the lower Point of an Island near the Star^d Shore		N.	8	529		4014	Ind^s Vis^t us in 7 canoes
" Cahwahnakiooks River	200	N.	1	530	3445	4015	
" the lower Point of *Wappato* Island		S.	1	—	—	4016	a Chan^l ¼ M^l wide
" Cathlahaws Creek and Village	18	N.	3	540	3455	4025	I thought was a I^d
" Lower extremity of Elallah or deer Island		S.	6	546	—	4031	Indian name. I seen 16 snakes
" the *Narrows* of the Mountain and lower part of the Columbian vally			7			4038	camped rained. killed a Pheasant.
" Coweliske River about the entrance and up this river the Skillute nation reside	150	N.	6	559	3474	4044	Ind^s acc^t
" Fannys Island & bottom		S.	16	575	3490	4060	bottom on the L^d is wide
" the Sea Otter Island			12	587	3502	4072	foggy
" " Upper Village of theWarkiacumsNation		N.	6	593	3502	4078	Petticoat women at this village
" the lower Village of the Warkiacum Nation of 7 houses under a high hill.		N	9			4087	landed a few M[inutes] bought a dog.

for the Clahclellah and Wahclellar villages.   The distances are seen to be the same.— ED.

From the Waukiacum Upper Village decending the Columbia on the South Side

Remarkable places decending the Columbia &c &c	the Side on which they are Sit-uated	Dis-tance from one place to an-other	Dis-tance De-cend-ing the Colum-bia	Distance from the Missis-sippi [direct route]	Distance from the Missis-sippi [actual route]	Latitude Remarks &c.
To Point *Samuel* on Star^d Side		M^s 6	M^s	Miles	4094	high land
To the Cath.lah-mâh Town of 9 houses South of the Seal Islands		8			4102	on high land
To Point William opposit the Shallow Bay		10			4111	point in this form

To Point Meriwether above Meriwethers Bay	S.	10	626	3541	4121	3 rivers mouth
" Fort Clatsop on the West Side of and 3 miles up the Netul river from Meri-wether bay and Seven miles East from nearest part of the Sea coast. at this fort Capt M Lewis and Capt Wm Clark wintered in the winter 1805–6	S	7	—	—	4128	
" Clat-Sop Village on the low point of Meriwethers Bay and 7 miles N W of *Fort Clatsop*	S.	10	634	3529	4138	large wood houses
" Point Adams at the enter-ance of Columbia into the Pacific ocean or Great South Sea in Latitude 46° 15′ North and Longt^d 124° 57′ West from Greenwitch	S.	6	640	*3555*	4144	low land[1]

[1] Here ends the final draft of the Summary (except for Lewis and Clark's pass, and the Yellowstone, given below). What follows is taken from the Summary in Codex I, and in Clark-Voorhis note-book No. 4. There is a slight discrepancy in the figures of these two accounts; the former makes the distance 4134 miles, the latter 4144. — ED.

Remarkable places decending the Columbia &c &c	the Side on which they are situated	Distance from one place to another	Distance Decending the Columbia	Distance from the Mississippi [direct route]	Distance from the Mississippi [actual route]	Latitude Remarks &c.
		M^s	M^s	Miles		
[*The Northern Shore of the River*]						
To the Shallow bay or nitch on the Star^d side 5m. Deep		16			4103 [1]	this bay is about 5m. deep and contains great numbers of fow[l]s.
To Point Distress	N	16	—	—	4119	lay 6 days
to Station Camp near an old Chinnook Village of 36 houses	N.	2	—	—	4121	delayed 10 days
to Cape Disapointment at the Enterance of the Columbia river into the Great Pacific Ocean in Lat^d *46º 19.' 11'' 1/10 N.* and Longitude *124º 57'. 0–W.*	N	11	—	—	4132	46° 19′ 11.1″

On the Sea Coast to the N N W of Cape Disapointment

To the Comencement of a Sandy Coast & low land	5	W. C. Saw the coast much further
Point Lewis High land N. of the Chinnook Villages is about	15	
to the *Chiltz* Nation. about	6	Indian information
to the *Cla-moi-to-micks* Tribe along the N W Coast		{ Indian account taken at different times
to *Potoashs* Tribe reside to the N West along the Coast		
to the *Quinielts* reside from the Potoash N W along the same coast about Cape Sh[o]alwater noumerous	15	
to *Qui eet so* reside from the Quinielts N W along the coast		
to *Chil-lâte-ho-kle* reside from Quieet-so N W along same coast about	19	
to *Quinechart* verry noumerous reside from the Chillatehokle N W along the same coast and on the slashes and creeks	60	NOTE. 50 mile of the above from the information of Indians.
Pailsh reside betwen the Potoash and Quinelt on the same coast.		

[1] This distance is measured from the "lower village of the Waukiacums." — ED.

On the sea coaste to the S. S. E.

From point Adams		Distances	Latitude, Remarks &c.
to *Ne-er-ca-war-re-ca* Creek & old Clatsop village	8	4152	3 houses remain
to the enterance of *Clât.sop* river 85 yards wide at 3 houses remains of an old Vilg.	9	4161	3 old towns
to the Salt works at the foot of a mountain near 4 houses	2	4163	2 old towns & Canoe vaults
to the most projected part of the Mountain of Clark's point of view near 1000 feet above the leavel of the Sea imediately under it	7	4170	one rock out steep assent
to an old *Kil-â-mox* Village	3	4173	abandoned N⁰. of rocks out
to the Mouth of *E-co-la* or whale Creek 35 yᵈˢ wide, and 4 huts of *Kil-a-mox* boiling whale blubber	6	4179	High rugid rocks out
to 6 huts of Kil-â-mox boiling blubber	2	4181	{ this was the extent of Capᵗ Clarks rout on this coast
to the Great *Kil-â-mox* Town at the enterance of Ni-ê-lee Creek	20	4201	Indˢ. ac. a sand bar out
to *Kil-har-hurst's* Town of Kil-â-mox at the Enterance *Kila-mox* Bay	about 5 miles		a rock in entrˢ
to *Kil-har-nar's* town of *Kil-a-mox* on the Bay at the mouth of a Creek	2		on the bay
to *Chish-ucks* town of *Kil-â-mox* at the Enterance of Kilamox river, which is about 100 yds 2 houses up this R	2		heads near Columbia
to Tow-er-quot-tons Creek & Town	2		
to *Chuck-tins* Town and Creek at the bottom of the Bay (which I call Kilamox Bay)	2		
Miles	70		

Note ☞ 30 miles of this course is from the information of Indians, collected from different persons. They further inform me that the *Kil á mox* have two Small villages on the Kil á mox river, it is very rapid without any purpindicular falls, that nation pass across from the head of this little river to the Columbian Vally, which is at no great Distance from its head at *Wappato* Island, and pass down the *Chock-âh' lil'.com* or Columbia river with the *Wappato* they purchase

[71]

NOTES, *from the Mouth of Columbia.*

To the Wappato Island, center is . .	. S. 20.° E 108 miles
To quick Sand river is	. S. 32.° E 121 "
To the grand rapids is	. S. 47.° E 128 "
to the Great falls is	. S. 65.° E. 172 "
to the Mouth of *Lewis's river* . . .	. East 240 "

From *the Mouth of Lewis'es river*

to the Mouth of Kooskooske is	N. 52.° E 96 Miles
to the Mouth of *Cho-pun-nich R* ⎱ at the Canoe Camp is ⎰	East 144 Miles
to the longshute or Narrows above	N. 28.° E. 55 Mile

[Lewis and Clark's Pass] [1]

Leaveing the Missouri below the Falls and passing by Land to the Navagable Waters of the Columbia River

Names of remarkable places	Width of the rivers & Creeks	Distance from one place to another	Distance from the falls of Missouri	Distance from the Mississippi
	yd	M.^{S}	M.^{S}	Miles
To the enterance of Medicine River passed 1st pitch of 87 feet, 2^d of 19 feet, 3^d of 47 feet 8 inches, and 4th of 26 feet 5 inches added to the rapids makes a fall of 362 feet	137	18	18	2593
To fort Mountain passing through the plains between Medicine river and the Missouri near the Missouri up the N. Side of the Missouri to the 1st bend above the entrance of Smiths river		15	33	2608
To the Rocky Mountains at a Gap on the ridge which divites the waters of the Missouri from those of the Columbia passing the N. p.^{t} of a Mt.^{n} and then crossing Dearborns river		35	68	2643
To a fork of Cohohlarishkit river from the N. passed 4 Creeks from N	45	40	108	2683
To Seamons Creek from the N	20	7	115	
To Werners Creek N	35	10	125	2700
" the East fork of Clarks river at the enterance of Cohohlarishkit R	120	30	155	2730
" Clarks River at the forks	150	12	167	2742
" Travellers rest Creek on the west Side of Clarks river above the forks	25	5	172	2747

[1] In the final draft, the following table was inserted between the Great Falls of the Missouri and "Remarkable places decending the Columbia." It gives the route by which Lewis returned from the Kooskooskee to the Missouri, in reversed order. — ED.

THE WHITE CASTLES, on the Upper Missouri

Names of remarkable places	Width of the rivers & Creeks	Distance from one place to another	Distance from the falls of Missouri	Distance from the Mississippi
	yd	M^s	M^s	Miles
To the Forks of Travellers rest Creek at a right hand road	10	18	190	
" the Hot Springs, on the N. side of the Creek	3	13	203	2778
" " Quawmash glades passing the head of the creek to a branch of Kooskooske River		7	210	
To the North branch of Kooskooske river, a left hand road leads off at 5 M^s		7	217	
To the junction of the roads on the top of a Snowey Mountain crossed a fork of Flathead R. at 2 Ms the left hand road passing by a fishery		10	227	2802
From the forks of the road on the Top of the Snow Mountains (from the left)				
To Hungary Creek from the right passing on a Dividing Mounteing between the Flathead and Chopunish passing on deep Snow except on two places which are open with a South exposure at 8 & 36 Miles		54	281	2856
[1]To a Glade up Hungary Creek		6	287	
To a Glade on a Small branch of d°		8	295	
To a Glade on Fish Creek	10	9	304	
" Collins's Creek	25	13	317	
" Quawmash flatts		11	328	2903
" Kooskooske or Flathead River in a pine Country	120	12	340	2915.

Note in passing from the falls of Missouri across the Rocky Mountains to the forks of Kooskooske, the nearest navagable waters of the Columbia you have 200 miles of Good road to Hot Springs on Clarks river; 140 miles of high Steep ruged mountain 60 miles of which is covered from 2 to 8 feet deep with Snow the last of June, 1806 Lat^d of the falls of Missouri 47° 8' 4" North. Clarks river forks Lat^d 46° 48' 0" North. Kooskooskia forks Lat^d 46° 34' 0' North.

[2] The rout by which we went out by the way of the Missouri to it's

---

1 The Clark-Voorhis note-book No. 4 gives the two following entries, instead of those in the text taken from Codex N:

"To the foot of the Rocky Mountains on the West side at a leavel country, 45 miles, 326 from the Falls, 2901 total. To the forks of Kooskooskea River from whence it is navigable, 14 miles, 340 from the Falls, 2915 total." — ED.

2 This long note on the route and the fur trade was added to the final draft before giving the Summary for the Yellowstone River. — ED.

head 3096 miles thence by land, by way of Lewis'es River over to Clarks river and down that to the enterance of travellers rest Creek where all the roads from different routs come together thence across the ruged part of the rocky Mountains to the Navagable branches of the Columbia 398 Miles. thence down that river 640 miles to the Pacific Ocean makeing a Total distance of 4134 miles. On our return in 1806 from Travellers rest Creek directly to the *falls* of the Missouri River Shortens the distance about 579 miles, and a much better rout, reduceing the distance from Mississippi to the Pacific Ocean to *3555* miles. 2575 miles of this distance is up the Missouri to the *Falls* of that river from thence passing through the plains and across the Rocky Mountains to the navagable part of Kooskooske river a branch of the Columbia *340* miles, 200 miles of which is a good road, 140 miles over a tremendious Mountain Steep and broken, 60 miles of which is covered Several feet deep with Snow on which we passed the last of June; from the navagable part of the Kooskooske we decended that rapid river 73 miles to its enterance into Lewis's river and down that river 154 miles to the Columbia and down that river 413 Miles to [its] enterance into the Pacific Ocian, about 180 miles of this distance is tide water. passed several bad rapids and narrows and one considerable fall 268 miles above the enterance of this river of 37 feet 8 inches the Total distance decending the Columbian waters 640 miles makeing a total of *3555* miles on the most direct rout from the Mississippi at the mouth of the Missouri to the pacific Ocean.

The fur trade may be carried on from the heads of the Missouri to the mouth of Columbia much cheaper than by any rout by which it can be conveyed to the East indias. form an establishment on the River Rochejhone for the reception of the furs of that river & South and one at Marias river below the great falls of Missouri. the Shoshones within the rocky mountains the Tushepaws on Clarks river and maney nations west of the Rocky mountains would visit those establishments from whome horses might be got on the most reasonable terms for the purpose of packing the furs across those mountains which may be passed from the 20.th of June untill the last of September.

You may leave those establishments on the Missouri 15 or 20 of June and arive on the Kooskooske river between the 1st & 5th of July. from that time you have untill the middle of September to decend the River and return to the mountains in time to pass them before the Snow becomes too Deep to cross them.

[The Yellowstone River.]

A Sumary Statement of the Rivers, Creeks, and the most remarkable places assending the *River Rochejhone*, their distances from each other and from the Missouri as estimated by me in 1806 also the Total distances from the Mississippi.

Names of Places &c	the Side on which they are situated	Width of the rivers and Creeks in yards	Distances from one place to another in miles	Distances from the Missouri assending	Computed Distances from the Mississippi assending
	Side	yds	M^s.	M^s.	Total M^s.
from Missouri up the River Rochejhone					1888
To the enterance of Jo^s Fields River	S E.	35	8	8	1896
" " yellow rock (river narrow)	S E		6	14	
" " Buffalow Crossings a low plain east side			33	47	
" " Ibex River	S E.	30	31	78	1966
" " Samuels Creek	N.W	30	12	90	
" " Buffalow Creek	N W	30	18	108	
" " Pine Brook	S.E.	20	29	137	
" " Cat fish Creek	S E.	20	10	147	
" " Gibson River	S E	60	8	155	2043
" " Oak-tar-pon-er stone Coal River	S E	40	18	173	2061
" " Shabonos River	N.W.	100	7	188	2068
" " Wolf rapid (not bad)			12	192	2080
" " Wah-har-sop, redstone River	S E	100	3	195	2083
" " Yorks dry river	N.W.	88	7	202	2090
" " Yellow Bear rapids (not bad)			1	203	2091
" " Buffalow Shoals (not bad)			20	223	2111
" " Dry River	N.W.	100	9	232	
" " Lezeka or Tongue River	S.E.	150	11	243	2131
" " Turtle Creek	S.E.	40	20	263	
" " *Mar-Shas-kap* River	S.E.	25	22	285	2173
" " Wood Brook	S.E.	30	16	301	
" " upper *Stone Coal* Bluffs	S.E.		6	307	2195
" " Little Horn River	S.E.	100	11	318	2206
" " Table River	N.W.	70	2	320	
" " Little Wolf River	N.W.	80	30	350	
" " Chimney Bluffs	N.W.		28	368	
" " White Creek	N.W.	30	17	385	
" " Laabeechs River	S.E	60	7	392	2281
" " Windsers River	N.W.	50	26	418	2307
" " Elk river	N.W.	40	4	422	
" " Big horn River	S.E.	220	15	437	2326
" " Island Brook	N W		16	453	
" " White Clifts (below the pine hills)	N.W.		27	480	
" " Halls River	N.W.	40	9	489	2378
" " Shannons river from which place party decended in Buffalow Skin Canoes	S.E.	22	10	499	2388

Names of Places &c.	the Side on which they are Situated	Width of the rivers and Creeks in yards	Distances from one place to another in miles	Distances from the Missouri assending	Computed Distances from the Mississippi assending
	Side	yds	M§	M§	Total M§
To the Pompeys Tower 200 feet high & 400 yds around in an open bottom	S.E.		9	508	2397
" " Tumbling Bluff	N.W.		12	520	
" " Big Dry brook	N.W.	60	16	536	
" " Pryors Creek in the big bend	S.E.	25	10	546	2435
" " Rock Creek	N.W.	18	5	551	
" " Pryors River	S.E.	35	6	557	2446
" " Yellow Clifts	S.E.		9	566	
" " Horse Creek	S E.	20	10	576	
" Clarks fork (the lodge where all dance)	S.E.	150	23	599	2487
" " Black bluffs opposit to the place ☞ Capt C. built 2 Canoes to ded	S.E.		27	626	2514
" " Bluffs above the extencive open bottoms on the N W Side	N.W.		26	652	
" " Rose Bud river	S.E.	40	6	658	2546
" " Dry Creek	N.W.	20	19	677	
" " Muddy Creek	N.W.	15	16	693	
" " Weasel Creek	S.E.	10	16	709	
" " Brattens River	S.E.	25	10	719	2607
" " Otter River	N.W.	30	12	731	2638
" " Beaver river	S.E.	30	$\frac{1}{4}$	731$\frac{1}{4}$	
" " Thy Snaged Creek	S.E.	20	5$\frac{3}{4}$	737	
" " Rivers a Cross	both	28	10	747	2635
" a small rapid not bad			24	771	
" Stinking Cabin Creek	S.E.	20	14	735	
" Shields River boald	N.W.	35	16	805	
" the foot of the Rocky Mountains covered with Snow 15 of July in Latd 45° 22′ 34″ North			16	817	2905

Note the distance by land from Clarks fork to the Mountain is only 120 miles. all the Streams falling in above Clarks fork are boald.

Portage from the River Rochejhone to the Head of the Missouri at the *three* forks.

	Miles	Miles across from the Rochejhone
From the Rochejhone 2 miles below the Rocky Mountain on a Course nearly S 75° W. to the top of the dividing ridge which divides the wate[r]s of the rochejhone from those of the Missouri, passing up on the N. Side of portage run to the forks of the road the Country open, assent gentle		9

	Miles	Miles across from the Rochejhone
To the Middle branch of the East fork of Galletins River takeing the left hand road, this Stream running to the left	$\frac{1}{2}$	$9\frac{1}{2}$
To a Gap in the Mountain passing up a Small branch on it's N. Side with a gradual ascent Country open and the course nearly west	$2\frac{1}{2}$	12
To the middle branch of the east fork of Galletins River passing down on the N. Side of a branch crouded with beaver dams	3	15
To the three forks of the East fork of Galletins river passing on the S. Side	3	18
To the main fork of Galletins river passing through a leavel plain N 78° W	12	30
To the arm of the river which forms beaver Island, passing through the island a leavel open plain on a course N. 70° W. an emencity of Beaver dams &c. on each side	6	36
To Galletins River below the forks passing through an open leavel plain on a course N. 78° W. on the S. Side of the R.	6	42
To the Missouri imediately below the three forks, Jeffersons Madisons and Galletins Rivers on a Course N. 35° W. through an open plain passing over 2 Small hills after crossing the river on its N. Side	6	48

Rout from the head of Jefferson River at the place we left the Canoes to the mouth of Travellers rest on Clarks river on my rout in July 1806.

From the forks where our Canoes were left in 1805 up the west branch on an old Shoshone road about nine miles	9	
To a Gap in the mountain which divides Willards Creek waters from those of wisdom river on a course N. 30° West	15	
To the boiling Hot Spring in a vally near the 3 forks of Wisdom river, crossed 2 forks of Wisdom river from the right hand	9	
To Glade Creek passing Wisdom river and 6 large creeks from a Snow toped Mountain to the west, passing a Spur of the mountain after crossing the last creek on a course N. 56° W	22	
To the head of Glade Creek keeping on an old roade which passes up on the N. Side	11	
To Oatlashoot vally leaveing Glade Creek an[d] heading to our right and passing over a dividing mountain which Seperates the waters of the Missouri from those of Clarks river	5	
To the Middle fork of Clarks river from the left hand in Oatlashshoots Vally	8	79
To flour Camp Creek from the S E.	10	
To the West fork of Clarks river from the W.	10	
To Scattered Creek from the East	38	
To Travellers rest Creek from the west where the different roads meet before the mountain is assended	23	81
		160

Note this rout is Generally leavel and firm and every par[t] of it will afford a very good waggon road by removeing a fiew logs and cutting a little on the hill Side.

Note The Indians inform us that there is an excellent road from the 3 forks of the Missouri through a low gap in the mountains to the East fork of Clarks river which passes down that fork to its junction and up on the west Side of the main fork to Travellers rest Creek which they travel with their families in 6 days the distance must be about 150 miles, that added to 48 which is the portage from the River Rochejhone is 198 miles which is 26 miles further than the rout by the way of the falls of the Missouri.

One other rout from the river Rochejhone which is also a good one but something further is from the head of the east fork of Galletins River on a direct course to the mouth of Wisdom River and up that river and Glade Creek and across to Clarks river in the Oatlashshoot vally and from thence down that river to the Travellers rest Creek, at which point all the roads in this quarter of the [world] appear to center at the foot of those tremendious mountains the best and most direct rout is by way of the falls of the Missouri and Travellers rest. Several roads pass from the Missouri above the falls to Travellers rest Creek.

[The following, taken from the fragment designated by Coues as Codex T, is in Clark's handwriting; we insert it here, as related to the preceding fragment from Codex N. It should be noted that this leaf called Codex T has been inserted in its manila cover by the wrong edge; it begins to read at top of p. 2 as thus inserted, and continues without break to the end of p. 1. — ED.]

[Blank space in MS.] Miles to the foot of the mountain where the party were obliged to delay from the 9th of May to the 24 of June for the snows of the mountains to subside sufficient to cross, and then passed over snow for 60 Ms Generally from 3 to 6 or 8 feet deep quit[e] Consolidated or Sufficiently so to bear a horse at the Enterance of the Travellers rest on Clarks river Capt. Lewis & Clark seperated. Lewis passed imediately to the falls of the Missouri on an old indian parth of good road left a party at that place to prepare geer & wheels and proceeded with 3 men to Explore a large N. fork of the Missouri called Maria River and met with a party of Indians & was compelled to kill 2 of them. Clark with [blank space in MS.] men passed up Clarks river and across the heads of several branches of the Missouri to the place the canoes had been left on his outward bound journey at the head of Jeffersons river, descended Jeffersons rivers to the 3 forks, and sent on the canoes down the Missouri under the direction of a Sergt. and proceded himself up Galitines River and passed over to the river Rochejhon or Yellow rock river from the South in Lat^d 45.22 N. and made canoes of wood & Buffalow canoes & Decended that river 818 miles, to its junction with the Missouri 1880 miles from St Louis.

II.   ETHNOLOGY

EDITORIAL NOTE. — During the winter at Fort Mandan, Lewis and Clark prepared a large table of the Indian nations east of the Rockies, with data respecting their trade, etc.   At least two copies were made, one of which was sent to the Secretary of War, and probably perished when the records of that department were burned in 1809, or in the stampede of 1814; what is apparently the second copy is now in the possession of the American Philosophical Society, at Philadelphia, and is a sheet 34½ x 27 inches, composed of six pieces of paper pasted together.   Owing to its unwieldy size and form, we have decided somewhat to recast the material as follows :

To each of the columns in the original manuscript we have, for purpose of identification, assigned the appropriate letter, as explained by the explorers under the heading " Notation," below.   In grouping into a paragraph, in narrative form, all the tabulated information concerning a tribe (which in the original manuscript occupies a line across the broad page), we have assigned to each item the letter [enclosed within brackets] corresponding to the column in which it appears in the original.

The numeral assigned to each tribe is that given in the original manuscript.

Upon the margin of the reverse of the manuscript, Clark made the following memorandum, showing that the copy sent to the Secretary of War contained considerable data not in the original tabulation :

additional Remarks made on the Copy Sent to the Secretary at war

1ˢᵗ the boundaries of the Countrey which they claim — the quantity of land & face of the Countrey

2ᵈ their Antient residence if known.

3   the State of their Trade whether it can be expected to increase and in what proportion.

4th their Trafick with other Indian nations, in what it consists and where carried on.

5th their Disposition towards the whites, and their conduct to their Traders.

6 to what place they might be provailed on to remove to make room for other nations.

7 whether they cultivate or not.

8 whether Stationary or roveing

9 whether the Nations is increasing or Deminishing.

Gen! remarks on the Trade & remittences and am! Estimated — Establishments in a Govm[nt] p! of view — Notations on Indian Names Sub Divisions of the Sioux Bands & names of their principal Chiefs.

From the tabulated statement prepared by Clark for the Secretary of War, with the above "additional Remarks," President Jefferson had prepared and presented to Congress *A Statistical View of the Indian Nations inhabiting the Territory of Louisiana and the Countries adjacent to its northern and Western boundaries* (printed by A. & G. Way, Washington, 1806).[1] We have selected from this publication all of the additional information contained therein, and appended the same to our compilation. Such matter we have indicated by two methods, according to the extent of the added data — (1) for mere words, phrases, figures, etc., printing the material in *Italics* and enclosing it within parentheses — *e.g.* (*except the Little Osage*); (2) for long sentences or paragraphs, printing it in smaller type. — ED.]

A. ESTIMATE OF THE EASTERN INDIANS

A List of the Names of the different Nations & Tribes of Indians Inhabiting the Countrey on the Missourie and its waters, and West of the Mississippi (above the Missourie) and a line from its head in Lat[d] 47.° 38′ N – & Long! 95.° 6′ W – to the N W extremity of the Lake of the Woods, in Lat! 49.° 37′ N – and Long[d] 94.° 31′ W – and Southerley & Westerley, of a West line from the Said Lake of Wood, as far as is known Jan? 1805. Expressive of the Names, Language, Numbers,

---

[1] See Bibliographical Data, vol. i, p. lxiii, *ante.*

Trade, water courses & countrey in which they reside claim & rove &c. &c. &c.

NOTATIONS [of Indian names].

— over a, denotes that a sounds as in caught, taught, &c.

∧ over a, denotes that it sounds as in dart, part, &c.

a without notation has its primitive sound as in ray, hay, &c. except only when it is followed by r or w, in which case it sounds as â

, set underneath denotes a small pause, the word being divided by it into two parts.

[a] The Names of the Indian nations, as usially spelt and pronounc'd by the English.

[b] Primitive Indian names of Nations and Tribes, English Orthography, the syllables producing the sounds by which the Ind⁵ themselves express the names of their respective nations.

[c] Nick-names, or those which have generally obtained among the Canadian Traders.

[d] The Language they speak if primitive marked with a * otherwise derived from, & approximating to.

[e] Nᵒˢ of Villages.

[f] N.ᵒˢ of Tents or Lodges of the roveing bands.

[g] Number of Warriours.

[h] The probable Number of Souls, of this Numbʳ deduct about $\frac{1}{3}$ generally.[1]

[i] The Names of the Christian Nations or Companies with whome they Maintain their Commerce and Traffick.

[j] The places at which the Traffick is usially carried on.

[k] The estimated amount of Merchindize in Dollars at the St. Louis prices for their annual consumption.

[l] The estimated amount of their returns in dollars, at the St. Louis prices.

[m] The kind of pelteries, & Robes which they Annually supply or furnish.

[n] The defferant kinds of Pelteres, Furs, Robes Meat Greece & Horses which each could furnish for trade.

[o] The place at which it would be mutually advantageous to form the principal establishment, in order to supply the Several nations with Merchindize.

---

[1] The numbers given in the following text are the corrected estimates, after deducting the one-third. — ED.

[p]   The names of the nations with whome they are at war.
[q]   The names of the nations with whome they maintain a friendly
      alliance, or with whome they may be united by intercourse or
      marriage.
[r]   The particular water courses on which they reside or rove.
[s]   The Countrey in which they usially reside, and the principal
      water courses on or near which the Villages are Situated, or the
      Defferant Nations & tribes usially rove & *Remarks.*

THE INDIAN TRADE. The sums stated under and opposite [k] are the amounts
of merchandise annually furnished the several nations of Indians, including all
incidental expenses of transportation, &c. incurred by the merchants which
generally averages about one third of the whole amount. The merchandise is
estimated at an advance of 125 per cent. on the sterling cost. It appears to me
that the amount of merchandise which the Indians have been in the habit of
receiving annually, is the best standard by which to regulate the quantities necessary for them in the first instance ; they will always consume as much merchandise as they can pay for, and those with whom a regular trade has been carried
on have generally received that quantity.

The amount of their returns stated under and opposite [1] are estimated by the
peltry standard of St. Louis, which is 40 cents per pound for deer skins ; (i. e.)
all furs and peltries are first reduced by their comparative value to lbs. of mer-
chantable deer skins, which are then estimated at 40 cents per lb.

These establishments are not mentioned as being thought important at present
in a governmental point of view.

1.   [a] Grand Osarge ; [b] Bar-har-cha ; [c] Grand Ose or zo ;
[d] * Osarge ; [e] 2 ; [f] ——— ; [g] 1200 ; [h] 5000 ; [i] a Co : at
St Louis ; [j] at their Village & the 3 forks of the Arkansaw River ;
[k] $15,000 ; [1] $20,000 ; [m] Skins of the small Deer, some Beaver
a fiew Bear, & otter skins ; [n] Beaver, otter, small Deer, Black Bear, &
racoons Skins ; [o] at the 3 forks of the Arkansaw 600 Miles up that
river and 60 Lg S. West of their Village [p] With all Nations of Indians (*except the Little Osage*) untill the United States took possession of
Louisiana ; [q] ——— (*with the Little Osage only*) ; [r] ——— ; [s] Their
villages are (80) Leagues up the Osarge River on the S. E. Side, they
claim all the Countrey included in the following boundrey. Viz begining at a S. E. branch of the Osarge called *Neangua* R up that river to
the head from thence Southerley to the Arkansaw 100 miles below the
three forks up the Arkansaw and a Southerly fork Some Distance above
the Great Saline, & the Ctry nearly to the Kanzus river. Cultivate
Corn, Beens &c. &c.

embracing the waters of the upper portion of the Osage river, and thence obliquely approaching the same to the beginning. The climate is delightful, and the soil fertile in the extreme. The face of the country is generally level, and well watered ; the eastern part of the country is covered with a variety of excellent timber; the western and middle country high prairies. It embraces within its limits four salines, which are, in point of magnitude and excellence, unequalled by any known in North America ; there are also many others of less note. The principal part of the Great Osage have always resided at their villages, on the Osage river, since they have been known to the inhabitants of Louisiana. About three years since, nearly one half of this nation, headed by their chief the *Big-track,* emigrated to the three forks of the Arkansas, near which, and on its north side, they established a village, where they now reside. The Little Osage formerly resided on the S. W. side of the Missouri, near the mouth of Grand river; but being reduced by continual warfare with their neighbors, were compelled to seek the protection of the Great Osage, near whom they now reside.

There is no doubt but their trade will increase : they could furnish a much larger quantity of beaver than they do. I think two villages, on the Osage river, might be prevailed on to remove to the Arkansas, and the Kansas, higher up the Missouri, and thus leave a sufficient scope of country for the Shawnees, Dillewars, Miames, and Kickapoos.

2. [a] Little Osarge ; [b] ooed-za-tar, [c] Petite Ose (or little zo; [d] [Same as for No. 1]; [e] 1 ; [f] ——— ; [g] 300; [h] 1300; [i] [Same as for No. 1]; [j] near their Village ; [k] $5000 ; [l] $8000 ; [m] [Same as for No. 1]; [n] [Same as for No. 1]; [o] [Same as for No. 1]; [p] (*With all their Indian neighbors, except the Great Osage*); [q] (*With the Great Osage only*); [r] on Kanzes R.; [s] [Included in No. 1 [s]].

3. [a] Kanzas; [b] Karsea; [c] Kah [d] * Osarge; [e] 1 ; [f] ——— ; [g] 300; [h] 1300; [i] The Merchants of S! Louis ; [j] at their Village and on the Missouri about the mouth of the Kanzes River; [k] $5000 ; [l] $8000 ; [m] (*The same as the Osage, with buffaloe grease and robes*); [n] Beaver, otter, Deer, Bear & Muskrat Skins; [o] 1 Mile up on the N. Side above the Mouth of the Kanzas R.; [p] with all nations ; [q] (*They are sometimes at peace with the Ottoes and Missouris, with whom they are partially intermarried*); [r] on Kanzes R.; [s] their village is 80 Leagues up the Kanzes River, they Hunt high up the Kanzes and Arkansaws they Cultivate Corn Beans &c. &c. Great robers.

The limits of the country they claim is not known. The country in which they reside, and from thence to the Missouri, is a delightful one, and generally well watered and covered with excellent timber: they hunt on the upper part of Kanzas and Arkanzas rivers : their trade may be expected to increase with proper management. At present they are a dissolute, lawless banditti; frequently plunder their traders, and commit depredations on persons ascending and descending the Missouri river: population rather increasing. These people, as well as the Great and Little Osages, are stationary, at their villages, from about the 15th of March to the 15th of May, and again from the 15th of August to the 15th of October: the balance of the year is appropriated to hunting.

4. [a] Ottoes; [b] War-doke-tar-tar; [c] la Zoto; [d] * Missoure, & Some words of osarge; [e] 1 [with the Missouris]; [f] ——; [g] 120; [h] 500; [i] the Merchants of S: Louis; [j] at their Village and at trading houses at different Places between the Grand Nemahar and Platt Rivers; [k] $4000 (*including the Missouris*); [l] $6000 (*including the Missouris*); [m] Beaver, otter, racoons, Deer & Black Bear Skins; [n] Beaver, otter, Muskat racoon, wolves Deer, bear, skins, bears oil & Buffalow tallow; [o] Council Bluffs 50 miles by water above R. Platt or there abouts, and about; [p] with all nations generally Partially at peace with the Panias and Kanzies nations; [q] with the Missouries; [r] 18 L^g up the Platt (*south side*); [s] The Village is 18 Leagues up the Platt River SE. Side, they hunt up the Salene and grand Ne-ma-har Rivers &c. they cultivate Corn Beans &c. &c This nation formerley lived on the Missoure river above the Platt river, they Speake Some words of the Osarge & Mahar (bad.

They have no idea of an exclusive possession of any country, nor do they assign themselves any limits. I do not believe that they would object to the introduction of any well disposed Indians: they treat the traders with respect and hospitality, generally. In their occupations of hunting and cultivation, they are the same with the Kanzas and Osage. They hunt on the Saline, Nimmehaw rivers, and west of them in the plains. The country in which they hunt lies well; it is extremely fertile and well watered; that part of it which borders on the Nimmehaw and Missouri possesses a good portion of timber: population rather increasing. They have always resided near the place their village is situated, and are the descendants of the Missouris.

5. [a] Missouries; [b] New-dar-cha; [c] Missourie; [d] * Missoure, & Some words of osarge; [e] 1 [with the Ottoes]; [f] ——; [g] 80; [h] 300; [i] the Merchants of St Louis; [j] [Same as for No. 4]; [k] included [in the Ottoes]; [l] included [in the Ottoes]; [m] [Same as the Ottoes]; [n] [Same as the Ottoes]; [o] [Same as the Ottoes]; [p] [Same as the Ottoes]; [q] With the Ottoes; [r] With the Ottoes; [s] With the Ottoes and hund[t] also above the Platt near the Missourie near the Corn Des cerf River; they Cultivate Corn Beans &c. This nation formerley lived below the grand River, and was noumerous, they Speake some words of the Osarge (bad.

These are the remnant of the most numerous nation inhabiting the Missouri, when first known to the French. Their ancient and principal village was situated in an extensive and fertile plain on the north bank of the Missouri, just below the entrance of the Grand river. Repeated attacks of the small pox, together with their war with the Saukees and Renars, has reduced them to their present state of dependence on the Ottoes, with whom they reside, as well in their village as on their hunting excursions. The Ottoes view them as their inferiors, and sometimes treat them amiss. These people are the real proprietors of an extensive and fertile country lying on the Missouri, above their ancient village for a considerable distance, and as low as the mouth of the Osage river, and thence to the Mississippi.

6. [a] Pania proper; [b] Parnee [c] Grand par; [d] * Pania; [e] ½; [f] ——; [g] 400; [h] 1600; [i] the Merchants of St Louis; [j] at their Village; [k] $3,200 [l] $5000; [m] Beaver otter & racoons Skins & Buffalow Robes; [n] Beaver, otter, racoon, cabra & a fiew Deer Skins, roabs, Buffalow meat & greas & horses; [o] Council Bluffs; [p] Ossar[ge]s, Kanzes, Pania Pickey, Padonces, Ali-tans & La-plays; [q] republickin Pania Loup & Mahas; [r] 30 Lgs up the Platt; [s] Their Village is 30 Leagues up the river platt on the S. E. Side, they Hunt on the heads of the Kanzes, and its N W waters and high up the Platt; they Cultivate Corn Beans &c. &c. (mild & well disposed)

With repect to their idea of the possession of soil, it is similar to that of the Ottoes : they hunt on the south side of the river Platte, higher up and on the head of the Kanzas. A great proportion of this country is open plains, interspersed, however, with groves of timber, which are most generally found in the vicinity of the water courses. It is generally fertile and well watered; lies level, and free of stone. They have resided in the country which they now inhabit, since they were known to the whites. Their trade is a valuable one, from the large proportion of beaver and otter which they furnish, and it may be expected yet to increase, as those animals are still abundant in their country. The periods of their residence at their village and hunting, are similar to the Kanzas and Osages. Their population is increasing. They are friendly and hospitable to all white persons ; pay great respect and deference to their traders, with whom they are punctual in the payment of their debts.

7. [a] Pania Loup (or Wolves; [b] Skee-e-ree; [c] La Loup (or Lou) Pania Maher; d * Pania; [e] 1; [f] ——; [g] 280; [h] 1000; [i] the Merchants of St Louis; [j] at the Pania Vilage; [k] $2400; [l] $3500; [m] [Same as Pania proper]; [n] [Same as Pania proper]; [o] Council Bluffs; [p] Ottoes & Missouries, and the same as the Panias; [q] The same as the Panias; [r] on the Loup R. [s] Their Village is 40 Leagues above the Panias on the right of the R. Loup

BISON DANCE OF THE MANDAN INDIANS
in front of their Medicine Lodge
IN-MIH-TUTTA-HANKUSH

which empties into the Platt 8 Lg^s above the Panias, they hunt on the rivers *platt* & Loup above their Village; they Cultivate Corn Beens &c. &c. (mild & well disposed)

These are also a branch of the Panias proper, who Separated themselves from that nation many years since, and established themselves on a north branch of the river Platte, to which their name was also given: these people have likewise no idea of an exclusive right to any portion of country. They hunt on the Wolf river above their village, and on the river Platte above the mouth of that river. This country is very similar to that of of the Panias proper; though there is an extensive body of fertile well timbered land between the Wolf river below their village and the river Corn de Cerf, or Elkhorn river. The particulars related of the other Panias is also applicable to them. They are seldom visited by any trader, and therefore usually bring their furs and peltry to the village of the Panias proper, where they traffic with the whites.

8. [a] Pania Republicans; [b] Ar-rah-pa-hoo [c] Republick; [d] * Pania; [e] ½; [f] ——; [g] 300 [h] 1400 [i] the Merchants of St Louis; [j] at the Pania Vilage; [k] $3,200 [l] $5000; [m] [Same as Panias proper]; [n] [Same as Panias proper]; [o] Council Bluffs; [p] the Same as the Panias; [q] The same as the Panias; [r] with the Panias; [s] Their village is with the Pania on the River Platt, they hunt on a branch of the Kanzus called the Republican fork, and near the Kanzes river also with the Panias; Cultivate Corn Beens &c. &c. (mild & well disposed).

Are a branch of the Pānia proper, or, as they are frequently termed, the *Big Paunch*. About ten years since they withdraw themselves from the mother nation, and established a village on a large northwardly branch of the Kanzas, to which they have given name: they afterwards subdivided and lived in different parts of the country on the waters of Kanzas river; but being harassed by their turbulent neighbors, the Kanzas, they rejoined the Panias proper last spring. What has been said with respect to the Panias proper is applicable to these people, except that they hunt principally on the Republican river, which is better stocked with timber than that hunted by the Panias.

9. [a] Mahar; [b] Oh-Mar-ha; [c] La Mar; [d] * Mahar with some words of the Osarge & Souix; [e] ——; [f] 80; [g] 150; [h] 600; [i] the Merchants at St Louis; [j] on the Missourie at different places between the old Mahar Village and River Platt; [k] $3000; [l] $5000; [m] Beaver, otter & racoons Skins & Buffalow Robes & B. Bear; [n] Beaver, otter, racoon, wolves Deer, Bear & Cabra Skins, & Buffalow robes, g[r]ees & oil; [o] Council Bluffs; [p] Ottoes & Missouries, all the Bands of Sieux, except the Yanktons of the burnt woods;

[q] Panias, Loup, republicks, Poncarer; [r] rove on the River Quicure; [s] Their Village was 1 League from the Missouree on the
S. W. Side, about 4 Leagues below Floyds river & 5 below the Grand
R Sieux, They now rove (haveing been reduced by the Small pox and
war with the Soues) on rapid river or quicure

They have no idea of exclusive possession of soil. About ten years since,
they boasted 700 warriors. They have lived in a village, on the west bank of the
Missouri, 236 miles above the mouth of the river Platte, where they cultivated
corn, beans, and melons : they were warlike, and the terror of their neighbors.
In the summer and autumn of 1802, they were visited by the small-pox, which
reduced their numbers to something less than 300 ; they burnt their village, and
have become a wandering nation, deserted by the traders, and the consequent
deficiency of arms and ammunition has invited frequent aggressions from their
neighbors, which have tended to reduce them still further. They rove principally
on the waters of the river Quicurre, or Rapid river. The country is generally
level, high, and open : it is fertile, and tolerably well watered. They might
easily be induced to become stationary : they are well disposed towards the
whites, and are good hunters : their country abounds in beaver and otter, and
their trade will increase and become valuable, provided they become stationary,
and are at peace. The Tetons Bois brûle' killed and took about 60 of them last
summer.

10. [a] Poncare; [b] Poong-car; [c] La Pong; [d] * Mahar with
some words of the Osarge, & Souix; [e] ———; [f] 20; [g] 50; [h] 200;
[i] the Merchants of St Louis; [j] [Same as the Mahar] [k] [included
with the Mahar]; [l] [included with the Mahar]; [m] Same as the
Mahar]; [n] [Same as the Mahar]; [o] Council Bluffs; [p] [Same as
the Mahar]; [q] the Mahars only; [r] with the Mahas; [s] Their
Village was 1 League up a Small river above the quicure called Pon-
cerres River, they being reduced by the Small pox, and their war with
the Soues rove in the plains with the Mahars, bad fellows, (a tribe of
Mahars) No Corn Beens to Cultivate at present, lost all in the late
maladay with the Small pox.

The remnant of a nation once respectable in point of numbers. They formerly
resided on a branch of the Red river of lake Winnipie : being oppressed by the
Sioux, they removed to the west side of the Missouri, on Porcar river, where
they built and fortified a village, and remained some years ; but being pursued by
their ancient enemies the Sioux, and reduced by continual wars, they have joined,
and now reside with the Mahas, whose language they speak.

11. [a] Ricaras 8 tribes; [b] Star-rah-he; [c] Ree ; [d] Pania Cor-
rupted; [e] 3; [f] ———; [g] 500; [h] 2000; [i] a Co. at St Louis;

[j] at their Villages; [k] $2,500; [l] $6,000; [m] Buffalow roabes, Greese & a fiew fox skins, and a little Beaver; [n] Buffalow robes, Tallow Grece de mele, large & small fox skins, wolves; [o] Those four nations [Ricaras, Mandans, Shoe, and Minnetarries] would move to the River Yallowstone at or about that place would be a proper place for the establishment for them; [p] with the Gens des Serpent or Snake Indians; [q] the Tetons in their neighbourhood the Chyennes & nations to the S. West; [r] on the Missouri; [s] Their Villages one in an Island in the Missouries above the Maropa River 1430 Miles up, two others near each other 4 miles above on the S W Side; those villages are the remains of Eight different tribes of the Pania nation who have become reduced by the *Soues* and compelled to live together in fortified towns for their protection, their villages on Different parts of the Missouries from the Teton river to near the mandans they may be Stiled gardners for the Soues; they raise Corn Beans &c. & hunt in their Neighborhood Those people have a partial exchange with the Soues for guns powder Ball & for Horses & corn &c. &c.

Are the remains of ten large tribes of Panias, who have been reduced, by the small pox and the Sioux, to their present number. They live in fortified villages, and hunt immediately in their neighborhood. The country around them, in every direction, for several hundred miles, is entirely bare of timber, except on the water courses and steep declivities of hills, where it is sheltered from the ravages of fire. The land is tolerably well watered, and lies well for cultivation. The remains of the villages of these people are to be seen on many parts of the Missouri, from the mouth of Tetone river to the Mandans. They claim no land except that on which their villages stand and the fields which they cultivate. The Tetons claim the country around them. Though they are the oldest inhabitants, they may be properly considered the farmers or *tenants at will* of that lawless, savage and rapacious race the Sioux *Teton*, who rob them of their horses, plunder their gardens and fields, and sometimes murder them, without opposition. If these people were freed from the oppression of the Tetons, their trade would increase rapidly, and might be extended to a considerable amount. They maintain a partial trade with their oppressors the Tetons, to whom they barter horses, mules, corn, beans, and a species of tobacco which they cultivate; and receive in return guns, ammunition, kettles, axes, and other articles which the Tetons obtain from the Yanktons of N. and Sissatones, who trade with Mr. Cammeron, on the river St. Peters. These horses and mules the Ricaras obtain from their western neighbors, who visit them frequently for the purpose of trafficking.

12. [a] Mandans; [b] Ma-too-tonka 1st vilage; Roop-tar-ha 2nd Vil.; [c] Mandan; [d] * Mandan (some words like the Osarge & Sieux; [e] 2; [f] ———; [g] 350; [h] 1250; [i] Hudson Bay, N. W.

& X. Y. Companies from Assinniboin R. overland N. 150 m^s; [j] at
their Villages; [k] $2000; [l] $6000; [m] Buffalow robes, wolves a
fiew Beavers Elk Skins & a fiew Horses & Corn; [n] Beaver otter &
Small furs, also cabre, a few Deer & a fiew White Bear Skins; [o]
[See for the Ricaras]; [p] with Soues, & Snake indians; [q] with the
Shoe Tribe the big bellies, Cheyennes ravins & those to the S. W. who
visit them; [r] on the Missouri 16000 [1600] mls. up. [s] Their Villages are on both Sides of the Missouree 1605 miles up, those Villages
are the remains of thirteen different villages of this nation and have been
reduced by the Small Pox, and the wars which the *Soues* have caused
them to collect & form [War with the Soues is according] to their earliest tredition [they have] been Compelled to unite in two Villages and
drove back by the Sous, from the Countrey below White River to this
place, haveing made on their retreat below, at this place they have resided 9 years in 2 Stockaded Towns. they raise Corn Beans &c &
hunt a fiew miles around   They trade Horses with the Assinnaboins for
Sundrey articles which is not sufficiently furnished by their Traders from
the North.

These are the most friendly, well disposed Indians inhabiting the Missouri.
They are brave, humane and hospitable.   About 25 years since they lived
in six villages, about forty miles below their present villages, on both sides
of the Missouri.   Repeated visitations of the small pox, aided by frequent attacks
by the Sioux, has reduced them to their present number.   They claim no particular tract of country.   They live in fortified villages, hunt immediately in their
neighborhood, and cultivate corn, beans, squashes and tobacco, which form articles
of traffic with their neighbors the Assinniboin : they also barter horses with the
Assinniboins for arms, ammunition, axes, kettles, and other articles of European
manufacturer, which these last obtain from the British establishments on the Assinniboin River.   The articles which they thus obtain from Assinniboins and
the British traders who visit them, they again exchange for horses and leather
tents with the Crow Indians, Chyennes, Wetepahatoes, Kiawas, Kanenavich,
Staetan and Cataka, who visit them occasionally for the purpose of traffic.   Their
trade may be much increased.   Their country is similar to that of the Ricaras.
Population increasing.

13.   [a] Shoes Men; [b] Mah-har-ha; [c] Soulier; [d] * Menetarra
(big belly) [e] 1; [f] ——; [g] 50; [h] 200; [ı] [Same as for the
Mandans]; [j] at the Mandan Villages; [k] $300; [l] $1000; [m]
The same [as the Mandans]; [n] The same [as the Mandans] and
White Har[e]s and large Foxes; [o] [See for the Ricaras]; [p] [Same as
the Mandans]; [q] with the Big-bellies Mandans, Crows and those to
the S. W. who rove; [r] in sight of the Mandans; [s] This village is

Situated on the S W. Side of the Missouries at the mouth of Knife river in Sight of the Mandans above, those people came from the S. W. and are of the Big Belley nation, they raise Corn &c hunt in their neighborhood [Trade similar to the Mandans].

They differ but very little, in any particular, from the Mandans, their neighbors, except with the unjust war which they, as well as the Minetares, prosecute against the defenseless Snake Indians, from which, I believe, it will be difficult to induce them to desist. They claim to have been once a part of the Crow Indians, whom they still acknowledge as relations. They have resided on the Missouri as long as their tradition will enable them to inform.

14. [a] Big bellies; [b] 1st Vilg. Me-ne-tar-re Me-ta-har-ta; 2 vilg. Me-ne-tar-re; [c] Gross Ventre; [d] Me ne tar re; [e] 2; [f] ———; [g] 500; [h] 2500; [i] [Same as the Mandans]; [j] at their Villages; [k] $1000; [l] $3,500; [m] The same [as the Mandans] except robes; [n] the same [as the Mandans] & White bear; [o] [See for the Ricaras] [p] with Sioux, Snake Ind^s & partially with the upper tribes of the Assinniboins, to the N. W. [q] [Same as the Shoe]; [r] in sight of the Mandans; [s] Their Villages are on the Knive river near its mouth and about 2 Miles apart & 1 from the Missouri, they came from the S E as they say, they raise corn Beans &c. &c. and hunt on both Sides of the Missourie above their Villages. [Trade the same as the Mandans].

They claim no particular country, nor do they assign themselves any limits: their tradition relates that they have always resided at their present villages. In their customs, manners, and dispositions, they are similar to the Mandans and Ahwahhaways. The scarcity of fuel induces them to reside, during the cold season, in large bands, in camps, on different parts of the Missouri, as high up that river as the mouth of the river Yellow Stone, and west of their villages, about the Turtle mountain. I believe that these people, as well as the Mandans and Ahwahhaways, might be prevailed on to remove to the mouth of the Yellow Stone river, provided an establishment is made at that place. They have as yet furnished scarcely any beaver, although the country they hunt abounds with them; the lodges of these animals are to be seen within a mile of their villages. These people have also suffered considerably by the small-pox; but have successfully resisted the attacks of the Sioux. The N. W. company intend to form an establishment in the course of the next summer, and autumn, on the Missouri, near these people, which, if effected, will most probably prevent their removal to any point which our government may hereafter wish them to reside at.

15. [a] Ayauwais; [b] Ah-e-o-war; [c] dis Iaways or ne persa; [d] Ottoes; [e] 1; [f] ———; [g] 200; [h] 800; [i] Mr Crawford

from Michilimacknac; [j] at the Villages; [k] $3,800 [l] $6000;
[m] Deer Beaver otter Mink Black Bear, fox racoon Muskrat &c.
[n] Deer, Black Bear Beaver otter Mink Muskrats, Racoons Gray
foxes & Tallow & Bears Oile; [o] on the Missourie at the mouth of
Kanzus or at the; [p] no nation particularly, sometimes join the
Saukies; [q] with the Saukees & renars, and all nations East of the
Mississippi; [r] 36 L^{gs} up Demoin; [s] Their Village is 40 Leagues
up the River Deemoen, their Countrey join the Soues Lands and extend to the Missoure River they are a tribe of the Ottoes Nation and
formerley lived on the Missourie (a fiew miles below the Antient Ottoes
Town) or their Town was at the 1st Bluff above R. platt on the N.
Side, they cultivate corn Beans &c. &c.

They are the descendants of the ancient Missouris, and claim the country west
of them to the Missouri; but as to its precise limits, or boundaries, between
themselves and the Saukees and Foxes, I could never learn. They are a turbulent savage race, frequently abuse their traders, and commit depredations on those
ascending and descending the Missouri. Their trade cannot be expected to
increase much.

16. [a] Saukees; [b] O-sau-kee; [c] la Sauk; [d] * O. Sau kee
(like the Shaw-o nee and Au-Chipaway; [e] 2; [f] ——; [g] 500;
[h] 2000; [i] Merchants at the Prarie de Chein & St Louis & Illinois
& Mick-a-nah; [j] at their Villages at Prarie de Chien and on the
Mississippi; [k] $4000; [l] $6000; [m] Deer skins principally, [also]
Beaver otter, mink Black Bear, fox racoon Muskrats &c. [n] Deer,
Black Bear Beaver otter mink Muskrats, Racoons Gray foxes &
Tallow & Bears Oile; [o] At prarie de Chien; [p] With the Osarge
& different tribes of the Chipaways; [q] all the nations on the East of
the Mississippi & with the Ayaways; [r] on the West of the Mississippi
above rock river; [s] [Saukees and Renards] live in 3 villages a fiew
miles above the mouth of the mouth of Rock River on the West bank
of the Mississippi, their Countrey is principally on the E. Side of the
Missippi, they hunt on the waters of the Missourie low down, on the
Demoin & the Mississippi on both Side from the oisconsin river down
to the Illinois river.

Saukees and Renars, or Foxes. These nations are so perfectly consolidated
that they may, in fact, be considered as one nation only. They speak the same
language: they formerly resided on the east side of the Mississippi, and still
claim the land on that side of the river, from the mouth of the Oisconsin to the
Illinois river, and eastward towards lake Michigan; but to what particular boundary, I am not informed: they also claim, by conquest, the whole of the country

belonging to the ancient Missouris, which forms one of the most valuable portions of Louisiana, but what proportion of this territory they are willing to assign to the Ayouways, who also claim a part of it, I do not know, as they are at war with the Sioux, who live N. and N. W. of them, except the Yankton ahnah. Their boundaries in that quarter are also undefined : their trade would become much more valuable if peace was established between them and the nations west of the Missouri, with whom they are at war: Their population has remained nearly the same for many years: they raise an abundance of corn, beans and melons : These people are extremely friendly to the whites, and seldom injure their traders; but they are the most implacable enemies to the Indian nations with whom they are at war. To them is justly attributable the almost entire destruction of the Missouris, the Illinois, Cahokias, Kaskaskias, and Piorias.

17. [a] Renarz; [b] Ottar-car-me; [c] la Renars; [d] [Same as Saukees]; [e] 1; [f] ———; [g] 300; [h] 1200; [i] [Same as for Saukees]; [j] [Same as for Saukees]; [k] $2500; [l] $4000; [m] Same [as for Saukees] a greater pirpotion of otter skins; [n] [Same as for Saukees]; [o] At Prarie de Chien; [p] [Same as the Saukees]; [q] [Same as the Saukees]; [r] [Same as the Saukees]; [s] [Included with the Saukees].

18. [a] [All the tribes from 18 to 27 are entered as] Dar-co-tar's proper the Soos or Sioux; [b] Wah-pa-tone tribe; [c] Sioux; [d] * Darcotar or Sioux; [e] ———; [f] 80; [g] 200; [h] 700; [i] Mrs Campbell Dickson and other Merchants who trade to Michilimack; [j] on the R. St. Peters; [k] $10,000; [l] $18,000 [m] Deer Beaver otter, fox mink Black bear, racoons fishers Muskrats with a greater perpotion of Deer; [n] Deer Bever otter red fox Mink Martains, Muskrat fishers Black bear, racoon and wolves [o] on the Mississippi R about the Falls of St Anthony or mouth of St Peters; [p] with the Chipaways of La follavoine & leach Lakes (*defensive with the Saukees, Renars and Ayauwais*); [q] The Saukie & Renards and those who inhabit East of the R Mississippi, below the Chipaways; [r] rove on the Mississippi; [s] a Band of Sieux or Darcotars rove on both Sides of the Mississippi about the Mouth of River St Peters and claim jointly with the other bands of the Sieux or *Dar-co-tars* all the Countrey North of a East line from the Mouth of Little Sieux River to the Mississippi R on the west Side of that river to the Oisconsin, and up on both Sides of the Mississippi, and an Easterley & westerley line passing the otter tail portage & between the head of St Peters & river Rogue [Rouge] and westerley passing the heads of River Jacque (or James) to the head of *War re' con ne* River Down that to the Missourie, and on both Sides of that river (including the *Ricaries* Tribes) to the White river, thence on the West of the west Side of the Missourie to the little Soues R.

Claim the country in which they rove on the N. W. side of the river St. Peters, from their village to the mouth of the Chippeway river, and thence north eastwardly towards the head of the Mississippi, including the Crow-wing river. Their lands are fertile, and generally well timbered. They are only stationary while the traders are with them, which is from the beginning of October to the last of March. Their trade is supposed to be at its greatest extent. They treat their traders with respect, and seldom attempt to rob them. This, as well as the other Sioux bands, act, in all respects, as independently of each other as if they were a distinct nation.

19. [a] Sioux; [b] Min-da-war-car-ton tribe; [c] Gens de Lake; [d] * Dar-co-tar (or Sioux); [e] ———; [f] 120; [g] 300; [h] 1200; [i] [Same as Wah-pa-tone]; [j] on the Mississippi River St Peters not Stationary; [k] $8,700; [l] $16000; [m] [Same as Wah-pa-tone]; [n] [Same as Wah-pa-tone]; [o] on the Mississippi about the Falls of St Anthony or mouth of S Peters; [p] with the Chipaways of La folla-voine & leach Lakes never go to war on the Missouri; [q] [Same as Wah-pa-tone]; [r] rove on the Mississippi; [s] they rove above the mouth of the St Peters River, their Village is on the Mississippi they rove on both Sides of the river as far or high up as the Crow Wing river, they cultivate Corn Beans &c. &c.

'Tis the only band of Siouxs that cultivates corn, beans, &c. and these even cannot properly be termed a stationary people. They live in tents of dressed leather, which they transport by means of horses and dogs, and ramble from place to place during the greater part of the year. They are friendly to their own traders; but the inveterate enemies to such as supply their enemies, the Chippe-ways, with merchandise. They also claim the country in which they hunt, com-mencing at the entrance of the river St. Peters, and extending upwards, on both sides of the Mississippi river, to the mouth of the Crow-wing river. The land is fertile, and well watered; lies level and sufficiently timbered. Their trade can-not be expected to increase much.

20. [a] Sioux; [b] Wâh-pa'-coo-ta tribe; [c] people who shoot at leaves; [d] * Dar-co-tar (or Sioux); [e] ———; [f] 60; [g] 150; [h] 500; [i] [Same as Wah-pa-tone]; [j] on the Mississippi & River St Peters not stationary; [k] $3,800; [l] $6,000; [m] the Same [as the Wah-pa-tone] (a greater perpt^n of otter skins); [n] the Same [as the Wah-pa-tone; [o] on the Mississippi R about the Falls of St Anthony or mouth of St Peters; [p] with the Chipaways but sometimes go to war on the Missouri; [q] [The Same as the Wah-pa-tone]; [r] rove on the St Peters; [s] they rove on St Peters river claim the Countrey on the N W Side of the Mississippi to the Chipaway River and on both sides

above, their Villag is 18 L^{gs} up St Peters on the N. Side, do not Cultivate the land but live by hunting, and is only stationary when Traders are with them.

They rove in the country south west of the river St. Peters, from a place called the *Hardwood* to the mouth of the Yellow Medicine river : never stationary but when their traders are with them, and this does not happen at any regular or fixed point. At present they treat their traders tolerably well. Their trade cannot be expected to increase much. A great proportion of their country is open plains, lies level, and is tolerably fertile. They maintain a partial traffic with the Yanktons and Tetons to the west of them ; to these they barter the articles which they obtain from the traders on the river St. Peters, and receive in return horses, some robes and leather lodges.

21. [a] Sioux ; [b] Sis-sa-tone tribe ; [c] ——— ; [d] * Dar-co-tar (or Sioux) ; [e] ——— ; [f] 80 ; [g] 200 ; [h] 800 ; [i] Mr Cammeron who trades to Mackilimack ; [j] at the head of the St Peters river ; [k] $17,000 ; [l] $30,000 ; [m] the Same [as the Wah-pa-tone] (a greater perpotion of Beaver otter & Bear ; [n] The Same [as the Wah-pa-tone] ; [o] at the heads of St Peters and red river (or R Rouch) ; [p] with the Chipaways & Mandans Knistanoux & assinniboins ; [q] [Same as the Wah-pa-tone] & Ricarras ; [r] Head of St Peters ; [s] on the heads of St Peters — not seperate — claim the Countrey on the N. W Side of the Mississippi, only Stationary when Traders are with them do not cultivate the ground

They claim the country in which they rove, embracing the upper portions of the Red river, of lake Winnipie and St. Peters : it is a level country, intersected with many small lakes ; the land is fertile and free of stone ; the majority of it open plains. This country abounds more in the valuable fur animals, the beaver, otter and marten, than any portion of Louisiana yet known. This circumstance furnishes the Sissatones with the means of purchasing more merchandise, in proportion to their number, than any nation in this quarter. A great proportion of this merchandise is reserved by them for their trade with the Tetons, whom they annually meet at some point previously agreed on, upon the waters of James river, in the month of May. This Indian fair is frequently attended by the Yanktons of the North and Ahnah. The Sissatones and Yanktons of the North here supply the others with considerable quantities of arms, ammunition, axes, knives, kettles, cloth, and a variety of other articles ; and receive in return principally horses, which the others have stolen or purchased from the nations on the Missouri and west of it. They are devoted to the interests of their traders.

22. [a] Souix ; [b] Yanktons of the N. tribe ; [c] ——— ; [d] * Dar-co-tar (or Sioux) ; [e] ——— ; [f] 200 ; [g] 500 ; [h] 1600 ; [i] a partial Trade [with] Mr Cammeron no trader of their own ; [j] [Same as the

Sissatone]; [k] $1800; [l] $3000; [m] Buffalow robes & Wolves only; [n] [The Same as for the Wah-pa-tone]; [o] at the same place [as the Sissatone] or on the Missourie; [p] with the Chipaways & Mandans, Knistanoux & assinniboins; [q] [Same as the Sissatones]; [r] Hd^s of R Jacque E Side (*from the heads of the river St. Peters and Red river to the Missouri, about the great bend*); [s] on the heads of Rivers Jacque & Big Sioux on the N. W. Side of the Mississippi, no traders, & but little acquainted with whites.

This band, although they purchase a much smaller quantity of merchandise than the Sissatones, still appropriate a considerable proportion of what they do obtain in a similar manner with that mentioned of the Sissatones. This trade, as small as it may appear, has been sufficient to render the Tetones independent of the trade of the Missouri, in a great measure, and has furnished them with the means, not only of distressing and plundering the traders of the Missouri, but also, of plundering and massacreing the defenceless savages of the Missouri, from the mouth of the river Platte to the Minetares, and west to the Rocky mountains. The country these people inhabit is almost one entire plain, uncovered with timber; it is extremely level; the soil fertile, and generally well watered.

23. [a] Sioux; [b] Yank-tons-Ah-nah tribe or River Demoin; [c] ——; [d] * Dar-co-tar (or Sioux) [e] ——; [f] 80; [g] 200; [h] 700; [i] with Mr Crawford on river Demoin; [j] on the river Demoin 30 Leagues up that R. [k] $3000; [l] $5000; [m] Deer & racoon, Some Bear otter & Beaver; [n] Deer, rackoon, Bear otter Beaver Buffalow roabs & Grees Elk, wolves; [o] near the mouth of Chyenne or Dog River or at the Council Bluffs; [p] with the nations on the West and lower part of the Missourie River and with the Ricaras; [q] The Saukie & Renards and those who inhabit East of the R. Mississippi below the Chipaways & Ayauways; [r] River Demoin; [s] between the Missourie & River Desmoin, on the Little River Souix they rove   live by hunting do not cultivate the ground   not good or verry bad.

These are the best disposed Sioux who rove on the banks of the Missouri, and these even will not suffer any trader to ascend the river, if they can possibly avoid it; they have, heretofore, invariably arrested the progress of all those they have met with, and generally compelled them to trade at the prices, nearly, which they themselves think proper to fix on their merchandise: they seldom commit any further acts of violence on the whites. They sometimes visit the river Demoin, where a partial trade has been carried on with them, for a few years past, by a Mr. Crawford. Their trade, if well regulated, might be rendered extremely valuable. Their country is a very fertile one; it consists of a mixture of wood-lands and prairies. The land bordering on the Missouri is principally plains with but little timber.

24. [a] Sioux; [b] Teton Bous rouley (burnt woods) [c] Bous rouley; [d] * Dar-co-tar (or Sioux) [e] ——; [f] 120; [g] 300; [h] 900; [i] with Louisell &c. from S.ᵗ Louis; [j] at Cedar Island 1235 miles up the Missoure River; [k] $5000; [l] $7000; [m] Buffalow robes, Dress.ᵈ Buffalow Skins Greece in bladders & meat; [n] Buffalow roabs, Dressed Buffalow Skins, Grees, [o] near the mouth of Chyenne or Dog River [p] with the nations on the West and lower part of the Missourie River; [q] the Saukie & Renards and those East of the R Mississippi below the Chipeways & Ayauways; [r.] 400 Lgs. up M[issouri]; [s] rove on both Sides of the Missourie about the Grand de tour (or big bend & on Teton River above White River, they are but little acquainted with the whites, uncivilised rascals, they attempted to Stop the party for N W &c.

25. [a] Sioux; [b] Teton-O-kan-dan-das tribe; [c] ——; [d] * Dar-co-tar (or Sioux); [e] ——; [f] 50; [g] 120; [h] 360; [i] with Louisell &c. from S.ᵗ Louis; [j] above the mouth of Chien or *Shar ha* R; [k] $1500; [l] $2500; [m] [Same as for No. 24]; [n] Buffalow roabs, Dressed Buffalow Skins, Grees, Beaver, Deer, Cabbra, Skins; Small & large foxes mink otter, wolves & Hair. [o] near the mouth of Chyenne or Dog River. [p] with the Loup, Mahers, Pon[c]arer, Mandans & Big bellies; [q] the Saukie & Renards [and those East of the Mississippi] Shar ha & Ricreras; [r] on the Miss[ouri]; [s] rove on both Sides of the Missourie below the Mouth of *Shar ha* (Chien or Dog) river on the Teton River above White River, they are but little acquainted with the whites.

26. [a] Sioux; [b] Teton-Min-ne-kine-az-zo; [c] ——; [d] * Dar-co-tar (or Sioux); [e] ——; [f] 100; [g] 250; [h] 750; [i] no trader; [j] about the mouth of Chien and at Ceder Is.ᵈ; [k] $2000; [l] $3000; [m] [Same as Teton O-kan-dan-das]; [n] [Same as Teton O-kan-dan-das]; [o] near the mouth of Chyenne or Dog River; [p] with the Loup, Mahars, Pon[c]arer, Mandans, & Big bellies; [q] [Same as Teton O-kan-dan-das]; [r] on the Missouri up; [s] rove on both Sides of the Missourie above the *Sharha* or Chien river Visious but have behaved tolerably well to the only trader M.ʳ Haney, but little acquainted with the whites; Some intercourse with the Ricaras whome they Some-times treat well but oftener bad (a kind of an exchange exists between them.

27. [a] Sioux; [b] Teton-Sah-o-ne tribe; [c] ——; [d] * Dar-co-tar (or Sioux); [e] ——; [f] 120; [g] 300; [h] 900; [i] no Trader; [j] about the mouth of Chien and at Cedar Is.ᵈ; [k] $2,300; [l] $3500; [m] [Same as Teton O-kan-dan-das]; [n] [Same as Teton O-kan-

dan-das]; [o] [Same as Teton O-kan-dan das]; [p] [Same as Teton O-kan-dan-das]; [q] [Same as Teton O-kan-dan-das]; [r] above [Teton Min-ne-kine-az-zo] on the Missouri; [s] rove on both sides of the Missourie above & below the Ricaraas, [included in the description[s] of Teton Min-ne-kine-az-zo].

Tetons Bois Brulé, Tetons Okandandas, Tetons Minnekineazzo, Tetons Sahone. These are the vilest miscreants of the savage race, and must ever remain the pirates of the Missouri, until such measures are pursued, by our government, as will make them feel a dependence on its will for their supply of merchandise. Unless these people are reduced to order, by coercive measures, I am ready to pronounce that the citizens of the United States can never enjoy but partially the advantages which the Missouri presents. Relying on a regular supply of merchandise, through the channel of the river St. Peters, they view with contempt the merchants of the Missouri, whom they never fail to plunder, when in their power. Persuasion or advice, with them, is viewed as supplication, and only tends to inspire them with contempt for those who offer either. The tameness with which the traders of the Missouri have heretofore submitted to their rapacity, has tended not a little to inspire them with contempt for the white persons who visit them, through that channel. A prevalent idea among them, and one which they make the rule of their conduct, is, that the more illy they treat the traders the greater quantity of merchandise they will bring them, and that they will thus obtain the articles they wish on better terms ; they have endeavored to inspire the Ricaras with similar sentiments, but, happily, without any considerable effect. The country in which these four bands rove is one continued plain, with scarcely a tree to be seen, except on the water-courses, or the steep declivities of hills, which last are but rare : the land is fertile, and lies extremely well for cultivation ; many parts of it are but badly watered. It is from this country that the Missouri derives most of its colouring matter ; the earth is strongly impregnated with glauber salts, alum, copperas and sulphur, and when saturated with water, immense bodies of the hills precipitate themselves into the Missouri, and mingle with its waters. The waters of this river have a purgative effect on those unaccustomed to use it. I doubt whether these people can ever be induced to become stationary ; their trade might be made valuable if they were reduced to order. They claim jointly with the other bands of the Sioux, all the country lying within the following limits, viz. beginning at the confluence of the river Demoin and Mississippi, thence up the west side of the Mississippi to the mouth of the St. Peters river, thence on both sides of the Mississippi to the mouth of Crow-wing river, and upwards with that stream, including the waters of the upper part of the same ; thence to include the waters of the upper portion of Red river, of lake Winnepie, and down the same nearly to Pembenar river, thence a south westerly course to intersect the Missouri at or near the Mandans, and with that stream downwards to the entrance of the Warrecunne creek, thence passing the Missouri it goes to include the lower portion of the river Chyenne, all the waters of White river and river Teton, includes the lower portion of the river Quicurre, and returns to the Missouri, and with that stream downwards to the mouth of Waddipon river, and thence eastwardly to intersect the Mississippi at the beginning.

The subdivisions of the Darcotar or Sioux nation, with the names of the principal chiefs of each band and subdivision.[1]

Names of the Bands	Names of the sub-divisions	Names of the chiefs	Remarks
Mindawarcarton.	Mindawarcarton. Kee-uke-sah. Tin-tah-ton. Mah-tah-ton.	*Ne-co-hun-dah. Tar-tong-gar-mah-nee. Cha-tong-do-tah.	Those marked with a star are the principal chiefs of their respective bands, as well as their own subdivisions.
Wahpatone.	Wah-pa-tone. O-ta-har-ton	*Tar-car-ray. War-bo-sen-dat-ta.	
Wahpacoota.	Wah-pa-coo-ta. Mi-ah-kee-jack-sah.	*War-cah-to. Chit-tah-wock-kun-de-pe.	
Sissatone.	Sissatone. Caw-ree.	*Wack-he-en-do-tar. Tar-tung-gan-naz-a.	
Yankton, (of the north.)	Kee-uke-sah. Sah-own. Hone-ta-par-teen. Hah-har-tones. Hone-ta-par-teen-waz. Za-ar-tar.	*Mah-to-wy-ank-ka. Arsh-kane. Pit-ta-sah. Mah-pe-on-do-tak. Tat-tung-gar-weet-e-co.	Said individually to be very friendly to the whites He possesses great influence in his band and nation.
Yankton ahnah.	Yank-ton,-sa-char-hoo. Tar-co-im-bo-to.	*Nap-pash-scan-na-mah-na. War-ha-zing-ga . . .	Accepted a medal and flag of the United States. Do. a medal.
Teton, (Bois brûle.)	E-sah-a-te-ake-tar-par. War-chink-tar-he. Choke-tar-to-Oz-ash. [womb. Me-ne-sharne.	*Tar-tong-gar-sar-par . . . Man-da-tong-gar . . . Tar-tang-gar-war-har. Mah-zo-mar-nee. Wah-pah-zing-gar.	Do. do. & flag of U. S. A great scoundrel; we gave him a medal before we were acquainted with his character.
Teton, O-Kan-dan-das.	She-o. O-kan-dan-das.	*O-ase-se-char Wah-tar-pa.	
Teton, min-na-kine-az-zo.	Min-na-kine-az-zo. Wan-nee-wack-a-ta-o-ne-lar. Tar-co-eh-parh.	*Wock-ke-a-chauk-in-dish-kah. Chan-te-wah-nee-jah.	
Teton, sah-o-ne.	Sah-o-ne. Tack-chan-de-see-char. Sah-o-ne-hont-a-par-par.	*Ar-kee-che-tar. War-min-de-o-pe-in-doo-tar Sharh-ka-has-car.	

[1] This is probably a copy of the table referred to by Clark as having been sent to the Secretary of War. — ED.

28.   [a] Chyennes; [b] Shar-ha; [c] Chien (Dog); [d] * Chyenne;
[e] ——; [f] 110; [g] 300; [h] 1200; [i] No Trader; [j] on the
Chien River (*not stationary*) and at the Ri[c]aras (*villages*); [k] (*$1500*)
[l] (*$2000*); [m] buffalow robes (*of best quality*); [n] Buffalow roabs,
Dressed Buffalow Skins, Grees, Beaver, Deer, Cabbra, Skins; small &
large foxes otter, wolves & Big horn anamal Skins; [o] at the Mouth
or *Shar ha* River or at the Mouth of Yellowstone R.; [p] a Defensive
War with Sioux (or Darcotas) and at war with no other that I know of;
[q] with the Ricaras, Mandans, Menatares, and all their neighbours in
the plains to the S. W. [r] on Chien R.; [s] No Settled place they
rove to the S. W. of the *Ricaras*, and on both Sides of the Cout Noir or
black hills, at the heads of the Chien River, do not cultivate the Soil,
they formerley lived in a Village and Cultivated Corn on the Cheyene
River a fork of the red river of Lake Winipique, the Souis drove them
from that quater across the Missourie, on the S. W. bank of which they
made a Stand (a fort) a little above the *ricares* a fiew years, and was
compelled to rove   well disposed In.^{ds}

They are the remnant of a nation once respectable in point of number : formerly resided on a branch of the Red river of Lake Winnipie, which still bears
their name.   Being oppressed by the Sioux, they removed to the west side of the
Missouri, about 15 miles below the mouth of the Warricunne creek, where they
built and fortified a village, but being pursued by their ancient enemies the Sioux,
they fled to the Black hills, about the head of the Chyenne river, where they
wander in quest of the buffaloe, having no fixed residence.   They do not cultivate.   They are well disposed towards the whites, and might easily be induced
to settle on the Missouri, if they could be assured of being protected from
the Sioux.   Their number annually diminishes.   Their trade may be made
valuable.

29.   [a] Wetapaha to [and] Cay-au-wa (Kiâwâs) nation;[1] [b] We
ta pa ha to & Cay-au-wah; [c] ——; [d] ——; [e] ——; [f] 70;
[g] 200; [h] 700; [i] no Traders that visit them, what little trinkets
they possess is acquired from their neighbouring Tribes or Nations; [j]
Sometimes visit the Ricaras; [k] ——; [l] ——; [m] ——; [n] [Same
as Chyennes] and Horses; [o] at the Mouth of the *Shar ha* River or
at the Mouth of Yellowstone R.; [p] a Defensive War with Sioux
(or Darcotas) and at war with no other that I know of; [q] with
the Ricaras, Mandans, Menatares, and all their neighbours in the plains
to the S. W; [r] Rivers platt & Loup; [s] rove on the Paducar fork

---

[1] In the printed *Statistical View* these tribes are given separately, but with no additional matter.—ED.

of the river platte [and] on the Wolf or Loup river a N. W. branch of
the Platt to the S W. of the Black hills or *Cout niree* a little to the S.
of West from the mouth of the *Chien or Sharha* River   they are but
little known, they Sometimes Come to the ricaras and trade horses to
them.

They are a wandering nation, inhabit an open country, and raise a great number of horses, which they barter to the Ricaras, Mandans, &c. for articles of
European manufactory.   They are a well disposed people, and might be readily
induced to visit the trading establishments on the Missouri.   From the animals
their country produces, their trade would, no doubt, become valuable.   These
people again barter a considerable proportion of the articles they obtain from
the Menetares, Ahwahhaways, Mandans, and Ricaras, to the Dotames and
Castapanas.

30.   [a] Ca-ne-na-vich [and] Sta-e-tan tribes; [1] [b] Ca-ne-na-vich
[and] Sta-e-tan; [c] Kites; [d] ——; [e] ——; [f.] 190; [g] 500;
[h] 1900; [i] No Traders visit them, what little trinkets they possess
is acquired from their neighbouring Tribes or Nations; [j] Some times
visit the Ricaras; [k] ——; [l] ——; [m] ——; [n] [Same as the
Chyennes] and horses; [o] at the Mouth of the Cheyenne or the River
Roche-joune (yellow Rock); [p] [Same as Wetapahato]; [q] Mandans, Ricaras, and all their neighbours; [r] Heads of the R. Loup;
[s] no limits can be discribed for any of the Nations and tribes in this
quarter as *war* with their neighbours frequently happen which force one
party to remove a considerable distance from the others, untill peace is
restored, at which period all lands are Generally in common, yet it is not
common for two tribes to camp to gether for any long time or hunt in
the Same place.   [applies also to the We ta pa ha to and Kiawas].

31.   [a] Cataka Tribe; [b] Cat'akâ; [c] Ha ka [?] [d] ——; [e] ——;
[f] 25; [g] 75; [h] 300; [i] No Traders that visit them, what little
trinkets they possess acquired from their neighbouring Tribes or Nations;
[j] Some times visit the Ricaras; [k] ——; [l] ——; [m] ——; [n]
[Same as for the Canenavich]; [o] [Same as for the Canenavich];
[p] [Same as for Wetapahato]; [q] Mandans, Ricaras, and all their
neighbours; [r] Heads of R Loup above; [s] Those tribes [Cataka,
Nemousin, Dotame] rove on the heads of the *Wolf* or *Loup* River and
on the head waters of the S. E branches of the *river, Rochejoune* or *yellow*

---

[1] In the printed *Statistical View* these tribes are given separately: 150 lodges, 400
warriors, and 1,500 people are assigned to the Kanenavish; and 40 lodges, 100 warriors, and 400 people to the Staetan; otherwise there is no additional information.—ED.

rock, and between the Cout Noire and rock or Shineing mountains —
one of those tribes is known to Speak the Padoucan Language. Their
Territories are in Common as above Stated [of the Canenavich]; do
not Cultivate the Soil but live by hunting in a countrey abounding in
animals, inhabit a fine [country] for Beaver Otter &c.

Neither these people, the Wetepahatoes, Kanenavish, Staetan, Cataka, nor the
Chyennes have any idea of exclusive right to the soil.

32. [a] Nemousin Tribe; [b] Ni-mi-ou-sin; [c] ——; [d] ——;
[e] ——; [f] 15; [g] 50; [h] 200; [1] [Same as for Cataka]
[j] Sometimes visit the Ricaras; [k] ——; [l] ——; [m] ——;
[n] [Same as for the Canenavich]; [o] [Same as for the Canenavich];
[p] [Same as for the Wetapahato]; [q] [Same as for the Cataka];
[r] Heads of R. Loup above; [s] [Included in Cataka].

These differ from the others (viz. Wetepahatoes, Kiawas, Kanenavich, Staetan
and Cataka) in as much as they never visit the Ricaras; in all other respects they
are the same.

33. [a] Do-ta-me tribe; [b] Do-ta ma; [c] ——; [d] Padouces;
[e] ——; [f] 10; [g] 30; [h] 120; [i] (*No Trader*); [j] Some
times visit the Ricaras; [k] ——; [l] ——; [m] ——; [n] [Same
as for the Canenavich]; [o] [Same as for the Canenavich]; [p] [Same
as for the Wetapahato]; [q] [Same as for the Cataka]; [r] Heads of
the R. Loup above; [s] [Included in Cataka[s]].

The information I possess, with respect to this nation, is derived from Indian
information: they are said to be a wandering nation, inhabiting an open country,
and who raise a great number of horses and mules. They are a friendly, well
disposed people, and might, from the position of their country, be easily induced
to visit an establishment on the Missouri, about the mouth of Chyenne river.
They have not, as yet, visited the Missouri.

34. [a] Cas-ta-ha-na N; [b] Cas-ta-ha-na *Nation*; [c] Gens des
Vache; [d] Me na tare (or big belly); [e] ——; [f] 500; [g] 1300;
[h] 5000; [i] No Traders; [j] Some visit the Mandans & Minataries;
[k] ——; [l] ——; [m] ——; [n] [Same as preceding tribes] (*and
skins of the lynx or louverin; and martens in addition*); [p] at the mouth
of Rochejoune (or Yellow Stone R); [p] a Defensive War with the
Sioux & Assinniboins, at war with no other nation that I know of;
[q] Mandans, Big bellies and their wandering neighbours; [r] Yellow
rock river & Loup; [s] rove on a S. E. fork of the *Yellow Rock* River
called Big horn River, and the heads of the Loup. Their Territories
are in common as above stated [of the Canenavich] do not cultivate the
Soil but live by hunting.

What has been said of the Dotames is applicable to these people, except that they trade principally with the Crow Indians, and that they would most probably prefer visiting an establishment on the Yellow Stone river, or at its mouth on the Missouri.

35. [a] *Ravin* nation (*Crow Indians*); [b] Kee'-hât-sâ; [c] Corbeaus; [d] Menetare (or big belly) [e] ———; [f] 350; [g] 900; [h] 3500; [i] No Traders; [j] Some visit the Mandans & Minataries; [k] ———; [l] ———; [m] ———; [n] [Same as for the Castahana]; [o] At the Mouth of Rochejoune (or Yellow Stone R); [p] a Defensive War with Sioux & Assinniboins & Ricares; [q] Mandans Big bellies and their wandering neighbours; [r] on the Yellow Rock R. low down; [s] rove on both Sides of the River Rochejone (or Yellow Stone) some distance above the mouth. Their territories are in Common, do not cultivate the Soil but live by hunting, Ther Countrey is full of anamals or Game of every Kind perticularly Beaver, a great perpotion Wood L[an]d.

These people are divided into four bands, called by themselves Ahâh'-âr-ro'-pir-no-pah, Noo'-ta-, Pa-rees-car, and E-hârt'-sâr. They annually visit the Mandans, Minetares, and Ahwahhaways, to whom they barter horses, mules, leather lodges, and many articles of Indian apparel, for which they receive in return, guns, ammunition, axes, kettles, awls, and other European manufactures. When they return to their country, they are in turn visited by the Paunch and Snake Indians, to whom they barter most of the articles they have obtained from the nations on the Missouri, for horses and mules, of which those nations have a greater abundance than themselves. They also obtain of the Snake Indians, bridle-bits and blankets, and some other articles which those Indians purchase from the Spaniards. The bridle-bits and blankets I have seen in the possession of the Mandans and Minetares. Their country is fertile and well watered, and in most parts well timbered.

36. [a] (*Paunch tribe*); [b] Kee-hât-sâ (*Al-la-kâ'-we-âh*); [c] Gens des panse; [d] Menetarre; [e] ———; [f] 300; [g] 800; [h] 2,300; [i] No Traders; [j] Some visit the Mandans & Minataries; [k] ———; [l] ———; [m] ———; [n] [Same as for the Castahana]; [o] at the mouth of the Rochejoune (or Yellow Stone R; [p] a Defensive War with the Sioux & Assinniboins; [q] Mandans, Big bellies and their wandering neighbours; [r] on the Yellow Rock R. high up; [s] rove on the River *Rochejone* high up their countrey abounds in animals of Different kinds. Their Territories are in Common do not cultivate the Soil but live by hunting.

[103]

These are said to be a peaceable, well disposed nation. Their country is a variegated one, consisting of mountains, vallies, plains, and wood-lands, irregularly interspersed. They might be induced to visit the Missouri, at the mouth of the Yellow Stone river; and from the great abundance of valuable fured animals which their country, as well as that of the Crow Indians, produces, their trade must become extremely valuable. They are a roving people, and have no idea of of exclusive right to the soil.

37. [a] [The three tribes 37, 38, 39 are called] Assiniboins T[ribe]s as calᵈ by the Chipaways or Stone Sious; [b] Ma-ne-to-par Tribe; [c] or Band lar Gru (crain) or canoe; [d] Soues (Darcota) with a little corruption; [e] ——; [f] 100; [g] 200; [h] 750; [i] Hudsons Bay N. W. & X. Y. Companies; [j] The Establishments at the mouth of Mous R. on the Assiniboin River & at the Establishmᵗˢ on R. Cappell abᵗ 150 mˡˢ N. of Fort Mandan; [k] $4,500; [l] $7,000; [m] some Beaver a fiew Roabs, Grees, meat wolves & penistigon; [n] (*Buffalow robes, tallow, dried and pounded meat and grease, skins of the large and small fox, small and large wolves, antelopes, (or cabri) and elk in great abundance, also some brown, white and grissly bear, deer and lynx*); [o] at the mouth of the Roche-joune (or Yellow Stone R; [p] Sioux Snake Indians and partially with Ricaras & Several nations on the S. W. of Missouri; [q] the Knistanoes (or Cristanoes & their own tribes only; [r] on Mous river & R. Rogue; [s] rove on the Mouse River and the branches of River Assinaboin North of the Mandans, those people do not cultivate the ground, they are Vicious. they live by hunting pay but little respect to their engagements, great Drunkards.

38 [a] Assiniboins; [b] Na-co'-ta O-see-gah; [c] Gens des fees or Girls (*Gens des Tee*); [d] Soues with a little corruption; [e] ——; [f] 100; [g] 250; [h] 850; [i] [Same as for Manetopa tribe]; [j] [Same as for Manetopa tribe]; [k] $6,000; [l] $6,500; [m] [Same as for Manetopa tribe]; [n] [Same as for Manetopa tribe]; [o] At the mouth of Roche-joune (or Yellow Stone R; [p] [Same as for Manetopa tribe; [q] [Same as for Manetopa tribe]; [r] between the R. Rouche & Missouri; [s] Rove on the heads of the Mouse river & River Capell (or that Calls) and on a N. West branch of the Missourie called White earth River, vicious & do not Cultivate the land live by hunting pay but little respect to their engagements, great Drunkards.

39. [a] Assiniboins; [b] Na-co'-ta Mah-to-pâ-nar-to; [c] Big Devils (*Gens des grand diable*); [d] Soues with a little corruption; [e] ——; [f] 200; [g] 450; [h] 1600; [i] [Same as for Manetopa tribe]; [j]]Same as for Manetopa tribe] (*and occasionally at the establish-*

ments on the river *Saskashawan*); [k] $8,000; [l] $8000; [m] [Same as for the Manetopa tribe]; [n] [Same as for Manetopa tribe] (*with more bears and some marten*); [o] At the mouth of Roche-joune (or Yellow Stone R; [p] [Same as for the Manetopa tribe]; [q] [Same as for the Manetopa tribe]; [r] between the R. Rouche & Missouri & up white earth R; [s] rove in the plains in Different parties between the *Missouris* & the Saskashowan rivers above the Yellow Stone River & heads of the Ossiniboins River, they are vicious do not Cultivate the Soil live by hunting

Manetopa. Oseegah. Mahtopanato. Are the descendants of the Sioux, and partake of their turbulent and faithless disposition: they frequently plunder, and sometimes murder, their own traders. The name by which this nation is generally known was borrowed from the Chippeways, who call them *Assinniboan*, which, literally translated, is *Stone Sioux*, hence the name of Stone Indians, by which they are sometimes called. The country in which they rove is almost entirely uncovered with timber; lies extremely level, and is but badly watered in many parts; the land, however, is tolerably fertile and unincumbered with stone. They might be induced to trade at the river Yellow Stone; but I do not think that their trade promises much. Their numbers continue about the same. These bands, like the Sioux, act entirely independent of each other, although they claim a national affinity and never make war on each other. The country inhabited by the Mahtopanato possesses rather more timber than the other parts of the country. They do not cultivate.

40. [a] Knistanoes or Cristanoes; [b] Knis-ta-nau 2 *bands*; [c] Crees; [d] Corupted Chipaway; [e] ———; [f] 150; [g] 300; [h] 1000; [i] Hudsons Bay N. W. & X. Y. Companies; [j] The Establishments at the mouth of Mous R. on the Assiniboin River & at the Establish^mts on R. Cappell ab^t 150 m^ls N. of Fort Mandan; [k] $10,000; [l] $15,000; [m] Beaver, wolves, otter, Carkajeu (or wolverine or Beaver robes) Dressed Elk or Mo[o]se little fox Loucirva Picou or Lynx, Mink Martin &c; [n] (*The skins of the beaver, otter, lynx, wolf, wolverine, marten, mink, small fox, brown and grizzly bear, dressed elk and moose-deer skins, muskrat skins, & some buffaloe robes, dried meat, tallow and grease.*) [o] at the mouth of Rochejoune (or Yellow Stone R; [p] Sioux the fall Indians Blood Indians, Crow, &c.; [q] Algonquins Chipaways Assiniboins Mandans Grovantre &c. and the Ah-nah-ha-ways or Shoe Indians; [r] Assiniboin River; [s] rove on Heads of Ossiniboin & its waters and to the Missouri in the Countrey of the Assiniboins, principally on the head [of] Assiniboin, not Stationary.

They are a wandering nation ; do not cultivate, nor claim any particular tract of country. They are well disposed towards the whites, and treat their traders with respect. The country in which they rove is generally open plains, but in some parts, particularly about the head of the Assinniboin river, it is marshy and tolerably well furnished with timber, as are also the Fort Dauphin mountains, to which they sometimes resort. From the quantity of beaver in their country, they ought to furnish more of that article than they do at present. They are not esteemed good beaver hunters. They might, probably be induced to visit an establishment on the Missouri, at the Yellow Stone river. Their number has been reduced, by the small pox, since they were first known to the Canadians.

41. [a] Fall Indians ; [b] (*A-lân-sâr*); [c] Fall Indians or Gen de rapid ; [d] Menetarre ; [e] ——; [f] 260; [g] 660 ; [h] 2,500 ; [i] N. W. Company; [j] Eagle Mountain (*upper establishment on the Saskashawan ; but little trade.*); [k] $1,000 ; [l] $4,000; [m] [Same as for Assiniboins] ; [n] [Same as for Assiniboins] and Big horned animal skins and all other no[r]thern animals inhabiting a N. climate except racoons & fisher ; [o] about the falls of Missouri ; [p] (*Defensive war with the Christenoes*); [q] ——; [r] near Rock M[ountains]; [s] rove between the Missouries and Askaw or Bad river a fork of the *Saskashawan*, a tribe of *Menetaries* but little known, they rove as far as the Rock mountains.

The country these people rove in is not much known : it is said to be a high, broken, woody country. They might be induced to visit an establishment at the falls of the Missouri : their trade may, no doubt, be made profitable.

42. [a] Cattanahaws; [b] Cat-an-a-haws; [c] none ; [d] ——; [all blank to] [m] [Same as for Cristanoes]; [n] [Same as for Falls Indians]; [o] about the falls of Missouri; [r] near Rock M ; [s] on the heads of the South fork of the Sas-kas-ha-wan, and North branches of the Missouri about the rock Mountains but little known.

What has been said of the Fall Indians is, in all respects, applicable to this nation. They are both wandering nations.

43. [a] Blue Mud Indians; [b] ——; [c] Blue Muds; [d] to [r] [Same as for Cattanahaws]; [s] In the Rock or Shineing mountains on the S. Side of a River Called *Great Lake* River, Supposed to run into the *Columbia* river, but little known.

44. [a] Alitan or Snake Indians; [b] A-li-tan ; [c] Gens de Serpent; [d] * Alitan ; [e] `[f] [g] [h] verry noumerous ; [i] Some of those Indians trade with the Spaniards S. of them ; [j] New Mexico; [k]

[l] [m] ——— ; [n] Carkajous wolverine or Beaver eaters Loucirva Picpou or Links (*they have in addition immense quantities of horses, mules and asses*); [o] Head of Platt or Arkansaws R. (*At or near the Falls of Missouri*); [p] Act on Defensive as far as I can lern, the most of the nearer nations make war upon them; [q] with those who wish to be friendly; [r] in and about Rockey Mount^ns; [s] rove on both Sides from the falls about 2500 miles up near the Rock mountain to the head and about those mountains Southerley quite to the heads of Arkansaw, verry noumerous all the nations on the Missouries make war on them & Steal their horses Those I have seen are mild and appear well disposed (I am told they are the best nation known) those to the South have some trade with the Spaniards of N. Mexico from whom those on the Missouries get some articles they abound in horses.

[The Statistical View divides this nation into three tribes as follows:]

Aliatans, *Snake Indians*. These are a very numerous and well disposed people, inhabiting a woody and mountainous country; they are divided into three large tribes, who wander at a considerable distance from each other; and are called by themselves So-so-na, So-so' bu-bar, and I-a-kar; these are again subdivided into smaller tho' independent bands, the names of which I have not yet learnt; they raise a number of horses and mules which they trade with the Crow Indians, or are stolen by the nations on the east of them. They maintain a partial trade with the Spaniards, from whom they obtain many articles of cloath· ing and ironmongery, but no warlike implements.

Of the West. These people also inhabit a mountainous country, and some-times venture in the plains east of the Rocky mountains, about the head of the Arkansas river. They have more intercourse with the Spaniards of New Mexico, than the Snake Indians. They are said to be very numerous and warlike, but are badly armed. The Spaniards fear these people, and therefore take the pre-caution not to furnish them with any warlike implements. In their present un-armed state, they frequently commit hostilities on the Spaniards. They raise a great many horses.

La Playes. These principally inhabit the rich plains from the head of the Arkansas, embracing the heads of Red river, and extending with the mountains and high lands eastwardly as far as it is known towards the gulph of Mexico. They possess no fire arms, but are warlike and brave. They are, as well as the other Aliatans, a wandering people. Their country abounds in wild horses, besides great numbers which they raise themselves. These people, and the West Aliatans, might be induced to trade with us on the upper part of the Arkansas river. I do not believe that any of the Aliatans claim a country within any particular limits.

45. [a] Padoucas; [b] ——; [c] Padoo; [d] * Padoucies; [e] Several v[illages]; [f] ——; [g] [h] very noumerous; [i] Some of those Ind^s trade with the Spaniards S. of them; [j] New Mexico; [k] [l] [m] ——; [n] [Same as Snake Indians] except Moose Marten Picou & carckjou skins; [o] near the head of Platt, or Arkansaw Rivers; [p] act on the Defensive as far as I can lern, the most of the nearer nations make war upon them; [q] with those who wish to be friendly; [r] Heads of Platt & Arkansaws R; [s] This nation live in Villages on the heads of River Platt & Arkansaws noumerous, well disposed, abound in horses, have Some [trade] with New Mexico, I can obtain no certain account of their Situation numbers &c. &c.

This once powerful nation has, apparently, entirely disappeared; every inquiry I have made after them has proved ineffectual. In the year 1724, they resided in several villages on the heads of the Kansas river, and could, at that time, bring upwards of two thousand men into the field (see Monsr. Dupratz history of Louisiana, page 71, and the map attached to that work). The information that I have received is, that being oppressed by the nations residing on the Missouri, they removed to the upper part of the river Platte, where they afterwards had but little intercourse with the whites. They seem to have given name to the northern branch of that river, which is still called the Paducas fork. The most probable conjecture is, that being still further reduced, they have divided into small wandering bands, which assumed the names of the subdivisions of the Paducas nation, and are known to us at present under the appellation of Wetepahatoes, Kiawas, Kanenavish, Katteka, Dotame, &c. who still inhabit the country to which the Paducas are said to have removed. The majority of my information led me to believe that those people spoke different languages, but other and subsequent information has induced me to doubt the fact.

46. [a] Chipaways; [b] Oo-chi-pa-wau; [c] Souteau; [d] * Oochepawau; [e] 1; [f] ——; [g] 400; [h] 1600; [i] British N. W. Co. [j] near their Village; [k] $12,000; [l] $16,000 [m] Beaver, Otter, racoon fox Min [k] Deer & B[lack] Bear Skins & Martens; [n] Beaver otters, racoon, fox, Mink, Deer & B. Bear Skins & Martens; [o] head of Mississippi or at Red Lake; [p] Sioux (or Darcotas) (*Saukees, Renars, and Ayouwais*); [q] all the tribes of Chipaways and the nations about the Lakes & Down the Missippi; [r] in an Island in Leach Lake; [s] a village in a lake near the head of the Mississippi and an expansion of the Same Called Leach, they own all the Countrey West of L. Super[i] or & to the Sous line —— wild rice which is in great abundance in their [Country] raise no Corn &c.

Chippeways, *of Leach Lake.* Claim the country on both sides of the Mississippi, from the mouth of the Crow-wing river to its source, and extending west of the Mississippi to the lands claimed by the Sioux, with whom they still contend for dominion. They claim, also, east of the Mississippi, the country extending as far as lake Superior, including the waters of the river St. Louis. This country is thickly covered with timber generally; lies level and generally fertile, though a considerable portion of it is intersected and broken up by small lakes, morasses and swamps, particularly about the heads of the Mississippi and river St. Louis. They do not cultivate, but live principally on the wild rice, which they procure in great abundance on the borders of Leach Lake and the banks of the Mississippi. Their number has been considerably reduced by wars and the small pox. Their trade is at its greatest extent.

47. [a] Chipaways about L. Dubois (or wood) (*Red Lake*) and the head of the Mississippi; [b] Algonquins 100 men & chipaways 200; [c] Souteaus; [d] * Oochepawau; [e]——; [f] ramble; [g] 300 (200, 100); [h] 1050 (700, 350); [i] British N. W. Co. [j] at Def! Camps; [k] $12,000; [l] $16,000; [m] Beaver, otters, racoon fox Min[k] Deer & B. Bear skins & Marten & some Berch Canoes; [n] Beaver, otters, racoon, fox, Mink Deer & B. Bear skins & Martens & Canoes; [o] head of the Mississippi or at Red Lake; [p] Sioux (or Darcotas); [q] all the tribes of Chipaways and the nations about the Lakes & Down the Missippi & partially with the Assiniboin; [r] about the head of Mississippi & L. of Woods; [s] in defferant parts of the Countrey from the heads of the Mississippi Northerley to the N. W. part of Lake Dubois do not cultivate the land but live on Wild rice hunting &c. &c.

[Chippeways] *of Red lake.* Claim the country about Red lake and Red lake river, as far as the Red river of lake Winnipie, beyond which last river they contend with the Sioux for territory. This is a low level country, and generally thickly covered with timber, interrupted with many swamps and morasses. This, as well as the other bands of Chippeways, are esteemed the best hunters in the north west country; but from the long residence of this band in the country they now inhabit, game is becoming scarce; therefore, their trade is supposed to be at its greatest extent. The Chippeways are a well disposed people, but excessively fond of spirituous liquor.

48. [a] Chipaways on River Rouge; [b] Oo-che-pa-wau; [c] Souteau; [d] * Oochepawau; [e]——; [f] ramble; [g] 100; [h] 800; [i] N. W. & X. Y. Co.; [j] at the mouth of Pembinar river; [k] $7,000; [l] $10,000; [m] [same as Chipaways of Leach Lake] and no Canoes; [n] Beaver, otters, racoon, fox, Mink, Deer & B. Bear skins & martens, Lynx, Wolverine & wolves; [o] head of the Mississippi or at

Red Lake; [p] Sioux (or Darcotas); [q] all the tribes of Chipaways and the nations about the Lakes & Down the Missippi & cristinoes; [r] on R. Ruge about the Mouth of Pembina; [s] ramble near the Establishment on the River Assiniboin & fork of red River running into Lake Winipicque, This tribe of Chipaways formerley lived on the Mississippi at Sand Lake and encouraged by the British traders to hunt on River Rogue [Rouge].

[Chippeways] *of river Pembena.* These people formerly resided on the east side of the Mississippi, at Sand lake, but were induced, by the north west company, to remove, about two years since, to the river Pembena. They do not claim the lands on which they hunt. The country is level and the soil good. The west side of the river is principally prairies or open plains ; on the east side there is a greater proportion of timber. Their trade at present is a very valuable one, and will probably increase for many years. They do not cultivate, but live by hunting. They are well disposed towards the whites.

49. [a] Algonquin; [b] Oo Chipawau; [c] Souters; [d] * Oochipawau; [e] ——; [f] ramble; [g] 200; [h] 600; [i] N. W. & X. Y. Co.; [j] Portage de prarie (*Establishments on the Assiniboin at Fort de Prairie*); [k] $8,000; [l] $11,000; [m] Beaver, otter, racoon, fox mink, Deer & B. Bear Skins & marten; [n] Beaver, otters, racoon, fox, Mink, Deer & B. Bear Skins & martens Lynx & Wolverines [o] Mouth of Assinnoboin about the place the West line will cross from the L. of Wo [o] ds in Lat. 49° 37' North or thereabouts (*At the Red river establishment*); [p] Sioux (or Darcotas); [q] [Same as Chippaways of River Pembena]; [r] about the Mouth of the assiniboin; [s] Those bands [including No. 50] rove on the river Rogue from the Pembauer down to the Lake Winipicque and about the Lake *Manitauber*, removed from the East encouraged by the British traders to hunt on River Rogue Those people do not cultivate the earth but hunt beaver & valuable furs.

Algonquins, *of Rainy Lake, &c.* With the precise limits of the country they claim, I am not informed. They live very much detached, in small parties. The country they inhabit is but an indifferent one ; it has been much hunted, and the game, of course, nearly exhausted. They are well disposed towards the whites. Their number is said to decrease. They are extremely addicted to spirituous liquor, of which large quantities are annually furnished them by the N. W. traders. in return for their bark canoes. They live wretchedly poor.

50. [a] Algonquin; [b] Oo Chipawau; [c] Souteau; [d] * Oochipawau; [e] ——; [f] ramble; [g] 100; [h] 500; [i] N. W. & X. Y. Co.; [j] Portage de prarie (*Establishments on the rivers Winnipie an*

DACOTA WOMAN AND ASSINIBOIN GIRL

Rainy Lake, and at their hunting camps); [k] $4,000; [l] $5,000; [m]
[Same as Algonquins of Rainy Lake]; [n] [Same as Algonquins of Rainy
Lake & wolverines wolves & Muskrats]; [o] [Same as Algonquins of
Rainy Lake]; [p] Sioux (or Darcotas); [q] [Same as Chippeways of
River Pembena] & Algonquins; [r] low down the red R.; [s] [Included
in No. 49 s].

Algonquins, *of Portage de Prairie.* These people inhabit a low, flat, marshy
country, mostly covered with timber, and well stocked with game. They are
emigrants from the lake of the Woods and the country east of it, who were
introduced, some years since, by the N. W. traders, in order to hunt the country
on the lower parts of the Red river, which then abounded in a variety of animals
of the fur kind. They are an orderly, well disposed people, but like their relations on Rainy lake, extremely addicted to spirituous liquors. Their trade is at
its greatest extent.

51. [a] Black foot Indians; [b] ——; [c] la peain noir; d ——;
[e] [f] [g] [h] [i] [j] [k] [l] ——; [m] Beaver, otter, racoons, fox,
mink Deer Black Bear martens & Elk; [n] Beaver, otter, racoon, fox,
Mink, Deer, Black Bear, Marten, Lynx, wolverines, wolves, Muskrats Elk & Bighorn; [o] about the falls of Missouri; [p] [q] ——; [r]
near the Rock M.; [s] Blackfots rove near the Rock mountains on the
East Side on the waters of the Missouries. but little known. Those
nations [including Flat heads] being little known the information is from
the Menetarres.
52. [a] Flat head In.ds; [b] (*Tut-see'-wâs*); [c] Tate Platt; [d] [e]
[f] [g] [h] ——; [i] (*No trader*); [j] [k] [l] [m] ——; [n] [Same as
Blackfoots]; [o] ——; [p] (*Defensive war with Minetares*); [q] ——;
[r] on the W. of Rock M.; [s] Flatheads live on a river running
to the N. W. beyond the Missouri, Supposed to be a branch of the
Columbia.

The information I posses with respect to these people has been received from
the Minetares, who have extended their war excursions as far westerly as that
nation, of whom they have made several prisoners, and brought them with them
to their villages on the Missouri: these prisoners have been seen by the French-
men residing in this neighborhood. The Minetares state, that this nations resides
in one village on the west side of a large and rapid river, which runs from south
to north, along the foot of the Rocky mountains on their west side; and that
this river passes at a small distance from the three forks of the Missouri. That
the country between the mountains and the river is broken, but on the opposite
side of the river, it is an extensive open plain, with a number of barren, sandy
hills, irregularly distributed over its surface as far as the eye can reach. They are
a timid, inoffensive, and defenceless people. They are said to possess an
abundance of horses.

53.   [a] Pania Pickey ;   [b] ———— ;   [c] Pania Pickey;   [d] * Pania ;
[e] 2 ;   [ɪ] ———— ;   [g] 500 ; [h] 2000 ;   [i] [j] [k] [l] [m] [n] ———— ;
[o] 3 Forks of Arkansaw   [p] Little & Big Ossage Kanses & Panias ;
[q] ———— ;   [r] on the head of Red River of Mississippi ;

[s] These people have no intercourse with the inhabitants of the Illinois; the information, therefore, which I have been enabled to obtain, with respect to them, is very imperfect.   They were formerly known by the name of the *White* Panias, and are of the same family with the Panias of the river Platte.   They are said to be a well disposed people, and inhabit a very fertile country ; certain it is that they enjoy a delightful climate.

[Here end both the printed *Statistical View* and Clark's MS. table. In the additional space at the foot of the table, Clark added the following information on the Southern tribes.— ED.]

54.   [a] Dellaways Kickapoos about the mouth of the Missouri; [c] Loups ;   [d] Dillaway &c. ;   [f] ramble; [g] 20 ; [h] 60 ; [r] above the Mouth of Missouri & up that river as high as Osarge Womans River
55.   [a] Dellaways Miamis &c. about Dilliard & S. Louis;   [c] Loups ;   [d] Dellaway &c. ;   [f] ramble; [g] 25 ; [h] 80 ; [r] about S. Louis & Dilliard village.
56.   [a] Piories & Illinois; [f] camps;   [g] 18 ; [h] 50 ; [r] near S. Genivieve ;
57.   [a] Shawonies ; [d] Shawonies; [e] 3 ; [g] 150 ; [h] 600 ; [r] on apple River near Cape Gerardeau
58.   [a] Dillaways; [c] Loups [d] Dillawais; [e] 2 ; [g] 200 ; [h] 800 ; [r] on a Small Creak near Cape Girardeau.
59.   [a] Cherikees Creeks &c. delewais & Chickasaws ; [f] ramble; [h] varies ; [r] near New Madrid.
60.   [a] Chickasaws, Chocktaws & Cherikees ; [f] ramble; [h] varies ; [r] Between the Mississippi & Arkansaws Rivers.

in Lower Louisiana

61.   [a] Arkansaws ; [b] O-zar-jees ; [d] Osage ; [e] 2 ; [g] 260 ; [h] 1000 ; [r] Near the mouth of the Arkansaws R.
62.   [a] Chacktaws ; [f] ramble ; [g] 300 ; [h] 1560 ; [r] from the Natchetouchs to the Mississippi.
63.   [a] Biloxes ; [e] 2 ; [g] 40 ; [h] 150 ; [r] on red River below the Natchetouches.
64.   [a] Chacktaws ; [e] 1 ; [g] 25 ; [h] 100 ; [r] 26 Leagues up Red R. at the Rapids.

65. [a] Biloni N. [e] 2; [g] 15; [h] 60; [r] on Red River near Avoyelles.

66. [a] Cadoquies [e] 1; [g] 400; [h] 1600; [r] on Red River 80 Leagues above Natchitoches.

67. [a] Conchates; [f] Dispersed; [g] 100; [h] 350; [r] Dispersed through the Opilousas countrey.

68. [a] Alibamas N: [e] 1; [g] 30; [h] 100; [r] near Opilousas Chirch.

69. [a] Bilexis & Chacktaws; [e] 1; [g] 15; [h] 50; [r] Rochedile Beyou.

70. [a] Atacapas; [f] Dispersed; [g] 30; [h] 100; [r] Dispersed on Vermillion Creek.

71. [a] Chitenachas [d] Natchas; [e] 3; [g] 30; [h] 100; [r] 12 Leagues from the Sea on bayou Teeche.

72. [a] Tounicas; [e] 1; [g] 18; [h] 60; [r] Point Coupee E. Side.

B. ESTIMATE OF THE WESTERN INDIANS

[Editorial Note. — During the winter passed at Fort Clatsop, Lewis and Clark drew up an " Estimate of the Western Indians," referring thereby to tribes west of the Rocky Mountains. This was entered in Codex I, pp. 147–155 (though in reverse order).[1] The first six pages were written by Clark, and the tribal names seem to have been jotted down without order or system. On pp. 148, 149, Lewis entered his estimate, beginning with the tribes that roamed between the upper waters of the Columbia and those of the Missouri, and following these in the order of their residence down to the tribes of the coast. On p. 147, Clark has added a number of other tribes situated north and south along the coast, compiled from Indian information. The sum total of this population, as here estimated, was 69,040. On the return journey, the explorers came into further contact with the tribes, and learned more

[1] As evidence in regard to the date of the original draft, the following note of Lewis (Codex I, p. 148) may be considered : " Feb. 8th 1805 [sc. 1806]. *Note* there are several other nations residing on the Columbia below the grand rappids and on some streams which discharge themselves into the same whose names we have learnt but have not any proper data from which to calculate ther probable number ; therefor omitted." See also text of journal for June 13, 1806, (volume v, p. 133), when the original draft as entered in Codex I was doubtless completed. — Ed.

of those residing southward on the Multnomah River; this information they added to the original draft. At some later time, Clark revised his enumeration, compiling from this original estimate, and numbering the tribes in the order in which he intended to describe them. He then wrote in red ink across the foot of p. 150, Codex I: "The estimate of the Nations and tribes West of the Rocky Mountains May be seen more Correctly Stated in a Supplement accompanying these Books. W. C. 80,000 Soles."

This "supplement" (now in possession of the American Philosophical Society) consists of four sheets of heavy paper, 13½ × 9½ inches, written upon one side, all in Clark's handwriting, and emended by himself in red ink. In this supplement, the populations of certain tribes were considerably enlarged. The differences between this final estimate and the original draft in Codex I are, in the following table, indicated by foot-notes.]

Names of Indian Nations and their places of General Residence	No of Houses or Lodges	Probable No of Souls
1. SHO-SHO-NE [1] Nation reside in Spring and Summer on the East fork of Lewis's river a branch of the Columbia, and winter and fall on the Missouri	60	800
2. OATE-LASH-SCHUTE [2] Tribe of the *Tush-she-pah* Nation reside in Spring and Summer in the Rocky Mountains on Clarks river, and winter and fall on the Missouri and its waters	33	400
3. CHOPUNNISH Nation residing on the Kooskooske river below the forks and on Colters Creek &ᶜ and who sometimes pass over to the Missouri	large Lodges	2,000
4. PEL-LOAT-PAL-LAH Band of *Chopunnish* reside on the Kooskooske above the forks and on the small streams which fall into that river west of the rocky mountains, & chopunnish river, and sometimes pass over to the Missouri	dº	1,600
		4,800

[1] In the original draft Lewis begins with the Oatelashschute tribe, and leaves the Shoshones until later. Clark appears to have entered them first, as these were the first Western Indians whom they encountered. — ED.

[2] The Clark-Voorhis note-book No. 4 adds: "a part of the Tushshepaw Nation includes the Tush she pah, ho hill pos & Micksicksealtom Tribes all of them rove on Clark's River and occasionally cross over to the Missouri for the purpose of making robes and dried meat &c." — ED.

Names of Indian Nations and their places of General Residence	No. of Houses or Lodges	Probable No of Souls
5. KI-MOO-E-NIM Band of *Chopunnish* N. reside on Lewis'es river above the enterance of the Koos-kooske as high up that river as the Forks	d°	4,800 800
6. Y-E-LET PO Band of Choponish reside under the S. W. Mountains on a Small river which falls into Lewis's river above the enterance of the Koos-kooske which they call *we-are-cum*	d°	250
7 WIL-LE-WAH Band [of] Choponish on a river of the same name which discharges itself into Lewis's river on the S. W. side below the forks of that river	d°	500
8 SO-YEN-NOW Band of Choponiesh [1] on the N. side of the E. fork of Lewis's river from it's junction to the rocky Mountains and on La-mal-tar Creek	d°	400
9 CHOPUNNISH of Lewis's river below the enterance of Kooskooske on either Side of that river to it's junction with the Columbia	h[ouses] Lodges 30 10	2,300
10 SOKULK Nation reside on the Columbia above the enterance of Lewis's river as high up as the enterance of Clarks river	120	2,400
11 CHIM-NAH-PUM on the N. W. side of the Columbia both above and below the enterance of Lewis's river and on the Tapteel R.[2] which falls into the Columbia 15 M. above Lewis's R.	42	11,450 1,860
12 WAL-LOW-WAL-LOW Nation on both sides of the Columbia from the enterance of Lewis's river as low as the Muscle shell rapid and in winter pass over to the waters of the Tapteel river.	46	1,600 [3]
13 PISH-QUIT-PAH's Nation reside from the Muscle rapid & on the N. side of the Columbia to the Commencement of the high Country this N. winter on the waters of the Tapteel river	71	2,600 [4]
14 WAH-HOW-PUM Nation reside on the N. bank of the Columbia in different Bands from the pish-quitpales as low as River Lapage the differt bands of this nation winter on the waters of Tapteel & Catteract Rvs	33	700
15 E-NE-CHUR Nation reside at the Great falls of Columbia on either side are stationary	41	1,200
16 E-SKEL-LUTE Nation reside at the upper part of the Great Narrows of Columbia on the N. Side (is the great mart for all the Country)	h[ouses] 21	1,000 [5] 31,860

[1] The preceding six tribes of the Chopunnish nation were entered in the original draft as follows : " Chopunnish of the Kooskooske River, 220 lodges, 3600 souls ; Chopunnish of Lewis's River above the entrance of the Kooskooske, 80 lodges, 1200 souls." Later was added Willeletpo and Willelahs with substantially the same description as given here. — ED.

[2] In the original draft this river is nameless. — ED.

[3] In the original draft " 1000." — ED.

[4] In the original draft " 1600." — ED.

[5] In the original draft the spelling is " E-che-lute," and the number " 600." — ED.

Names of Indian Nations and their places of General Residence	No of Houses or Lodges	Probable No of Souls
		31,860
17 CHIL-LUCK-KIT-TE-QUAW N. resideing next below the narrows and extending down on the N. side of the Columbia to River Labeech	h[ouses] 32	1,400 [1]
18 SMOCK-SHOP Band of Chil-luck-kit-te-quaw reside on the Columbia on each side from the Enterance of River Labiech to the neighbourhood of the Great rapids of that river	24	800
19 SHA-HA-LA [2] Nation reside at the Grand Rapids of the Columbia and extend down in different Villages as low as the Multnomah river consisting of the following tribes, viz : *y-e-huh* above the rapids, Clah-clel-lah below the rapid, the Wah-clel-lah below all the rapids and the *Ne-er-cho-ki-oo* 1 House 100 sole on the S. side a fiew miles above the Multnomah R.	62	2,800
20 NE-CHA-CO-KEE Tribe reside on the S. side of the Columbia a fiew miles below quick Sand river & opposit the dimond Island — (remains) —	1	100
SHOTO Tribe resides on the N. side of the Columbia back of a pond ½ mile from the river and nearly opposit the Enterance of the Multnomah river	8	460
MULT-NO-MAH Tribe reside on Wap-pa-tow Island in the Mouth of the Multnomah, the remains of a large nation	6	800
CLAN-NAH-QUEH'S Tribe of Moltnomah's on Wap-pato Island below the Multnomars	4	130
NE-MAL-QUIN-NER'S a Tribe of Multnom's reside on the N. E. side of the Multnomah River 2 m^s above its mouth	4	200
CATH-LAH-COM-MAH-TUP'S a Tribe of Multnom's South Side of the Wappato Island on a slew of the Miltn^t	3	170
CATH-LAH-NAH-QUI-AH'S Tribe of Multnomes reside on the SW. side of Wappato Island	6	400
CLACK-STAR-N. resides on a small river which discharges itself on the S. W. Side of Wappato Island	28	1,200
CLAN-IN-NA-TA'S resides on the S. W. Side of Wap-pa-to Island	5	200
CATH-LAH-CUM-UPS on the main Shore South West of Wappato Island	6	450
CLAN-NAR-MIN-NA-MUN'S on the S.W. side of the Wappato Island	12	280
		42,150

Wap-pa-to Indians [3] (bracketed label at left of rows 20 through end)

[1] In the original draft "1000." — ED.

[2] Of the different branches of the Shahala nation, only the Neerchokioo is mentioned in the original draft, and the numbers are given as "1340." — ED.

[3] All these tribes of Wappato Indians are given in the first draft substantially as here, save that the numbers are here considerably enlarged. — ED.

Names of Indian Nations and their places of General Residence		No of Houses or Lodges	Probable No of Souls
			42,150
Wap-pa-to Indians continued	QUATH-LAH-POH-TLE'S. N. reside on the N.W. of the Columbia above the Enterance of *Cah-wah-na-hi-ooks* river opposit the Low p. of Wappato Is.	14	900
	CAL-LA-MAKS reside on a creek which falls into the Columbia on the N. side at the lower part of the Columbian Vally N. Side	10	200
21	SKIL-LUTE Nation resides on the Columbia on each sides in different Villages from the lower part of the Columbian Vally as low as the Sturgeon Island and on either Side of the *Cow-e-lis-kee* River *Hull-loo-el-lell* on the Cow-e-lis-kee [1]	50	2,500
22	WACK-KI-A-CUMS reside on the N. Side of the Columbia opposit the Marshey Islands	11	200
23	CATH-LÂH-MÂHS reside on the S. side of the Columbia opposit to the Seal Islands	9	300 [2]
24	CHIN-NOOK'S reside on the N. side of the Columbia to its enterance & on Chinnook river	28	400
25	CLÂT.SOP'S N. reside on the S. Side of the Columbia and a fiew miles along the S.E. coast on both Sides of point Adams	14	200
26	KIL-LA-MUCKS N. from the Clâtsops of the coast along the S.E. coast for many Ms.	50	1,000
Indian information reside to Indian information, those nations speak the Killamox the South of the Killamox & speak Diff. Languages 27 [3]	LUCK-TONS reside on the sea coast to the S SE of the Kil-la-mucks.	houses	200
	KA-HUN-KLE'S d⁰ d⁰ d⁰ S.SE of the Luck-tons	"	400
	LICK-A-WIS d⁰ d⁰ d⁰ to the S.SE. large town	"	800
	YORICK-CONE'S d⁰ d⁰ d⁰ d⁰ d⁰ houses	"	700
	NECK-Ê-TO'S d⁰ d⁰ d⁰ d⁰ large town	"	700
	UL-SE-ÂH'S d⁰ d⁰ d⁰ d⁰ small town	"	150
	YOU-ITTS d⁰ d⁰ d⁰ d⁰ d⁰	"	150
	SHE-A-STUCK-KLE'S d⁰ d⁰ d⁰ d⁰ large town	"	900
	KIL-LA-WATS d⁰ d⁰ d⁰ d⁰ d⁰	"	500
28	COOK-KOO-OOSE Nation reside on the Sea coast to the South of the Kil-la-wats [4]	hous	1,500
	SHAL-LA-LAH Nation on the Same course to the South	"	1,200
	LUCK-KAR-SO Nation on the Same course to the South &c	"	1,200
	HAN-NA-KAL-LAL Nation on the Same course to the South &c	"	600
			56,850

[1] This tribe appears to have been entered as an after-thought, is not in original draft, and is here unnumbered and unestimated.

[2] The numbers for the three preceding tribes have been much enlarged ; the Skillutes increased from 1500 to 2500, the Wackkiacums from 100 to 200, the Cathlâhmâhs from 200 to 400. — ED.

[3] The list of Indians southeast of the Killamucks is also to be found in the Clark-Voorhis note-book No. 4. — ED.

[4] Clark adds following note in the original draft, also in the Clark-Voorhis note-book No. 4: ''I saw Several prisoners from this nation with the Clatsops and Kila-mox, they are much fairer than the common Indians of this quarter, and do not flatten their heads.'' — ED.

	Names of Indian Nations and their places of General Residence	No of Houses or Lodges	Probable No of Souls
			56,850
29 (Information of different Indians on the N.W. Coast)	Kil-laxt-ho-kle's T. on the Sea coast from the Chinnooks to the N. N. W.	8	100
	Chiltz N. from the Killaxthokles along the N. N. W coast	38	700
	Cla-moc-to-mick's from the chiltz along the N. N. W. coast	12	260
	Potoash's reside on the Same Coast N. westwarly of the Clamochokle [1]	10	200
	Pailsh T. reside from the potash on the N. W. coast &c	10	200
	Qui-ni-ilt's from the pailsh along the N. W. coast &c	60	1,000
	Qui-eet-so's from the Quiniilts along the N W. coast &c	18	250
	Chil-lâte's from the quieettso along the N. W. coast &c	8	150
	Ca-lâst-ho-cle from the Chillâte N. W. allong the same coast	10	200
	Quin-ne-chart N. reside on the sea coast & Creeks N. & N W. of the calâsthocles [2]		2,000
30	Clark-a-mus Nation reside on a large river of the Same name which heads in Mt. Jefferson and discharges itself into the Multnonah 40 M. up that river on its N. E. Side. this N. has several villages on either side	Houses	1,800 [3]
31	Cush-hooks N. reside on the N.E. bank of the Multnomah imediately below the fall of that river about 60 M. above its enterance into the Col.m	d°	650 [4]
32	Char-cow-ah N. reside on the S.W. bank of the Multnomah imediately above the falls and take the salmon in that river	d°	200
33	Cal-lah-po-e-wah Nation inhabit the country on both sides of the Multnomah above the Charcowahs for great extent	"	2,000
34	Sho-Sho-ne (or Snake indians) residing in Winter and fall on the Multnomah river. Southerly of the S. W. Mountains, and in Spring and summer on the heads of the *To-war-ne-hi-ooks*, *La Page*, *You-ma-tol-am*, and *Wal-lar-wal-lar* rivers, and more abundantly at the falls of the Towarnehiooks, for the purpose of fishing	"	3,000
			69,560

[1] The original draft has here "Clamoctomich." — Ed.

[2] The Clark-Voorhis note-book No. 4 adds at this point, "and on the Slashes & Creeks off the coast."

[3] In the original draft "800." — Ed.

[4] In the original draft "250." — Ed.

MS. page, Whitehouse's Journal
for January 1, 2, 1805.

Names of Indian Nations and their places of General Residence	No of Houses or Lodges	Probable No of Souls
35 SHO-SHO-NE's on the Multnomah and its waters, the residence of them is not well known to us. or Inds.-of-the Columbia say ab.ᵗ	"	69,560 6,000
36 SHO-BAR-BOO-BE-ER Band of Shoshones reside on the S. W. side of the Multnomah river, high up the Said river	"	1,600 [1]
37 SHO-SHO-NE's. resideing on the S. fork of Lewis's river and on the Nemo, Walshlemo, Shallett, Shushpellanimmo, Shecomskink, Timmooenum-larwas, and the Cop cop pahark rivers branches of the South fork of Lewises river	"	3,000
38 SKÂD.DÂTS N. reside on Cattaract river 25 M. N. of the big narrow live by hunting	"	200
SQUÂN-NAR-OOS. dᵒ dᵒ below the Skaddals	"	120
SHAL-LÂT-TOS. dᵒ dᵒ above dᵒ	"	100
SHAN-WAP-POM's reside on the heads of Catter-act river & Tapteel river	"	400
39 CUTS-SÂH-NIM Nation reside on both Sides of the Columbia Above the Sokulks & on the Northerly branches of the Tapteel river and also on the *Wah-na-a-chee* river	60	1,200
LA-HÂN-NA Nation reside on both Sides of the Columbia above the enterance of Clarks river [2]	120	2,000
COOS-PEL-LAR's Nation reside on a river which falls into the Columbia to the N. of Clarks river [3]	30	1,600
WHE-EL-PO Nation reside on both Sides of Clarks river from the enterance of the *Lastaw* to the Great falls of Clarks R	130	2,500
HI-HIGH-E-NIM-MO Nation from the enterance of the Lastaw into Clarks river on both Sides of the Les-taw as high as the forks	45	1,300 [4]
LAR-TI-E-TO's Nation at the Falls of the Lastaw river below the great Waytom Lake, on both Sides of the river	30	600
SKEET-SO-MISH Nation resides on a Small river of the Same name which discharges itself into the Lastaw below the falls around the Waytom Lake, and on two islands within the said Lake	120	2,000
MICK-SUCK-SEAL-TOM Tribe of the *Tushshepah* reside on Clark river above the great falls of that river, in the rocky Mounᵗˢ	25	300 92,480

We Saw parts of those Tribes at the long narrows (marginal note, beside items 38–39)

[1] In the original draft " 1000." — ED.

[2] The original draft adds here: " and as fur up the Columbia as is known by the Chopunnish & other nations which we have Seen on the Columbian Waters." — ED.

[3] In the original draft: " reside on a large fork of the Columbia which discharges itself into that river on it's East Side above the enterance of Clarks river, and heads with the waters of Hudsons bay." — ED.

[4] In the original draft " 800." — ED.

Names of Indian Nations and their places of General Residence	No of Houses or Lodges	Probable No of Souls
Ho-hil-pos. a tribe of dº on Clarks river above the *Micksuck-seal-toms* in the Rocky Mountains	25	92,480 300
Tush-she-pah's Nation reside on a N. fork of Clarks river and rove on Clarks river in Spring and Summer and the fall and winter on the Missouri.[1] The Oat-lash-shute is a band of this nation	35	430 80,000
West of the Rocky Mountains is		[93,210] 80,000 Sol

[1] The original draft adds: "Sometimes pass over to the Missouri to kill Buffalow." — Ed.

III.   ZOÖLOGY[1]

NOTES BY CLARK, in Codex N, pp. 154, 155. Italicized words and figures enclosed in parentheses were interpolated in red ink, apparently by Biddle. — ED.]

The Prarie Fowl common to the Illinois are found as high up as the River Jacque above which the Sharpe tailed Grows [grouse] commence (*950 M.*)

---

[1] At the time of Lewis and Clark's expedition, practically nothing was known of the zoölogy of the United States west of the Mississippi river, consequently the opportunities for valuable discoveries in this field by members of the party were exceptional. Unfortunately there seems to have been no systematic zoölogist among those who made up the expedition, and consequently no new species of animals were named in the report.

The authors did, however, include in their narrative good descriptions of such of the mammals and birds as especially attracted their attention, and subsequent naturalists have established proper technical names upon these descriptions. The eccentric Rafinesque evidently had their description in mind when he named the mule deer (*Odocoileus hemionus*, Raf.); and George Ord, in his zoölogical appendix to Guthrie's *Geography*, named the whistling swan (*Olor columbianus*, Ord) entirely from the description of the bird given by Lewis and Clark.

Of more interest than their descriptions, however, are the actual specimens brought back by the explorers. These were by no means numerous, and were all deposited in the then famous repository for natural history curiosities, Peale's Museum, in Philadelphia. They were mounted by Peale, and submitted to the famous ornithologist, Alexander Wilson — who was then publishing his great work on North American birds — in order that plates and descriptions of the novelties might appear therein. Wilson found that three species (possibly all that they secured) were new to science, and named them "Louisiana tanager," "Clark's crow" [i. e., nutcracker], and "Lewis's woodpecker" — or, as they stand today in our technical lists, *Piranga ludoviciana* (Wilson); *Nucifraga columbiana* (Wilson), and *Melanerpes torquatus* (Wilson). The three will be found together on plate 20, vol. iii, of the *American Ornithology*. With the decline and disintegration of Peale's Museum, the ornithological specimens were scattered; but recently some of them appeared in Boston, and found their way into the possession of Charles J. Maynard. Among them, Mr. Maynard informs me, is a specimen of Lewis's woodpecker, without much doubt the original specimen, and probably the only one of this historic collection that is still extant. — WITMER STONE, conservator of the Ornithological Section of the Academy of Natural Sciences of Philadelphia.

Racoons is found from the Calumet Bluffs (*650*) downwards & on the Pacific Coast also the *honey locus* and *coffee nut*

Indian Hen & Small Species of kildee which frequent drift is found as high up as the Enterance of the Little Sieoux river (*733 M:*)

The large *Black* and *Brindle Wolf* is found as high up as the Mahars Village (*836 M⁵·*)

The Small burrowing wolf of the prarie is found as low as the Mahars & some fiew near the Miss[iss]ippi

The Black Bear is found in abundance as high as the little Sieoux river, (*733 M⁵*) and the[y] are found much higher but scerce. The *Ass smart* is also found in the Same neighborhood.

Parotqueet is seen as high as the Mahar Village (*836 M:·*)[1]

Opossum is found as high as the River platt. (*600 M:*)

Grey Squrels are found as high up as little Sieoux R (*733*)

Turkeys first appear at the enterance of Tylors River above the big bend 1200 (*1206*) miles up this river (*Missouri*)

The pointed tail Prarie fowl are found above the Big bend (*1200 M⁵ up*) upwards. box elder as high as the Mandans (*1600*)

The party coloured Corvus or *Magpy* commence at or about Corvus Creek and from thence upwards. (*1130*)

The *Fox Squirel* first appear a fiew miles above the Dome where we first met with the *burrowing* or *Barking Squirels*. (*1030 Mils. up the*) Missouri whipperwill is the common attendant of those squirels.

The Big horn animal is found as low as the Beaver bends (*1800 M ᵘᵖ*) a fiew miles below the enterance of the rochejhone.

The Antilope or Cabra are found in great abundance as low as the Chyenne River, and are seen scattering as low down as the neighbourhood of the Mahar village. (*or 800 Ms. ᵘᵖ*)

Mule or Black tail Deer is met with (*on the Snowey Mt⁵*) and are found as low (*down the Missouri*) as the antient fortification & on Boon homm Island or good mans Island 1000 m.

Brarow are found as low as Council Bluffs (*650 M⁵ up*)

[Rough notes by Lewis, apparently intended to be later entered in his diary; found in Codex Q, pp. 4–56. — Ed.]

[1] The parroquet has now practically been exterminated throughout the West; but it was found in abundance in the region of Jefferson City, Missouri (and probably even farther down the river), up to the middle of the nineteenth century. — J. N. BASKETT.

A Journal Commenced at River Dubois — monday 14th 1804

may 14th 1804 Showorey day Capt Clark Set out at
3 oclock P m for the western expidition the party
Consisted of 3 Sergeantes and 38 woking hands which maned
the Battow and two Progues we Sailed up the missouria
6 miles and encamped on the N side of the River

Tuesday may 15th 1804 Rainey morning fair wind the
later part of the day Sailed 5 om and encamped on
the N side some Sand Cleared the Soil verry rich —

Wensday may 16th 1804 Set out Criley this morning plesent
arrived at St Charles at 12 oclock P m one hurry third
a great number of French people Came to See the Boat
&c this place was an old French village y Rouen

First Page of Floyd's Journal.

ZOÖLOGY

August 2^{cd} 1804.

This day one of our Hunters brought me a *white Heron*. [*Herodias egretta* — Coues] this bird as [is] an inhabitant of ponds and Marasses, and feeds upon tadpoles, frogs, small fish &c. they are common to the Mississipi and the lower part of the *ohio*. River, (ie) as high as the falls of that river.

this bird weighed two lb? it's plumage is perfectly white and very thin from extremity of beak to the extremity of toe [it measured] 4. F 7.$\frac{1}{4}$ I from tipp to tip of wing on the back 4 F. 11. I.

it's beak is yellow, pointed, flated crosswise and 5. Inches in length. from the upper region of the bill to the eye is one inch in length, covered with a smoth yellow skin the plumage of the head projecting towards the upper bill and coming to a point a[t] an Inch beyond the eyes on the center of the upper bill. The mouth opens to distance of the eyes. The eye is full and projecting reather, it is 7/10 of half an inch. four joints in the wing

1st	joint from body in length	6. Inches	
2nd,		$8\frac{1}{4}$;	
3rd,		$3\frac{1}{2}$;	
4th		1.	
1st	Joint Number of feathers	7	Length of 3
2nd	. . . .	.18	
3rd	. . . .	6.	from 10 to 12
4th	. . . .	5.	12

it's legs are black, the neck and beak occupy $\frac{1}{2}$ it's length. it has four toes on a foot, the outer toe on the right foot is from the joining of the leg to extremity of toe nails 4 Inch. & $\frac{1}{4}$ has four joints exclusive of the nail joint, the next is $4\frac{3}{4}$ inches has three joints exclusive of the nale joints. the next is $3\frac{3}{4}$ and has two joints, the heel toe has one joint only and is 3 Inches in length. the nails are long sharp and black. the eye is of a deep seagreen colour, with a circle of pole yellow around the sight forming a border to the outer part of the eye of about half the width of the whole eye. the tale has 12 feathers of six inches in length. the wings when *foalded are the same* length with the tale.

has 2 remarkable tufts of long feathers on each side joining the body at the upper joint of the wing. these cover the feathers of the 1st joint of the wings when they are even extended

[123]

Killed a serpent [*Pityophis melanolenca* — COUES] on the bank of the river adjoining a large prarie.

Length from nose to tail	5 F	2. Inch
Circumpherence in largest part		4½
Number of scuta on belly		221.
Dº on Tale		53

No pison teeth therefore think him perfectly inocent, eyes, center black with a border of pale brown yellow   Colour of skin on head yellowish green with black specks on the extremity of the scuta which are pointed or triangular   colour of back, transverse stripes of black and dark brown of an inch in width, succeeded by a yellowish brown of half that width the end of the tale hard and pointed like a cock's spur the sides are speckled with yellowish brown and black.   two roes of black spots on a lite yellow ground pass throughout his whole length on the upper points of the scuta of the belly and tale ½ Inch apart this snake is vulgarly called the cow or bull snake from a bellowing nois which it is said sometimes to make resembling that anamal, tho' as to this fact I am unable to attest it never having heard them make that or any other nois myself.

I have frequently observed an aquatic bird [*Sterna antillarum* — COUES] in the cours of asscending this river but have never been able to procure one before today, this day I was so fortunate as to kill two of them, they are here more plenty than on the river below.   they lay their eggs on the sand bars without shelter or nest, and produce their young from the 15ᵗʰ to the last of June, the young ones of which we caught several are covered with down of a yellowish white colour and on the back some small specks of a dark brown.   they bear a great resemblance to the young quale of ten days oald, and apear like them to be able to runabout and peck their food as soon as they are hatched.   this bird, lives on small fish, worms and bugs which it takes on the virge of the water it is seldom seen to light on trees an qu[i]te as seldom do they lite in the water and swim tho' the foot would indicate that they did it's being webbed   I believe them to be a native of this country and pr[ob]ably a constant resident.   the weight of the male bird is one ounce and a half, it[s] [l]ength from b[e]ak to toe 7½ inches. from tip to tip of wing across the back one foot seven inches and a half [the beak] is one ⅛ inch long, large where it joins the head flated on the sides and tapering to a sharp point, a little declining and curvated, a fine yellow, with a shade of black on the extremity of upper beak; the eye is prominent, black and on a angular scale of ½ Inc; occupyse

3. 3. in width. the upper part of the head is black from the beak as low as the middle of the eye and a little below the joining of the neck except however some white which joins the upper part of the beak which forks and passing over the sides of the forehead terminate above each eye. the under part of the bird, that is the thr[o]at and cheeks as high as the eye, the neck brest belly and under part of the wings and tail are of a fine white, the upper part of the neck, back, and wings are of a fine, quaker coulour, or bright dove colour with reather more of a bluish tint — except however the three first or larger feathers in the wing which on upper side are of a deep black. the wing has four joints

No. Joint	Length of joint	No. of feathers.	Length of do.
1.	1 ½	a Clump of feathers not strong but loosly connected with the flesh of the wing	1 ¼
2. . . .	2	16	2
3. . . .	1 ½	7	from 2 ½ to 4 ½
4 . . .	¾	3	5 ½

the tail has eleven feathers the outer of which are an inch longer than those in the center gradually tapering inwards which gives the tale a forked appearance like that of the swally the largest or outer feathe[r] is 2 ¾ that of the shortest 1 ¾. the leg and thye are three inches long the leg occupying one half this length the thye is covered with feathers except about ¼ of an inch above the knee the leg is of a bright yellow and nails, long sharp and black the foot is webbed and has three toes forward; the heel or back toe is fixed to the leg above the palm of the foot, and is unconnected by a web to the other toes, it has no nail. the wings when foalded lap like that of the swallow and extend at least an inch and a half beyond the tale. this bird is very noysey when flying which it dose extreemly swift the motion of the wing is much like that of *Kildee* it has two notes one like the squaking of a small pig only on reather a higher kee, and the other kit'-tee'-kit'-tee'- as near as letters can express the sound. the beak of the female is black and the black and quaker colour of the male in her is yellow[i]s[h] brown mixed with dove colour

August 8th 1804.

we had seen but a few aquatic fouls of any kind on the river since we commenced our journey up the Missouri, a few geese accompanied by their young, the wood duck which is common to every part of this country & crains of several kinds which will be discribed in their respective places this day after we had passed the *river* Souix as called by Mr Mackay (or as is more properly called the stone river, I saw a great number of feathers floating down the river   those feathers had a very extraordinary appearance as they appeared in such quantities as to cover prettey generally sixty or seventy yards of the breadth of the river. for three miles after I saw those feathers continu[e] to run in that manner, we did not percieve from whence they came, at length we were surprised by the appearance of a flock of Pillican [*Pelecanus erythrorhynchus*] at rest on a large sand bar attatched to a small Island the number of which would if estimated appear almost in credible; they apeared to cover several acres of ground, and were no doubt engaged in procuring their ordinary food; *which is fish*; on our approach they flew and left behind them several small fish of about eight inches in length, none of which I had seen before.   the Pellican rested again on a sand bar above the Island which we called after them from the number we saw on it. we now approached them within about three hundred yards before they flew; I then fired at random among the flock with my rifle and brought one down; the discription of this bird is as follows.

HABITS.

They are a *bird* of *clime*   remain on the coast of Floriday and the borders of the Gulph of mexico & even the lower portion of the Mississippi during the *winter* and in the Spring (see for date my *thermometrical observations at the river Dubois*), visit this country and that fa[r]ther north for the purpose of raising their young.   this duty seems now to have been accomplished from the appearance of a young Pilacon which was killed by one of our men this morning, and they are now in large flocks on their return to their winter quarters.   they lay usually two eggs only and chuise for a nest a couple of logs of drift wood near the water's edge and with out any other preperation but the thraught formed by the proximity of those two logs which form a trought   they set and hatch their young which after[wards they] nurture with fish their common food

MEASURE.

	F	I
F[r]om beak to toe	5.	8
Tip to tip of wing	9 .	4.
Beak Length	1 .	3.
D? Width from	.	2. to 1 ½
	F	
Neck Length	1 .	11.
1st Joint of wing	1 .	1.
2ed D?	1 .	4.½
3rd D?	— .	7.
4th D?	— .	2 ¾
Length of leg including foot	.	10.
D? of thy	.	11.

Discription of Colour &c. The beak is a whiteish yellow the under part connected to a bladder like pouch, this pouch is connected to both sides of the lower beak and extends down on the under side of the neck and terminates in the stomach this pouch is uncovered with feathers, and is formed [of] two skins the one on the inner and the other on the outer side a small quantity of flesh and strings of which the anamal has at pleasure the power of moving or drawing in such manner as to contract it at pleasure. in the present subject I measured this pouch and found it's contents 5. gallons of water The feet are webbed large and of a yellow colour, it has four toes the hinder toe is longer than in most aquatic fouls, the nails are black, not sharp and ½ an inch in length. The plumage generally is white, the feathers are thin compared with the swan goose or most aquatic fouls and has but little or no down on the body. the upper part of the head is covered with black f[e]athe[r]s short, as far as the back part of the head. the yellow skin unfeathered extends back from the upper beak and opening of the mouth and comes to a point just behind the eye The large f[e]athers of the wings are of a deep black colour the 1st & 2nd joint of [the wings] from the body above the same is covered with a second layer of white feathers which extend quite half the length of those large feathers of the wing the thye is covered with feathers within a quarter of an inch of the knee.

1st Joint of wing has feather[s]		No 21 Length.	9 Inch
2ed	Do	No 17 Length	Black 13 Inch
3rd	Do	No 5 Length . . .	18. Inch
4th	Do	No 3 Lenth . . .	19. Ich

it has a curious frothy subs[t]ance which seems to divide its feathers from the flesh of the body and seems to be composes of Glob[u]les of air and perfectly imbraces the part of the feather which extends through the skin. the wind pipe terminates in the center of the lower part of the upper and unf[e]athered part of the pouch and is secured by an elastic valve commanded at pleasure.

The green insect known in the U'States by the name of the *sawyer* or *chittediddle*, [Katydid — Coues] was first heard to cry on the 27th of July, we were then in latitude 41° some minutes.

The *prarie hen* or *grouse*, was seen in the praries between the Missouri and the river *platte*

July the 30ᵗʰ

this day Joseph Fields killed a *Braro* [badger] as it is called by the French *engages*. this is a singular anamal not common to any part of the United States. it's weight is sixteen pounds. it is a carniverous anamal. on both sides of the uper jaw is fexed one long and sharp canine tooth. it's eye is small black and piercing. [See description in full, under date of Feb. 25, 1806.]

August the 25ᵗʰ

on our return from the mound of sperits saw the first *bats* that we had observed since we began to assend the Missouri.

also saw on our return on the Creek that passes this mound about 2 M. distant S. a bird of heron kind as large as the Cormorant short tale long leggs of a colour on the back and wings deep copper brown with a shade of red. we could not kill it therefore I can not discribe it more particularly.

Sept 5ᵗʰ

saw some wild goats or antelopes on the hill above the Glauber Salts Springs   they ran off   we could not discover them sufficiently distinctly to discribe even their colour.   their track is as large as a deer reather broader & more blont at the point.

This day one of our hunters brought us a Serpent beautifully vari-agated with small black spotts of a romboydal form on a light yellow white ground   the black p[r]edominates most on the back the whiteis[h] yellow on the sides, and it is nearly white on the belly with a few party couloured scuta on which the black shews but imperfectly and the col-ouring matter seems to be underneath the Scuta.   it is not poisonous it hisses remarkably loud; it has 221 Scuta on the belly and 51 on the tale, the eyes are of a dark black colour   the tale terminates in a sharp point like the substance of a cock's spur.   Length 4 F. 6. I

Sepᵗ 9ᵗʰ

Capt. Clark found on the Lard shore under a high bluff issuing from a blue earth a bittuminus matter resembling molasses in consistance, colour and taste.

Sepᵗ 10ᵗʰ

On the Lard. side of the river about 2 miles from the river Sergt. Pryor and Drewyer discovered a bold salt spring of strong water.

killed a *bluewinged teal* [*Querquedula discors* — COUES] and a *Porcupine* [*Erethizon dorsatum*]; found it in a Cottonwood tree near the river on the Lar^d Shore. the leaves of the Cottonwood were much distroyed as were those of the Cottonwood trees in it's neighbourhood. I therefore supposed that it fed on the folage of trees at this season, the flesh of this anamal is a pleasant and whoalsome food. the quills had not yet obtained their usual length. it has four long toes, before on each foot, and the same number behind with the addition of one short one on each hind foot on the inner side. the toes of the feet are armed with long black nails particularly the fore feet. they weigh from 15 to 20 lbs they resemble the *slowth* very much in the form of their hands, or fore feet. their teeth and eyes are like the bever

September 14th 1804.

this day Capt. Clark killed a male *wild goat* [antelope] so called it's weight 65 bs.

	F	I
length from point of nose to point of tail	4.	9.
hight to the top of the wethers	3.	
D? behind	3.	
girth of the brest	3.	1.
girth of the neck *close to the* sholders	2.	2.
d? near the head	1.	7

Eye deep see green, large percing and reather prominent, & at or near the root of the horn within one ¼ inches.

Sept. 14th 1804.

Shields killed a *hare of the prarie* weight six pounds and ¼

	F		I.
Length from point of hind to extremity fore feet	2	.	11
hight when standing erect	1	.	1 ¾
length from nose to tale	2	.	1.
girth of body	1	.	2 ¾
length of tale		.	6 ½
length of the year [ear]		.	5 ½
width of d?. d?.		.	3 ⅛
	F	.	I
fiom the extremity of the hip to the toe of the hind foot	1	.	3 ½

---

[1] Part of the following was used by Lewis in describing the animals of the Columbian plains, under date of Feb. 28, 1806; but the measurements differ, and in the journal proper (volume iv, p. 119) he adds other particulars. — ED.

the eye is large and prominent the sight is circular, deep sea green, and occupyes one third of the width of the eye the remaining two thirds is a ring of a bright yellowish silver colour.   the years ar[e] placed at the upper part of the head and very near to each other, the years are very flexable, the anamall moves them with great ease and quickness and can contra[c]t and foald them on his back or delate them at pleasure.   the front outer foald of the year is a redis[h] brown, the inner foalds or those which ly together when the years are thrown back and w[h]ich occupy two thirds of the width of the year is of a clear white colour except one inch at the tip of the year which is black, the hinder foald is of a light grey.   the head back sholders and outer part of the thighs are of a ledcoloured grey the sides as they aproache the belly grow lighter becomeing greadually more white   the belly and brest are white with a shad[e] of lead colour.   the furr is long and fine.   the tale is white round and blount[l]y pointed the furr on it is long and extreemly fine and soft   when it runs it carry's it's tale strait behind in the direction of the body.   the body is much smaller and more length than the rabbit in proportion to it's height.   the teeth are like those of the hair or rabbit as is it's upper lip split.   it's food is grass or herbs.   it resorts the open plains, is extreemly fleet and never burrows or takes shelter in the ground when pursued,   I measured the leaps of one which I surprised in the plains on the 17th Inst and found them 21 feet the ground was a little decending   they apear to run with more ease and to bound with greater agility than any anamall I ever saw.   this anamal is usually single seldom associating in any considerable numbers

Sept 18th

this day saw the first brant on their return from the north.

Sept 17th

one of the hunters killed a bird of the *Corvus genus* and order of the pica [*Pica pica hudsonica* — COUES] & about the size of a jack-daw. with a remarkable long tale.   beautifully variagated.   it[s] note is not disagreeable though loud — it is twait-twait-twait, twait ; twait, twait twait twait.

	F	I
from tip to tip of wing	1	. 10
D? beak to extremity of tale	1	. 8 ½
of which the tale occupys		. 11
from extremity of middle toe to hip	5	. 5 ½

it's head, beak, and neck are large for a bird of it's size; the beak is black and of a convex and cultrated figure, the chops nearly equal, and it's base large and beset with hairs. the eyes are black encircled with a narrow ring of yellowish black it's head, neck, brest & back within one inch of the tale are of a fine glossey black, as are also the short f[e]athers of the under part of the wing, the thies and those about the root of the tale. the belly is of a beatifull white which passes above and arround the but of the wing, where the feathers being long reach to a small white spot on the rump one inch in width. the wings have nineteen feathers, of which the ten first have the longer side of their plumage white in the midd[l]e of the feather and occupying unequal lengths of the same from one to three inches, and forming when the wing is sp[r]ead a kind [of] triangle, the upper and lower part of these party coloured feathers on the under side of the wing being of dark colour but not jut or shining black. the under side of the remaining feathers of the wing are darker. the upper side of the wing, as well as the short side of the plumage of the party-coloured feathers is of a dark blackis[h] or bluish green sonetimes presenting as light orange yellow or bluish tint as it happens to be presented to different exposures of lig[h]t. the plumage of the tale consists of 12 feathers of equal lengths by pair[s], those in the center are the longest, and the others on each side deminishing about an inch each pair. the underside of the feathers is a pale black, the upper side is a dark blueish green and which like the outer part of the wings is changable as it reflects different portions of light. towards the extremity of these feathers they become of an orrange green, then shaded pass to a redish indigo blue, and again at the extremity assume the predominant colour of changable green. the tints of these feathers are very similar and equally beatiful and rich as the tints of blue and green of the peacock. it is a most beatifull bird. the legs and toes are black and imbricated. it has four long toes, three in front and one in rear, each terminated with a black sharp tallon of from $3/8$ths to $1/2$ an inch in length. these birds are seldom found in parties of more than three or four and most usually at this season single as the halks and other birds of prey usually are. it's usual food is flesh. this bird dose not spread it's tail when it flys and the motion of it's wings when flying is much like that of a Jay-bird.

The White turkey of the black hills from information of a french lad who wintered with the Chien Indians About the size of the common wild turkey. the plumage perfectly white this bird is booted as low as the toes

October 16*th*

This day took a small bird alive [*Phalænoptilus nuttalli* — Coues] of the order of the [blank space in MS.] or goat suckers. it appeared to be passing into the dormant state. on the morning of the 18th the murcury was at 30 a. o. the bird could scarcely move. I run my penknife into it's body under the wing and completely distroyed it's lungs and heart yet it lived upwards of two hours this fanominon I could not account for unless it proceeded from the want of circulation. of the blo[o]d the recarees call this bird to'-na it's note is at-tah-to'-na' at-tah'to'-na, to-nah, a nocturnal bird, sings only in the night as dose the whipperwill. it's weight [is] 1 oz 17 Grains Troy

20*th* *October*

Peter Crusat this day shot at a white bear he wounded him, but being alarmed at the formidable appearance of the bear he left his tomahalk and gun ; but shortly after returned and found that the bear had taken the oposite rout. soon after he shot a buffaloe cow broke her thy, the cow pursued him he concealed himself in a small raviene.

May 1*st* 1805.

Shannon killed a bird of the plover kind [avocet, *Recurvirostra americana* — Coues]. the weight one pound. eye black percing and prominent.[1]

MEASURE.

	F		Inches
from the tip of the toe to the extremity of the beak	1	.	10
from tip to tip of wing when extended	2	.	5.
length of beak	—	.	3 ⅝
length of tale	—	.	3 ⅛
length of leg and toe	—	.	10.

the legs are flat, of a pale skye blue colour and but slightly imbricated. the second joint, as low as the mustle extends is covered with feathers which is about half it's length. it has three toes on a foot connected by a web. there is also a small toe on each foot placed about the eighth of an inch up the leg behi[n]d. the nails are black and short and those of the middle toes ar[e] singular — there being two nails on each the

[1] This description of the plover is the first draft of that entered by Lewis in the journal proper (Codex D, pp. 72, 73 ; in our volume i, pp. 357, 358). It is very nearly the same ; but we here give the original draft, to exhibit the method of working up the subject. — ED.

one above the other the upper one the longest and sharpest. the tale contains eleven feathers of the same length of a bluish white colour. the body and under side of the wings except the large feathers of the 1 & 2.ᶜᵈ joints of the wings are white, as are also the feathers of the upper part of the 4ᵗʰ joint of the wing. and some of those of the 3ʳᵈ adjoining. the large feathers of the pinion or first & the second joint are black ; a part of the larger feathers of the third-joint on the upper side and all the smaller feathers which cover the upper part of these joints ar[e] black ; as are also the tuft of long feathers on each side of the body above the joining of the wing, leaving however a stripe of white between them on the back. the head and neck are shaped much like the grey plover, and is a light brick-dust brown. the beak is black and flat, largest where it joins the head and from thence tapering every way gradually to a very sharp point the upper beak being $\frac{1}{8}$ of an inch the longest turning down at the point. the nostrils are parallal with the beak and are long narrow and connected. the beak is curvated and inverted ; the Curvature being upwards in stead of downwards as those of most birds are the substance of the beak is as flexable as whalebone and at a little distance precisely resembles that substance. their note is like that of the common whistling or grey plover tho' reather louder, and more varied, and their habits are the same with that bird so far as I have been enabled to learn, with this difference however that this bird sometimes lights in the water and swims. it generally feads about the shallow bars of the river ; to collect it's food, it immerces it's beak in the water, and th[r]ows it's head and beak from side to side at every step it takes.

May 9ᵗʰ 1805.

I killed four plover this evening of a different kind [*Symphemia semipalmata* — COUES] from any I have yet seen.[1] it resembles the grey or whistling plover more than any other of this family of birds, tho' it is much larger. it is about the size of the yellow leged plover common to the U'States, and called the jack curloo by some. the legs are of a greenish brown ; the toes, three and one high at the heel unconnected with a webb, the breast and belly of a brownish white ; the head neck upper part of the body and coverts of the wings are of a dove coloured brown which when the bird is at rest is the predomanent colour. the tale has 12 feathers of the same length of which the two in the center are black with transverse bars of yellowish bron, the others are a brown-

---

1 This description is extended by Lewis in Codex D, p. 111 (in our volume i, p. 17), with some alterations, and rearrangement. — ED.

ish white. the large feathers of the wings are white tiped with black. the eyes are black with a small ring of dark yellowish brown the beak is black 2½ inches long, cilindrical, streight, and roundly or blountly pointed. the notes of this bird are louder and more various than of any other species which I have seen.

May 26th 1805.

One of the party killed a bighorned [*Ovis montana*], the head and horns of which weighed 27 lbs. a hare was also killed which weighed 8½ lbs. the hare are now of a pale lead brown colour

Discription of the blue Crested corvus bird [*Cyanocitta stelleri* — Coues] common to the woody and western side of the Rockey mountains, and all the woody country from thence to the Pacific Ocean It's beak is black convex, cultrated, wide at its base where it is beset with hairs, and is 1¼ inches from the opening of the chaps to their extremity, and from the joining of the head to the extremity of the upper chap 1⅛ inches, the upper exceeds the under chap a little; the nostrils are small round unconnected and placed near the base of the beak where they lye concealed by the hairs or hairy feathers which cover the base of the upper chap. the eye reather large and full but not prominent and of a deep blueish black, there being no difference in the colour of the puple and the iris. the crest is very full the feathers from 1 to 1½ Inches long and occupye the whole crown of the head. the head neck, the whole of the body including the coverts of the wings, the upper disk of the tail and wings are of a fine g[l]ossey bright indigo blue Colour the under disk of the tail and wings are of a dark brown nearly black. the leg and first joint of the thye are 4¼ In. long, the legs and feet are black and the front covered with 6 scales the hinder part smothe, the toes are also imbrecated, four in number long and armed with long sharp black tallons. the upper disk of the first four or five feathers of the wing next to the boddy, are marked with small transverse stripes of black as are also the upper side of the two center feathers of the tail; the tail is five inches long & is composed of twelve feathers of equal length. the tail 1 & ½ as long as the boddy. the whole length from the point of the beak to extremity of the tail 1 Foot 1 Inch; from the tip of one to the tip of the other wing 1 Foot 5½ Inches. the size & the whole Contour of this bird resembles very much the *blue jay* or *jay-bird* as they are called in the U'States. like them also they seldom rest in one place long but are in constant motion hoping from spra to spray. what has been said is more immediately applicable to the male, the colours of the female are somewhat different in her the head crest neck half the back downwards and the coverts of the wings are of a dark brown, but sometimes there is a little touch of the Indigo on the short feathers on the head at the base of the upper chap. this bird feeds on flesh when they can procure it, also on bugs flies and buries. I do not know whether they distroy little birds but their tallons indicate their capacity to do so if nature, has directed it. their note is loud and frequently repeated châ'-â' châ'-â'. &c. also twat twat twat, very quick.

[The rest of Codex Q consists of Clark's copies of Lewis's notes. — Ed.]

[Note by Clark, in Codex R. — Ed.]

Fort Clatsop. December 18*th* 1805.

This day one of the men shot a bird of the Corvus genus, which was feeding on some fragments of meat near the camp. this bird is about the size of the king bird or *bee martin*, and not unlike that bird in form. the beak is ¾ of an inch long, wide at the base, of a convex, and cultrated figure. beset with some small black hairs near it's base. the chaps are of nearly equal lengths tho' the upper exceeds the under one a little, and has a small nich in the upper chap near the extremity perceptable only by close examineation. the colour of the beak is black. the eye is large and prominent, the puple black, and iris of a dark yellowish brown. the legs and feet are black and imbricated. has four toes on each foot armed with long sharp tallons, the hinder toe is nearly as long as the middle toe in front, and longer than the two remaining toes. the tale is composed of twelve feathers the longest of which are five inches, being six in number placed in the center. the remaining six are placed 3 on either side and graduly deminish to four inches which is the shortest and outer feathers. the tail is half the length of the bird, the wh[ol]e length from the extremity of the beak to the extremity of the tale being 10 Inches. the head from it's joining the neck forward as far as the eyes nearly to the base of the beak and on each side as low as the center of the eye is black. arround the base of the beak the throat jaws, neck, brest and belley are of a pale bluish white. the wings back and tale are of a bluish black with a small shade of brown. this bird is common to this piny country are also found in the rockey mountains on the waters of the columbia river or woody side of those mountains, appear to frequent the highest summits of those mountains as far as they are covered with timber. their note is *que*, quit-it, quit-it, que-hoo; and tâh, tâh, &[c]. there is another bird of reather larger size which I saw on the woddy parts of the rockey mountains on the waters of the Missouri, this bird I could never kill tho' I made several attempts, the predominate colour is a dark blue the tale is long and they are not crested, I believe them to be of the corvus genus also. their note is *châr, châr*, char-ar, char; the large blue crested corvus bird of the Columbia river is also   [See description by Lewis, pp. 134, 135, above. — ED.]

[Note by Lewis, on fly-leaf of Codex R. — ED.]

note of the corvus bird killed at Fort Clatsop. que-quit. it; que hos. repeated, & chat, chat, chat

[Note by Clark, on fly-leaf of Codex B. — ED.]

Oake cha ke har the Corvuss bird.

[Codex P — marked on the outer cover, " W. Clark's Natural History Notes, &c, Apr. 9, 1805–Feb. 17, 1806 " — was apparently written up by Clark at a much later period (the handwriting corresponds to his later habit); it consists almost entirely of extracts copied from the text of the journals — those portions in the latter, relating to natural history and crossed out with red lines.   The only additional items are the following:
April 13th, 1805, in describing the magpie's nest, Clark adds in parentheses these words: " (and frequently found Near and sometimes immediately under the nest of the bald eagle)."
Jan. 10th, 1806, after completing the description of beaver bait, he adds: " The bate is put on the point of a stick and stuck in the ground so as the bait will be over the trap which is under the water Set for the beaver." — ED.]

ORIGINAL JOURNALS

OF THE

LEWIS AND CLARK EXPEDITION

1804–1806

WITH FACSIMILES, MAPS, PLANS, VIEWS, PORTRAITS, AND A BIBLIOGRAPHY

VOLUME SIX

PART II

Botany, Mineralogy, Meteorology, Astronomy, and Miscellaneous Memoranda

*Of this Edition on Van Gelder Hand-made Paper
two hundred copies only have been printed
of which this is*

No.

PSIHDJÄ-SÁHPA. A Yanktonan Indian

ORIGINAL JOURNALS

OF THE

LEWIS AND CLARK EXPEDITION

1804-1806

PRINTED FROM THE ORIGINAL MANUSCRIPTS
in the Library of the American Philosophical Society and
by direction of its Committee on Historical Documents

TOGETHER WITH

MANUSCRIPT MATERIAL OF LEWIS AND CLARK
from other sources, including Note-Books, Letters, Maps, etc.,
and the Journals of Charles Floyd and Joseph Whitehouse

NOW FOR THE FIRST TIME PUBLISHED IN FULL
AND EXACTLY AS WRITTEN

Edited, with Introduction, Notes, and Index, by

REUBEN GOLD THWAITES, LL.D.

Editor of " The Jesuit Relations and Allied Documents," etc.

VOLUME SIX

PART II

NEW YORK

DODD, MEAD & COMPANY

1905

Copyright, 1905
By The State Historical Society of Wisconsin

Copyright, 1905
By Julia Clark Voorhis
Eleanor Glasgow Voorhis

Copyright, 1905
By The American Philosophical Society

Copyright, 1905
By Dodd, Mead & Company

Published July, 1905

THE UNIVERSITY PRESS
CAMBRIDGE, U.S.A.

CONTENTS TO VOL. VI

PART II

LIST OF ILLUSTRATIONS

VOL. VI — PART II

IV. BOTANY

FROM a small blank-book of Lewis's,[1] which he had also used when an army paymaster in 1800. These notes were apparently written during the winter of 1803–04, at River Dubois. The book also contains meteorological data, which will be given *post.* — ED.]

The Kickapoo calls a certain water plant with a large Circular floating leaf found in the ponds and marshes in the neighbourhood of Kaskaskias and Cahokia, *Po-kish'-a-co-mah'*, of the root of this plant the Indians prepare an agreeable dish, the root when taken in it's green state is from 8 to 14 inches in circumpherence is dryed by being exposed to the sun and air or at other times with a slow fire or smoke of the chimnies, it shrinks much in drying. The root of this plant grows in a horrizontal direction near the surface of the rich loam or mud which forms the bottoms of their ponds or morasses, generall[y] three, sometimes four or more of these roots are attatced together by a small root or string of a hearder substance of a foot or six inches in length, the root of the plant thus annually progresses shooting out a root from a bud at the extremity of the root of the presceeding years groath, this in the course of the summer p[r]oduces a new root prepared with a bud for the progression of the next season, also one leaf and one seed stalk the stem of the former supporting or reather attatched to a large green circular leaf 18 inches to two feet in diameter which fl[o]ats while green usually on the serface of the water, the sta[l]k is propotioned to the debth of the water, and of a celindrical form, is an inch and a half in circumpherence at or near it's junction of the root thence regularly tapering to the leaf where it is perhaps not more than an inch, the large fibers of the leaf project from the extremity of the stalk in every direction at right angles from it to the circumpherence of the leaf like rays from the center, there are from twelve to eighteen of those fibers. the leaf is nearly a circle smoth on both sides and even and regular on it's edges near the same part of the root from which the leaf stalk project the seed stalk dose also it is about the same size and form of it but usually a foot longer standing erect and bearing it[s]

---

[1] In possession of American Philosophical Society. — ED.

blossum above the surface of the water which I am informed is of a white colour.

The seed vessel or matrix is the form of a depressed cone the small extremity of which is attatc [h] ed to the uper end of the stalk; before it has attained it's groath it resembles an inverted cone but when grown the base obtains a preponderancy and inclining downwards rests it's edge against the stalk   the base is a perfect circular plain from eighteen to twenty inches in circumpherence in it's succulent state, and from two to three inches in hight.   the surface of the cone when dryed by the sun and air after being exposed to the frost is purforated with two circular ranges of globular holes from twenty to 30 in number arond one which forms the center placed at the distance of from an eighth to ¼ of an inch assunder, each of those cells contains an oval nut of a light brown colour much resembling a small white oak acorn smothe extreemly heard, and containing a white cernal of an agreeable flavor; these the native [s] frequently eat either in this state or roasted; they frequently eat them also in their succulent state   the bear feed on the leaves of this plant in the spring and summer   in the autumn and winter the Swan, geese, brant, ducks and other acquatic fowls feed on the root. the cone is brown, pithy and extreemly light, and when seperated from the stalk flots on the suface of the water with its base down.   the Indians procure it and prepare it for food in the following manner — they enter the ponds where it grows, barefooted in autumn, and feel for it among the mud which being soft and the root large and near the surface they readily find it   they easily draw it up it having no fiborus or colateral roots to attatch it firmly to the mud   they wash and scrape a thin bleack rind off it and cut it croswise into pieces of an inch in length   when it is prepared for the pot it is of a fine white colour boils to a pulp and makes an agreeable soupe in which way it is usually dressed by the natives   when they wish to preserve it for any length of time they cut it in pieces in the manner before discribed string it on bark or leather throngs of a convenient length and hang it to dry in the sun, or expose it to the smoke of their chimnies,   when thus dryed it will keep for several years, it is esteemed as nutricius as the pumpkin or squash and is not very dissimilar in taste   The Chipiways or sateaus call this plant *Wab-bis-sa-pin* or Swan-root   The ferench or Canadians know it by two names the Pois de Shicoriat or Graine de Volais.   the roots of this plant are from one foot to eighteen inches in length.

The common wild pittatoe also form another article of food in savage life   this they boil untill the skin leaves the pulp easily which it will do in the course of a few minutes   the outer rind which is of a dark brown coulour is then sc[r]aped off the pulp is of a white coulour, the pettatoe thus prepared is exposed on a scaffold to the sun or a slow fire untill it is thoroughly dryed, or at other times strung upon throngs of leather or bark and hung in the roofs of their lodges where by the influence of the fire and smoke it becomes th[o]roughly dryed, they are then prepared for use, and will keep perfectly sound many years, these they boil with meat or pound and make an agreeable bread of this pittaitoee may be used in it's green or undryed state without danger provided it be well roasted or boiled it produces a vine which runs to a considerable length usually intwining itself about the neighbouring bushes and weeds, the vine is somewhat branched, and in it[s] progress at the distance of 2½ inches it puts forth one leaf stem at right angles with the vine, which is furnished with two par of ovate leaves and turminated by one of a similar shape, these are of a pale green colour not indented on their edges, reather a rough appearance, the vine is small and green except near the ground where it sometime[s] assumes a redish hue. the fruit is connected by a small liggament at both ends extending for many yards in length and attatching together in some instances six eight or more of these pittaitoes it's root is pereniel the vine annual.

There is also another root found in ma[r]shey land or ponds which is much used by the Kickapoos Chipaways and many other nations as an article of food it is called by the Chipeways *Moc-cup-pin* this in it's unprepared state is not only disagreeable to the taste but even dangerous to be taken even in a small quantity; in this state it acts as a powerfull aemetic. a small quantity will kill a hog yet prepared by the Indians it makes not only an agreeable but a nutricious food. I have not seen the plant and can therefore only discribe it from information the leaf is said to be broad and to float on the water the root is from 10 to 12 inches in length and about ⅔.^{ds} as much in thickness it has a rough black skin, the pulp is white and of a mealy substance when properly prepared the preparation is this — having collected a parsel of these roots you cut and split a sufficient parsel of wood which is set on end as the coliers commence the base of their coal pitts, the [l]engths of these sticks of wood being as nearly the same as you can conveniently cut them and about 4 feet in length thus forming when put together an even surface at top on this is thrown soft earth of from two to 3 Inches in debth the roots are laid on this and earth thrown over the whole forming the Colliers kiln complete fire is then communicated to the wood beneath and it is suffered to burn slowly for several days untill the wood is exausted or they concieve their roots are sufficiently cooked they then take them out scrape them & cut them into slices crosswise of half an inch thick and laying them on a scaffold of small sticks build small fires under them and dry them untill they become perfectly firm thus prepared they are fit for uce and will keep for years if not exposed to wet. they are either boiled to a pulp in their soupe or less boiled eat them with bears oil or venison and bears flesh they sometimes pound it and make a bread of it.[1]

[Data by Clark, found in Codex N, pp. 154, 155. The italicized words and figures in parentheses are interlineations, also by Clark, in red ink. — ED.][2]

NOTE. The *Lynn* commence about the Calumet Bluffs and downwards. (*950 M⁺ up the Missouri*)

The Black Walnut is found as high up as White Stone river and from thence down on the high rich lands. (*900 M⁺*)

Mulberry is found as high up as Grand River de Sieoux. (*858.*)

Prickly pear is not Common below the Queequerre (*1000 M⁵*)

Hickory is to be found below the Mahars and black birch in the Same country, also the *horn beem* (*830 M⁺*)

Hack berry and *Hasel bushes* are found as high up as the Council bluff (*650 M⁺*) also red oake and *Sycamore* several species of oake Iron wood

---

[1] "Po-kish-a-co-mah" is unmistakably the native nelumbium, *Nelumbo lutea*. The "wild pittatoe" is probably *Ipomœa pandurata*, though the leaf description is very misleading. "Moc-cup-pin" is probably *Nymphœa reniformis*, also sometimes called *Nymphœa tuberosa* or *Castalia tuberosa*. — WILLIAM TRELEASE, director of Missouri Botanical Garden, St. Louis.

[2] Dr. Trelease furnishes us with the following memoranda on the plants and trees named in the following list.

"Prickly pear" is an *Opuntia* — probably *O. Missouriensis*, from its geographical position.

Several species of oak less than 480 miles from the mouth of the Missouri River would undoubtedly be, besides the red oak noted (*Quercus rubra*, or more probably *Q. Schneckii*), *Q. velutina* (sometimes called *Q. tinctoria*), *Q. Marylandica* (sometimes called *Q. nigra*), *Q. imbricaria*, *Q. alba*, *Q. minor* (sometimes called *Q. stellata*), *Q. macrocarpa* and *Q. platanoïdes* (sometimes called *Q. bicolor*).

"Iron wood" may refer to *Carpinus Caroliniana* or to *Ostrya Virginica*.

"Popaw" is *Asimina triloba*.

"Arrow wood," though this sometimes has been applied to the Osage orange, probably refers to *Viburnum dentatum* or *V. molle*.

"Green Bryar" is probably *Smilax rotundifolia*.

"Pacan" is *Carya olivaeformis*, sometimes known as *Hicoria pecan*.

"Grapes of the small kind" are probably *Vitis riparia*.

The "White oak" is *Quercus alba*, but, from the locality (1370 miles from the mouth of the river), I should think that the Burr oak, *Q. macrocarpa*, might be referred to here; or, more probably, the common oak of the Rocky Mountain region, *Q. Garryaria*, or some one of the forms segregated from this.

"Shoemate" is *Rhus*, and possibly may be *R. typhana*, also sometimes called *R. hirta*.

KOUTANI INDIAN

Popaws arrow wood and elder are found as high as the little Nemahaw
(*480 Mil*) also Sugar tree

Buckeye is found as high up as the old Kanzas village above Independance
Creek (*285 M*⁰·)

Green Bryar found as high up as [blank space in MS.]

Pacans are found as high up as Osarge River (*400*.)

In decending the Missouri & Rochejhone

The Grapes of the Small kind first appear on the River Rochejhone near
it's enterance into the Rocky mountain (*2700 Mⁱˢ*) but are not abundant on that river, the grape are abundant below cannon ball river,
(*1500 Mˢₐₚ*) and from thence down to the enterance of the river into
the Mississippi. no grapes of the large kind

Wild plumbs first appear at the cut off or Mandan Isᵈ (*1580 Mˢ*) below
the mandans tho' they are Scerce and Small they becom abundant
and fine in the neighbourhood of the enterance of White River.

White oaks first appear 60 miles below the Ricaras Vil.g (*1370 ᴹˢ Uᵖ*)
and are found in considerable quantity in the river bottoms just above
the enterance of Corvus Creek.

White Ash at ash rapid on the Missouri (*2443 Mls ᵁᵖ*). and on the
River rochejhone 60 miles above it's enterance.

Elm is found something higher up the rivers than the ash (*2500*)

Prickly ash first appears a fiew miles above Bull Island (*2800*) in the
river bottoms. Shoemate commences.

Yellow Oker above the upper old Kanzas Village in a bend on the S side

Chock Cherry found between the 2 Nemahars Rivers 500 miles up the
Missouri also another species of Cherry.

Sycamore is found at Ball pated prarie.

[Data by Lewis, found in Codex R, pp. 4–53, and not
entered elsewhere. The rest of Codex R consists of Clark's
copies of Lewis's natural history notes on the Columbia; as
these are contained in the journals proper, they are here
omitted. — Eᴅ.]¹

¹ The following identifications of plants and trees named in Lewis's list are furnished by Dr. Trelease :

1. "Cress" is a species of *Nasturtium*, probably *N. obtusum, sessiliflorum*, or *sinuatum*,
sometimes called *Roripa*.

3. Probably is the hop tree, *Ptelea trifoliata*.

4. "Cottonwood" is *Populus monilifera*, sometimes called *P. deltoides*. The trans-Missouri
cottonwood is a variety of this sometimes called var. *occidentalis* and sometimes var. *intermedia*.

5. "Cress" is probably a species of *Nasturtium*.

A List of specimines of plants collected by me on the Mississippi and Missouri rivers contain such observations on the vegitable kingdom spread to our view in this rich country as they have occurred to my mind. or as the several subjects have presented themselves to my view.

N°. 1. a species of Cress taken at S^t. Louis May 10th. 1804. it is common in the open grown[d]s on the Mississippi bottoms, appears in the uncultivated parts of the lots gardens and orchards, the seed come to maturity by the 10^h of May in most instances.

N°. 2. was taken on the 22^{ed}. of May 1804 on the bank of the Missouri about 8 miles above S^t. Charles it is common in the botom lands —rises to the hight of two feet, and rarely puts forth more than two stalks from the same root and most commonly only one it's root is spiral.

N°. 3. Was taken on the 23rd of May 1804., near the mouth of the Osage Woman's creek, it is a srub and resembles much in growth the *bladder scenna*, it rises to [the] hight of eight or ten feet and is an inhabitant of a moist rich coil. usually the verge of the river bank. it is a handsome Shrub

N° 4. Was taken at a small Village North side of the Missouri called Sharetton on the 25th. of May 1804. this is the last settlement on the Missouri ; and consists of ten or twelve families mostly hunters. this specimine is the seed of the Cottonwood which is so abundant in

6. " Kail," possibly *Brassica Sinafistrum.*

8. " Yellow root " may be *Hydrastis Canadensis.*

10. "Wild ginger " is a species of *Asarum,* perhaps *A. Canadense,* or more likely, *A. reflexum.*

11. Seems to be *Astragalus Mexicanus.*

12. " Purple courant " is probably *Ribes floridum.*

13. " Narrow leaf willow " is *Salix longifolia.*

14. "Wide leaf willow," from the pale under surface of the leaf, is pretty clearly *Salix amygdaloides.*

15 and 16 may possibly be, respectively, *Petalostemon violaceus* and *P. candidus,* also known sometimes as *Kuhnistera purpurea* and *K. candida.*

17. From the description of the fruit would seem to be a *Rhamnus,* and it might possibly be *R. alnifolia,* though the leaves are very small for that.

18. Is *Desmanthus brachylobus.*

26. Is probably *Lonicera Sullivantii.*

27. Is probably another wild potato, *Ipomœa leptophylla ;* though I am surprised that, if so, he did not learn from the Indians that its root was used by them.

29. Is probably *Cassia Chamaecrista.*

30. " Wild sage " may possibly have been *Salvia Pitcheri.*

31. "Sand rush " is *Equisetum arvense.*

32. Is *Gutierrezia Euthamiae.*

33. Is *Arctostaphylos Uva-ursi.*

40. Is *Grindelia squarrosa.*

104. Is *Juniperus sabina procumbens.*

105 and 106, "Tobacco," are *Nicotiana quadrivalvis.*

this country, it has now arrived at maturity and the wind when blowing strong drives it through the air to a great distance being supported by a parrishoot of this cottonlike substance which gives the name to the tree in some seasons it is so abundant as to be troublesome to the traveler. this tree arrives at great sise, grows extremly quick the wood is of a white colour, soft spungey and light, perogues are most usually made of these trees, the wood is not durable nor do I know any other valuable purpose which it can answer except that just mentioned. this tree forms a great majority of the timber bordering the rivers Missouri and Mississippi; it extends itself throughout the extensive bottom lands of these streams and seases to appear when the land rises into hills when these rivers form new lands on their borders or Islands in their st[r]eams, which they are per[pe]tually doing, the sweet willow is the first tree or shrub which usually makes it's appearance, this continues one two or three years and is then supplanted by the Cottonwood which invariably succeedes it. this tree resembles much in it's air and appearance that beatifull and celibrated tree the Lombardy poplar; and more particularly so when in its young state; the young plants grow very close untill they have attained the age of four or five years, a proportion of them then begin to dye and the forrest opens and gives place to sundry other shrubs and plants which will be noticed in their proper places.

N°. 5. was taken on the 27th. of May 1804, near the mouth of the Gasconade; it is a species of cress which grows very abundantly alonge the river beach in many places; my men make use of it and find it a very pleasant whol[e]some sallad.

N°. 6. Was taken on the 27th of May 1804, near the mouth of the Gasconade; it is a species of rope or kail, it grows on the beach of the river, when young my men used it [as] a boiled green and found [it] healthy and pleasant.

N° 7. was found on the 27th of May 1804, near the water side about 10 miles below the mouth of the Gasconade, it rises to the hight of three feet and puts forth many large suculent branched stalks from the same root, this plant is a stranger to me.

N° 8. Was taken the 29th. of May 1804, below the mouth of the Osage Riv: this plant is known in Kentuckey and many other parts of this western country by the name of the yellow root. it is a sovereighn remidy for a disorder common in this quarter called the soar eyes this complaint is common it is a violent inflamation of the eyes attended with high fevers and headach, and is extreemly distressing, and frequently attended with the loss of sight. this root affords a speady and efficasieus remidy for this disorder prepared & used in the following manner.—— let the roots be geathered washed and carefully dryed in the shade; brake them in pieces of half an inch in length and put them in a bottle or viol, taking care to fill the vessel about two thirds full of the dryed root, then fill the vessell with could water, rain water is preferable; let it remain about six hours shaking it occasionally and it will be fit for use; the water must remain with the root and be applyed to the eyes frequently by weting a piece of fine linin [and] touching them gently with it. this root is a fine aromatic bitter, and a strong asstringent; it is probable that it might be applyed in many cases as a medicene with good effect, but I have not learnt that any experiment has been made by an inward application. it makes an excellent mouth water, and a good outward applycation for wounds or inflamations of every kind. native of rich bottom lands on the rivers.

N° 9. Was taken on the 30th of May 1804, below the mouth of the Osage river; it rises from 18 Inches to 2 feet in hight; is a beautifull green plant found most generally on the sides of rich hills in the forrest it's radix is fiberous.

N° 10. This plant was taken the 1st of June at the mouth of the Osage river; it is known in this country by the name of the *wild ginger,* it resembles that plant somewhat in both taste and effect, it is a strong stomatic stimelent, and freequently used in sperits with bitter herbs. it is common throughout the rich lands in the Western country.

N° 11. Was taken the 3rd of June above the mouth of the Osage river; it is the groath of high dry open praries; rises to the hight of 18 inches or two feet puts forth many stems from the same root; the radix is fiborous; the Indians frequently use the fruit of this plant to alay their thirst as they pass through these extensive dry praries common to many parts of the country bordering on the Missouri; it resembles much the Indigo in the appearance of it's growth. it bears it's fruit much like the indigo, a stem projects about three inches from the main stem at an angle of about 20 degrees, and bears from [two] to four podds, which in their succulent and unripe state as at this season of the year are about the size of a pullet's egg, somewhat flattened on two sides; the matrix is formed in two lobes and the seed are like pees and attatched to the matrix in the same manner, single and adhering to the center the pulp is crisp & clear and tasts very much like the hull of a gardin pee. when ripe the fruit is of a fine red coulour and sweet flavor. it dose not ripen untill the middle of June.

N° 12. 1st of august 1804, one of our hunters brought us a bough of the purple courant, which is frequently cultivated in the Atlantic states; the fruit was ripe; I presume it is a native of North America here it grows generally in the praries but is not very abundant. N°. 12 is a specimine of it's leaves.

N°. *13*. The *narrow leaf willow* taken on the 14th of June. this tree is male and female, the female bearing it[s] seed in a small pod (small ova form) of three lobes, or devisions these pods are attatched to a stem which projects from the small boughs, and are from thirty to fifty in number, about this season they begin to ripen, when the pods burst and a great number of small seeds each furnished with a parri-shoot of a cottonlike substance are discharged from those cels. they readily float in the air and are driven by the wind to a great distance, they are so abundant at some times as to be disagreeable to the travel-ler. the *male* plant has a sucession of it's flowers, commencing to bloom about the 1st of June and continuing untill the 1st of August, they are a small tausel of a half, or ¾ of an inch in length, round, and tapering to the extremity, puting frort[h] from it's sides an infinite number of small stamens of a brown colour. it's leaves are numerous narrow, slightly indented, of a yellowish green, on the uper side, and whiteish green underneath, pointed, being widest in the middle which rarely exceeds ⅛th of an inch, it is smoth, tho' not glossey.

This tree is invariably the first which makes it's appearance on the newly made Lands on the borders of the Mississippi and Missouri, and seems to contribute much towards facilitating the operation of raisin[g] this ground still higher; they grow remarkably close and in some instances so much so that they form a thicket almost impenetrable the points of land which are forming allways become eddies when over-flown in high water these willows obstruct the force of the water and makes it more still which causes the mud and sand to be deposited in greater quantities; the willow is not attal imbarrassed or injured by this inundation, but puts forth an innumerable quantity of small fibrous roots from every part of its trunk near the surface of the water which further serve to collect the mud, if there happens not to be a sufficient quantity of mud depossited in the one season to cover the trunk of the willow as high as these capillery roots when the water subsides they fall down and rest on the trunk of the tree and conceal it for 18 or 20 Inches; these capillery roots now perish and the willow puts forth other roots at the surface of the ground which enter it and furnish the tree with it's wanted nutriment this willow never rises to any con-siderable size, it is seldom seen larger than a mans arm, and scarcely ever rises higher than 25 feet. the wood is white light and tough, and is generally used by the watermen for *setting poles* in preference to any thing else. as the willow incre[a]ses in size and the land gets higher by the annu[a]l inundations of the river, the weeker plants decline dye and give place to the cottonwood which is it's ordinary successor, and these last in their turn also thin themselves as they become larger in a similar manner and leave the ground open for the admission of other forest trees and under brush. these willow bars form a pleasant beacon to the navigator at that season when the banks of the river are tumbling in, as they [are] seldom high and rearly falling in but on the contrary most usually increasing.

Nº 14. The *wide leaf willow* or that species which I believe to be common to most parts of the Atlantic States. it grows in similar situations to that discribed with rispect to the narrow leaf willow, but is never found in such abundance, it arrives to greater size some times to forty feet in hight and eighteen inches in diameter, the leave is smoth ovate, pointed, finely indented, a pale green on the upper side and of a whiteis[h] green or silver colour underneath. like the narrow leaf willow the leaf is widest in the middle where it is from one inch to ¾ wide. it bears it's seed in the manner discribed of the other and the plants ar[e] likewise male and female.

Nº 15. Was taken on the 20ᵗʰ of July, a bieniel plant, an inhabitant of the open praries or plains, high situations, where the grass is low. the flower is a pale purple colour small form a kind of button of a long cone like form which terminate[s] it's branches which are numerous. it grows abo[u]t 2½ or three feet high. it is a stranger to me. the leaves are small and narrow, and divided into three on a stem

Nº 16. this is much the same as Nº 15. with this difference that the blume of the conic tausel are white in stead of purple and it's leaves single fewer and longer.

Nº 17. Taken on the 27ᵗʰ of July, the appearance of the bush is much like the privy and about the same hight it grows about the borders of the open praries it's leaf is a deep green, ovate 1½ to 1¼ inches long ½ inch wide finely indented plan[t] piennial. the buries or fruit a small round bury of a deep perple coulour nearly black, has three seed formed like the third part of a globe split by the meeting of two plains at it's axcis. I do not know whether birds eat them or not. they look handsome but tast insipid. this is a groath with which I am not acquainted.

Nº 18. was taken 30ᵗʰ July grows in the praries in high situations, it's radix is pe[r]ennial, it grows about three ½ or 4 feet high it has a long top root is but little branced, it's colateral brances are short and furnished with many leaf stems which are garnished by a great number of small leaves which are attatch[ed] by pairs on either side and resemble some of the sensative bryers, tho I could not discover that this plant partook of that quality. it's flower is of a gloubelar form composed of a number of fibers of a yellowish white, and produces as a fruit a bunch of little pees which are all bent edgeways into the form of a semicircle and so closely connected and compressed as to form a globular figure of a curious appearance.

N° 19. Taken at the old village of the little Osages ; the seed were now ripe; it grew in great abundance in the prarie from five to six feet high; it gave the plain much the appearance of an extensive timothy meadow ready for the sythe, the small birds feed on the seed which are very abundant resembling in size shape and colour those of the flax; when ripe they fall very easily from the stem. the leaf of this grass dose not decline or wither as many others do at the time the seed ripens but still continues succulent and green. it continues throughout the summer to put up a succession of young succors which in turn bear a large quantity of seed : this succession of crops continues throughout the season without the declining or withering of the stalk or leaves of the mother plant. the horses were very fond of this grass and I am disposed to believe that it would make a valuable grass for culture. this grass is common in the praries or bottom lands as high as the river Platte and perhaps further   it is a fine sweet grass and I am confident would make good hay.

N° 20. A specemine of wild Rye taken on the 27th of July, this grass is common to all the low praries above the Cancez river. it rises to the hight of six feet and upwards and resembles the rye extreemly in appearance   the geese and ducks feed on it when young, as they do also on the grain when ripe   in September and October it produces much grain tho of an inferior quality compared with cultivated rye.

N° 21. is another species of the wild rye it dose not grow as tall as N°. 20. neither does it like that species confine itself so much to the open ground ; it is sometimes found in the timbered land.   the grain it produces is [n]either so large or so abundant as the former.

N°'s 22, 23, 24 & 25, Are various species of grasses which appear in the praries,   N° 23. is the most common of any other grass, it rises to the hight of from 4 to 8 feet and never bears any flower or seed that I ever observed and suppose therefore that it must propegate by means of the root : *common* to all praries in this country.

N° 26. — Taken on the 2ed of August in the p[r]arie at the Cuncil bluff.   it is a species of honeysuccle and the tube of the flour is very small and short they smell precisely like the English Honeysuccle so much admired in our gardens; this is a shrub and dose not run or vine. the vining honesuckle which bears a red flour is also common to the Illinois and is found as high up the Missoury as the mouth of the Kancez river above which I have not observed it. this species of shrub Honesuccle has some of it's leaves much indented; the fruit nearly ripe when the plant is still in blume; it makes a pretty groath and is a pleasant looking pla[n]t rises to three or four feet high and limbs are much branched.

N^o *27.* taken 4th of August, and furst observed at the bald prarie it is [a] beatifull plant with a variagated leaf these leaves incompass the flowers which are small and in the center of them; at a small distance they resemble somewhat a white rose the leaf near the large stem is green and is edged with white; they grow smaller and more numerous as they approach the flower or the extremity of the limb. the plant is much branched; the leaf is smoth on both sides and edge, of an ovate form and pale green colour, rises to five or six feet, is annual. at every point that it branches it has a pair of opposite leaves and from th[r]ee to four branches.

N° 28. taken on the 17th July at the bald prarie is a large convolvalist [of] a fine white colour; the vines are very extensive and run in every direction intwining themselves about the larger weeds and bending them down is [in] such manner as to make the open grownds or praries where they grow almost impassable; the root is about the size and shape of the vine and enters it so deep that I could not find it's brances tho' I dug as much as 2 feet in surch of it. the leaf is of a tonge like form pale green even on the edges. leaf thus

N^o *29.* Taken on the 18th of July. an annuel plant puting up many branches from the root has a leaf like the pateridge bea[n], is jointed bears a number of yellow *pea-like* flowers which grow on the seed stems which project from the main branches and which are unattended with leaves; these flowers grow all arround this stem and give it the appearance of a tausell. the [l]eaf stems ar[e] long and have 24 par of leaves.

N^o *30.* was taken at the bald praries and is common to both low and high praries it usually grows in a single stem and appears to be an annual groath the leaves are white and like the stem appear to be covered with a white down. this is common to all the praries above the Kancez river; from it's resemblence in taste smell &c to the *common Sage* I have called it the wild Sage.

N^o *31.* Taken on the 10th of August, a species of sand rush, jointed and so much branched as to form a perfect broom; it is common to every part of this river at least as far as Latitude 42. N. it grows near the water's edge in moist sand; the horses are remarkably fond of it.

N° 40   Taken at our camp at the Maha vilage August 17th 1804. it is a handsome plant about 3 feet high much branched bears a yellow circular flower carnished with meany small narrow ovate petals of the same colour, the leaf about an inch and a quarter in length thick smoth indent[ed] finely, incompassing the stalk about ⅔'s and of a tongue like form; annual plant is covered with a gumlike substance which adheres to the fingers and yealds a pleasent smell.

N^o (100) Nov^b 17th the seed of a plant given me by the recara chief who accompanyed us to the mandanes he informed me that a tea of the seed was a strong diaerettic. and that the squaws chewed them and rubed their hair with them as a perfume.

N^o (101) the root w[h]en pounded in either green or dryed state makes an excellent poltice for swellings or soar throat. information of the same chief.

N° 102) by the information of the same chief — is an excellent purge. the root is dryed and pounded in that state as much as you can hold between the finger and thumb thrise is a doze. it is the growth of the open praries has many small stalks 2 feet high radix piennl [biennial].

N° 103. is the growth of the open praries. it seldom grows higher it is said to be good for inflamed eyes the leaves are immerced in water and being bruised with the fingers a little the water is squeezed from it and occasionally droped when could upon the eyes.

(104 N^o) October the 16th a dwarf cedar of the open praries seldom ever rises more than six inches high it is said to be a stimilating shrub it is used as a tea by the Indians to produce sweat. they would make a handsome edging to the borders of a gardin if used as the small *box* sometime is.

N° 105. seed of the Larger species of recarre tobacco pre[se]nted us by *Lepoy* an Indian chief of that nation commanding the *middle town*.

N° 106 is the corrollars of the same prepared for smoking. they are plucked and dryed in the shade.

N° 107 is the seed of the smaller species.

The recarres cultivate two species of tobacco for the purpose of smoking in which way they use it altogether as they neither snuff nor chew.

The *Larger species* (see specimine plants Nº 108) rises to the hight
of three feet   it's round green and succulent   much branched when
suffered to grow singly.   in that sittuation it branches near the ground
and continues to branch and rebranch as it rises at the distance of an
inch or 2 inches, thus forming an infinite number of boughs at the top
which are terminated by the flowers which are tubelar, trunnicated
scalluped on the edges and five pointed, white colour, order, *pentandria
moniginia*,   the leaf is of a toung-like form   the larger of which are
attatched to the lower part of the stalk, one inch wide in the broadest
part & 2½ inches long.   the [y] demin[i]s[h] as they are higher on the
stalk, tho' they increas in numbers.   The indians cultivate it in the
following manner   they prepare hills at the distance of about 2½ feet
from each other, and leavel the top nearly leaving it somewhat convex.
in those hills they sew the seed as early in the spring as the climate will
permit them to prepare the earth say latter end of April; they keep the
hills clear of weeds and grass by plucking it from among the stalks of
tobacco with their fingers   and sometimes allso thin the stalks of
tobacco by plucking up the weaker stalks tho they leave many stalks
to grow on each hill.   when the tobacco begins to form it's seed poods
it is then ready for the knife when a great portion from each hill is cut
and hung on sticks untill it is nearly dry   when they form them into
carrots of the thickness of a mans arm   role them closely with willow
bark and hang them in the smoke of their lodges to dry.   in forming
the carrot they put the butts or lower parts of the stalks together.
where the tobacco is cultivated with a view to make carrots the stalks
are so thick that they do not attain a thickness at the largest part of the
stem greater than that of a small quill.   They esteem much more the
corroller dryed for the purpose of smoking and for this purpose leave
some plant[s] more widely seperated from each other   in which situation they produce a greater abundance of flowers & seed   they begin to
blume in the month of [blank space in MS.] and continue untill the
first frost; during the full blume of the flower they pluck the corrollar
together with the flower and discarding the latter suffer the former to
dry in the shade   when perfectly dryed it resembles at first view the
green *tea* and in that state it is smoked by the indians and I found it
very pleasent.   it dose not affect the nerves in the same manner that
the tobacco cultivated in the U'S. dose.   The smaller species of this
plant differs but little from this just discribed.   it is cultivated in the
same manner and bears a flower like the other only smaller.   the only
difference is the form of the leaf, which is larger say 4 times the size
and *ovate*   they dry this on sticks and use it in that manner   it is

note found them our hunters gone on a
the mountains rough and rocks which appear
above the timber like towers in some places
the day proved pleasant. we proceeded on upon
a high mountain. over took the hunters who
had killed a Deer 2 of them but broke one of
Capt Lewis horse. we crossed the dividing ri
dge found it only about half a mile from
the head spring of the water running Eas
to a branch running west. and heading
in an open country which is level and
full of springs. came ___ miles this day and
camped on the branch running west whe
we had good feed for our horses.
Saturday 14th Sepr 1805. a cloudy morning
we eat the last of our meat. and set
out as usual ascended a mountain cove
with pine. at ___ miles we descended it down
on the creek at a fork where it ran very
rapid and full of rocks. we then ___
ascended a verry high mountain about
2 miles from the forks of this creek to the
top of it went some distance on the top
then descended it about 5 miles. some
places verry steep. came down at
another fork of the creek where it
was considr larger. the natives had a
place made deep in form of our
weirs in 2 places and worked in with
willows verry ingeniously for the
current verry rapid. we crossed at the
forks and proceeded on down the creek
passed several little Indian encampmen
our guide tells us that the
natives catch a great number of salmon

reather stronger than the large kind and is seldom made into carrots by the Recares.

☞ it is worthy of remark that the recares never use *sperituous liquors*. Mr Tibeau informed me that on a certain occasion he offered one of their considerate men a dram of sperits, telling him it's virtues the other replyed that he had been informed of it's effects and did not like to make himself a fool unless he was paid to do so that if M^r. T. wished to laugh at him & would give him a knife or *breech-coloth* or something of that kind he would take a glass but not otherwise.

[The following is copied verbatim from the American Philosophical Society's Donation Book of the period — a small volume in limp board covers, 7⅝ × 12½" in size. These entries, covering sixteen pages, and apparently in the handwriting of Dr. John Vaughn, doubtless closely followed the original notes by Lewis. The letter " H " is apparently the checkmark of a receiving clerk. — Ed.][1]

---

[1] Stewardson Brown, assistant to the curators, in charge of the herbarium of the Botanical Section of the Academy of Natural Sciences of Philadelphia, furnishes us with the following note upon the herbarium of Lewis and Clark :

The importance of the results of the Lewis and Clark expedition to American botany may be appreciated when we consider what a large proportion of the plants brought back by these pioneers were of species then unknown to science. The work of identifying the material appears to have been entrusted to Frederick Pursh, a young botanist, who at the time of the return of the expedition, was in Philadelphia, having come there from Dresden several years previous for the purpose of making as thorough a study as possible of the flora of this country ; in this he achieved considerable success — largely, it would appear, through the munificence of Dr. Benjamin Smith Barton, then professor of botany at the University of Pennsylvania, under whose patronage much of Pursh's work was made possible.

In 1814 Pursh published (in London) the first edition of his *Flora Americæ Septentrionalis*, two octavo volumes, of 725 pages of text and 24 plates, which contained descriptions of the plants under consideration. Speaking of these in the preface of his work, after a brief reference to his having made the acquaintance of Meriwether Lewis, Pursh says : " A small but highly interesting collection of dried plants was put into my hands by this gentleman in order to describe and figure those thought new, for the purpose of inserting them in the account of his Travels which he was then engaged in preparing for the press. . . . The collection of plants just spoken of was made during the rapid return of the expedition from the Pacific Ocean to the United States. A much more extensive one, made on the slow ascent toward the Rocky Mountains and the chain of the Northern Andes, had unfortunately been lost, by being deposited among other things, at the foot of those mountains. The loss of this collection is the more to be regretted when I consider that the small collection communicated to me, consisting of about one hundred and fifty-five specimens, con-

Donations November 16, 1805 from Meriwether Lewis Dried
Plants &c put into Dr B. S Bartons hands for examination.[1]

tained not above a dozen plants known to me to be natives of North America — the
rest being either entirely new or little known, and among them at least six distinct and
new genera. This may give an idea of the discerning eye of their collector, who had
but little practical knowledge of the Flora of North America. . . . The descriptions
of these plants so far as the specimens were perfect I have inserted in the present work,
in their respective places distinguishing them by the words ' *v. s. in Herb. Lewis.*' "
Here he refers in his descriptions to one hundred and twenty-three (123) species which
he ascribes as above, the majority of which he considered to be new to science.

For many years the bulk of these plants were entirely lost to the botanical world,
it being assumed that Pursh had taken them with him for further study when he went
to England in 1811, and had subsequently left them with his friend and benefactor,
Mr. A. B. Lambert, vice-president of the Linnean Society, under whose roof the task
of completing the work on his *Flora* was accomplished.

Whatever the facts in the case may be, it is certain that a number of plants marked
as coming from Lambert's herbarium and representing the type specimens of many of
the species described by Pursh in his *Flora* (among which are seven of the plants
received by him from Lewis) now form a part of the herbarium of the Academy of
Natural Sciences of Philadelphia ; but in what manner they came into the possession of that institution, the early records fail to show. It is not improbable, however, that they were purchased abroad, and presented to the Academy by some early
benefactor.

These few specimens were supposed to constitute all that existed of the one hundred
and fifty-five specimens referred to by Pursh, until, in making room for improvements
at the American Philosophical Society about six years ago, were revealed among
other botanical collections in their possession several bundles of plants, the labels of
which bore a handwriting which proved to be that of Pursh ; and this, together with
the data there contained, identified the plants without doubt as the missing specimens
of Lewis and Clark.

During the more than three-quarters of a century while they had been hidden from
the light of day, the beetles had not been altogether idle ; and in a few cases the specimens had been entirely reduced to dust, nothing remaining to aid in identification
except the labels, while in other cases only fragments were left. Generally, however,
they were in fair condition, and now form a part of the herbarium of the Academy of
Natural Sciences, having been placed there on deposit by the Philosophical Society
shortly after their discovery. As might be expected, Pursh in his work of identification had fallen into some errors, as a subsequent critical study of the collection by
Messrs. Robinson and Greenman of the Gray Herbarium demonstated ; but never-
theless fully one-half of the one hundred and twenty-three species referred to by Pursh
in the text of his *Flora*, stand as such to-day.

The collection has also been found to contain, in addition to these, a number of
species not recognized by Pursh as distinct, but which have proven to be the earliest
collections of many of the species of subsequent authors. That some of these, although clearly quite new to Pursh, may have remained undescribed from what he

---

[1] Dr. Benjamin Smith Barton had agreed to edit the scientific notes of Lewis and
Clark, for publication. See vol i, p. xlv, *ante.* — ED.

No. 1   At St Louis May 10th 1804
2   May 10th 1804
3   May 23, 1804
4   May 25th 1804

The Cottonwood found on every part of the Missouri as high as the mandans, generally grows in the river bottoms & near its borders. — *H*

considered a lack of sufficiently perfect material, seems probable, as the following quotation would indicate : " Here I cannot refrain from drawing the attention of future botanists traveling in those regions to two highly interesting plants of which I have only seen imperfect specimens.   The first is what Mr. Lewis in his journal calls the ' Osage Apple or Arrow wood of the Missouri.' "   This plant is without doubt the osage orange (*Toxylon pomiferum*, Raf.), a specimen of which, with no label, is contained in the collection.   Pursh, in continuation of the paragraph above quoted, describes at considerable length the characteristics of the tree — or, as he terms it, shrub — dwelling on its importance to the Indians in the making of arrows.   He further refers to specimens grown at Philadelphia from seed brought back by Lewis, considering it in all respects a most desirable acquisition as an ornamental shrub ; and yet, with all this, he fails to give it a name.   Three years after the date of the publication of Pursh's *Flora*, the plant was described by Rafinesque under the name designated above, he possibly drawing his descriptions largely from the specimens which originated from Lewis's seed, planted twelve years before.   Whether or not this be true there seems but little doubt that the first information regarding the plant came through Lewis.

The collection, as preserved in the Herbarium of the Academy of Natural Sciences to-day, consists of specimens of one hundred and seventy-three recognizable species, mostly in fair condition ; these include fifty-five of Pursh's types recognized as species at the present time, with thirty-eight additional ones, now for various reasons not considered tenable.   The number lacks but fifteen of the species referred to by Pursh as contained in the Lewis Herbarium ; of these, some may be included among the existing specimens but, if so, are not recognizable from their descriptions.

In Pursh's *Flora* he describes but five new genera ; of this number four are based upon the plants received by him from Lewis, all of the specimens still existing in fairly good condition.

Of these, three still retain the names conferred upon them by Pursh, two in honor of the heads of the expedition — represented each by a single species : *Lewisia rediviva* (Pursh Fl. 368), and *Clarkia pulchella* (Pursh Fl. 260, with an excellent figure) ; and the third *Calochortus*, the genus of a handsome group of liliaceous plants confined to the Western United States and Mexico.

The name selected by Pursh for the fourth new genus represented in the collection had, unfortunately, been proposed as early as 1775 by Aublet for another plant, which necessitated a new name.   The discrepancy was noted by De Candolle, who in 1817 in the transactions of the Linnean Society, the original medium of publication of Pursh's new genera, renamed the genus in honor of Pursh.   The species collected by Lewis, which is represented by an excellent specimen, now bears the name of *Purshia tridentata* (Pursh), D. C.

5	May 27, 1804
6	May 27, 1804
7	May 27, 1804
8	May 29, 1804.

This plant is known in Kentucky & many other parts of the Western Country by the name of the yellow root. It is said to be a sovereign remedy in a disorder common to the Inhabitants of the Country where found, usually termed sore eyes — frequently attended with high fever & sometimes terminates in the loss of sight, always gives great pain & continues for a length of time in most cases. The preparation & application of the root is as follows — having procured a quantity of the roots, wash them clean & suffer them to dry in the Shade, break them with the fingers as fine as you conveniently can, put them in a glass vessel, taking care to fill it about ⅔ with the Broken root, then add rain or river water until the Vessel is filled, shake it frequently & it will be fit for use in the course of 6 hours. The Water must not be decanted but remaining with the root is to be frequently applied by wetting a piece of fine linnen and touching thee Eyes gently with it. This root has a fine aromatic bitter taste, it is probable that it might be applied internally in many cases with good effect, but I have not learnt that any experiments have yet been made with it in that way. It makes an excellent *mouth water* & is an excellent outward application in cases of wounds or local application of any kind. It is the Growth of rich bottom lands.   M. Lewis

9

10   Usually called wild ginger   grows in rich bottom Land   June 1, 1804

11.   June 3ᵈ 1804

12   The purple Currant.   1 Augᵗ 1804

13   Narrow leaf willow common to the borders of the Missouri. June 14, 1804.

14   Broadleaf Willow found on the Missouri   not so common as the Narrow leaf willow but grows much larger sometimes rising to 30 feet   June 14, 1804

15   found in the open plains.   20 July, 1804   H

16   same as Nº 16   H

17   found on the Edges of the Prairies,   rises about 8 foot high the leaf is a deep green, the bush has a handsome appearance with its fruit.   27 July, 1804   H

18. growth of the high plains taken the 30 July, 1804.

20 S.

20 Growth of the rich Prairie bottoms found 27 July. 1804 S

21 Another Speceis of the Wild Rye it does not grow as tall as N° 20 S 27 July

22 N 22, 23, 24, 25 are various species of grass which grow in the prarie Bottom lands of the Missouri N 23 is the most common it rises to the height of 4 & 5 feet & never bears any Seed or flower, it propagates itself by the root   27 July

23

24   *H*

25   *H*

26

26 Species of Honey Suckle common to the prairies this Specimen was obtained at the Council Bluffs 2ᵈ Aug, 1804   *H*

27 Growth of the Prairie Bottoms taken on the 4ᵗʰ Aug, 1804

28 D° — D° — 15 July 1804

29 Growth of the open praries   18 July 1804

30. D° — D° — 13 July

31 Growth of the Sand Bars near the Banks of the Rivers   10 Aug 1804

32 Specimens of the aromatic plants on which the Antelope feeds these wer obtained 21 Sep. 1804 at the upper part of the Big bend of the Missouri —   *H*

33 an evergreen plant which grows usually in the open plains, the natives smoke its leaves mixed with Tobacco called by the french engages *Sacacommé* obtained at Fort Mandon

34 The leaf of Oak which is common to the Prairies. 5 Sep. 1804

35 Sept. 18. The Growth of the Prairies   *H*

36 Sep. 18 Growth of the high Prairies.

37 Sep. 22 D° — D° —

38 Oct. 15, 1804 Growth of the high Prairies or Plains.

39 Obtained at the mouth of the River Quicourre from which place upwards, it is abundant in the Missouri bottoms, it is a pleasant Berry to eat, it has much the flavor of the Cranbury & continues on the bush thro' the Winter. This is an Evergreen shrub —

Some plants are sent down by the barge to the care of Capt Stoddart at Sᵗ Louis.   *H*

40. 17 Aug 1804 Growth of Prairies at our Camp near the old Maha Village. *H*

41. 2ᵈ Sep. 1804 On the Bluffs grows in open high situations. *H*

42. 27ᵗʰ Aug. At the Chalk Bluff grows in the mineral earth at the base of the Hill *H*

43. 25ᵗʰ Augᵗ Growth of the open Prairies. *H*

44. Sepʳ 1ˢᵗ Dº. Dº *H*

45. Oct. 12. Specimen of Tobacco the Indians cultivate called Ricaras Tobacco — at the Ricares Town

46. Sep. 15, 1804 The growth of the Upper Prairies *H*

47. Oct. 17. Species of Juniper common to the Bluffs *H*

48. Oct. 17 a Decoction of this plant used by the Indians to wash their Wounds 103

49. Oct. 16. (104) never more than 6 Inches high Dwarf Cedar.

50. Oct. 18. The small rose of the Prairies it rises from 12 to 14 Inch high does not vine *H*

51. Oct. 3ᵈ 1804 Radix Perrenial three to 8 Stalks as high as the specimen growth of the high sides of the Bluff (Camomile taste)

52. Sep. 15, 1804 Growth of the plains. *H*

53 Oct. 3ᵈ Flavor like the Cammomile Radix Perennial — High Bluffs.

53 (A) Sep. 2 The Indians use it as an application to fresh wounds they bruise the leaves add a little water & use it.

54. Oct. 2ᵈ grows from 18 Inches to 2½ feet many stalks from the same root, from which they issue near the ground. The Radix perrenial. The goat or antelope feed on it in the winter, it is the growth of the high bluffs *H*

55 Oct. 2ᵈ 1804 Growth of the high Bluffs

56 Oct. 2ᵈ 1804. Growth of the open plains

57 Oct. 1, 1804 first discovered in the neighborhood of the Kancez River — now very common, the growth of the little Cops, which appear on the steep declivities of the Hills where they are sheltered from the ravages of the fire. *H*

58 2ᵈ Oct. 1804 A species of Cedar found on the Bluffs the trees of which are large, some 6 feet in the Girth. *H*

58 12 Sepʳ growth of the high dry Prairie *H*

| 59 | 19th Sepr. 1804   The growth of the high & bare Prairies which produce little Grass — Generally mineral earth. | *H* |

59   19th Sepr. 1804   The growth of the high & bare Prairies which
       produce little Grass — Generally mineral earth.   *H*

59.   Growth of moist & very wet prairies — 8 Sep.   *H*

60.   Octr 1, 1804. another variety of wild Sage growth of high &
       bottom Prairies.   *H*

Seeds

61   Wild Prairie Timothy Seeds   *H*

62   Seeds of a Species of Pine with a Pod   *H*

The Fang of a Rattle Snake, they are abundant on the Missouri.

Specimen of the fur of the Antelope, this animal affords but little, it is intermixed with the coarse hair & is not perceptible but by close examination.

Two Small quadrupeds.

a few Insects.

The corolla of the Indian Tobacco as prepared for the purpose of smoking by the Mandans, Ricaras, Minetares & Ahwahhaways, in this State it is mixed with a small quantity of Buffaloes Tallow, previous to charging the pipe.   It is esteemed a great delicacy among these people, they dispose of it to their neighbors the Assinouboins & others who visit them for the purpose of Traffick from whom they obtain a high price.

———

FORT MANDAN March 5, 1805.

This specimen of a plant [*H.*] common to the praries in this quarter was presented to me by Mr Hugh heney a gentleman of rispectability and information who has resided many years among the natives of this country from whom he obtained the knowledge of its virtues.   Mr. Haney informed me that he had used the root of this plant frequently with the most happy effect in cases of the bite of the mad wolf or dog and also for the bite of the rattle snake   he assured me that he had made a great number of experiments on various subjects of men horses and dogs particularly in the case of madness where the symptoms were in some instances far advanced and had never witnessed it's failing to produce the desired effect.   the method of using it is by external application, to half an ounce of the root finely pulverized, add as much water as is necessary to reduce it to the consistency of a common poltice and apply it to the bitten parts, renewing the dressing once in twelve hours. in cases of the bite of the mad dog where the wound has healed before the symptoms of madness appear, the bitten part must be lacerated or sca[r]efyed before the application is made.   the application had always better be made as early as possible after the injury has been sustained.

I have sent herewith a few pounds of this root, in order that experiments may be made by some skillful person under the direction of the P[h]ilosophical society of Philadelphia.

I have the honor to be with much rispect,

Your Ob't Serv.ᵗ

MERIWETHER LEWIS.[1]

Thomas Jefferson
President U.' States }

---

[1] The following identifications of the specimens named in the Donation Book, above, are furnished by Dr. Trelease :

4. Cottonwood — *Populus monilifera.*	45. *Nicotiana quadrivalvis.*
8. Yellow root — *Hydrastis Canadensis.*	46. *Astragalus Mortoni.*
10. Wild ginger — *Asarum Canadensis,* or, probably *A. reflexum.*	47. Juniper — *Juniperus communis.*
	48. *Psoralea argophylla.*
12 Purple currant — *Ribes floridum.*	49. Dwarf cedar — *Juniperus sabina procumbens.*
13. Narrow leaf willow — *Salix longifolia.*	50. Small rose — *Rosa Woodsii.*
14. Broad leaf willow — *Salix amygdaloides.*	51. *Artemisia frigida.*
26. Honeysuckle — *Lonicera Sullivantii.*	52. " " *dracunculoides.*
31. *Equisetum arvense.*	53. " " *longifolia. Liatris scariosa* also seems to have been collected under this number.
32. *Gutierrezia Euthamiae.*	
33. *Arctostaphylos Uva-ursi.*	
34. Prairie oak — *Quercus macrocarpa depressa.*	54. *Bigelowia graveolens.*
35. *Liatris pycnostachya.*	55. *Artemisia cava.*
36. *Astragalus Missouriensis.*	57. *Rhus aromatica trilobata,* also called *R. Canadensis trilobata.*
38. *Euphorbia heterophylla.*	
39. *Sheperdia argentea.*	58. Cedar — *Juniperus occidentalis.*
40. *Grindelia squarrosa.*	59. *Gutierrezia Euthamiae,* of September 19th ; *Zizania aquatica* of September 8th.
41. *Artemisia frigida.*	
43. *Cleome integrifolia.*	

This Barton list is evidently made out from specimens collected when the numbers in the preceding list were entered in Lewis's note-book, and agrees with this up to 40.   Numbers 104 to 107 of the Lewis list (p. 149, *ante*) are evidently to be matched off by lower numbers in the Barton list.

V. MINERALOGY

FROM the Donation Book of the American Philosophical Society, already described under the division of Botany — p. 151, *ante*. The language of the original entry is apparently that of Lewis and Clark themselves. The italicized comments in brackets are doubtless by some contemporary scientist connected with the Society's museum. The letter *H* is, apparently, the check mark of a receiving clerk. — ED.]

M. Lewis' Donation continued   16 Nov. 1805.

No. 1. Specimen of compact salt formed by concretion & found adhering to the rocks, thro' which a Salt fountain Issues, situated on the South Side of the Southern Branch of the Arcansas River, called by the osage Indians Ne-chu-re-thin-gar. [*Muriat of Soda. This salt beyond all doubt is formed in consequence of water, we held it in solution, having been evaporated in consequence of exposure to the sun's rays & atmosphere. The crystals are small cubes heaped together and in every respect resemble those procured by art.*]

2. Found just above the entrance of the cannon Ball river, the butt[e] is principally composed of this sand & strongly impregnated with a substance supposed to be blue vitriol. [*Sulphat of Iron in consequence of the decomposition of Pyrites.*]

3. Flint found at the white Chalk Bluffs 1804.

4. 23 Aug, 1804, found exuding from a Strata of sand rock on [one] of the Bluffs. [*Much resembles the " Atrament stein" of the Germans found near Goslar, and consists principally of Sulphate of Iron derived from decomposed Sulphuret of Iron, intermixed with Clay.*]

5. Specimen of the Sand of the Missouri. [*It is siliceous sand with a mixture of particles of Mica.*]

6. Augt 21, 1804. In the Interstices of a blue clay which forms the majority of the Bluffs, Strata of all earth or Stone make their appearance & Horizontal. [*Alum formed in consequence of a decomposition of aluminous Shistus* [schist] — *& Sulphat of Lime on the lower surface crystallized.*]

7. Petrefaction on the Missouri, May 30, 1804.

8. Found among the loose earth of the Bluff 23 Aug. 1804 [*regular crystals of Gypsum or Sulphat of Lime. Trapezoid.*]

9. a Petrified Jawbone of a fish or some other animal found in a cavern a few miles distant from the Missouri S. side of the River. 6 Aug. 1804, found by Searjant Gass.

10. a Specimen of Earth which forms a narrow Strata in the Bluffs above the Sand rock & beneath a large strata of blue earth Aug. 22, 1804. [*Tripoli nearly colourless & shistose.*]

11. Generally met with on the Surface of the earth in the level plains & is very common from the calumet Bluff to Fort mandan. [*Clay with aluminous impregnation derived from decomposed shistus.*]

12. Pebble found at the entrance of the River Quicourré. [*Agatised Flint.*]

13. 22ᵈ Aug. 1804. found occupying the interstices of a blue clay which forms the middle Strata of the Bluff & is about 15 feet in Depth. [*same as No. 6.*]

14. Specimen of the granulated spontaneous Salt, found at the licks on Salt River bran[ch] of the River Platte, obtained from the Oteoes. [*Muriat of Soda in form of an efflorescance.*]

15. Sept. 1, 1804. found exuding from a Strata of firm, blue earth which forms the majority of the River Bluffs [*a yellowish clay, probably arising from decomposed Slate.*]

16. Presented to me by a Mʳ Griffith near the entrance of the Missouri. This mineral was presented me by a Mʳ Griffith who informed me that it had been procured from an earth, found in a cave of limestone rock on the Mississipi a few miles from the entrance of the Missouri, by the same process observed in extracting saltpêtre from the earth of Caverns. [*a mixture of different kinds of Salts.*]

17.

18. Aug. 22   On the Upper part of the Bluff.

19

20. Aug. 22, 1804   Is usually found incrusting or overlaying a black Rock which crowns the Summits of most of the river Hills in this quarter. [*Sulphat [of] Lime ?*]

21. a specimen of a firm blue earth which formed a large strata of the Bluffs which we passed from 21 Augᵗ to 15 Sep. 1804. [*Aluminous Shistus in a state of decomposition.*]

22. found at the Calumet Bluff. [*also resembling " Atramentstein " similar to No. 4.*]

23. Salt obtained the 17 Sep. 1804 overlaying a dark blue Clay on

the sides of the river hills, it is so abundant that it impregnates the little rivulets in Such a degree that the water is unfit to drink. [*Alum intermixed with Clay.*]

24. Carbonated wood found on the St.ᵈ side of Riv[er] near fort Mandane 60 feet above high water mark in the Bank Strata 6 Inch thick.

25. Precipitate of one pint of Missouri water weight 80.65 grs [*p*[*r*]*incipally common Clay.*]

26. Pebbles common to the Sand Bars of the Missouri. [*Agatised flint & small quartzose pebbles.*]

27. Specimen of lead ore of Bertons mine on the Marimeg River. [*Galena or sulphuret of Lead.*]

28. *Green Earth*, Presented by Mʳ Charbono, who informed me that the natives procure this earth in the neighborhood of the Rocky mountains, but cannot point out the place. The Indians mix this Earth with glue & paint their arrows with it, when thus boiled with Glue it gives a fine green color to wood, but easily yields to Water the Indians also paint their skins with it. M. L. Feb'ʸ 13, 1805 [*Green Clay coloured by Iron.*]

29. Specimen of the lead ore of Bertons' mine on the Marrimic River Upper Louisiana. [*Galena.*]

30. Sep. 15, 1804 found in the interstices of a Brown rock which Sometimes makes its appearance in a strata of 6 or 8 feet usually about half of the Elevation of the Bluffs. [*Similar to 4 & 22.*]

31. Specimen of quartz [*Carbonat of Lime*] found on many parts of the Missouri common to the Mississipi & Ohio, probably a mixture of Glauber, common & Epsom salts with alumine. [*Rhomboidal carbonat of Lime.*]

32. Specimen of Globar Salts taken in Prairie of St.ᵈ Shore 22 Oct.ʳ 1804 many bushels could have been obtained. [*a mixture of various kinds of Salt with alumine.*]

33. Specimen of the Sand of the river Quicourre or Rapid River, [*quartz ore sand of a greyish white colour.*]

34. Obtained at the Calumet Bluffs [*principally fragments of argillaceous Iron ore.*]

35. Found on the N. Side of the River quicourre just above its entrance. [*Slate in a state of decomposition — with some Sulphat of Lime.*]

36. Found Sep. 6 on Larbord Shore encrusting a Rock — [*Alumine probably from decomposition of Shistus with saline impregnation tho' very slight.*]

37. Found at the upper part of the Big Bend.

38. found at the base of the Bluffs intermixed with loose earth 22 Aug. 1804. [*Pyrites.*]

39. Petrefactions obtained on the River Ohio in 1803.

40. Specimen of the Sand rock which forms the base of the Limestone Clifts in the neighborhood of the osag-Woman's river on the Missouri. [*fine grained sand stone.*]

41. Specimen of Earth which constitutes the majority of the Bluffs 23.ᵈ Aug 1804. when taken was in a firmer state than at present. [*Slate decomposed with Pyrites decomposed.*]

42. found at the upper Point of the Big Bend of the Missouri.

43. found above the white chalk Bluff in the Interstices of the Chalk rock [*Shistus decomposing with small crystals of Gypsum.*]

44. Aug. 23. 1804. Specimen of a bituminous substance found on the face of a sand rock, from which it appears to exude & forms by exposure to the air. This strata of sand rock is about 10 feet thick & forms a proportion of the lower part of the River Bluffs. [*Aluminous shistus in a state of decomposition.*]

45. Specimen of the Earth which forms the base of the Banks of the Missouri H. [*fine grey coloured sand.*]

46. Found at the Burning Cliffs 23 Aug. 1804. [*Pyrites.*]

47. Specimen of the Earth of which the Hills of the Missouri are principally formed from the entrance of the river Sioux to fort mandan & if Indian information may be depended upon, for several hundred miles further up It is in this tract of country that the Missouri acquires it[s] coloring matter of which it abates but little to its junction to the Mississipi. This earth when saturated by the rains or melting snows becomes so soft for many feet in depth, that being unable to support its own weight, it seperates into large masses from the hills & Slipping down their sides precipitates itself into the Missouri & mingles with its waters — great quantities of this earth are also thrown into the river by its subsidiary Streams & rivulets which pass thro' or originate in this tract of open Country. M. L. [*Slate in a decomposed state.*]

48. Sep. 10.ᵗʰ found on the side of the Bluffs not very abundant [*same as 47 — with streaks of green clay.*]

49. Aug. 22, 1804 found overlaying & intermixed with the Earth which forms the bluffs of the River. [*crystallized sulphate of Lime.*]

50. Aug. 24, 1804 Specimen of Pirites at the base of the Bluffs on the South side of the Missouri. [*Principally cubic Pyrites imbedded in argillaceous Shistus.*]

REMARKABLE HILLS ON THE UPPER MISSOURI

51. Specimen of Pirites found 22 Aug. 1804 at the base of the bluffs on the S. Side of the Mississipi. (only the label)

52. A Specimen of the Chalk found at the white Clay Bluffs on the S. Side of the Missouri. [*Argill?*]

53. Found at the White Clay Bluffs on S. side Missouri [*Pyrites in a state of efflorescence.*] (only the label)

54. from 24 Aug. to 10 Sep. 1804 Pyrites found intermixed promiscuously with the earth which form the Bluffs of the Missouri in a great variety of places. [*same as 53.*]

55. Incrustations of large round masses of rock which appear in a Sand bluff just above the entrance of the Cannonball river. This river derives its name from the appearance of these Stones many of them are as perfectly globular as art could form them. [*Carbonate of Lime be caustious that you do not confound this with the globular Pyrites. See No. 58 below.*]

56. Found on the side of the River bluffs. 22^d Aug. 1804 Irregularly intermixed with the Earth. [*Pyrites.*]

57. Pyrites found along the borders of the Missouri from 20 Augt to 10 Sep^r, they are very common on the borders of all the little Rivulets in this open Country. [*Some of these Pyrites are in a state of efflorescence.*]

58. Found 23^d Aug. 1804 at the base of the Bluff. [*Carbonat of Lime indeterminately crystallized & invested by compact carbonat of Lime.*]

59. A Specimen of calcareous rock, a thin Stratum of which is found overlaying a soft Sand rock which makes its appearance in many parts of the bluffs from the entrance of the River Platte to Fort Mandon. [*Mass of shells.*]

60. Found on the River Bank 1 Aug. 1804 (petrified [blank space in MS.] nest.)

61.

62. Specimen of the pummice Stone found amongst the piles of drift wood on the Missouri, sometimes found as low down as the mouth of the osage river. I can hear of no burning mountain in the neighborhood of the Missouri or its Branches, but the bluffs of the River are now on fire at several places, particularly that part named in our chart of the Missouri *The Burning Bluffs*. The plains in many places, throughout this great extent of open country, exhibit abundant proofs of having been once on fire. Witness the Specimens of Lava and Pummice-stone found in the Hills near fort mandon. [*Pumice.*]

63. Specimen of a Substance extremely common & found intermixed

with the loose Earth of all the Cliffs & Hills from the Calumet Bluff to Fort Mandon. [*crystallized Gypsum. Sulphated Li[me]*]]

64. Specimen of Carbonated wood with the loose sand of the sand-Bars of the Missouri & Mississipi, it appears in considerable quantities in many places [*carbonated wood.*]

65. Specimen of stone commonly met with on the surface of the Earth thro' a great proportion of the plain open country above the River Platte. [*Carbonat of Lime.*]

66. Found in the Bluffs near Fort Mandan. [*Petrefied wood.*]

67. A Specimen of Lava & pummice Stone found in great abundance on the sides of the Hills in the Neighborhood of Fort Mandan 1609 miles above the mouth of the Missouri — exposed by the washing of the Hills from the rains & melting Snow. These are merely the river Hills which are the banks only of a Valley formed by the Missouri, passing thro' a level plain — from the tops of these hills the country as far as the eye can reach is a level plain. The tract of Country which furnishes the Pummice Stone seen floating down the Missouri, is rather burning or burnt plains than burning mountains. [*Lavas.*]

68. Brought us by one of our hunters, John Shields who found it at the Allum Bluff 22 Aug. 1804. [*Pyrites on slate.*][1]

[The following note is found on the back fly-leaf of Codex R, in Lewis's hand.]

Sep. 20th

on the lard shore at the commencement of the big bend observed a clift of black porus rock which resembled *Lava* tho' on a closer examination I believe it to be calcarious and an imperfect species of the French *burr*   preserved a specemine, it is a brownish white, or black or yellowish brown.

---

[1] Comments by Prof. Edwin H. Barbour, curator of the geological museum, University of Nebraska : I scarcely dare guess just what is meant by some of the specimens referred to in the notes of Lewis and Clark. By "slate," to which frequent reference is made, is doubtless meant Pierre shale. By "tripoli" is probably meant volcanic ash or dust, which is very common throughout the great plains ; while tripoli, or diatomaceous earth, is rather rare. No. 21 is doubtless shale of the Benton or Pierre formations. No. 24 probably refers to lignite found in the region mentioned. The white deposits spoken of at times, are probably common salt and lime sulphate, which make a white coating.

VI. METEOROLOGY

LEWIS and Clark kept careful record of the weather and of various meteorological phenomena. Their data under this head appear scattered through various codices, having apparently been at different times written up from original memoranda. Seeking to avoid undue repetition, the Editor has combined all this material into one consecutive account, in form as nearly like the original as practicable. The accompanying notes explain the essential changes and combinations. — ED.]

Thermometrical observation[s] [1] shewing also the rise and fall of the Mississippi, appearances of weather winds &c at the mouth of the river Dubois commencing 1ˢᵗ Jany 1804. in Longitude 89° 57′ 45″ W. Latitude 38° 55′ 19″. 6. N. Thermometer on the N. Side of a large tree in the woods

Explanations

In the Miscellanious column or column of remarks are noted, the appearance quantity and thickness of the floating or stationary ice, the appearance and quantity of drift-wood, the appearance of birds, reptiles and insects in the spring disappearance in the fall, leafing flowering and seeding of plants, fall of leaf, access and recess of frost, debth of snows, their duration or disappearance.

Notation of the weather

   f. means fair
   c.   "   Cloudy
   r.   "   Rain
   s.   "   Snow
   h.   "   Hail

---

[1] The following explanations, in Lewis's handwriting, are found in a small blank-book which he had previously used in 1800, when paymaster in the army. They are also found (abridged) in Clark's handwriting, Codex C, p. 245; and repeated by Clark in Codex I, p. 13, where he arranges the weather diary from Fort Mandan. — ED.

t. means Thunder
l. " Lightning
a. " after — as f.a.r. means that it is *fair after rain* which has intervened
    since the last observation.
        c.a.s. — *Cloudy after Snow* intervening
        c.a.r.s. — cloudy after rain & snow.

Notation of the River
  R. means *risen* in the last 24 Hours ending at ☉ rise
  F. " *fallen* in the same period.
  Notation of Thermometer   *a. o* means *above naught* & *b. o visa versa*

REMARKS *on the* Thermometer [1]

1ᵗ — By two experiments made with Ferenhiets Thermometer which
was used in these observations, I assertained it's error to be 8° too
low or additive   I tested it with water and Snow mixed for the
friezing point, and boiling water for the point marked boiling
water.

Note when there is not room in the column for the necessary
remarks   it is transfired by the refference of numbers to an adjoining
part of this book. [2]

Diary *of the weather for* January, *1804.* [3]

Day of the month	Them: at ☉ rise	Weather	Wind	Them: at 4 o'Clock	Weather	Wind	River		
							rise or fall	Feet	In
1804 Jany 1	. . .	Cloudy	. . .	. . .	c	. . .	. . .	. .	. . .
" 2	. . .	c.a.s	. . .	. . .	c	. . .	. . .	. .	. . .
" 3	. . .	. . .	. . .	2½ a.	f.	N. W. by W	. . .	. .	. . .
" 4	11.a.	f.	W.	. . .	. . .	W	. . .	. .	. . .
" 5	. . .	f.	W.	. . .	f.	W.	. . .	. .	. . .
" 6	. . .	f.	W N W	30° a	f.	W. N. W	. . .	. .	. . .
" 7	. . .	h.	S. W.	. . .	c.a.r.h.	S. W	. . .	. .	. . .
" 8	. . .	f.	S. W.	. . .	f.	S. W	. . .	. .	. . .
" 9	. . .	f.	W. N. W.4	1° b.	c.	N. W. by W.	. . .	. .	. . .
" 10	. . .	f.	. . .	. . .	f.	. . .	. . .	. .	. . .

[1] This was entered in Lewis's book of thermometrical observations under caption
" *Notes of refference for Jany 1804,*" and is all that is entered thereunder. It is
found in Clark's Codex C, p. 246. — ED.

[2] This note is found at the head of the column " Remarks " in Lewis's book of
thermometrical observations. Clark placed it in Codex C, p. 246. — ED.

[3] This table was begun by Lewis in his book used for that purpose ; but after
January 1 the handwriting is all Clark's, as Lewis was absent in St. Louis. Clark
also copied this in his own set of tables, Codex C, p. 244, and in Clark-Voorhis note-
book No. 4. — ED.

[4] The absence of entries for January 10, 11, 12, 15, and 16, is explained by the
note " W. C. very sick."

Day of the month	Them: at ☉ rise	Weather	Wind	Them: at 4 o'Clock	Weather	Wind	River rise or fall	Feet	In
1804									
Jan᷃ 11	. . .	. . .	. . .	. . .	. . .	. . .	. . .	. .	. . .
" 12	. . .	. . .	S. W	. . .	. . .	. . .	. . .	. .	. . .
" 13	. . .	c.s.	S. W	. . .	r & s.	S. W.	. . .	. .	. . .
" 14	. . .	f a.s.	. . .	. . .	f.	. . .	. . .	. .	. . .
" 15	. . .	. . .	. . .	. . .	. . .	. . .	. . .	. .	. . .
" 16	. . .	. . .	. . .	. . .	. . .	. . .	. . .	. .	. . .
" 17	8.b	f.	N. W.	1½.b.	f.	N. W	f.	. .	6
" 18	1.b.	c.	N. W. W.	1.a	f.a.s	N W. W.	f.	. .	. . .
" 19	13 a	c.	N. W.	11.a	c.	N. W.	f	. .	. . .
" 20	5 b.	f	N. W.	8.a	c.	N. W.	f.	. .	. . .
" 21	7.a	c.s.	N. E.	17.a	s.h.	N. E.	f.	. .	. . .
" 22	11.a	s.	shifting	13.a.	s.	N. W.	f.	. .	. . .
" 23	11.a	c.	N. E.	17 a.	c.	N	f.	. .	. . .
" 24	4.a	c.	N. W.	11.a.	c.	W	f.	. .	. . .
" 25	2 b	f	W. N. W.	16.a.	f.	W	f.	. .	. . .
" 26	. . .	c	S W	. . .	c	S W	f	. .	. . .
" 27	. . .	f	. . .	. . .	f	. . .	. . .	. .	. . .
" 28	5.a	c.s	N W	18.a	c.a.s	N W	r	. .	. . .
" 29	16 a	f	W	23.a	f	. . .	r	. .	. . .
" 30	22.a	c. & s	N	16.a	f.a.s	. .	r	. .	. . .
" 31	10.a	f	S W by W	15.a	f.	W	r	. .	. . .

Remarks for January, 1804.[1]

1ˢᵗ Snow one Inch Deep
2ⁿᵈ Some Snow last night
3ʳᵈ hard wind
4ᵗʰ River covered with *ice* out of the Missouri
5ᵗʰ River Dubois rise
6ᵗʰ dᵒ dᵒ dᵒ snow
7ᵗʰ dᵒ dᵒ dᵒ
8ᵗʰ Ice run down River Dubois
9ᵗʰ Some Snow last night
10ᵗʰ Missouri rise
13ᵗʰ Snow'd last night Ice 5 In thick
14ᵗʰ dᵒ dᵒ dᵒ.
17ᵗʰ River Covered With Ice Some 5½ In: thick
19ᵗʰ No ice running
20ᵗʰ No ice passing to day snow 2½ hrs.
21ˢᵗ Ice running out of the Missoury 9 In. thick Snow 2½ Inches deep

---

1 These remarks are found in Codex C, p. 231. All remarks regarding events
have been transferred to text of journals, vol. i, pp. 4, 5, *ante.*— ED.

22nd Ice running out of the Missouri, Snow 5¾ In Deep.
23rd Ice Stoped
24th The Trees covered with ice
26th worm day
27th d°
28th ice running, cold &c.
26th worm [warm] day.
28th cold and Ice running
29th no Ice running
31st ice running

Diary of the weather for February, 1804.[1]

Day of the month	Them: at ⊙ rise	Weather	Wind	Them: at 4 oClock	Weather	Wind	River		
							rise or fall	Feet	In
1804 Feby 1	10.a	f.	S. W.	20.a	f.	S. W S	r.	.	1½
2	12.a	f.	N. W.	10 a	f.	N. W.	r.	..	1½
3	12.a	f.	S. W.	19.a	f.	W.	...	..	.
4	17.a	f.	S. W.	28.a	f.	S.	r.	..	½
5	18.a	f.	S. E.	31.a	c.a.f.	S. E. S.	r.	2	6½
6	19.a	f.	N. W.	15.a	c	S	...	..	...
7	29 a	r.a.c	S. E.	30.a	r & c.	S E.	f.	..	8
8	22 a	c.a.r	N. W.	20.a	c.a.s.	N.	r.	1	...
9	10 a	f.a.s	N. N. E.	12.a	c	N. E.	r.	2	...
10	3.a	f.	N. E.	17.a	f.	S. W.	r.	1	4
11	18.a	c.a.h.	S. E.	31.a	s a.h.f	S. E.	r.	1	...
12	15.a	f.	S. S. E	25.a	f.	S. W.	f.	..	2
13	12.a	f.	N. W.	20.a	f.	W.	r. & f.	..	1
14	15.a	f.	S. W.	32.a	f.	S. W.	...	..	...
15	18.a	f.	S. W.	32.a	f.	W.	.	..	...
16	28.a	c.	S. E.	30.a	c.a.r.	S. E.	r.	..	2½
17	15.a	c.a.r.	S. W.	32.a	f.	W.	r.	..	2
18	10.a	f.	N. W.	...	.	...	r.	..	7½
19	10.a	f.	N. W.	...	...	...	...	..	...
20	10 a	f.	N. W.	28.a	...	S. W.	f.	..	2½
21	20.a	f.	N. W.	34.a	...	N. W.	f.	..	1½
22	14.a	f.	N. E.	26.a	...	N. E.	r.	..	1½
23	6.a	f.	N. W.	24.a	...	N. W.	r.	..	1
24	6.a	f.	N. E.	26.a	...	N. E.	f.	..	2
25	20.a	f.	N. E	28.a	...	S. S. W.	...	..	...
26	16.a	f.	N. E.	30.a	...	N. E.	f.	.	½
27	4.a	c.	N. E.	24 a	r. & s.	N. W.	f.	..	1
28	4.a	c.s.	N. W.	6.a	c.a.s.	N. W.	f.	..	2
29	8.a	h.s.	N. W.	12.a	c.a.s.	N. W.	f.	..	2½

[1] The weather diary for February is found in the same places as that for January. Lewis made his own entries until the 15th; the rest of the month is in Clark's handwriting. — ED.

[*Remarks for February, 1804.*]¹

Feby 1st the wind blew hard,   no frost, snow disapearing fast

2nd Frost this morning,   the Snow has disapeared in Spots.

3rd Frost this morning,   the Snow thaws considerably   raised the Boat &c.

4th Frost,   number of Swan & Gees from N. & S.

5th emmence quantity of ice running, some of Which is 11 Inches thick

6th a quantity of soft ice running   white frost,   the snow disappeared   Swans passing.

7th a Small quantity of floating *ice* passing   Swans passing.

8th Many Swans from N W.   Creek rose & took of[f] the water mark.

9th The River rose 2 feet   large quantity of drift ice from the Missouri.

10th Ice Still drifting in considerable quantities   Some Gees pass from the S.

11th The Sugar Maple runs freely,   Swans pass from the North.

12th Pigeons Gees & Ducks of Various kinds have ret^d

13th the first appearance of the blue crain.

14th but little drift *ice*   the Mississippi is not broken up.   Sugar trees run

15th emmence quantity of Swan in the mars[h].

21st in the evening the river began to rise ½ Inch.

23^d [river] fall in the evening ½ Inch.

25th River on a stand.

27th The River rose 3 inches and fell imediately

28th began to Snow and continued all day

29th Snow all night & untill 11 oClock a.m. & Cleared away the weather had been clear since Capt Lewis lef[t] Camp untill this.²

---

¹ See note for January, 1804. — ED.

² This note is found in Clark's Codex C, p. 230, and in Lewis's Codex P, fly-leaf. — ED.

Diary of the weather for March, 1804.[1]

Day of the month	Them:[2] at ☉ rise	Weather	Wind	Them:[2] at 4 oClock	Weather	Wind	River rise or fall	Feet	In
1804 March 1	20 b	f.	N. W.	4 b	...	N. W.	f.	..	9
2	19.b	f.	N. W.	14 a	...	E.	f.	..	3
3	18.b	f.	E.	10.a	...	S. W.	f.	..	6½
4	4.b	f.	N. E.	12.a	...	E.	f.	..	5
5	2.a	f.	N. W.	12.a	...	N. W.	f.	..	3
6	4.b	f.	N. W.	2.a	...	N. W.	f.		3
7	16.b	c & s.	N. W.	10.a	s.	N. W.	...	..	...
8	2.b	c & s	N. W.	12.a	s.	N. W.	f.	..	1½
9	10.a	c.	N. W.	20.a	c.	N. W.	r.	..	2
10	6.a	c & f.	N. W.	24 a	f.	N. W.	r.	..	2½
11	12.a	f.	E.	20.a	f.	S. W.	f.	..	2½
12	14.a	f.	N. E.	16.a	f.	N. E.	r.	..	1½
13	8.a	f.	N. W.	12.a	f.	N. W.	f.	..	1½
14	4.a	f.	N. E.	10.a	f.	N. E.	f.	..	4½
15	6.b	c & s	N. W.	40.a	r. a. s	N. E.	r.	..	5
16	2.b	f.	E.	40.a	f.	S. S. W.	r.	..	11
17	12.a	f.	N. E.	38.a	f.	N. E.	r.	..	7
18	2.a	f.	E.	44.a	f.	N. E.	f.	..	3
19	2.a	f.	N. E.	52.a	f.	S. S. W	f.	..	2½
20	4.a	f.	E.	60.a	f.	S. S. W.	f.	..	1½
21	26.a	f.	S. S. W.	46.a	f.	N. W.	f.	..	2
22	22.a	f.	N. W.	40.a	f.	N. W.	f.	..	2
23	14.a	f.	N. E.	44.a	f.	N. E.	r.	..	4
24	6.a	f.	E.	52.a	f.	S. S. W.	r.	1	5½
25	16.a	f.	S. S. W.	46.a	f.	E.	r.	2	...
26	18 a	f.	E.	44.a	f.	E.	r.	..	10
27	34.a	r & t.	E.	42.a	f. a. r.	N. E.	r.	..	7
28	34 a	c.	N. E.	44.a	c.	E.	r.	..	5½
29	20.a	r. a. t	N. E.	30 a	h. r.	N. E.	r.	..	1
30	...	c. a. r	N. W.	...	f.	N. W.	r.	..	2
31	...	f.	N. W.	...	f.	N. W.	r.	..	2

[Remarks for March, 1804.][3]

March 7th Saw the first Brant return.

    8th Rain Suceeded by Snow & hail

    9th Cloudy in the morning and cleared up.

[1] The diary of the weather for March, 1804, is found in Lewis's book of thermo-metrical observations (chiefly in Clark's handwriting) and in Clark's Codex C, p. 242. — ED.

[2] The thermometer having been tested and found 8° too low (see previous note), that amount was added to the records by Lewis in his diary, but not by Clark. Clark's figures are here given. — ED.

[3] The following remarks are found in Lewis's handwriting on the fly-leaf and p. 1 of Codex P; in Clark's handwriting, in Codex C, pp. 228, 229. The references to events have been transferred to text of journal, volume i, p. 4, *ante.* — ED.

20.th The Weather has been generally fair but verry cold, the ice run for Several days in such quantities that it was impossible to pass the River. Saw the 1.st *Snake* which was the kind usially tirmed the *Garter* Snake, saw also a *Beatle* of black colour with two red stripes on his back passing each other Crosswise, from the but of the wing towards the extremity of the Same.

20th Heard the first frogs

25th Saw the 1.st White *Crains* return

26th the weather warm and fair.

27.th The buds of the Spicewood appeared, and the tausels of the mail Cotton wood were larger than a large mulberry, and Which [were] the Shape and colour of that froot, Some of them had fallen from the trees. the grass begins to Spring. The weather has been warm, and no falling weather untill this time tho the atmispere has been verry Smokey and thick, a heavy fall of rain commenced which continued untill 12 at night, attended with thunder, and lightning. Saw large insects which resembled musquitors, but doubt whether they are really those insects or the fly which produces them, they attemped to bite my horse, but I could not observe that they made any impression with their Beaks.

28th day cloudy and warm.

31st Windey.

Diary of the weather for April, 1804.[1]

Day of the month	Them:[2] at ☉ rise	Weather	Wind	Them:[2] at 4 oClock	Weather	Wind	River rise or fall	Feet	In
1804 April 1	. . .	f.	N. E.	. . .	f.	N. E.	r.	.	2 ½
2	8.a.	f.	. . .	. . .	f.	N. E.	r.	. .	3 ½
3	42.a	f.	N. E.	. . .	r.	N. E.	r.	. .	3 ½
4	44.a	c.a.r.	N. W.	. . .	. . .	. . .	r.	. .	11
5	24.a	c.a.r.	N. E.	. . .	t.a.r.	. . .	r.	. .	2
6	18.a	c.a.r.	N. W.	. . .	s.a.r.	. . .	f.	.	4 ½

[1] The diary of the weather for April, 1804, is found in Lewis's book of thermometrical observations (chiefly in Clark's handwriting) and in Clark's Codex C, p. 241. — ED.

[2] The thermometrical notations should be amended here by the addition of 8°, as explained in note for March diary. — ED.

Day of the month	Them: at ☉ rise	Weather	Wind	Them: at 4 oClock	Weather	Wind	River rise or fall	Feet	In.
1804 April 7	10.a	f.a.c.	N. W.	. . .	c.	. . .	f.	. .	2
8	10.a	c.	N. E.	. . .	c.r.	. . .	f.	. .	2 ½
9	18.a	f.a.c.	N. E.	. . .	c.	. . .	f.	. .	2
10	10.a	f.	N. W.	. . .	f.	. . .	f.	. .	6 ½
11	10.a	f.	N. E.	. . .	f.	. . .	f.	. .	7 ½
12	16.a	c.	N. W.	. . .	f.a.c.	. . .	f.	. .	7
13	26.a	c.	N. E.	. . .	c.	. . .	f.	. .	6 ½
14	22.a	f.	S. W.	. . .	f.	. . .	f.	. .	5
15	22 a	f.	N. W.	. . .	. . .	. . .	f.	. .	6 ½
16	36.a	c.	N. W.	. . .	f.a.c.	. . .	f.	. .	5 ½
17	26.a	f.a.c.	N. W.	. . .	f.	. . .	f.	. .	5
18	16.a	f.a.c	N. N. W.	. . .	c.	. . .	f.	. .	3
19	34.a	r.	S. S. E.	. . .	. . .	. . .	f.	. .	4
20	34 a	c.r.	S. E.	37.a	r.	S. E.	f.	. .	3 ½
21	31.a	r.	S. W.	42.a	f.a.r.	W.	r.	1	2
22	28.a	c.	N. W.	34 a	c.	N. W.	r.	1	6
23	22.a	f.	N. W.	64 a	f.	W.	f.	. .	1
24	36.a	f.	N. W.	44.a	f.	N. W.	r.	. .	8
25	26 a	f.	N. W.	38.a	c.	N. W.	r.	. .	2 ½
26	16.a	f.	N. W.	58.a	f.	N. W.	f.	. .	6
27	28.a	c. & r.	W.	62.a	f.	S. W.	f.	. .	8
28	30.a	f.	N. W.	64.a	f.	N. W.	f.	. .	7
29	32.a	f.	N. W.	52.a	f.	S. E.	f.	. .	7
30	18.a	f.	S. E.	56.a	f.	N. E.	f.	. .	6

[*Remarks for April 1804.*[1]]

April 1st The Spicewood is in full bloe, the dogs tooth violet, and may apple appeared above ground, a northern light appeared at 10 oClock P.M. verry red.

3d a cloudy day.

5th the buds of the peaches, apples & Cherrys appear

6th A large flock of Pellicans appear.

7th the leaves of some of the Apple trees have burst their coverts and put forth, the lieves of the green wood bushes have put foth. Maney of the wild plants have Sprung up and appear above ground. Cold air.

9th Windey

10th no appearance of the buds of the Osage apple, the Osage Plumb has put forth their leaves and flower buds : tho it is not yet completely in bloe.

---

[1] The following remarks are found partly in Lewis's book of thermometrical observations and partly in Codex C, pp. 227, 228. The references to events have been transferred to our volume i, pp. 4, 7, *ante.* — ED.

13th The peach trees are partly in blume   the brant, Geese, Duck, Swan, Crain and other aquatic birds have disappeared verry much, within a fiew days and have gorn further North I prosume.   the Summer duck raise their young in this neighbourhood and are now here in great numbers

17th Wind verry high every day since the 3rd instant.   Some frost today.   Peach trees in full Bloome,   the Weaping willow has put forth its leaves and are $^{1}/_{5}$ of their size,   the *violet* the *doves foot*, & *cowslip* are in bloe,   the *dogs* tooth violet is not yet in blume.   The trees of the forest particularly the Cotton wood begin to obtain from their Size of their buds a Greenish cast at a distance   the Gooseberry which is also in this countrey and lilack have put forth their leaves.

18th Windey Day

26th The White frost Killed much froot near Kahokia, while that at St Louis escaped with little injurey.

30th White frost, Slight did but little injurey.

Diary of the weather for May, 1804.[1]

Day of the month	Them:[2] at ☉ rise	Weather	Wind	Them:[2] at 4 oClock	Weather	Wind	River		
							rise or fall	Feet	In
1804 May 1st	20.a	f.	S. E.	54.a	f.	N. E.	f.	. .	4½
2	19.a	f.	S. E.	68.a	f.	S. S. E	f.	. .	6
3	24.a	f.	S. S. E.	72.a	f.	S. S W	f.	. .	4½
4	40 a	t.l.c.r	S.	56.a	c.a.r.	S.	r.	. .	2
5	42.a	t.l.r.	W.	58.a	c.a.r	f.	r.	. .	2½
6	34.a	f.	S. W.	70.a	f.	S. W.	f.	. .	2½
7	38.a	f.	S. E.	52.a	f.	S. S. W.	f.	. .	4½
8	44.a	f.	N. E.	62.a	f.	S. W.	f.	. .	4
9	42.a	f.	E.	76.a	f.	S. W.	f.	. .	2
10	46.a	c.	N. E.	67.a	f.	N W.	f.	. .	3½
11	40.a	f.	E.	70.a	f.	S. W.	f.	. .	2½
12	36 a	f.	E	72 a	f.	W.	f.	. .	3
13	42.a	c.a.r.	W.	40.a	c.a.r.	N. W.	f.	. .	2
14	34.a	c.	S. E.	56.a	f.	N.	. . .	. .	. . .

1 The diary for May is found in the same places as that for April.   For some unexplained reason no notations were kept after leaving River Dubois, until September 19, 1804. — ED.

2 Lewis's diary adds 8° to each figure in these columns, as previously explained. — ED.

[Remarks for May, 1804.] [1]

May 5th Thundered & lightened excessively this morning
10th distant Thunder, Sultrey this evening.
12th the wind at 4 was uncommonly hard.
14th Set out from the River Dubois up the Missouri
25th Strawberries in the Praries ripe & abundant
27th Survis berries or wild currents ripe & abundant.
30th Mulberries begin to ripen, abundant in the Bottom of the river.

Remarks for June and July 1804. [2]

June 10th Perple Rasberreis ripe & abundant
11th many Small birds are now setting. Some have young, the whipper Will Setting.
16th The Wood Duck now have it's young, this Duck is abundant, and except one solitary Pelican and a fiew gees, these ducks were the only aquatic fowls we have yet seen.
July 1st Saw Some Geese With their young, caught Several, they are not yet feathered nor can they fly. the old geese are in the same Situation at this season.
4th a great number of young geese and Swan in a *lake* opposit to the mouth of the 4th of July Creek, in this lake there is also an abundance of fish of various Species, the pike, perch, carp, or *buffaloe fish* cat. Sunperch &c. &c.
12th The Deer and Bear begin to get scearce and the Elk begin to appear
23rd Cat fish is verry Common and easy taken in any part of this river. Some are nearly White perticilarly above the Platte River.

[1] Combined from Lewis's book of thermometrical observations and Clark's Codex C, pp. 226, 227. — ED.
[2] Combined from Lewis's book of thermometrical observations and Clark's Codex C, p. 226. — ED.

Diary of the weather for September, 1804.[1]

Day of the month	Them: at ☉ rise	Weather	Wind	Them: at 4 oClock	Weather	Wind	River rise or fall	Feet	In
1804 Sept 19	46.a	f.	S. E.	71.a	f.	S. E.	. . .	. .	. . .
20	51.a	f.	S. E.	70.a	f.	S. E.	. . .	. .	. . .
21	58.a	f.	S. W.	88.a	f.	S. W.	. . .	. .	. . .
22	52.a	f.	E.	82.a	f.	S. E.	. . .	. .	. . .
23	50.a	f.	S. E.	86.a	f.	S. E.	. . .	. .	. . .
24	54.a	f.	E.	82.a	f.	W.	. . .	. .	. . .
25	50.a	f.	S. W.	79.a	f.	W.	. . .	. .	. . .
26	54.a	f.	W.	78.a	f.	S. W.	. . .	. .	. . .
27	52.a	f.	W.	86.a	f.	S. W.	. . .	. .	. . .
28	45.a	f.	S. E.	80 a	f.	S. E.	. . .	. .	. . .
29	45 a	f.	S. E.	67.a	f.	S. E.	. . .	. .	. . .
30	42.a	c. a. r.	S. E.	52.a	c. a. r.	S. E.	. . .	. .	. . .

Remarks for September, 1804.[2]

September 19th The leaves of Some of the Cottonwood begin to fade, yesterday saw the 1st brant passing from the N. W. to S.E.

20th The Antilope is now ruting, the swallow has disapeared 12 days.

21st The Elk is now ruting the Buffalow is nearly ceased the latter Commence the latter end of July or 1st of August.

22nd a little foggy this morning, a great number of green leged plover passing down the river, also some Geese & Brant.

23rd The Aire remarkably dry. plumbs & grapes fully ripe. in 36 hours two Spoonfuls of water aveporated in a Sauser.

27th Saw a large flock of white gulls with wings tiped with black

---

1 The weather diary for this portion of September, 1804, is found in Lewis's book of thermometrical observations and Clark's Codex C, p. 239. — ED.

2 The following remarks are found in Lewis's book of thermometrical observations and Clark's Codex C, p. 225. References to events described in text of journals are here omitted. — ED

Diary of the weather for October, 1804.[1]

Day of the month	Them: at ☉ rise	Weather	Wind	Them: at 4 oClock	Weather	Wind	River		
							rise or fall	Feet	In
1804 Oct. 1	40.a	c.	S. E.	46.a	c.	S E	. . .	. .	. . .
2	39.a	f.	S. E.	75.a	c.	N. W.	. . .	. .	. . .
3	40.a	c.	N. W.	45.a	c.a.r.	N. W.	. . .	. .	. . .
4	38.a	c.a.r.	N. W.	50.a	c.	N W.	. . .	. .	. . .
5	36.a	f.	N. W.	54.a	f.	N. W.	. . .	. .	. . .
6	43.a	f.	N. W.	60.a	f.	N. W.	. . .	. .	. . .
7	45.a	c.	S. E.	58.a	f.	S E.	. . .	. .	. . .
8	48.a	f.	N. W.	62.a	f.	N. W.	. . .	. .	. . .
9	45.a	c.	N. E.	50.a	c.a.r.	N.	. . .	. .	. . .
10	42.a	f.a.r.	N. W.	67.a	f.	N. W.	. . .	. .	. . .
11	43 a	f.	N. W.	59.a	f.	N. W.	. . .	. .	. . .
12	42.a	f.	S.	65.a	f.	S E.	. . .	. .	. . .
13	43.a	f.	S. W.	49.a	c.a.r.	S E.	. . .	. .	. . .
14	42.a	r.	S. E.	40.a	r.	S E.	. . .	. .	. . .
15	46 a	r.	N.	57.a	f.a.r.	N. W.	. . .	. .	. . .
16	45.a	c.	N. E.	50.a	f.	N. E	. . .	. .	. . .
17	47.a	f.	N. W.	54.a	f.	N. W.	. . .	. .	. . .
18	30 a	f.	N. W.	68.a	f.	N. W.	. . .	. .	. . .
19	43.a	f.	S. E.	62.a	f.	S.	. . .	. .	. . .
20	44.a	f.	N. W.	48.a	f.	N.	. . .	. .	. . .
21	31.a	s.	N. W.	34.a	s.	N. W.	. . .	. .	. . .
22	35.a	c.a.s.	N. E.	42.a	c.	N. E.	. . .	. .	. . .
23	32.a	s.	N. W.	45.a	c.	N. E.	. . .	. .	. . .
24	33.a	s.a.f.	N. W	51.a	c.a.s.	N. W.	. . .	. .	. . .
25	31.a	c.	S. E.	50.a	c.	S. E.	. . .	. .	. . .
26	42.a	f.	S. E.	57.a	f.	S. E.	. . .	. .	. . .
27	39.a	f.	S. W.	58 a	f.	S. W.	. . .	. .	. . .
28	34.a	f.	S. W.	54.a	f.	S. W.	. . .	. .	. . .
29	32.a	f.	S. W.	59.a	f.	S. W.	. . .	. .	. . .
30	32.a	f.	S. W.	52.a	f.	S. W.	. . .	. .	. . .
31	33.a	f.	W.	48.a	f.	W.	. . .	. .	. . .

Remarks for October, 1804.[2]

October 1st The leaves of the ash, poplar and most of the shrubs begin to turn yellow and decline.

3rd The earth and sand which forms the bars of the river are so fully impregnated with salt that it shoots and adhers

---

[1] The following table is found in Lewis's book of thermometrical observations and Clark's Codex C, pp. 238, 239. — ED.

[2] The following remarks are found in Lewis's book of thermometrical observations and Clark's Codex C, pp. 222–224. References to events described in text of journals are here omitted. — ED.

to the little sticks which appear on the surface,   it is pleasant & seems niterous.

5ᵗʰ Slight white frost last night   Geese & Brant passing South.

6ᵗʰ frost as last night   saw teal, mallards & Gulls large.

9ᵗʰ Wind blew hard this morning drove the boat from her ancker, came to Shore,   Some Brant & Gees passing to the South.

11ᵗʰ no fogg or dew this morning nor have we seen either for many days (i. e.) since the 21ˢᵗ of Septʳ.

14ᵗʰ Cotton wood all yellow, and the leaves bigin to fall, abundance of Grapes & red berries.   the leaves of all the trees as Ash, elm, &c except the Cotton wood is now fallen.

17ᵗʰ saw a large flock of White Brant with Black wings, Antelopes are passing to the Black mountains to winter as is their custom.

18ᵗʰ Hard frost last night,   the clay near the water edge was frozen as was the water in the vessels exposed to the air.

19ᵗʰ No mule Deer Seen above the Chyanne R. none at the Recares

20ᵗʰ Much more timber than usual.   Saw the first black haws that we have seen for a long time.

21ˢᵗ The snow fall ½ inch deep.

25ᵗʰ this evening passed a rapid and shole place in the river were obliged to get out and drag the boat.   all the leaves of the trees have now fallen.   the snow did not lye.

28ᵗʰ Wind so hard that we could not go into council.

29 We Spoke to the Indians in Council tho' the winds was so hard that it was extremely disagreeable, the Sands was blown on us in clouds.

30 Examoned the Countrey in advance for Several Leagues for a place for winter encampment without finding a Spot Calculated for one

Diary of the weather for November, 1804[1]

Day of the month	Them: at ☉ rise	Weather	Wind	Them: at 4 oClock	Weather	Wind	River rise or fall	Feet	In.
Nov. 1	31.a	f.	N. W.	47 a	f.	N. W	...	..	...
2	32.a	f.	S. E.	63.a	f.	S. E.	...	..	...
3	32.a	f.	N. W.	53.a	f.	N. W.	...	..	...
4	31.a	f.	N. W.	43.a	c.	W.	...	..	...
5	30.a	c.	N. W.	58.a	c.	N. W.	...	..	...
6	31 a	c.	S. W.	43.a	c.	W.	...	..	...
7	43.a	c.	S.	62.a	c.	S.	...	..	...
8	38.a	c.	S.	39.a	c.	W.	...	..	...
9	27 a	f	N. W.	43.a	f.	N. W.	...	..	...
10	34.a	f.	N. W.	36.a	c.	N. W.	...	..	...
11	28.a	f.	N. W.	60.a	f.	N. W.	...	..	...
12	18.a	f.	N.	31.a	f.	N. E.	...	..	...
13	18.a	s.	S. E.	28.a	c. a. s.	S. E.	f.	..	1½
14	24 a	s	S. E.	32.a	c. a. s	S. E.	r.	..	1
15	22.a	c.	N. W.	31.a	c. a. s.	N. W.	r	..	½
16	25 a	c.	N. W.	30.a	f.	S. E.	r.	..	¼
17	28.a	f	S. E.	34.a	f.	S. E.	r.	..	¼
18	30 a	f.	S. E.	38.a	f.	W.	r.	..	¼
19	32.a	f.	N. W.	48.a	f.	N. W.	r.	..	1
20	35 a	f.	N. W.	50.a	f.	W.	r.	..	1¼
21	33.a	c.	S.	49.a	f.	S. E.	r.	..	...
22	37.a	f.	W.	45 a	f.	N. W.	r.	..	½
23	38 a	f.	W.	48.a	f.	N. W.	...	..	...
24	36.a	f.	N. W.	34.a	f.	N. W.	...	..	...
25	34 a	f.	W.	32.a	f.	S. W.	...	..	...
26	15.a	f.	S. W.	21.a	f.	W.	...	..	...
27	10.a	f.	S. E.	19.a	c.	S. E.	f.	..	3
28	12.a	s.	S. E.	15.a	s.	E.	f.	..	4
29	14.a	c. a. s	N. E.	18.a	f.	W.	f.	..	2½
30	17.a	f.	W.	23 a	f.	W.	f.	2	...

Remarks for November, 1804.[2]

Nov. 1st The winds blew so hard to day that we could not decend the river to a proper place to Camp, untill after 5 P.M. when the Boat droped down

3rd Wind blew hard all day

4th Wind hard this evening.

---

[1] The following table is found in Lewis's book of thermometrical observations and in Clark's Codex C, pp. 238, 239. — ED.

[2] The following remarks are found in Lewis's book of thermometrical observations and Clark's Codex C, pp. 220,221. References already entered in text of journals are here omitted. — ED.

6th Some little hail about noon.

7th a fiew drops of rain this evening saw the Arrora. boriales at
10 P.M. it was very brillient in perpendicular Columns
frequently Changeing position.

8th Since we have been at our present Station the River has
fallen about 9 inches

9th verry hard frost this morning.

10th maney Gees passing to the S. saw a flock of the crested
Cherry birds passing to the South

13th large quantity of drift ice running this morning the river
haveing appearancies of closing for the winter.

16th very hard frost this morning attached to the limbs and
boughs of the trees.

17th The frost of yesterday remained on the trees untill 2 P.M.
when it decended like a Shower of Snow, Swans passing
from the N.

20th little soft ice this morning, that from the board[er] of the
river came down in such manner as to endanger the
boat.

26th wind blew verry hard.

27th much drift ice running in the river.

29th the snow fell 8 inches deep, it drifted in heaps in the open
ground.

30th the indians pass over the river on the ice. Capt. Clark
returned in the evening on the ice.

Diary of the weather for December, 1804.[1]

Day of the month	Them: at ⊙; rise	Weather	Wind	Them: at 4 oClock	Weather	Wind	River		
							rise or fall	Feet	In
Dec. 1	10 b.	f.	E.	6.a	f.	S. E.	r.	1	. . .
2	33.a	f.	N. W.	36.a	f.	N. W.	r.	. .	1
3	26.a	f.	N. W.	30.a	f.	N. W.	r.	. .	1
4	18.a	f.	N.	29 a	f.	N.	r.	. .	1
5	14.a	c.	N. E.	27.a	s.	N. E.	. . .	. .	. . .
6	10.a	s.	N. W.	11.a	c.a.s.	N. W.	. . .	. .	. ½
7	0.	f.	N. W.	1.b	c.	N. W.	r.	2	½
8	12.b	s.	N. W.	5.b	f.a.s.	N. W.	. . .	. .	. . .
9	7.a	f.	E.	10 b	f.	N. W.	. . .	. .	. . .
10	10.b	c.	N.	11.b	c	N.	r.	. .	1 ½

1 The following table is found in Lewis's book of thermometrical observations
and Clark's Codex C, pp. 236, 237, and Clark-Voorhis note-book No. 4. — ED.

Day of the month	Them: at ☉ rise	Weather	Wind	Them: at 4 oClock	Weather	Wind	River		
							rise or fall	Feet	In.
Dec. 11	21.b	f.	N.	18.b	f.	N.	f.	..	½
12	38.b	f.	N.	16.b	f.	N.	...	..	...
13	20.b	f.	S. E.	4.b	c.	S. E.	...	..	..
14	2.b	c.	S. E.	2.a	s.	S. E.	f.	..	1
15	8.b	c.a.s.	W.	4.b	c.a.s.	W.	...	..	...
16	22.b	f.	N. W.	4.b	f.	N. W.	f.	..	1
17	43.b	f.	N.	28.b	f.	N.	r.	..	3
18	32.b	f.	W.	16.b	f.	S. W.	r.	..	1
19	2.b	c.	S. W.	16.a	f.	S.	r.	..	1
20	24.a	c.	N. W.	37.a	f.	N. W.	r.	..	3½
21	22.a	f.	N. W.	22 a	c.	N. W.	r.	..	2
22	10.a	f.	N. W.	23.a	f.	N. W.	r	..	2½
23	18.a	c.	S. W.	27.a	c.	W.	f	..	1
24	22.a	s.	S. W.	31.a	c.a.s.	W.	f.	..	2½
25	15.a	s.	N. W.	20.a	c.a.s.	N. W.	f.	..	1
26	18.a	c.	N. W.	21.a	f	N. W.	...	..	...
27	4 b	c.	N. W.	14.a	c.	N. W.	...	..	...
28	12.a	f.	N.	13.a	f.	N. W.	r.	..	2½
29	9.b	f.	N.	3.a	f.	N.	r.	..	1
30	20 b	f.	N.	11.b	f.	N.	r.	..	½
31	10.b	f.	S. E.	12.a	c.	S. W.	r.	..	1½

Remarks for December, 1804.[1]

Dec. 1st   Ice thick.

2nd   wind hard

Dec. 5th   Wind blew excessively hard this night from the NW.

7th: last night the river blocked up with ice which was 1½ inches thick in the part that had not previously frozen. The Buffaloe appear   Capt. Lewis go out with a party in quest of them kill 14.   the Mandanes take two.

8th: Capt. Clark was hunting the Buffaloe this day with 16 Men. severall of the men frosted   killed 3 buffaloe himself and the party killed 5 others.

9th: [Capt. Lewis] went hunting with a party of fifteen men killed 10 Buffaloe and 1 deer   staid out all night.   no blanket

14th: Capt. Clark sets out with a hunting party on the ice with three small sleds.

15th: Snow fall ½ inch.   visited by the big man & the big white inform me that many buffaloe have visited the Grosventers

---

[1] The following remarks are found in Lewis's book of thermometrical observations and Clark's Codex C, pp. 219, 220, also Clark-Voorhis note-book No. 4. Such records of events have been retained as indicate features of the weather. — ED.

on the opposite side of the river they came from the west.

17th this evening the Ther.[r] stood at 42 b. o

24th Snow verry considerable

26th Much frost

27th The trees are all white with frost which attached itself to their boughes

28th It blew verry hard last night the frost fell like a Shower of Snow

Diary of the weather for January, 1805.[1]

Day of the month	Them: at ☉ rise	Weather	Wind	Them: at 4 oClock	Weather	Wind	River		
							rise or fall	Feet	In
1805 Jany 1	18.a	s.	S. E.	34.a	f.	N. W.	r.	..	1
2	4.b	s.	N. W.	8.b	f.a.s.	N.	...	..	...
3	14.b	c.	N.	4.b	s	S. E.	...	..	...
4	28.a	c.a.s.	W.	4.b	c.	N. W.	r.	..	2½
5	20.b	c.	N. W.	18.b	s.	N.E.	r.	..	2
6	11.b	c.a.s.	N. W.	16.b	f.	N. W.	r.	..	3
7	22.b	f	N. W.	14.b	f.	W.	f.	..	1
8	20.b	f.	N. W.	10.b	f.	N. W.	r.	..	1
9	21.b	f.	W.	18.b	f.a.c.	N. W.	...	..	...
10	40.b	f.	N. W.	28.b	f.	N. W.	r	..	1
11	38.b	f.	N. W.	14.b	f.	N. W.	f.	..	½
12	20.b	f.	N. W.	16.b	f.	N. W.	r.	..	1
13	34.b	f.	N. W.	20.b	f.	N. W.	r	..	2
14	16.b	s.	S E.	8.b	c.a.s.	S. E.	...	..	...
15	10.b	f.	E.	3.a	c.	S. W.	r.	..	1
16	36.a	c.	W.	16.a	f.	S. W.	r.	..	2½
17	2.b	c.	W.	12.b	f.	N. W.	...	..	...
18	1.b	f.	N. W.	7.a	f a.c.	N. W.	f.	..	1
19	12.a	c.	N. E.	6.b	f.	N. W.	r.	..	1
20	28.a	f.	N. E.	9.b	c.	S. E.	r.	..	½
21	2 b	c.	N. E.	8.a	f.	S. E.	...	..	...
22	10 a	f.a.h	N W.	19.a	c.	N. W.	r.	..	1¾
23	21.b	s.	E.	2 b	c.a.s.	N.	f.	..	2½
24	12.b	c.	N. W.	2.b	f.	N. W.	r.	..	¼
25	26.b	f.	N. W.	4.b	f.a.c.	W.	...	..	...
26	12.a	c	N. E.	20.a	f.a.c	S. E	...	..	...
27	20.a	c.	S. E	16.a	c.	N. W.	r.	..	2
28	2.b	f.	N. W.	15.a	f.	S. W.	...	..	...
29	4.a	f.	S. W.	16.a	f.	W.	r.	..	½
30	6.a	c.	N. W.	14.a	c.	N. W.	r.	..	1
31	2.b	c.a.s.	N. W.	8.a	f.a.c.	N. W.	f.	..	1

[1] The following table is found in Lewis's book of thermometrical observations and Clark's Codex C, pp. 235, 236, also Clark-Voorhis note-book No. 4. — ED.

Remarks for January, 1805.[1]

January 3ʳᵈ   the Snow is 9 Inches Deep

6ᵗʰ   at 12 oClock to day two Luminous Spots appeared on either side of the Sun extreemely bright.

8ᵗʰ   The Snow is now ten inches deep accumolateing by frosts

12ᵗʰ   Singular appearance of three distinct *Halo* or luminus rings about the moon, appeared this evening at ½ after 9 P. M. and continued one hour. the moon formed the center of the middle ring, the other two which lay N. & S. of the moon & had each of them a limb passing through the Moons Center and projecting N. & S. a Simidiamiter beyond the middle ring to which last they were equal in Dimentions, each ring appearing to subtend an angle of 15 degrees of a great Circle.

15ᵗʰ   a total eclips of the moon last night visible here, but partially obscured by the clouds.

18ᵗʰ   at Sun rise 12° below 0.

19ᵗʰ   Ice now 3 feet thick on the most rapid part of the river.

22ⁿᵈ   mist the afterno[o]n observation.

23ʳᵈ   The Snow fell about 4 inches deep last night and continues to Snow.

25ᵗʰ   it frequently happens that the ☉ rises fair and in about 15 or 20 minutes it becomes suddenly turbid, as if the ☉ had some chimical effect on the atmosphere.

31ˢᵗ   The Snow fell 2 inches last night.

Diary of the weather for February, 1805.[2]

Day of the month	Them : at ☉ rise	Weather	Wind	Them : at 4 oClock	Weather	Wind	River		
							rise or fall	Feet	In
Feby 1ˢᵗ	6.a	c.	N. W.	16.a	f.	N. W.	r.	. .	2½
2	12.b	f.	N. W.	3.a	f.	S.	f.	. .	1
3	8.b	f.	S. W.	2.a	f.	W.	. . .	. .	. . .
4	18.b	f.	N. W.	9.b	f.	W.	. . .	. .	. . .
5	10.a	f.	N. W.	20.a	f.	N. W.	r.	. .	1
6	4.b	f.	N. W.	12.a	f.	W.	r.	. .	½

[1] The following remarks are found in Lewis's book of thermometrical observations, Clark's Codex C, pp. 218, 219, and Clark-Voorhis note-book No. 4. — Eᴅ.

[2] The following table is found in Lewis's book of thermometrical observations and Clark's Codex C, pp. 234, 235. — Eᴅ.

MS. page of Weather Diary for January 15, 1805.

Day of the month	Them: at ☉ rise	Weather	Wind	Them: at 4 oClock	Weather	Wind	River rise or fall	Feet	In.
Feb᷎ 7	18.a	f.	S. E.	29.a	c.	S.	r.	..	½
8	18.a	f.	N. W.	28.a	c.	N. E.	f.	..	1
9	10 a	f.	S. E.	33.a	c.	S. E.	...	..	...
10	18.b	c.a.s	N. W.	12.a	c.	N. W.	...	..	...
11	18.b	f.	N. W.	2.b	f.	N. W.	...	..	...
12	4.b	f.	S. E	2.a	f.	W.	...	..	...
13	12.a	c.	S. E.	10.a	c.	N. W.	f.	..	1
14	2.a	c.a.s.	N. W.	2.b	f.	N. W.	...	..	...
15	16.b	f.	S. W.	6.b	f.	W.	...	..	...
16	2.a	f.	S. E.	8.a	f.	W.	f.	..	1
17	4.a	c.	S. E.	12.a	f.	N. W.	...	..	...
18	4.a	s.	N. E.	10.a	f.	S.	...	..	...
19	4.a	f.	S. E.	20.a	f.	S.	...	..	...
20	2.a	f.	S.	22.a	f.	S.	...	..	...
21	6.a	f.	S.	30.a	f.	S.	...	..	...
22	8.a	c.	N.	32.a	c. r & s.	N. W.	...	..	...
23	18.a	f.	N. W.	32.a	f.	W.	r.	..	½
24	8.a	f.	N. W.	32.a	f.	W.	...	..	...
25	16.a	f.	W.	38.a	f.	N. W.	...	..	...
26	20 a	f.	N. E.	31.a	f.	N.	...	..	...
27	26.a	f	S. E.	36.a	f.	E.	f.	..	½
28	24.a	f.	E.	38.a	c.	S. E.	...	..	...

Remarks for February, 1805.[1]

Feb᷎ 8th The Black & white & Speckled woodpeckers has returned.

14th The Snow fell 3 Inches deep last night

23d got the poplar perogue out of the ice.

24th loosed the boat & large perogue from the ice.

27th got the Boat and Perogues on the bank.

Diary of the weather for March, 1805.[2]

Day of the month	Them: at ☉ rise	Weather	Wind	Them: at 4 oClock	Weather	Wind	River rise or fall	Feet	In
March 1	28.a	c.	W.	38.a	f.	N. W.	...	..	...
2	28.a	f.	N. E.	36.a	f.	N. E.	r.	..	1½
3	28.a	c.	E.	39 a	f.	N. W.	...	..	...
4	26.a	f.	N. W.	36.a	f.	N. W.	...	..	...
5	22.a	f.	E.	40.a	f.	N. W.	...	..	...

1 The remarks for February are found in Lewis's book of thermometrical observations and Clark's Codex C, p. 218. Lewis's are chiefly in regard to events, and are omitted here, unless having some relation to weather conditions. — Ed.

2 The following table is found in Lewis's book of thermometrical observations and Clark's Codex C, pp. 233, 234. — Ed.

Day of the month	Them: at ☉ rise	Weather	Wind	Them: at 4 oClock	Weather	Wind	River rise or fall	Feet	In
1805									
March 6	26.a	c.	E.	36.a	f.	E.	r.	..	2
7	12.a	f.	E.	26.a	c.	E.	r.	..	2
8	7.a	c.	E.	12 a	f.	E.	r.	..	2½
9	2.a	c.	N.	18.a	f.	N. W.	r.	..	2
10	2.b	f.	N. W.	12 a	f.	N. W.	r.	..	3½
11	12 a	c.	S. E.	26.a	f. a. c.	N W.	r.	..	4½
12	2.b	f. a. s.	N.	10.a	f.	N. W.	r.	..	5
13	1 b	f.	S. E.	28.a	f.	S. W.	r.	..	3½
14	18.a	f.	S. E.	40.a	f	W.	...	..	..
15	24.a	f	S E.	38 a	f.	W	f.	..	1
16	32.a	c.	E.	42.a	c.	W.	f.	..	3
17	30.a	f.	S. E	46 a	f.	S. W.	r.	..	2
18	24.a	c.	N.	34.a	c.	N.	f.	..	1
19	20.a	c. a. s.	N.	31.a	f.	N. W.	r.	..	1
20	28.a	c.	N. W.	28.a	f.	N. W.	r.	..	3
21	16.a	c.	E.	26.a	s. & h.	S.	...	..	..
22	22 a	f. a. s.	S.	36.a	f.	S. W.	f.	.	4
23	34 a	f.	W.	38 a	c. a. r	N. W.	f	..	4
24	28 a	c. a. s.	N. E.	30.a	c. a s.	N.	r.	..	1
25	16 a	f.	E.	32.a	f.	S.	r.	..	5
26	20.a	f.	S. E.	46.a	f.	W.	r	..	4½
27	28 a	f.	S E.	60.a	f.	S. W.	r.	..	9
28	40 a	f.	S. E.	64.a	f.	S. W.	r.	..	1
29	42 a	f.	N. W.	52.a	f.	N. W.	f.	..	11
30	28.a	f.	N. W.	49.a	f	N. W.	r	1	1
31	35 a	c. a. r.	S. E.	45.a	c.	S. E.	r	..	9

Remarks for March, 1805.[1]

March 2d The Snow has disappeared in many places the river partially broken up.

3rd a flock of Ducks passed up the river this morning.

9th wind hard all day.

12th Snow but Slight disappeared to day

18th collected Some roots, herbs & plants in order to Send by the boat perticularly the root said to cure the bites of a mad dog and rattle snake.

19th But little snow not enough to cover the Ground

20th The Indians raise a kind of artechokes which they Say is [now] common in the praries. well tasted

21st Some Ducks seen to light in the river opposit the fort.

23d but little rain.

---

[1] The following remarks are found in Lewis's book of thermometrical observations and Clark's Codex C, pp. 217, 218. — ED.

24ᵗʰ but little Snow.

25ᵗʰ a gang of *Swan* return to day the ice in the river has given way in maney places, and it is with Some difficulty it can be passed.

26ᵗʰ The ice gave way in the river abᵗ 3 P.M. and came down in emence sheets verry near Distroying our new Canoes Some Geese pass to day.

27ᵗʰ The first insect I have seen was a large black knat to day. the *ice* drifting in Great quantities.

28ᵗʰ ice abates in quantity wind hard river rise 13 inches & fall 12 inches.

29ᵗʰ a variety of insects make their appearance, as flies bugs &c. the *ice* ceases to run Supposed to have formed an obstruction above

30ᵗʰ The *ice* Come down in great quantities the Mandans take Some floating Buffalow.

31ˢᵗ Ducks and Gees passing the *ice* abates in quantity.

Thermometrical observations

Showing also the rise and fall of the Missouri, appearances of Weather Wind &ᶜ &ᶜ. assending above *Fort Mandan* In Latitude 47°–12′–47″. North & Longitude *99° 24′. 45″ $\frac{1}{10}$ West*

Diary of the weather for April, 1805.[1]

Days of the month	State of the thermometer at Sun rise	Weather	Winds at Sun rise	State of the thermometer at 4 oClock P. M	Weather	Winds at 4 oClock P M	State of the river.		
							raised or fall	feet	Inches
april									
1ˢᵗ	33.a	c.	N. W.	43.a	{ c.a.t. { l.r & h	W.	f.	. .	11
2ⁿᵈ	28.a	c.a.r.	N. W.	38.a	f.a.c	W.	f.	. .	5
3ʳᵈ	24.a	f.	N.	44.a	f.	N.	f.	. .	4
4ᵗʰ	36.a	f.	S.	55.a	f.	N. W.	f.	. .	4
5ᵗʰ	30.a	f.	N. W.	39.a	f.	N.	f.	. .	2
6ᵗʰ	19.a	f.	N.	48.a	c.	N. W.	f.	. .	1
7ᵗʰ	28.a	f.	W.	64.a	f.	S. W.	r.	. .	2
8ᵗʰ	19.a	f.	N. W.	56.a	f.	N. W.	f.	. .	2

[1] Lewis's book of thermometrical observations and Clark's weather entries in Codex C end with the departure of the expedition from Fort Mandan, April 7, 1805. Lewis's diary of the weather for April, 1805, is found in Codex Fe, and Clark's in Codex I, p. 14. As before, the items in the column of "Remarks" have been transferred to the "Remarks" for the month, following the notation. — ED.

Days of the month	State of the thermometer at Sun rise	Weather	Winds at Sun rise	State of the thermometer at 4 oClock P M	Weather	Winds at 4 oClock P M	State of the river		
							raised or fall	feet	Inches
april									
9th	38.a	f.	S. E.	70.a	f.	S. W.	f.	. .	$\frac{1}{2}$
10th	42.a	f.	E.	74.a	f.	S. W.	r.	. .	$\frac{1}{2}$
11th	42.a	f.	N. W.	76.a	f.	W.	f.	. .	$\frac{1}{2}$
12th	56.a	f.	N. W.	74.a	c.a.r.t.&l	W.	r.	. .	$\frac{1}{8}$
13th	58.a	f.	S. E.	80.a	f.	S. E.	f.	. .	1
14th	52.a	c.	S. E.	82.a	f.	S. W.	f.	. .	$\frac{3}{4}$
15th	51.a	f.	E.	78.a	f.	S. W.	f.	. .	$\frac{1}{2}$
16th	54.a	f.	S. E.	78.a	f.	S·	f.	. .	$\frac{1}{2}$
17th	56.a	f.	N. E.	74.a	c.	S. W.	f.	. .	$\frac{1}{2}$
18th	52.a	f.	N. E.	64 a	c.	N.	. . .	. .	. . .
19th	45.a	c.	N. W.	56.a	c.	N. W.	. . .	. .	. . .
20th	40.a	c.	N. W.	42.a	c.a.s.	N. W.	. . .	. .	. . .
21st	28.a	f.	N. W.	40 a	c.	N. W.	f.	. .	$\frac{1}{2}$
22nd	34.a	f.a.c.	W.	40.a	f.	N. W.	r.	. .	2
23rd	34.a	f.	W.	52 a	c.	N. W.	r.	. .	2
24th	40.a	f.	N.	56.a	f.	N.	r.	. .	1
25th	36.a	f.	N.	52 a	f.	N. W.	r.	. .	2
26th	32.a	f.	S.	63.a	f.	S. E.	r.	. .	3
27th	36.a	f.	S. W.	64.a	f.	N. W.	f.	. .	2
28th	44.a	f.	S. E.	63.a	f.	S. E.	f.	. .	$1\frac{1}{2}$
29th	42.a	f.	N. E.	64.a	f.	E.	f.	. .	$1\frac{1}{2}$
30th	50.a	f.	N. W.	58.a	f.	S. E.	f.	. .	$\frac{1}{2}$

Remarks for April, 1805.[1]

April 1st but little ice, put our Boat Perog[ue]s & canoes in the water. A fine refreshing shower of rain fell about 2 P. M. this was the first shower of rain that we had witnessed since the fifteenth of September 1804. tho' it several times has fallen in very small quantities, and was noticed in this diary of the weather. the cloud came from the west, and was attended by hard thunder and Lightning. I have observed that all thunder clouds in the Western part of the continent, proceed from the westerly quarter, as they do in the Atlantic States. the air is remarkably dry and pure in this open country, very little rain or snow e[i]ther winter or summer. the atmosphere is more transparent than I ever obse[r]ved it in any country through which I have passed.

2nd. rained hard and without intermission last night.

---

[1] The following remarks are compiled from Lewis's book of thermometrical observations, Lewis's Codex Fe, Clark's Codex C, pp. 216, 217, and Clark's Codex I, pp. 14–17. — ED.

Day of the month	Hour of obsn.	Weather	Wind	State of ther.	Weather	Wind at 4 o'Clk P.M.	State of the river		Remarks and references
April 1st	33 a	c	N.E.	43 a	c a r	W.	f	11	a fine shower of rain at 4 P.m. & ice ceased to run
2d	28 a	c a r	N.W.	38 a	f a c	W.	f	5	rained hard and continued the thermomr. last night
3d	24 a	f	N.	44 a	f	W.	f	4	frost last night
4th	36 a	f	S.	55 a	f	N.W.	f	4	wind hard, a flock of brant pass up the river
5th	30 a	f	N.W.	39 a	f	N.	f	2	
6th	19 a	f	N.	48 a	c	N.W.	f	1	the cherry or cedar bird returns, this bird has thin
7th	28 a	f	W.	64 a	f	S.W.	a	2	set out on our voyage at 6 P.m.
8th	19 a	f	N.W.	56 a	f	N.W.	f	2	the Killdee & large plovers
9th	38 a	f	S.E.	70 a	f	S.W.	f	½	storms have returned & the
10th	42 a	f	E	74 a	f	S.W.	a	½	currus bird disappears. Musculous appears.
11th	44 a	f	N.W.	76 a	f	W.	f	½	the redbury and broad leaf willow in bloom.
12th	56 a	f	N.W.	74 a	c	W.	a		small shower from the W. attended with hard wind
13th	58 a	f	S.E.	80 a	f	S.E.	f	1	
14th	52 a	c	S.E.	82 a	f	S.W.	f	2 4	
15th	51 a	f	E	78 a	f	S.W.	f	½	
16th	54 a	f	S.E.	78 a	c	S.	f	½	thunder shower passed
17th	56 a	f	N.E.	74 a	c	S.W.	f	½	above us from S.W. to N.E. no rain where wind very violent
18th	52 a	f	N.E.	64 a	c	N.			wind very violent
19th	45 a	c	N.W.	56 a	c	N.W.			wind violent
20th	40 a	c	N.W.	42 a	c a s	N.W.	f		wind violent
21st	28 a	f	N.W.	40	c	N.W.	f	½	wind violent
22d	34 a	f a c	N.	40	f	N.W.	a	2	wind very hard greater part of the day
23d	34 a	f	N.	52	c	N.W.	a	2	fair do. do.
24	42 a	f	N.	56	f	N.	a	1	do. this morning.
25	36 a	f	N.	52 a	f	N.W.	a	2	do. until 5 o'clock P.m.
26	32 a	f	S.	63 a	f	S.E.	a	3	
27	36 a	f	S.W.	63 a	f	N.W.	f	2	wind very hard from
28	44 a	f	S.E.	63 a	f	S.E.	f	1½	11 to 4 o'clock
29	42 a	f	N.E.	64 a	f	E.	f	1½	
30	50 a	f	N.W.	58 a	f	S.E.	f	½	

MS. page, Lewis's Weather Diary
for April 1, 1805.

3rd a white frost, Some ice attached to the edges of the water

4th Observed a flock of brant passing up the river today, the wind blew very ha[r]d as it dose frequently in this quarter; there is scarcely any timber to brake the wind from the river, & the country on both sides being level plains, wholy destitute of timber, the wind blows with astonishing violence. in this open country the winds form a great obstruction to the navigation of this river particularly with small vessels, which can neither ascend or decend should the wind be the least violent.

6th This day a flock of *cherry* or *cedar* birds were seen, one of the men killed several of them which gave me an opportunity of examining them. they are common in the United States; usually ascociate in large flocks and are freequently distructive to the chery orchards, and in winter in the lower parts of the states of Virginia & Maryland feed on the buries of the Cedar. they are a small bluish brown bird, crested with a tuft of dark brown feathers. with a narrow black stripe passing on each side of the head underneath the eye from the base of the upper beak to the back of the head. it is distinguished more particularly by some of the shorter feathers of the wing, which are tiped with a red spots that have much the appearance at a little distance of sealing wax. All the birds that we believe visit this country have now returned.

7th wind very high. Set out on our voyage at 5 P. M.

8th the Kildee, and large Hawk have returned. the only birds that I obse[r]ved during the winter at Fort Mandan was the Missouri Magpie, a bird of the Corvus genus, the raven in immence numbers, the small woodpecker or *sapsucker* as they are sometimes called, the beautifull eagle, or *calumet bird*, so called from the circumstance of the natives decorating their pipe-stems with it's plumage, and the Prairie Hen or grouse.

9th the Crow has also returned saw the first today. the Musquitoes revisit us, saw several of them. Capt Clark brought me a flower in full blo. it is a stranger to me.

10th The Prarie lark, bald Eagle, & the large plover have returned. the grass begins to spring, and the leaf buds of the willow to appear. Cherry birds disappear

11th The lark woodpecker, with yellow wings, and a black spot on the brest common to the U' States has appeared, with sundry small birds. many plants begin to appear above the ground. saw a large white gull today the Eagle is now laying their eggs, and the gees have mated. the Elm, large leafed, willow and the bush which bears a red berry, called by the engages *greas de buff* are in blume.

12th small shower from the W.[est] attended with hard wind.

13th The leaves of the Choke cherry are about half grown ; the Cotton wood is in blume the flower of this tree resembles that of the aspen in form, and is of a deep perple colour.

15th several flocks of white brant with black wings pass us today, their flight was to the N. W. the trees now begin to assume a green appearance, tho' the earth at the debth of about three feet is not yet thawed, which we discovered by the banks of the river, falling in and disclosing a strata of frozen earth.

16th saw the first leather winged bat. it appeared about the size of those common to the U' States.

18th a heavy dew this morning. which is the first and only one we have seen since we passed the council bluffs last summer. there is but little dew in this open country. saw a flock of pillecan pass from S. W. to N. E. they appeared to be on a long flight. wind very violent.

19th The trees have now put forth their leaves. the goosbury, current, servisbury, and wild plumbs are in blume. wind violent.

20th wind violent.

21st white frost last night. the earth friezed along the water's edge. wind violent

22nd wind very hard greater part of the day.

23d d° d° d° d° d° d° saw the first robbin. also the brown Curloo.

24th wind very hard this morning.

25th d° d° d° until 5 oClock P. M.

27th wind very hard from 11 to 4 oClock.

28th Vegetation has progressed but little since the 18th, in short the change is scarcely perceptible.

Diary of the Weather for the Month of May, 1805 [1]

Day of the Month	State of the thermometer at Sun rise	Weather	Wind at Sun Rise	State of the thermometer at 4 oClock P M	Weather	Wind at 4 oClock P.M.	State of the River		
							raised or fallen	Feet	Inches
1st	36.a	c.	E.	46.a	c.a.f.	N. E.	f.	..	1½
2nd	28.a	s.	N. E.	34.a	c.a.s.	N. W.	f.	..	1
3rd	26.a	f.	W.	46.a	c.	W.	f.	..	¼
4th	38.a	c.	W.	48.a	f.a.c.	W.	..	..	..
5th	38.a	f.	N. W.	62.a	f.a.r.	S. E.	r.	..	1
6th	48.a	f.	E.	61.a	c.a.r.	S. E.	r.	..	2
7th	42.a	c.	S.	60.a	f.	N. E.	r.	..	1½
8th	41.a	c.	E.	52.a	c.a.r.	E.	f.	..	¼
9th	38.a	f.	E.	58.a	f.	W.	r.	..	¾
10th	38.a	f.a.c.	W. N. W.	62.a	c.a.r.	N. W.	f.	..	¾
11th	44.a	f.	N. E.	60.a	c.	S. W.	..	..	..
12th	52.a	f.	S. E.	54.a	c.a.r.	N. W.	r.	..	2
13th	52.a	c.a.r.	N. W.	54.a	f.a.c.	N. W.	f.	..	2¼
14th	32.a	f.	S. W.	52.a	c.	S. W.	f.	..	1¾
15th	48.a	c.a.r.	S. W.	54.a	c.	N. W.	f.	..	¾
16th	48.a	c.	S. W.	67.a	f.	S. W.	..	..	..
17th	60.a	f.	N. E.	68.a	f.	S. W.	..	..	..
18th	58.a	f.	W.	46.a	c.a.r.	N. W.	f.	..	1
19th	38.a	f.	E.	68.a	f.a.c.	S. W.	..	..	..
20th	52.a	f.	N. E.	76.a	f.	E.	f.	..	1
21st	50.a	f.	S. W.	76.a	f.	N. W.	..	..	..
22nd	46.a	c.	N. W.	48.a	c.	N. W.	f.	..	½
23rd	32.a	f.	S. W.	54.a	f.	S. W.	f.	..	½
24th	32.a	f.	N. W.	68.a	f.	S. E.	r.	..	3½
25th	46.a	f.	S. W.	82.a	f.	S. W.	r.	..	2
26th	58.a	f.	S. W.	80.a	f.	S. W.	r.	..	½
27th	62.a	f.	S. W.	82.a	f.	S. W.	..	..	..
28th	62.a	c.	S. W.	72.a	c. & r.	S. W.	r.	..	½
29th	62.a	c.a.r.	S. W.	67.a	r.	S. W.	r.	..	1
30th	56.a	c.a.r.	S. W.	50.a	r.	S. W.	r.	..	5
31st	48.a	c.a.r.	W.	53.a	c.a.r.	S. W.	r.	..	1½

Remarks for May, 1805. [2]

1st   wind violent from 12 oC. to 6 P.M.

2nd   the wind continued so high from 12 oClock yesterday, untill 5 this evening that we were unable to proceed. the snow which fell last night and this morning one inch deep has not yet

---

1 The following table is found in Lewis's Codex Fe, and Clark's Codex I, p. 18.— ED.

2 The following remarks are found in Lewis's Codex Fe, and Clark's Codex I, pp. 18-20. They are compiled from column of " Remarks," and data following the table of weather notations. — ED.

disappeared, it forms a singular contrast with the trees which are now in leaf.

3.ᵈ hard frost last night. at 4 P. M. the snow has not yet entirely disappeared. the new horns of the Elk begin to appear.

4.ᵗʰ the snow has disappeared. saw the first grasshoppers today. there are great quantities of a small blue beatle feeding on the willows. the black martin makes its appearance.

5ᵗʰ a few drops of rain only.

6.ᵗʰ rain very inconsiderable as usual.

8.ᵗʰ rain inconsiderable. a mear sprinkle the bald Eagle, of which there are great numbers, now have their young. the *turtledove* appears.

9ᵗʰ The choke Cherry is now in blume.

10.ᵗʰ rain but slight a few drops.

11ᵗʰ frost this morning

12.ᵗʰ rain but slight.

13ᵗʰ dᵒ dᵒ dᵒ

14ᵗʰ white frost this morning

15.ᵗʰ slight shower.

17ᵗʰ the Gees have their young ; the Elk begin to produce their young, the Antelope and deer as yet have not. the small species of Goatsucker or whiperwill begin to cry the blackbirds both small and large have appeared. we have had scarcely any thunder and lightning. the clouds are generally white and accompanyed with wind only.

18ᵗʰ saw the wild rose in blume. the brown thrush or mocking bird has appeared. had a good shower of rain today, it continued about 2 hours ; this is the first shower that deserves the appellation of *rain*, which we have seen since we left Fort Mandan. no thunder or lightning

19ᵗʰ heavy fog this morning on the river.

22.ⁿᵈ the wind excessively hard all night. saw some particles of snow fall today it did not lye in sufficient quantity on the ground to be perceptible.

23.ʳᵈ hard frost last night ; ice in the eddy water along the shore, and the water friezed on the oars this morning. Strawburies in bloom. saw the first king fisher.

24ᵗʰ frost last night ice ⅛ of an inch thick.

25.ᵗʰ saw the king bird, or bee martin ; the grouse disappear. killed three of the bighorned antelopes.

26.ᵗʰ The last night was much the warmest we have experienced, found

the covering of one blanket sufficient. the air is extremely dry
and pure.

27th wind so hard we are unable to proceed in the early part of
the day

28th a slight thunder shower; the air was turbid in the forenoon and
appeared to be filled with smoke; we supposed it to proceed
from the burning of the plains, which we are informed are
frequently set on fire by the Snake Indians to compell the
antelopes to resort to the woody and mountanous country
which they inhabit. saw a small white and black woodpecker
with a red head; the same which is common to the Atlantic
states.

29th rained but little, some dew this morning

30th the rain commenced about 4 Oclock in the evening, and continued moderately through the course of the night; more rain
has now fallen than we have experienced since the 15th of
September last.

31st The Antelope now bring forth their young. from the size of
the young of the bighorned Antelope I suppose they bring
forth their young as early at least as the Elk. but little rain.

Diary of the Weather for the Month of June, 1805 [1]

Day of the Month	State of the thermometer at ☉ rise	Weather	Wind at Sun rise	State of the thermometer at 4 oClock P M	Weather at 4 oClock	Winds at 4 oClock P M	State of the River:		
							raised or fallen	Feet	Inches
1st	50.a	c.	S. W.	62.a	c.	S. E.	r.	. .	1½
2nd	56.a	c.a.r.	S. W.	68.a	f.	S. W.	. . .	. .	. . .
3rd	46.a	f.	S. W.	60.a	f.	S. W.	. . .	. .	. . .
4th	48.a	f.a.c.	N E.	61.a	f.	S. W.	f.	. .	⅜
5th	40.a	r.	S. W.	42.a	c.a.r.	N. E.	f.	. .	¾
6th	35.a	c.a.r.	N. E.	42.a	r.a.r.	N. E.	f.	. .	1½
7th	40.a	c.a.r.	S. W.	43.a	r.a.r.	S. W.	f.	. .	1½
8th	41.a	r.a.r.	S. W.	48.a	f.a.r.	S. W.	f.	. .	1¼
9th	50.a	f.	S. W.	52.a	f.	S. W.	f.	. .	1
10th	52.a	f.	S. W.	68.a	f.a.r.	S. W.	r.	. .	2
11th	54.a	f.	S. W.	66.a	f.	S. W.	. . .	. .	. . .
12th	54.a	f.	S. W.	64.a	f.a.r.	S. W.	. . .	. .	. . .
13th	52.a	f.	S. W.	72.a	f.	S. W.	r.	. .	¾
14th	60.a	f.	S W.	74.a	f.	S. W.	f.	. .	¾
15th	60.a	f.	S. W.	76.a	f.	S. W.	f.	. .	1½
16th	64.a	c.a.r.	S. W.	58.a	f.	S. W.	r.	. .	½

[1] The following table is found in Lewis's Codex Fe and Clark's Codex I,
p. 21.— ED.

Day of the Month	State of the thermometer at ☉ rise	Weather	Wind at Sun rise	State of the thermometer at 4 oClock P M	Weather at 4 oClock	Winds at 4 oClock P.M	State of the River:		
							raised or fallen	Feet	Inches
17th	50.a	c.	S. W.	57.a	c.	S. W.	f.	. .	¼
18th	48.a	c.	S. W.	64.a	f.a.c.	S. W.	f.	. .	½
19th	52.a	f.	S. W.	70.a	f.	S. W.	f.	. .	¼
20th	49.a	c.	S. W.	74.a	f.a.r.	S. W.	f.	. .	¼
21st	49.a	f.	S. W.	70.a	c.	S. W.	f.	. .	¼
22nd	45.a	c.	S. W.	54.a	f.	S. W.	f.	. .	½
23.d	48.a	f.	S. E.	65.a	c.	S. E.	f.	. .	¼
24th	49.a	c. a. r.	S. E.	74.a	f.a.c.	S. W.	f.	. .	. . .
25th	47.a	c. a. r.	S. W.	72.a	f.	S. W.	. . .		
26th	49.a	f.	S. W.	78.a	f.	S. W.	r.		¼
27th	49.a	f.	S. W.	77.a	f.a.r.h.t.&l.	S. W.	r.	1	¼
28th	46.a	f.	S. W.	75.a	c.a.f.	S. W.	r.	2	
29th	47.a	r.t.l.	S. W.	77.a	f.a.r.	S. W.	r.		4½
30th	49.a	f.	S. W.	76.a	f.	S. W.	r.		2¼

Remarks for June, 1805.[1]

2nd rained a few drops only

3d cought the 1st White Chub, and a fish resembling the Hickory Shad in the clear stream.

5th rained considerably some snow fell on the mounts great numbers of the sparrows larks, Curloos and other small birds common to praries are now laying their eggs and seting, their nests are in great abundance. the large batt, or night hawk appears. the Turkey buzzard appears, first saw the mountain cock near the entrance of Maria's river.

6th rained hard the greater part of the day.

7th rained moderately all day.

8th cleared off at 10 A. M.

13th some dew this morning.

15th The deer now begin to bring forth their young the young Magpies begin to fly. The Brown or grizzly bear begin to coppolate.

16th some rain last night

17th the thermometer placed in the shade of a tree on the north side at the foot of the rappids.

19th wind violent all day

20th wind still violent rain slight.

---

[1] The remarks for June are found in Lewis's Codex E, p. 140, and in Clark's Codex I, pp. 21–23, combined with those from the column of remarks that refer to meteorological matters. References to events described in text of journals are here omitted. — Ed.

21st wind not so violent.

22d. Thermometer removed to the head of the rappid and placed in the shade of a tree.

24th slight rain last night & a heavy shower this evening

27th. At 1 P M a black cloud which arose in the S. W. came on accompanied with a high wind and violent thunder and Lightning ; a great quantity of Hail also fell during this storm which lasted about two hours and a half the hail which was generally about the size of pigions eggs and not unlike them in form, covered the ground to one inch and a half. for about 20 minutes during this Storm hail fell of an inno[r]mus size driven with violence almost incredible, when they struck the ground they would rebound to the hight of 10 to 12 feet and pass 20 or 30 before they touched again. during this emence Storm I was with the greater part of the men on the portage the men saved themselves, Some by getting under a canoe others by putting Sundery articles on their heads two was k[n]ocked down & Sever[al] with their legs & thighs much brused Cap! Lewis weighed one of those hail Stones which weighed 3 ozs and measured 7 Inches in secumfrance ; they were generally round & perfectly Solid. I am Convinced if one of those had Struck a man on naiked head [it] would certainly [have] fractured his Skull. young blackbirds which are abundant in these Islands are now beginning to fly

28th. cat fish no higher.

29th. heavy gust of rain this morning & evening.

Diary of the Weather for July, 1805 [1]

Day of the month	State of the thermometer at ☉ rise	Weather	Winds at Sun rise	State of the thermometer at 4 oClock P M	Weather	Winds at at 4 P M	State of the River		
							raised or fallen	feet	Inches
1st	59.a	f.	S. W.	74.a	f.	S. W.	r.	..	½
2nd.	60.a	f.a.r.	S. W.	78.a	f.	S. W.	...	..	..
3rd.	56.a	f.	S. W.	74.a	c.a.f. & r.	S. W.	...	..	...
4th.	52.a	f.	S. W.	76.a	f.a.r.	S. W.	f.	..	¼
5th	49.a	f.a.h. & r.	S. W.	72.a	f.	S. W.	f.	..	½
6th.	47.a	c.a.h.r.t. &l.	S. W.	74.a	f.a.c.	S. W.	f.	..	¼
7th	54.a	c.a.f.	S. W.	77.a	r.a.c.	S. W.	f.	..	¼
8th	60.a	f.	S. W.	78.a	f.a.r.	S. W.	f.	..	¼
9th.	56.a	f.	S. W.	76.a	c.a.r.	N. W.	f.	..	¼

1 The following table is found in Lewis's Codex Fe and Codex P, p. 131, and in Clark's Codex I, p. 23. — ED.

Day of the month	State of the thermometer at ☉ rise	Weather	Winds at Sun rise	State of the thermometer at 4 oClock P M	Weather	Winds at 4 P M	State of the River raised or fallen	feet	Inches
10th	52.a	f.a.r.	S. W.	66.a	f.	S. W.	. . .	. .	. . .
11th	46.a	f.	S. W.	70.a	f.	S. W.	. . .	. .	. . .
12th	50.a	f.	S. W.	74.a	f.	S. W.	f.	. .	$\frac{1}{4}$
13th	42.a	f.	S. W.	76.a	f.	S. W.	f.	. .	$\frac{1}{4}$
14th	45.a	f.	S. W.	78.a	c.a.r.	S. W.	. . .	. .	. .
15th	60.a	f.a.r.	S. W.	76.a	f.	S. W.	f.	. .	$1\frac{1}{2}$
16th	53.a	f.	S. W.	80.a	f.	S. W.	f.	. .	$\frac{3}{4}$
17th	58.a	f.	S. W.	81.a	f.	S. W.	f.	. .	$1\frac{1}{4}$
18th	60.a	f.	S. W.	84.a	f.	S. W.	f.	. .	$\frac{1}{2}$
19th	62.a	f.	S. W.	68.a	c.a.h. &r.	S. W.	f.	. .	$\frac{1}{2}$
20th	59.a	f.a.r.	S. W.	60.a	f.	N. W.	. . .	. .	. .
21st	60.a	f.	N. W.	67.a	f.	N. W.	f.	. .	$\frac{1}{2}$
22nd	52.a	f.	N. W.	80.a	f.	N. E.	. . .	. .	. .
23rd	54.a	f.	S. W.	80.a	c.	S. W.	f.	. .	$\frac{1}{4}$
24th	60.a	f.	S. W.	90.a	f.	S. W.	f.	. .	$\frac{3}{4}$
25th	60.a	f.	S. W.	86.a	f.	S. W.	f.	. .	$\frac{1}{2}$
26th	60.a	f.	S. W.	82.a	c.a.r.	S. W.	f.	. .	$\frac{3}{4}$
27th	52.a	c.	S. W.	80.a	c.a.r.	S. W.	f.	. .	$\frac{3}{4}$
28th	49.a	f.a.r.	S. W.	90.a	f.	S. W.	f.	. .	$\frac{1}{2}$
29th	54.a	f.a.r.	N.	82.a	f.	N. E.	r.	. .	$\frac{1}{2}$
30th	50.a	f.	S. E.	80.a	f.	S. E.	. . .	. .	. . .
31st	48.a	f.	S. W.	92.a	f.	S. W.	. . .	. .	. . .

Remarks for July, 1805 [1]

1st   wind hard during part of the day.

2nd   some rain just before sunrise.

3d   slight rain in the evening.

4th   heavy dew this morning.   slight sprinkle of rain at 2 P.M.

5th   heavy shower of rain and hail at 9 P.M.   some thunder & L[ightning].

6th   a heavy wind from the S. W. attended with rain about the middle of the last night.   about day had a violent thunderstorm attended with hail and rain   the hail covered the ground and was near the size of Musquet balls.   one black bird was picked up killed with the hail.   I am astonished that more have not suffered in a Similar Manner as they are abundant and I should suppose the hail suffciently heavy to kill them.   wind high all day.

[1] The remarks for July, 1805, have been compiled from the column of remarks in the tables, and those following in Lewis's Codex Fe ; Codex P, pp. 130, 131 ; and Clark's Codex I, pp. 23, 24. Lewis's original entries appear to have been made in Codex P; those in Codex Fe are in Clark's handwriting after July 5. Events described in text of journal are here omitted. — Ed.

7th   a shower at 4 P. M.
10th   wind hard all day.
11th   wind hard all day
12th   wind violent all day.
13th   wind violent in the latter part of the day.
19th   Thunder storm ½ after 3 P. M.
25th   Snow appears on the mountains ahead.
27th   a considerable fall of rain unattended with Lightning.

Diary of the weather for the month of August, 1805. [1]

Day of the month	State of the thermometer at ☉ rise	Weather	Wind at ☉ rise	State of the thermometer at 4 P M.	Weather	Winds at 4 P M	State of the River		
							risen or fallen	feet	Inches
1st	54.a	f.	S. W.	91.a	f.	S. W.	f.	. .	1/2
2nd	48.a	f.	N. W.	81.a	f.	N. W.	f.	. .	1/2
3rd	50.a	f.	N. E.	86.a	f.	N. E.	f.	. .	1/4
4th	48.a	f.	S.	92.a	f.	S.	f.	. .	1/2
5th	49.a	f.	S. E.	79.a	f.	S. E.	f.	. .	1/4
6th	52.a	f.	S. W.	71.a	c.	S. W.	. . .	. .	. . .
7th	54.a	c. a. r.	S. W.	80.a	c.	S. W.	. . .	. .	. . .
8th	54.a	f. a. r.	S. W.	82.a	c. a. f.	S. W.	. . .	. .	. . .
9th	58.a	f.	N. E.	78.a	c.	S. W.	. . .	. .	. . .
10th	60.a	c. a. r. t. &l.	S. W.	68.a	t. l. &r.	S. W.	. . .	. .	. . .
11th	58.a	c. a. r. &h	N. E.	70.a	f.	S. W.	. . .	. .	. . .
12th	58.a	f. a. r. &h.	W.	72.a	f. a. r. &h.	N. W.	. . .	. .	. . .
13th	52.a	c. a. f.	N. W.	70.a	f. a. r.	N. W.	. . .	. .	. . .
14th	51.a	f. a. r.	N. W.	76.a	f.	N. W.	. . .	. .	. . .
15th	43.a	f.	S. E.	74.a	f.	S. W.	. . .	. .	. . .
16th	48.a	f.	S. W.	70.a	f.	S. W.	. . .	. .	. . .
17th	42.a	f.	N. E.	76.a	f.	S. W.	. . .	. .	. . .
18th	45.a	c.	S. W.	78.a	r.	S. W.	. . .	. .	. . .
19th	30.a	f. a. r.	S. W.	71.a	f. a. r.	S. W.	. . .	. .	. . .
20th	32.a	f.	S. W.	74.a	f.	S. W.	. . .	. .	. . .
21st	19.a	f.	S. E.	78.a	f.	E.	. . .	. .	. . .
22nd	22.a	f.	E.	70.a	f.	E.	. . .	. .	. . .
23rd	35.a	f.	E.	72.a	f.	S. E.	. . .	. .	. . .
24th	40.a	f.	S. E.	76.a	f. a. r.	S. E.	. . .	. .	. . .
25th	32.a	f. a. r.	S. E.	65.a	c.	S. E.	. . .	. .	. . .
26th	31.a	f.	S. E.	45.a	f.	S. E.	. . .	. .	. . .
27th	32.a	f.	S. E.	56.a	f.	S. E.	. . .	. .	. . .
28th	35.a	f.	S. W.	66.a	f.	S. W.	. . .	. .	. . .
29th	32.a	f.	S. W.	68.a	f.	S. W.	. . .	. .	. . .
30th	34.a	c.	N. E.	59.a	c.	N. E.	. . .	. .	. . .
31st	38.a	c. a. r.	N. E.	58.a	c. a. r. &h.	N. E.	. . .	. .	. . .

1 The following table is found in Lewis's Codex Fe ; Codex P, p. 128 ; and in Clark's Codex I, p. 25. — ED.

Remarks for August, 1805 [1]

7th. Thunder shower last evening from the N.W. the river which we are now ascending is so inconsiderable and the current so much of a stand that I relinquished paying further attention to it's state.

8th. a thunder shower last evening.

10th. rain commenced at 6 P.M. and continued showery through the night. Musquetors very bad.

11th. heavy dew last evening   killed a long tailed grouse.

13th. very cold last night.

15th. remarkably cold this morning

19th. ice on standing water $\frac{1}{8}$ of an inch thick.

20th. hard frost last night.

21st. ice $\frac{1}{2}$ an inch thick on standing water.   Most astonishing difference between the hight of the Murcury at ⊙ rise and at 4 P. M.   today there was 59.° and this in the Space of 8 hours, yet we experience this wonderfull transicion without feeling it near so sensibly as I should have expected.

22nd. snow yet appears on the summits of the mountains.

25th. white frost this morning

26th. hard white frost and some ice on standing water this morning.

27th. hard frost white this morning.

Diary of the weather for the month of September, 1805 [2]

Day of the month	State of the thermometer at ⊙ rise	Weather	Winds at ⊙ rise	State of the thermometer at 4 P M.	Weather	Winds at 4 P M	State of the river		
							fallen or raised	feet	Inches
1st.	38.a	c.	N. W.	67.a	c.	N. W.	. . .	. .	. . .
2nd.	36.a	c.a.r.	N. E.	60.a	c.a.r.h.	N. E.	. . .	. .	. . .
3rd.	34.a	c.a.r.	N. E.	52.a	c.a.r.	N. E.	. . .	. .	. . .
4th.	19.a	r.a.s.	N. E.	34.a	c.a.r.	N. E.	. . .	. .	. . .
5th.	*17.a*	c.a.s.	N. E.	*29.a*	c.a.r. & s.	N. E.	. . .	. .	. . .
6th 8	. . .	c.a.r.	N. E.	. . .	r.	N. E.	. . .	. .	. . .
7th.	. . .	c.a.r.	N. E.	. . .	c.a.r.	N. E.	. . .	. .	. . .

[1] The following data are compiled from the tables and remarks found in Lewis's Codex P, pp. 127, 128; Codex Fe — entries in Clark's writing until August 23, the rest in Lewis's; and Clark's Codex I, pp. 25, 26. The remarks on events described in text of journal are here omitted. — ED.

[2] The following table is found in Codex P, p. 125, in Lewis's writing; in Codex Fe, partly in Lewis's, and partly in Clark's writing; in Codex I, p. 27, in Clark's writing. — ED.

[8] The absence of further thermometrical entries is explained by note of Sept. 6. — ED.

Day of the month	State of the thermometer at ☉ rise	Weather	Winds at ☉ rise	State of the thermometer at 4 P.M.	Weather	Winds at 4 P.M.	State of the river fallen or raised	feet	Inches
8th	. . .	c.	N. E.	. . .	c. a. r.	N. E.	. . .	. .	. . .
9th	. . .	c. a. r.	N. E.	. . .	f. a. r.	N. E.	. . .	. .	. . .
10th	. . .	f.	N. W.	. . .	f.	N. W.	. . .	. .	. . .
11th	. . .	f.	N. W.	. . .	f.	N. W.	. . .	. .	. . .
12th	. . .	f.	N. W.	. . .	f.	N. E.	. . .	. .	. . .
13th	. . .	c.	N. E.	. . .	r.	N. E.	. . .	. .	. . .
14th	. . .	c. a. r.	S. W.	. . .	c. a. r.	S. W.	. . .	. .	. . .
15th	. . .	c. a. s.	S. W.	. . .	s.	S. W.	. . .	. .	. . .
16th	. . .	c. a. s.	S. W.	. . .	f.	S. W.	. . .	. .	. . .
17th	. . .	f.	S. W.	. . .	f.	S. W.	. . .	. .	. . .
18th	. . .	f.	S. W.	. . .	f.	S. W.	. . .	. .	. . .
19th	. . .	f.	S. W.	. . .	f.	S. W.	. . .	. .	. . .
20th	. . .	f.	S. W.	. . .	f.	S. W.	. 2 o .	. .	. . .
21st	. . .	f.	S. E.	. . .	f.	S. W.	. . .	. .	. . .
22nd	. . .	f.	S. W.	. . .	f.	S. W.	. . .	. .	. . .
23rd	. . .	f.	S. W.	. . .	f.	S. W.	. . .	. .	. . .
24th	. . .	f.	S. E.	. . .	f.	S. E.	. . .	. .	. . .
25th	. . .	f.	E.	. . .	f.	S. W.	. . .	. .	. . .
26th	. . .	f.	E.	. . .	f.	S. W.	. . .	. .	. . .
27th	. . .	f.	E.	. . .	f.	S. W.	. 2 o .	. .	. . .
28th	. . .	f.	E.	. . .	f.	S. W.	. . .	. .	. . .
29th	. . .	f.	E.	. . .	f.	S. W.	. . .	. .	. . .
30th	. . .	f.	E.	. . .	f.	S. W.	. . .	. .	. . .

Remarks for September, 1805.[1]

2nd Service berries dried on the bushes abundant and very fine.   black colour.

3d Choke Cherries ripe and abundant.

4th ice one inch thick.

5th Ground covered with snow.

6th *Thermometer* broke by the Box striking against a tree in the Rocky mountains.

8th Mountains covered with Snow to the S. W.   a singular kind of Prickly Pears.

12th Mountains to our left covered with snow.

14th snowed rained & hailed today.

16th [Lewis:] Snow commenced about 4 oClock A. M. and continued untill night.   it is about 7 inches deep.   ice one inch thick. [Clark:] the snow fell on the old Snow 4 inches deep last night.

---

1 The following remarks are compiled entirely from the columns of remarks in the tables.   References to events recorded in text of journals are here omitted. — Ed.

18th black frost this morning.

19th Snow is about 4 Inches deep. rose raspberry ripe and abundant.

24th a thunder cloud last evening.

25th warm day.

27th day very warm

29th Day very hot

30th Great numbers of small Ducks pass down the river. hot day.

Diary of the Weather for October, Nov^r & December, 1805 [1]

October			November			December		
Day of the month	Wind	State of the Weather	Day of the month	Wind	State of the Weather	Day of the month	Wind	State of the Weather
1st	E.	f.	1st	N. E.	f.	1st	E	c. a. r.
2d	N.	f.	2nd	S. W.	f.	2d	S. W.	c. a. r.
3rd	E.	f.	3rd	N. E.	f. a fog	3rd	E.	f. a. r.
4th	E.	f.	4th	W.	c. a. r.	4th	S. E.	r.
5th	E.	f.	5th	S. W.	r. c. r.	5th	S. W.	r.
6th	E.	f.	6th	S W	r. a. r.	6th	S. W.	r.
7th	E.	f.	7th	S. W.	r. a. fog	7th	N. E.	f. a. r.
8th	E.	f.	8th	S. W.	f. a. r.	8th	N. E.	c. a. r.
9th	S. W.	c.	9th	S.	r.	9th	N. E.	c. r.
10th	N. W.	f.	10th	N. W.	r. a. r.	10th	N. E.	r.
11th	E. & S. W.	c.	11th	S. W.	r.	11th	S. W.	r.
12th	E. & S. W.	f.	12th	S. W.	h. r. t. & l.	12th	S. W.	r.
13th	S. W.	f. a. r.	13th	S. W.	r.	13th	S. W.	r.
14th	S. W.	f.	14th	. . .	r.	14th	S. W.	r.
15th	S. W.	f.	15th	S. E.	f. a. r.	15th	S. W.	c. a. r.
16th	S. W.	f.	16th	W. S. W.	f.	16th	S. W.	r.
17th	S. E.	f.	17th	E.	c. a. f.	17th	S. W.	f. a. r. & h.
18th	S. E.	f.	18th	S. E.	f. a. c.	18th	S. E.	c. a. r. s. & h.
19th	S. E.	f.	19th	S. E.	c. a. r.	19th	S. W.	h. r. & c.
20th	S. W.	f.	20th	S. E.	f. a. r.	20th	S. W.	f. a. r. & h.
21st	S. W.	f.	21st	S. E.	c. a. r.	21st	S. W.	r.
22nd	S. W.	f.	22d	S. S. E.	r.	22d	S. W.	r.
23rd	S. W.	f.	23rd	S. W.	c. a. r.	23rd	S. W.	r. h. & l.
24th	W.	f.	24th	W.	f. a. r.	24th	S. W.	r.
25th	W.	f.	25th	E. S. E.	c. a. r.	25th	S. W.	c. r
26th	W.	f.	26th	E. N. E.	r.	26th	S. W.	r. a. t. & l.
27th	W.	f.	27th	S. W.	r.	27th	S. W.	r.
28th	N. W.	r. a. f.	28th	S. W. & N. W.	r.	28th	S. E.	r.
29th	W.	f. a. r.	29th	S. W.	r.	29th	S. E.	c. a. r.
30th	S. E.	r. a. r	30th	S. W.	f. a. r. & h.	30th	S. E.	f. a. r.
31st	S. W.	f. a. r.				31st	S. W.	r.

[1] The following table is found in Clark's Codex I, p. 29, and in Clark-Voorhis note-book No. 4. The succeeding notes have been retained in order that by marking the locality the table can be more readily studied. — ED.

Note from the 1ˢᵗ to the 7ᵗʰ of October we were at the mouth of Chopunnuish river makeing canoes to Decend the Kooskooske.

Note from the 7ᵗʰ to the 16ᵗʰ octʳ we were decending Kooskooske & Lewises river, the 17ᵗʰ 18⁽ᵗʰ⁾ at the mouth of Lewis River.

Note from the 18ᵗʰ to the 22ᵈ of octʳ decending the Great Columbia to the falls.

note from the 22ᵈ to the 29ᵗʰ about the great Falls of the Columbia river.

note from the 29ᵗʰ of Octʳ to the 3ᵈ of Novʳ in passing through the western mountains below falls.

note the balance of Novʳ and December betwen the Mountains & Pacific ocean.

Remarks for October, 1805.[1]

3ᵈ. The easterly winds which blow imediately off the mountains are very cool untill 10 A. M. when the winds shift about to different points and the latter part of the days are worm.

13ᵗʰ. rained moderately from 4 to 11 A. M. to day.

28ᵗʰ. a violent wind a moderate rain commenced at 4 oClock P. M. and continued untill 8 P. M. first Vulture of the Columbia seen today.

29ᵗʰ. rained moderately all day I shot at a vulture

30ᵗʰ. rained moderately all day. Saw a different Species of ash. to any I have ever seen. arrived at the grand rapids.

31ˢᵗ. Some rain last night and this morning.

Remarks for the Month of November, 1805[2]

3ʳᵈ a thick fog which continued untill 12 oClock at which time it cleared off and was fair the remainder of the day.

5ᵗʰ. Comenced raining at 2 P.M. and continued at intrvales all day. Saw 14 Striped Snakes to day

6ᵗʰ rained the greater part of the day moderately.

7ᵗʰ. a thick fog this morning which continued untill 11 A.M at which it cleared off and continued fair until meridian, and began to rain. Several heavy Showers dureing the evening

8ᵗʰ rained moderately

---

1 The following remarks for October are found in the column of remarks of the preceding table, Codex I, p. 29, and Clark-Voorhis note-book No. 4. — ED.

2 The following remarks for November are found in Codex I, p. 30, and in Clark-Voorhis note-book No. 4. Events recorded in text of journals are here omitted. — ED.

9th rained all day with wind
10th   d°   d°
11th   d°   d°
12th Violent wind from the S.W. accompanied with Hail Thunder and
    lightning, the Claps of Thunder excessively loud and continued
    from 3 to 6 A.M. when it cleared off for a short time, after a
    heavy rain suckceeded which lasted untill 12 oClock when it
    cleared off for an hour and again became cloudy, the rain has
    been pretty generally falling sinc the 7th inst
14th a blustering rainey day
15th The after part of this day is fair and calm for the first time since
    the 5th instant. and no rain. move our encampment.
18th Cloudy R. Field killed a Vulture
20th rained moderately from 6 oClock A.M. on the 20th untill 1 P M
    on the 22^{ed} after which it became cloudy without rain
22^d The wind violent from the S.S.E. throwing the water of the R
    over our camp and rain continued all day
23rd rained all last night   to day cloudy
24th rained moderately for a short time this morning
25th some showers of rain last night
26th rained all day, some hard showers wind not so hard as it has been
    for a fiew days past
27th rained moderately all day a hard wind from the S. W. which
    compelled us to lie by on the isthmus of point William on the
    south side
28th The wind which was from the S.W. Shifted in the after part
    of the day to the N. W. and blew a Storm which was
    tremendious. rained all the last night and to day without
    inter mission
29th rained all last night hard, and to day moderately
30th rained and Hailed at intervales throughout the last night, Some
    thunder and lightning.

Remarks for December, 1805 [1]

1st rained last night and some this morning
2nd rained all the last night. and untill meridian cloudy the remainder
    of the day
3rd fair from 12 to 2 P M. rained all the last night & this morning.

[1] The following remarks are found in Clark's Codex I, p. 28, and in Clark-Voorhis
note-book No. 4. Events mentioned in text of journal are here omitted. — ED.

rained at intervales the night of the 2^d instant with constant hard and sometimes violent winds.

5th rained yesterday, last night, and moderately today all day   wind violent in the after part of the day.

6th rained all last night and to day untill 6 oClock at which time it clear'd away and become fa[i]r.   the winds also Seased to blow violent.

7th raind from 10 to 12 last night   fair day   a hard wind from the N W and a Shower of rain at 2 P M

8th cloudy after a moderate rain last night

9th cloudy and rained moderately untill 3 P.M.

10th Rained all day and the air cool   a violent wind last night from the S W.

15th rained a[t] Short intervales from the 10th instant untill 8 A. M. today after which it was cloudy all day.

16th rained all the last night.   cold wind violent from the S. W. accompanied with rain.

17th rained all the last night and this morning untill 9 oClock when we had a Shower of Hail which lasted about an hour, and then Cleared off.

18th rained Snowed and hailed at intervales all the last night,   several showers of Hail and Snow untill Meridian

19th rained last night and several showers of hail and rain this evening. the air cool.

20th Some rain and Hail last night,   rain Continu[e]d untill 10 A. M.

21st rained all last night and today

22nd d^o d^o

23^d rained all last night and moderately all day with Several showers of Hail accompanied With hard claps of thunder and sharp lightning

24th rained at intervales last night and today.

25th d^o d^o d^o

26th raind and blew hard all last night and today   som hard claps of Thunder and Sharp Lightning.

29th rained moderately without much intermittion from the 26th untill 7 a M. this morning   hard wind from S. E.

30th hard wind and Some rain last night   to day tolerably fair.

31st rained last night and moderately all day to day.

Fort Clatsop 1806

Diary of the Weather for the month of January.[1]

Day of the Month	aspect of the Weather at ☉ rise	Wind at ☉ rise	Weather at 4 oClock	Wind at 4 oClock
1st	c.a.r.	S. W.	r.a.c.	S. W.
2nd	c.a.r	S. W.	r.	S. W.
3rd	c.a.r.h.t.l.	S. W.	c.a.r.h.f.	S. W.
4th	c.a.r. & h.	S. W.	r.a.f. & r.	S. E.
5th	r.	S. E.	r.	S. E.
6th	c.a.r.	S. E.	f.	E.
7th	f.	N. E.	c.a.f.	S. E.
8th	f.	N. E.	c.a.f.	S. E.
9th	f.	S. W.	c.a.f.	S. W.
10th	f.a.r.	S. W.	c.a.f.	S. W.
11th	c.	S. W.	c.a r.	S. W.
12th	f.a.c.	N. W.	c.	N. W.
13th	r.	S. W.	r.	S. W.
14th	f.a.r.	N. W.	c.a.f.	S.
15th	r.a.c. & r.	S. E.	r.a.r.	S.
16th	r.a.r.	S. W.	r.a.r.	S. W.
17th	c.a.r.	S. W.	c.	S. W.
18th	r.a.r.	S. W.	c.a.r.	S. W.
19th	c.a.r.	S.	c.a.r.	S. W.
20th	r.a.r.	S. W.	r.a.r.	S. W.
21st	c.a.r.	S. W.	c.a.r.	S. W.
22nd	r.a.r.	S. W.	c.a.r.	S. W.
23rd	c.a.r.h.t. & l.	S. W.	c.a.f.	S. W.
24th	c.a.r. & s.	S. E.	c.a.r.h. & s	E.
25th	h.a.r.h. & s.	N. E.	c.a.r.h. & s.	N. E.
26th	c.a.h. & s.	N. E.	c.a.s.	N. E.
27th	f.a.s.	N. E.	f.	N. E.
28th	f.	N. E.	f.	N. E.
29th	f.	N. E.	f.	N. E.
30th	s.a.s.	N.	c.a.s.	W.
31st	f.a.c.	N. E.	f.	N. E.

Remarks for January, 1806.[2]

1st sun visible for a few minutes about 11 A M. the changes of the weather are exceedingly sudden, sometimes tho' seldom the sun is visible for a few moments the next it hails & rains, then

---

[1] The following table is found in Lewis's Codex J, p. 152, and Clark's Codex I, p. 31. — ED.

[2] The following remarks are compiled from those found in the column of "Remarks," and the notes following in Lewis's Codex J, pp. 150–152; and Clark's Codex I, pp. 31–33. Notes on events described in text of journals are here omitted. — ED.

Fort Clatsop. 1806.

Diary of the weather for the month of January.

Day of the month	Wind at &c at 6 A.M.	Wind at O'clock	weather at 4 O'clock P.M.	Wind at 4 O'clock P.M.	Remarks
1st	car	S.W	rac	S.W	sun visible for a few minutes about 11 A.M.
2nd	car	S.W	r	S.W	
3rd	car&f	S.W	car&f	S.W	the sun visible for a few minutes only.
4th	car&f	S.W	ra&fr	S.E	the sun visible about 2 hours
5th	r	S.E	r	S.E	
6th	car	S.E	f	E	the shower about 5 hours this evening yet it
7th	f	N.E	ca&f	E	continued fair during the night it clouded up just about sun... but
8th	f	N.E	ca&f	S.E	but shortly after became fair lost my P.M. obs.t for Equal Altitudes
9th	f	S.W	ca&f	S.W	began th rain at 10 P.M. and continued all night
10th	f&r	S.W	ca&f	S.W	
11th	c	S.W	car	S.W	
12th	f&c	N.W	c	N.W	cool this morning but no ice, nor frost, at mid-day saw flies and insects in motion
13th	c	S.W	r	S.W	
14th	f&r	N.E	ca&f	S.	
15th	r&c&r	S.E	r&r	S	saw several insects, weather warm...
16th	r&r	S.W	r&ar	S.W	rained this morning rains incessantly all night
17th	car	S.W	c	S.W	rained incessantly all night; insect in motion
18th	rar	S.W	car	S.W	rained very hard last night
19th	car	S	car	S.W	rained the greater part of last night
20th	rar	S.W	rar	S.W	rain greater part of the night wind hard
21st	car	S.W	car	S.W	mild and this morning continued all day
22nd	rar	S.W	car	S.W	wind violent last night & this morning
23rd	car&f	S.W	ca&f	S.W	the sun shown about 2h in the fore noon
24th	car	S.E	car&f	E	this morning the snow covered the ground and more... than anything... we have had, but no ice
25th	f&r&s	N.E	car&s	N.E	the ground covered with snow this morning...
26th	car&f	N.E	ca&s	N.E	at 6 P.M. last evening the wind...
27th	f&s	N.E	f	N.E	at sun this morning 4 inches very icicles of 18 inches...
28th	f	N.E	f	N.E	
29th	f	N.E	f	N.E	
30th	s&s	N.	ca&s	N.	the weather by no means as cold as it has been... snow about an inch...
31st	f&c	N.E	f&r	N.E	this morning is pleasant, the night was clear and...

MS. page, Lewis's Weather Diary
for January, 1806.

ceases, and remains cloudy the wind blows and it again rains; the wind blows by squalls most generally and is almost invariably from S.W. these visicitudes of the weather happen two three or more times a day. snake seen 25ᵗʰ December

3ᵈ: the sun visible for a few minutes only. The thunder and lightning of the last evening was violent. a singular occurrence for the time of year. the loss of my thermometer I most sincerely regret. I am confident that the climate here is much warmer than in the same parallel of Latitude on the Atlantic Ocean tho' how many degrees is now out of my power to determine. since our arrival in this neighbourhood on the 7ᵗʰ of November, we have experienced one slight white frost only which happened on the morning of the 16ᵗʰ of that month. we have yet seen no ice, and the weather so warm that we are obliged to cure our meat with smoke and fire to save it. we lost two parsels by depending on the air to preserve it, tho' it was cut in very thin slices and sufficiently exposed to the air.

4ᵗʰ: the sun visible about 2 hours

6ᵗʰ: the sun shown about 5 hours this evening & it continued fair during the night.

7ᵗʰ: it clouded up just about sunset, but shortly after became fair.

8ᵗʰ: lost my P. M. obsⁿ for Equal Altitudes.

9ᵗʰ: began to rain at 10 P. M. and continued all night.

10ᵗʰ: Various flies and insects now alive and in motion.

12ᵗʰ: the wind from any quarter off the land or along the N.W. Coast causes the air to become much cooler. every species of waterfowl common to this country at any season of the year still continue with us. cool this morning but no ice nor frost at miday sand flies and insects in motion.

14ᵗʰ: weather perfectly temperate, I never experienced a winter so warm as the present has been.

15ᵗʰ: saw several insects, weather warm, we could do very well without fire. I am satisfied that the murcury would stand at 55 a. o.

16ᵗʰ: wind hard this morning rained incessently all night.

17ᵗʰ: rained incessantly all night, insects in motion.

18ᵗʰ: rained very hard last night.

19ᵗʰ: rained the greater part of last night.

20ᵗʰ: raind greater part of night wind hard.

21ˢᵗ: wind hard this morning cont[in]ued all day.

22ⁿᵈ: wind violent last night & this morning.

23ᵈ: the sun shown about 2 h. in the forenoon. when the sun is said to shine or the weather fair it is to be understood that it barely casts a shaddow, and that the atmosphere is haizy of a milkey white colour.

24th. this morning the Snow covered the ground and was cooler than any weather we have had but no ice.

25th the ground covered with snow this morning $\frac{1}{2}$ inch deep   ice on the water in the canoes $\frac{1}{4}$ of an inch thick. it is now preceptably coulder than it has been this winter.

26th. the snow this evening is 4 $\frac{3}{4}$ inches deep, the icesickles of 18 inches in length continued suspended from the eves of the houses during the day. it now appears something like winter for the first time this season.

27th the sun shone more bright this morning than it has done since our arrival at this place. the snow since 4. P. M. yesterday has increased to the debth of 6 Inches. and this morning is perceptibly the couldest that we have had. I suspect the Murcury would stand at about 20.° above naught; the breath is perceptible in our room by the fire.

28th last night exposed a vessel of water to the air with a view to discover the debth to which it would freiz in the course of the night, but unfortunately the vessel was only 2 inches deep and it f[r]eized the whole thickness; how much more it might have frozen had the vessel been deeper is therefore out of my power to decide. it is the couldest night that we have had, and I suppose the murcury this morning would have stood as low as 15.° above o.

29th not so could, water in a vessel exposed to the [air] during the night freized $\frac{3}{8}$ths of an inch only.[1]

30th the weather by no means as could as it has been   snow fell about an inch deep.

31st. this morning is pleasant, the night was clear and cold. notwithstanding the could weather the Swan white Brant geese & ducks still continue with us; the sandhill crain also continues. the brown or speckled brant are mostly gone some few are still to be seen   the Cormorant loon and a variety of other waterfowls still remain. The Winds from the Land brings us could and clear weather while those obliquely along either coast or off the Ocean bring us warm damp cloudy and rainy weather. the hardest winds are always from the S.W. The blue crested

---

[1] We infer that this note was intended for January 29; but it may have been written for the preceding day. — ED.

Corvus bird has already began to build it's nest.   their nests
are formed of small sticks; usually in a pine tree.

Great numbers of Ravens, and a small black Crow are con-
tinually about us.   The pale yellow Streiked and dove coloured
robin is about, also the little brown ren or fly-catsch which is a
little larger than the humming bird.

Diary of the weather for the month of February, 1806.[1]

Day of Month	aspect of the weather at ☉ rise	wind at ☉ rise	aspect of the weather at 4 OCl P. M.	wind at 4 O'Clock P M.
1st	f.	N. E.	f.	N. E.
2nd	f.	N. E.	c. a. s.	S. W.
3rd	c. a. s. & r.	N. W.	c. a. f.	N. E.
4th	f.	N. E.	f.	N. E.
5th	f.	N. E.	f.	N. E.
6th	f.	N. E.	c.	S. W.
7th	c.	S. W.	c.	S. W.
8th	c. a. s. r. & h.	S. W.	c. a. f. r. h. & s.	S. W.
9th	c. a. r. & h.	S. W.	c. a. r. & h.	S. W.
10th	c. a. r. h. & s.	N.	c. a. f. & c.	S. W.
11th	c. a. f. & c.	S. W.	r. a. f. & r.	S. W.
12th	r. a. r. & c.	S. W.	r. a. c. & r.	S. W.
13th	c. a. r.	S. W.	c. a. r.	S. W.
14th	c. a. f. & s.	S. W.	r. a. r. f. & r.	S. W.
15th	c. a. r. & f.	S.	c. a. r. & f.	S. W.
16th	r. a. s. & r.	S. W.	r. a. f. & r.	S. W.
17th	c. a. r. h. & s.	S. W.	r. a. f. h. s. & r.	S. W.
18th	c. a. r. & h.	S. W.	r. a. r. & h.	S. W.
19th	r. a. r.	S. W.	r. a. r.	S. W.
20th	c. a. r.	S. W.	c. a. r.	S. W.
21st	r. a. c. & r.	S. W.	r. a. c. & r.	S. W.
22ed	f. a. r.	N. E.	c. a. f.	N. E.
23rd	f.	S. W.	c. a. f.	S. W.
24th	c. a. f. & c.	S. W.	r. a. c. & r.	S.
25th	r. a. r.	S.	r. a. r.	S.
26th	f. a. r.	N. E.	c. a. f. & r.	S.
27th	c. a. r.	S. W.	r. a. r.	S. W.
28th	r. a. r.	S. W.	c. a. c. & f.	S. W.

Remarks for February, 1806.[2]

1st   the weather by no means as cold as it was tho' it freized last
night.

---

[1] The following table is found in Lewis's Codex I, p. 149, and Clark-Voorhis
note-book No. 2. — Ed.

[2] The following remarks are combined from the column of remarks in the preceding table, and those succeeding in Lewis's Codex J, pp. 148, 149, and the last pages
of Clark-Voorhis note-book No. 2. — Ed.

2nd the bald Eagle still remains.

3^d the snow fell about half an inch, but the rain which succeded soon melted it   at 9 A. M. the sun shone.   the rain which fell in the latter part of the night freized and formed a slight incrustation on the snow which fell some days past, and also on the boughs of the trees &c.   yesterday it continued fair until 11. A.M. when the wind vered about to S.W. and the horizon was immediately overcast with clouds, which uniformly takes place when the wind is from that point.

4th the last night clear and cold   the Netul frozen over in several places.   All the waterfowls before innumerated still continue with us.   the bird which resembles the robbin have now visited us in small numbers   saw two of them yesterday about the fort ; they are gentle.

6th very cold last night think it reather the coldest night that we have had.   cloudy at 9 A. M.

7th continued cloudy all night   a little snow at 10 A. M.

8th it was principally rain which fell since 4 P. M yesterday and has melted down the snow w[h]ich has continued to cover the ground since the 24th of January ; the feeling of the air and other appearances seem to indicate, that the rigor of the winter is passed ; it is so warm that we are apprehensive that our meat will spoil, we therefore cut it in small peices and hang it seperately on sticks.   Saw a number of insects flying about. the small brown flycatch continues with us.   this is the smallest of all the American birds except the humming bird.

9th principally rain which has fallen.

10th snow covered the ground this morning disappeared before evening. sun shown 2 hours.

12th it rained the greater part of last night

13th Wind very hard last evening and all night.

14th very small quantity of snow fell last night   not enough to cover the ground   somewhat colder this morning.   the sun shown only a few moments.

15th fair most of last night   hard frost this morning.   the ground white with it.

The robbin returned and were singing which reminded me of spring.   some other small birds passed on their flight from the South, but were so high that we could not distinguish of what kind they were.   the robbin had left this place before our arrival in November.

16th   but a small quantity of snow nearly all disolved by morning with the succeeding rain. at 11. A.M. it became fair and the insects were flying about. at ½ after 12. O'C.ᵏ it again clouded up and began to rain.

17th   the hail and snow covered the ground this morning.

18th   wind violent greater part of the day and all night.

19th   wind violent all day.

20th   wind violent all night and the greater part of the day.

21st   the wind continues high this morning & untill evening.

22nd   the wind scarcely perceptable

23d   heavy white frost this morning. at eleven A. M. it c[l]ouded up and continued so all day.

24th   much warmer this morning than usual. the aquatic and other birds heretofore enumerated continue with us still. the Sturgeon and a small fish like the Anchovey begin to run. they are taken in the Columbia about 30 or 40 milˢ above us. the anchovey is exquisitely fine. the wind became hard this evening.

25th   the wind violent all night and this morning continued untill late in the evening when it c[e]ased.

26th   at 9 A.M. it clouded up again.

28th   it rained constantly during the last night. the sun shown about 9 A. M. partially a few minutes.

saw a variety of insects in motion this morning some small bugs as well as flies. a brown fly with long legs about half the size of the common house fly was the most common. this has been the first insect that appeared. it is genrally about the sinks, or filth of any kind. the yellow and brown flycatch has returned. it is a very small bird with a tail as long proportiably as a Sparrow.

Diary of the weather for the month of March, 1806.[1]

Day of the month	aspect of the weather at sun rise	wind at ☉ rise	aspect of the weather at 4 O'Ck P M	wind at 4 OCk P M
1st	f. a. r. & c.	S. W.	r. a. c. & r.	S. W.
2ed	r. a. c. & r.	S.	r. a. c. & r.	S.
3rd	c. a. r.	S.	c. a. r.	S.
4th	r. a. c. & r.	S.	r. a. r.	S.
5th	c. a. r.	N. E.	c. a. r.	S.
6th	f. a. r.	S. E.	c. a. f.	S. E.
7th	r. a. r. & h.	S. E.	r. a. f. r. h. c & f.	S. E.
8th	h & r. a. h. r. & s.	S.	r. a r. & h.	S. E.
9th	s. & h. a. r. s & h.	S. W.	r. a. h & r.	S. W.
10th	s. & r. a. h. r. & s.	S. W.	f. a. r. h. & s.	S. W.
11th	f. a. r. h. & s.	S. E.	f. a. r. & h.	S. E.
12th	f. a. c.	N. E.	c. a. f.	N. E.
13th	f. a. r.	N. E.	f.	N. E.
14th	c. a. f.	N. E.	c.	N. E.
15th	c. a. c.	N. E.	f.	N. E.
16th	r. a. f. & c.	S. W.	c. a. f. c. r	S. W.
17th	c. a. r.	S. W.	r. a. f h. s. & r.	S W.
18th	r. a. c. & r.	S. W.	r. a. f. r. & h.	S. W.
19th	r. & h. a. c. r. & h.	S. W.	r. a. f. r. & h.	S. W.
20th	r. a. r. & h.	S. W.	r.	S. W.
21st	r. a. r.	S. W.	c. a. r.	N. E.
22ed	r. a. r.	S. W.	r. a. c. & r.	S. W. or N. W. & N. E.
23rd	r. a. r.	S. W.	f. a c. & r.	S. W.
24th	r. a. c. & r.	S. W.	f. a. c.	N. W. a S. W.
25th	c. a. f.	S. E.	r. a. c. & r.	S. E.
26th	c. a. r.	N. W.	c. a. f. & c.	S. E.
27th	r. a. c.	S. E.	r. a. c. & r.	S. E.
28th	c. a. r.	N.	f. a. f. & r.	S. W.
29th	c. a. r. & f.	S.	c. a. r.	S. W.
30th	c.	S.	f. a. c.	S. W.
31st	f.	S. E.	f.	S. E.

Remarks for March 1806.[1]

1st a great part of this day was so warm that fire was unnecessary, notwithstanding it's being cloudy and raining. The clouds interfered in such manner that no observations could be made this morning.

3d rained and the wind blew hard all night. air perfectly temperate.

---

[1] The following table is found in Lewis's Codex J, p. 147, and in Clark-Voorhis note-book No. 2. — ED.

[1] The following remarks are found in Lewis's Codex J, pp. 145–149, and in Clark-Voorhis note-book No. 2. — ED.

4th. rained constantly most of the night, saw a Snail this morning, they are very large.

5th. the air is considerably colder this morning but nothing like freizing.

6th. altho' it is stated to be fair this morning the sun is so dim that no observations can be made. Saw a spider and an insect resembling a Musquetoe this morning, tho' the air is perceptably colder than it has been since the 1st inst. at 9 A.M. it clouded up and continued so the ballance of the day. even the Easterly winds which have heretofore given us the only fair weather which we have enjoyed, seem now to have lost their influence in this respect.

7th. Sudden changes & frequent, during the day, scarcly any two hours of the same discription. the Elk now begin to shed their horns. a bird of a scarlet colour as large as a common pheasant with a long tail has returned, one of them was seen today near the fort by Capt. Clark's black man, I could not obtain a view of it myself.

8th. the ground covered with hail and snow this morning, air cool but not freezing.

9th. snow and hail 1 inch deep this morning air still cold more so than yesterday but not freezing.

10th. snow nearly disappeared by this morning. the air considerably warmer.

11th. snow 1 inch deep this morning air cold, but no ice. some insects seen in the evening in motion. I attem[p]ted to make an observation for Equal Altitudes but the P.M. Obsern. was lost in consequence of clouds. it became cloudy at 10 A.M. and rained attended with some hail at six it P.M. it became fair and the wind changing to N. E. it continued fair during the night. the snow had all disappeared by 4. P.M. this evening.

12th. white frost this morning and ice in the pools of standing water. it being fair in the morning I again attempted Equal Altitudes but it became cloudy at 3. P.M. and continued so during the day, without any rain

13th. slight frost this morning. a little rain fell in the latter part of the night. saw a number of insects in motion ; among others I saw for the fi[r]st time this spring and winter a downey black fly about the size of the common house fly. the plants begin to appear above the ground, among others the rush of which the natives eat the root. and the plant, the root of which resembles in flavor the sweet potato also eaten by the natives. it is small.

14th yesterday and last night were the most perfectly fair wether we have seen at this place.

15th the temperature of the air is perfectly pleasant without fire. became fair at 8 A. M. the sorrel with an oval obtuse and ternate leaf has now put forth it's leaves. some of them have nearly obtained their growth already.[1] the birds were singing very agreably this morning particularly the common robin.

16th wind hard greater part of the day. The Anchovey has ceased to run; the white salmon trout have succeeded them. the weather so warm that the insects of various speceis are every day in motion.

17th rained all night. air somewhat colder this morning. frequent and sudden changes in the course of the day.

18th frequent showers through the day

19th frequent and sudden changes during the day wind not so hard as usual.

20th rained all day without intermission.

21st rained all night   at 9 A. M. wind changed to N. E. and the rain ceased.   cloudy the ballance of the day.

22nd rain continued without intermission greater part of the night. air temperate. the leaves and petals of the flowers of the green Huckleburry have appeared. some of the leaves have already obtained ¼ of their size.[2]

23d it became fair at 12 OCk. and continued cloudy and fair by intervales without rain till night.

24th at 9 A.M. it became fair and continued fair all day and greater part of the night. the brown bryery shrub with a broad pinnate leaf has began to put fourth it's leaves.[3] the polecat Colwort, is in blume. Saw the blue crested fisher. birds are singing this morning. the black Alder is in blume.

25th cold this morning but no ice nor frost. the Elder, Gooseberry, & Honeysuckle are now putting forth their leaves. the nettle [4] and a variety of other plants are now springing up. the flower of the broad leafed thorn is nearly blown. several small plants in blume.

[1] *Oxalis oregana* Nutt. — C. V. PIPER.
[2] This is probably the huckleberry known as *Vaccinium parvifolia*. —C. V. PIPER.
[3] Probably this is *Fatsia horrida*. — C. V. PIPER.
[4] The nettle is *Urtica lyallii* Wats — C. V. PIPER.

26th. cold and rainy last night. wind hard this morning fair at 9 A.M. cloudy at 1 P. M. The humming bird has appeared. killed one of them and found it the same with those common to the United States.

27th. blew hard about noon. rained greater part of the day. the small or bank martin appeared today, saw one large flock of them. waterfowl very scarce, a few Comorant, geese, and the red-headed fishing duck are all that are to be seen. the red flowering currant are in blume, this I take to be the same speceis I first saw in the Rocky Mountains ; the fruit is a deep purple berry covered with a gummy substance and not agreeably flavored. there is another speceis uncovered with gum which I first found on the waters of the Columbia about the 12th of August last.[1]

28th. rained by showers greater part of last night frequent showers in the course of the day. this evening we saw many swan passing to the North as if on a long flight. vegitation is not by several days as forward here as at Fort Clatsop when we left that place. the river rising fast, the water is turbid ; the tide only swells the water a little, it dose not stop the current. it is now within 2 feet of it's greatest hight, which appears to increase as we assend.

29th frequent showers through the night. very cold this morning.

30th. at 10 A. M. it became fair and continued so weather moderately warm. Saw a leather winged bat. the grass is about 16 Inches high in the river bottoms. the frogs are now abundant and are crying in the swamps and marshes.

31st The Summer Duck has returned. I saw several to day in a small pond. This evening the Musqueters were verry troublesom this evening, it is the first time they have been so this spring. The waterfowls are much plentyer about the enterance of quick sand river than they were below. observed a species of small wild onion growing among the moss of the rocks, they resemble the Shives of our gardens and grow remarkably close together forming a perfect tuft, they are quite as agreeably flavoured as the shives.

---

1 The red-flowering currant is *Ribes sanguineum*. The Rocky Mountain species referred to is *Ribes viscossissimum*, similar in foliage but not in flowers. Lewis brought back types of both. — C. V. PIPER.

Diary of the Weather for the month of April, 1806.[1]

Days of the month	State of the weather at ☉ rise	Wind at ☉ rise	State of the Weather at 4 P M	Wind at 4 P M	State of the Columbia River		
					raised or fallen	Feet	Inches & parts
1st	c.a.f.	S. E.	c.a.f.	S. E.	r.	. .	1.
2ed	c.	S. E.	c.a.f.	S. E.	f.	. .	7/8
3rd	c.a.r.	S. W.	c.a.r.	W.	f.	. .	3 1/2
4th	c.a.r.	S. W.	c.a.r.	S. W.	f.	. .	4 1/2
5th	c.a.r.	S. W.	c.a.f. & c.	S. W.	f.	. .	2 1/2
6th	f.a.c.	S. W.	f.	S. W.	f.	. .	1.
7th	f.	S. W.	f.	S. W.	r.	. .	1/2
8th	f.	E.	f.	E.	r.	. .	1 1/2
9th	f.	W.	f.	W.	. . .	. .	. . .
10th	c.a.r.	W.	c.a.r.	S. W.	r.	. .	1.
11th	r.a.r.	W.	c.a.r.	S. W.	r.	. .	2
12th	c.a.r.	W.	r.a.c. & r.	W.	r.	. .	2
13th	r.a.c. & r.	W.	c.a.r. & f.	W.	r.	. .	2 1/2
14th	f.	W.	f._	W.	r.	. .	1
15th	f.	W.	f.	W.	. . .	. .	. . .
16th	f.a.c.	S. W.	f.	S. W.	f.	. .	2.
17th	f.	N. E.	c.a.f.	S. W.	f.	. .	2
18th	f.a.r.	S. W.	f.	S. W	f.	. .	1
19th	c.a.r.	S. W.	c.	Ɛ. W.	f.	. .	3
20th	f.a.r.	S. W.	c.a.r.	S. W.	f.	. .	2 1/2
21st	f.	N. E.	f.	E.	f.	. .	2
22nd	f.	N. W.	f.	W.	f.	. .	1
23rd	f.a.c.	E.	f.	N. E.	f.	. .	4
24th	f.	N. W.	f.	N. W.	f.	. .	2
25th	f.	N. E.	f.	N. E.	f.	. .	2
26th	f.a.c.	N. W.	f.	N. E.	f.	. .	2 1/2
27th	f.a.r.	S. E.	f.	N. W.	f.	. .	1 1/2
28th	f.a.t.	S. W.	f.	N. E.	f.	. .	2
29th	f.a.c.	N. W.	f.	N. W.	f.	. .	.1
30th	c.a.r.	N. W.	f.a.c.	N. W.	f.	. .	2

Remarks for April, 1806.[2]

1st at 6 P. M. last evening it became cloudy. Cotton wood in blume. From the best opinion I could form of the state of the Columbia on the 1st of April it was about 9 feet higher than when we decended it in the begining of November last. the rising and falling of the river as set down in the diary is that only which took place from sunseting to sunrise or thereabouts it being the time that we usually remain at our encampments.

2nd heavy dew last night. cloudy all night.

---

[1] The following table is found in Lewis's Codex K, p. 150, and in the Clark-Voorhis note-book No. 3.—ED.

[2] The following remarks are found in Lewis's Codex K, pp. 150-152. — ED.

3.ᵈ a slight rain about day light this morning.

4.ᵗʰ the rains have been very slight.

5.ᵗʰ rain but slight, air colder than usual this morning.

6.ᵗʰ this is the most perfectly fair day that we have seen for a Some time musquetoes trouble some this evening in the bottoms the cottonwood has put forth its leaves and begin[s] to assume a green appearance at a distance. the sweet willow has not yet generally birst its budscales while the leaves of the red and broad leafed willow are of some size; it appears to me to be the most backward in vegetating of all the willows. the narrow leafed willow is not found below tide water on this river.

7.ᵗʰ the air temperate, birds singing, the pizmire, flies, beetles, in motion.

8.ᵗʰ wind commenced at 5 A. M. & continued to blow most violently all day air temperate. the male flowers of the cottonwood are falling. the goosburry has cast the petals of it's flowers, and it's leaves obtained their full size. the Elder which is remarkably large has began to blume. some of it's flowerets have expanded their corollas. the serviceburries, chokecherries, the growth which resembles the beach, the small birch and grey willow have put forth their leaves.[1]

9.ᵗʰ the wind lulled a little before day, and became high at 11 A. M. continued till dark. the vineing honeysuckle, has put forth shoots of several inches the dogtoothed violet is in blume as is also both the speceis of the mountain holley, the strawburry, the bears claw, the cowslip, the violet, common striped; and the wild cress or tongue grass.[2]

10.ᵗʰ some snow fell on the river hills last night. morning cold, slight showers through the day.

11.ᵗʰ cold raining night the geese are yet in large flocks and do not yet appear to have mated. what I have heretofore termed the broad leafed ash is now in blume. the fringe tree has cast the corolla and it's leaves have nearly obtained their full size.[3] the sacacommis is in blume.

---

1 Most of these plants have been identified in the text of journals. The small birch is not the species mentioned April 30, 1806, but *Betula glandulosa* Mx. — C. V. PIPER.

2 The honeysuckle, dogtooth violet, mountain holly, and strawberry have been identified in text of journals. The "bear's claw" is some species of *Delphinium*; the cowslip, *Dodecaltheon sp.*; the violet is probably *Viola sp.*; and the cress or tongue grass, *Cardamine sp.* — C. V. PIPER.

3 The "fringe-tree" is probably *Nuttallia cerasi formis.* — C. V. PIPER.

12th cold   snowed on the mountains through which the river passes
at the rapids.   the duckinmallard which bread in this neighbourhood, is now laying it's eggs, — vegetation is rapidly progressing in the bottoms tho' the snow of yesterday and to day
reaches within a mile of the base of the mountains at the rapids
of the Columbia.

13th cold rainy night.   rained by showers through the day.   wind
hard.

14th wind arrose at 8 A.M. and continued hard all day   service berries
in blume.

15th wind blew tolerably hard to day after 10 A.M.   observed the
Curloo and prairie lark.

16th morning unusually warm.   vegitation rapidly progressing.   at the
rock fort camp saw the prarie lark, a species of the peawee, the
blue crested fisher, the partycoloured corvus, and the black
pheasant.   a species of hiasinth native of this place blumed to
day, it was not in blume yesterday.

17th weather warm; the sweet willow & white oak begin to put forth
their leaves.

18th rain but slight.   wind very hard all day.

19th raind.   moderate showers, very cold   snow on the tops of the
low hills.

20th weather cold   rain slight   snow on the hills adjacent   wind violent.   some frost this morning.

21st heavy white frost this morning.   remarkably cold last night.

22nd night cold the day warm.

26th the last evening was cloudy it continued to threaten rain all night
but without raining.   the wind blew hard all night.   the air
cold as it is invariably when it sets from the westerly quarter.
the sweet willow has put forth its leaves.

27th had a shower of rain last night.

30th rain slight.

Diary of the Weather for the month of May, 1806.[1]

Days of the month	State of the Weather at ☉ rise	Wind at ☉ rise	State of the Weather at 4 P M	Wind at 4 P M	State of the Kooskooskee		
					rased or fallen	Feet	Inc. & parts
1st	c.a.r.	S. W.	c.	S. W.			
2d	f.a.c.	N. E.	f.	S. W.			
3rd	c.a.h.r. & s.	S. W.	c.a.r.h. & s.	S. W.			
4th	f.a.h.	S. W.	c.a.r. & h.	S. W.			
5th	f.	S. W.	f.	S. W.			
6th	r.a.c. & r.	N. E.	f.a.r.	N. E.			
7th	f.a.c.	N. E.	f.	S. W.			
8th	f.	S. W.	f.	S. W.			
9th	f.	S. W.	f.a.c.	W.			
10th	c.a.r. & s.	S. W.	f.a.s.	S. W.			
11th	f.a.r.	S. W.	f.a.c.	S. W.			
12th	f.	E.	f.	S. W.			
13th	f.	S. W.	f.	S. W.			
14th	f.	S. W.	f.	S. W.			
15th	f.	N.	f.a.c.	N. W.			
16th	c.	S. E.	c.a.r.	S. E.	r.	..	6
17th	r.a.r.	S. E.	c.a.r.	S. E.	r.	..	10¾
18th	c.a.r.	S. E.	c.	S. E.	r.	..	2
19th	r.a.r.	S. E.	c.a.r.	S. E.	f.	..	4
20th	r.a.r.	N. W.	c.a.r.	S. E.	r.	..	2
21st	c.a.r.	S. E.	f.a.c.	S. E.	f.	..	1
22nd	f.	S. E.	f.	S E.	f.	..	2
23rd	f.	N. W.	f.	N. W. & S. E.	f.	..	1½
24th	f.	S. E.	f.	N. W.	f.	..	1
25th	c.a.r & t.	N. W.	f.	N. W.	r.	..	9½
26th	f.a.r.	S. E.	f.	N W.	r.	..	6
27th	c.	S. E.	r.a.f.r. & t.l.	S E.	r.	..	6½
28th	c.a.r.t.l.	S. E.	c.a.f.r.t. & l.	S. E.	r.	..	11
29th	c.a.r. & t.	S. E.	c.a.r.	N. W.	r.	1	5
30th	c.a.r.	S. E.	f.	S. E.	f.	..	6
31st	c.a.f.	S. E.	f.	S. E.	r.	1	1

Remarks for May, 1806.[2]

1st had a pretty hard shower last night. cold morning. having left the river we could no longer observe it's state; it is now declining tho' it has not been as high this season by five feet as it appears to have been the last spring. the indians inform us that it will rise higher in this month, which I presume is caused by the snows of the mountains.

2ed cold this morning, some dew.

1 The following table is found in Lewis's Codex K, p. 149, and in the Clark-Voorhis note-book No. 3. — ED.

2 The following remarks are found in Lewis's Codex K, pp. 147–149, and in the Clark-Voorhis note-book No. 3. — ED.

3rd the mountains to our right seem to have experienced an increase of their snow last evening. rained last night and snowed & hailed this morning. the air cold and wind hard.

4th heavy white frost this morning ice ⅙ of an inch thick on standing water.

5th hard frost this morning ice ⅛ of an inch thick on vessels of water.

7th the Kooskooske is rising water cold and clear.

9th Musquetors troublesom

10th it began to rain and hail about sunseting this evening which was shortly after succeeded by snow. it continued to fall without intermission untill 7 A.M. and lay 8 inches deep on the plain where we were. the air was very keen. a suddon transition this. yesterday the face of the country had every appearance of summer. after nine A.M. the sun shown but was frequently obscured by clouds which gave us light showers of snow. in the after part of the day the snow melted considerably but there was too great a portion to be disipated by the influence of one day's sun.

11th the Crimson haw is not more forward now at this place than it was when we lay at *rock fort camp*. in April.

12th the natives inform us that the salmon have arrived at the entrance of the Kooskooske in great numbers and that some were caught yesterday in Lewis's river opposite to us many miles above the entrance of that river. from this village of the broken ,arm Lewis's river is only about 10 miles distant to the S. W. the natives also inform us that the salmon appear many days sooner in Lewis's river above the entrance of the Kooskooseke than they do in that stream.

15th the Kooskooske rising fast, the water is clear and cold.

16th last night was uncommonly warm river rising fast. say 9 Inches.

17th rained hard the greater part of the night wet the Chronometer by accedent. river rise 11 inches the indians caught 3 salmon at their village on the Kooskooske above our camp some miles. they say that these fish are now passing by us in great numbers but that they cannot be caught as yet because those which first ascend the river do not keep near shore ; they further inform us that in the course of a few days the fish run near the shore and then they take them with their skimming netts in great numbers.[1] rained untill 12 Oc^k by intervails.

---

[1] This information in regard to the salmon is not found in text of journal and seems somewhat inconsistent therewith. See text of journal for May 14, 18, 22, 25, 26, and June 2 and 3. — ED.

19th rained hard last night and untill 8 A. M.

20th rained violently the greater part of the night. air raw and cold.
a nest of the large blue or sand hill crain was found by one of
our hunters. the young were in the act of leaving the shell.
the young of the partycoloured corvus begin to fly.

22nd air colder this morning than usual white frost tho' no ice. the
air is remarkably dry and pure it has much the feeling and
appearance of the air in the plains of the Missouri. since our
arrival in this neighbourhood on the 7th inst. all the rains noted
in the diary of the weather were snows on the plain and in
some instances it snowed on the plains when only a small mist
was perseptable in the bottoms at our camps. (The high plains
are about 800 feet higher than the small bottoms on the river
and creeks.)

23d the air is cold in the morning but warm through the day. some
dew each morning.

24th air remarkably pleasant all day.

25th rained moderately the greater part of last night and to day nearly
all day. Thunder.

26th the sun shone warm today, but the air was kept cool by the
N. W. breezes.

27th the dove is cooing which is the signal as the indians inform us of
the approach of the salmon. The snow has disappeared on the
high plains and seems to be diminishing fast on the spurs and
lower region of the Rocky Mountains.

28th had several heavy thunder showers in the course of the last
evening and night. the river from sunrise yesterday to sun
rise this morning raised 1 ft. 10 Ins. d[r]ift wood runing in
considerable quantities and current incredibly swift tho' smooth.

29th frequent and heavy showers attended by distant thunder through
the night. the river raised 6 inches in the course of yesterday
and 1 foot 5 I. in the course of the last night. it is now as
high as there are any marks of it's having been in the spring
1805. at 10 A.M. it arrived at it's greatest hight having
raised 1½ inches from sunrise to that time. in the ballance of
the day it fell 7 inches. the natives inform us that it will take
one more rise before it begins finally to subside for the season
and then the passage of the mountains will be practicable.

30th rain slight last night. the river continued to fall untill 4 A.M.
having fallen 3 Inches by that time since sunrise. it now was
at a stand untill dark after which it began again to rise.

31ˢᵗ within 3 Inches of its greatest hight on the 29ᵗʰ inst. and fell a little after which it rose again. The river rose 13 inches last night and continues to rise fast. from sunset on the 31ˢᵗ of May untill sun rise on the 1ˢᵗ of June it rose Eighteen inches and is now as high as any marks of it's having been for several years past. a heavy thunder cloud passed around us last evening about sunset. Some rain fell in the fore part of the night only.

Diary of the weather for the Month of June, 1806.[1]

Day of the Month	State of the weather at ⊙ rise	Wind at ⊙ rise	State of the weather at 4 P M	Wind at 4 P M.	State of the Koskooske at ⊙ rise		
					raised or fallen	Feet	Inches and parts
1ˢᵗ	f.a.r.t. & l.	S. E.	f.a.c.	N. W.	r.	1	6
2ᵉᵈ	c a.c.	N. W.	f.a.c.	S. E.	r.	..	8
3ʳᵈ	c.a.f. & c.	S. E.	c.a.f.	S. E.	r.	..	6
4ᵗʰ	c.a.r.	S. E.	f.a.c.	N. W.	r.	..	1−½
5ᵗʰ	f.	S. E.	f.	N. W.	r.	..	4
6ᵗʰ	f.	S. E.	f.	N. W.	f.	..	1
7ᵗʰ	c.a.r.	N. W.	c.a.f.r. & h.	N. W.	f.	..	3
8ᵗʰ	c.	S. E.	c.a f.	N. W.	f.	..	7
9ᵗʰ	c.	S. E.	f.a.c.	N. W.	f.	..	3−½
10ᵗʰ	f.	S. E.	f.	N. W.	f.	..	1
11ᵗʰ	f	S. E.	f.	N. W.	..	..	..
12ᵗʰ	f.a.r.t. l.	S. E.	f.	N. W.	..	..	..
13ᵗʰ	c.	S. E.	c.a.f.	N. W.	..	..	..
14ᵗʰ	f.	S. E.	f.	N. W.	..	..	..
15ᵗʰ	c.	N. W.	r.a.f & r.	N. W.	..	..	..
16ᵗʰ	f.a.c.	S. E.	c.a.f.	S. E.	..	..	..
17ᵗʰ	c.a.r.	E.	c.a.f. & r.	S. E.	..	..	..
18ᵗʰ	c.a.r.	E.	c.a.r. & h.	S. W.	..	..	..
19ᵗʰ	f.a.c.	S. E.	f.	N. W.	..	..	..
20ᵗʰ	f.	S. E.	f.	N. W.	..	..	..
21ˢᵗ	f.	S. E.	f.	N. W.	..	..	..
22ᵉᵈ	f.	N. W.	f.	N. W.	..	..	..
23ʳᵈ	f.	N. W.	f.	N. W.	..	..	..
24ᵗʰ	f.	N. W.	f a.c.	N. W.	..	..	..
25ᵗʰ	c.a.r.	S. E.	c.a.r.	N. W.	..	..	..
26ᵗʰ	c.a.r.	S. E.	f.	S. E.	..	..	..
27ᵗʰ	f.a.r. & t.	S. E.	f.	S. E.	..	..	..
28ᵗʰ	f.	S. E.	f.	S. E.	..	..	..
29ᵗʰ	f.	S. E.	f.a.r.h. & t.	S. E.	..	..	..
30ᵗʰ	f.	S. E.	f.	N W.	..	..	..

[1] The following table is found in Lewis's Codex L, p. 149; and in Clark's Codex M, p. 152. The latter has no notation for the river. — ED.

Remarks for June, 1806.[1]

1st about dark last evening had a slight rain from a heavy thunder cloud which passed to the E. & N. E. of us.

2nd have slept comfortably for several nights under one blankett only. The river from sunrise untill 10 A. M. yesterday raised 1½ inches; from that time untill dark fell 4½, and in the course of the last night raised again 8 Inches as stated in the diary. the Indians inform us that the present rise of the river is the greatest which it annually takes, and that when the water now subsides to about the hight it was when we arrived here the mountains will be passable. I have no doubt but that the melting of the mountain snows in the begining of June is what causes the annual inundation of the lower portion of the Missouri from the 1st to the Middle of July.

3d The weather has been much warmer for five days past than previously, particularly the mornings and nights.

4th rained greater part of last night but fell in no great quantity. yesterday the water was at it's greatest hight at noon, between which and dark it fell 15 inches and in the course of the night raised 1½ inches as stated in the diary. from the indian information the river will now subside and may therefore be said to have been at it's greatest annual hight on the 3rd inst at noon.

5th last night was colder than usual but no frost. the river fell 3½ inches in the course of the day and raised 4 I. last night as [s]tated in the diary. this fluctuating state of the river no doubt is caused by the influence of the sun in the course of the day on the snows of the mountains; the accession of water thus caused in the day does not reach us untill night when it produces a rise in the river. The wild rose is in blume.[2] the river fell 10 Ins in the course of this day.

6th in the course of the last night the river raised a little but fell by morning 1 inch lower than what it stood at last evening. the seven bark and the yellow vining honeysuckle are just in blume. a few of the does have produced their young. strawberries ripe near the river. hot sultery day.

7th rain but slight both last evening and today. but little hail tho'

---

1 The following remarks are found in Lewis's Codex L, pp. 148, 149; and in Clark's Codex M, pp. 150-152. References to events mentioned in text of journal are here omitted. — ED.

2 *Rosa nutkana* — C. V. PIPER.

large.   The river fell three inches last night and 7 yesterday. The goose berries fully grown also the servis berry.

8ᵗʰ   river fell 8 in. in the course of yesterday.   7 last night [as entered in the diary].

9ᵗʰ   river fell 9 In. yesterday

10ᵗʰ   river fell 5½ in. in course of yesterday.   having left the river today I could not longer keep it's state; it appears to be falling fast and will probably in the course of a few days be as low as when we first arrived there.   it is now about 6 feet lower than it has been.

12ᵗʰ   slight sprinkle of rain in the fore part of the night.

13ᵗʰ   The days for several past have been warm, the Musquetoes troublesome.

15ᵗʰ   it began to rain at 7 A. M. and continued by showers untill 5 P. M.

16ᵗʰ   on the tops of the hills the dog tooth violet is just in bloom, grass about 2 inches high, small Huckleberry just putting fourth it's leaves &c.[1]

17ᵗʰ   rained slightly a little after sunset   air cool.   rained from 1 to 3 P. M.

22ⁿᵈ   hard frost this morning tho' no ice.   Strawberries ripe at the Quawmash flats, they are but small and not abundant.

23ᵈ   hard frost this morning ice one eighth of an inch thick on standing water.

25ᵗʰ   rained a little last night; some showers in the evening.

26ᵗʰ   Slight rain in the fore part of last evening in the snowey region.

27ᵗʰ   Thunder shower last evening   some rain a little before dark last evening.

28ᵗʰ   nights are cool in these mountains but no frost.

29ᵗʰ   night cold   hard frost this morning.   the quawmash and Strawberries are just begining to blume at the flatts on the head of the Kooskooske.   The sun flower also just beginning to blume, which is 2 months later than those on the Sides of the Western Mountains near the falls of Columbia.[2]

30ᵗʰ   night cold   hard frost this morning.   We are here Situated on Clarks river in a Vally between two high mountains of Snow.[3]

---

[1] This species of huckleberry is *Vaccinium caespitosum*. — C. V. PIPER.

[2] The sunflower is *Balsamorrhiza sagittata* Nutt., of which Lewis brought back types that were collected, however, at another date and place. — C. V. PIPER.

[3] A long note by Clark following the remarks for June, 1806, in reference to crossing the mountains is transferred to text of the journal, vol. v, p. 175. — ED.

[**Lewis:**] *Diary of the weather for the Month of July, 1806* [1]

Day of the Month	State of the weather at ☉ rise	Wind at ☉ rise	State of the weather at 4 P.M.	Wind at 4 P.M.
1st	c.a.f.	N. W.	f.	N. W.
2ed	f.	S. E.	f.	S. E.
3rd	f.	S. E.	f.	N. W.
4th	f.	S. E.	f.	N. W.
5th	f.	N. E.	f.	S. W.
6th	f.	N. E.	f.	S. W.
7th	c.a.r.t. & l.	S. W.	c.a.f. & r.	W.
8th	f.	S. W.	f.	W.
9th	c.a.r.	N. E.	r.	N. E.
10th	f.a.r.	N. W.	f.	W.
11th	f.	N. W.	f.	N. W.
12th	f.	N. W.	f.	N. W.
13th	f.	N. E.	f.	N. E.
14th	f.	S. W.	f.	S. W.
15th	f.	S. W.	f.	E.
16th	f.	S. W.	f.	S. W.
17th	f.a.t.l.	S. W.	f.	S. W.
18th	f.	S. W.	f.	N E.
19th	f.	S. E.	f.	N. E.
20th	f.	E.	f.	N.
21st	f.	N.	f.	N. E.
22ed	f.	S. E.	f.	N. E.
23rd	f.a.t & l.	S. E.	f.	S W.
24th	c.a.r.t & l.	N. W.	c.a.r.t & l.	N. W.
25th	c.a.r.	N. W.	c.a.r.	N. W.
26th	c.a.r.	N.	f.	N. W.
27th	f.	N. W.	f.	S. W.
28th	f.a.r.t. & l.	N. E.	c.a.f.h.r.t. & l.	N. E.
29th	r.a.r.t. & l.	S. W.	c.a.r.	N. E.
30th	r a.r.	N. E.	r.	N. E.
31st	c.a.r.	N. E.	r.	N. W.

[**Lewis:**] *Remarks for July, 1806.* [2]

1st   a speceis of wild clover with a small leaf just in blume.

3rd   the turtle dove lays it's eggs on the ground in these plains and is now seting, it has two eggs only and they are white.

5th   a great number of pigeons breeding in this part of the mountains. musquetoes not so trobleome as near Clark's river. some ear flies of the common kind and a few large horse flies.

6th   the last night cold with a very heavy dew

---

1 Since Lewis and Clark took different routes in July, 1806, their weather diaries for that period differ, and are here reproduced separately. The following table is found in Lewis's Codex L, p. 147. — ED.

2 The following remarks are found in Lewis's Codex L, pp. 146, 147. —ED.

7th a cloud came on about sunset and continued to rain moderately all night.   rained at 3 P. M.

8th heavy white frost last night.   very cold.

9th rained slightly last night.   air cold.   it began to rain about 8 A. M. and continued with but little intermission all day   in the evening late it abated and we obtained a view of the mountains we had just passed they were covered with snow apparently several feet deep which had fallen during this day.   air extremely cold.

11th wind very hard in the latter part of the day

12th wind violent all last night and today untill 5 P. M. when it ceased in some measure

16th saw the Cookkoo or rain crow and the redheaded woodpecker. the golden rye now heading.   both species of the prickly pare in blume.   the sunflower in blume.

17th wind violent all day.   distant thunder last evening to the West.

23^d a distant thundercloud last evening to the west.   mountains covered with snow.

24th a violent gust of thunder Lightning last evening at 6 P. M.   rain and wind all night untill this evening with some intervales.

25th rained and wind violent all day and night.

26th wind violent   rain continues.

28th a thunder shower last night from N. W. but little rain where we were. heavy hail storm at 3 P. M. the prickly pear has now cast it's blume.

29th heavy rain last night, continued with small intervales all night.

30th rained almost without intermission

31st   d°   d°   d°   d°

[Lewis:] *Diary of the weather for the month of August, 1806.*[1]

day of the month	State of the weather at ☉ rise	Wind at ☉ rise	State of the weather at 4 P M.	Wind at 4 P M
1st	r.a.r.	N. E.	r.a.r.	N. W.
2^{ed}	f.a.r.	N. W.	f.	N. W.
3rd	f.	S. E.	f.	S. E.
4th	f.	S. E.	f.	S. E.
5th	c.a.f.	N. W.	f.	S. E.
6th	f.a.r.t. & l.	N. E.	f.	N. E.
7th	r.a.r.	N. E.	c.a.r.	N. E.
8th	f.	N. E.	f.	N. E.
9th	f.	N. E.	f.	S E.
10th	f.	N. E.	c.a.r.	N. E.
11th	f.	N. E.	f.	N. W.
12th	f.	N. W.		

[1] The following table completes Lewis's separate itinerary, as he rejoined Clark on August 12, 1806.   It is found in Lewis's Codex L, p. 145. — ED.

[Lewis:] *Remarks for August, 1806.*[1]

2nd it became fair soon after dark last evening and continued so.
6th a violent gust of Thunder Lightning wind and hail last night.
7th rained from 12 last night untill 10 A. M. to day.
8th wind hard but not so much so as to detain us.
9th heavy dew last night. air cold.
10th a slight shower about 3 P. M. wind hard.
11th air cool this evening wind hard.
12th wind violent last night.

[Clark:] *Diary of the Weather for the Month of July, 1806*[2]

Day of the month	State of the weather at Sun rise	Wind at sun rise	State of the weather at 4 P M.	Wind at 4 P M
1st	c.a.f.	N. W.	f.	N. W.
2nd	f.	S. E.	f.	N. W.
3rd	f.	S. E.	f.	S. W.
4th	f.	S. W.	f.	S. W.
5th	f.	N. E.	f.	S. W.
6th	f.	S. W.	c. a. r. t. l.	S. W.
7th	c. a. r.	W.	f. a. r.	S. W. by W.
8th	f. a. r.	W.	f.	S. W.
9th	c.	S W.	f.	S. W.
10th	f.	S. E.	f.	S. W.
11th	f.	S. E.	f.	N. N. E.
12th	f.	S. E.	f.	N. W.
13th	f.	S. S. E.	f.	N. E.
14th	f.	N. W.	f.	N. W.
15th	f.	S. E. by E.	f.	N. E.
16th	c.	N. E.	c.	N. E.
17th	f. a. r. h. t. & l.	S. E.	f.	S. W.
18th	f.	S. W.	f.	S. E.
19th	f.	N. W.	f.	S. E.
20th	f.	N. E.	f.	N. E.
21st	f.	N. E.	c.	N E.
22nd	f. a. t. l. & r.	N. E.	c.	N. E.
23rd	f.	N. E.	c.	S E.
24th	f.	S. W.	r.	S. W.
25th	c.	E.	c. a. r.	S. W.
26th	c.	S. S. W.	f. a. r.	N. W.
27th	f.	N. E.	f.	S. W.
28th	c. a. r.	N. E.	f.	N. W.
29th	c. a. r. t. & l	N. E.	f.	N.
30th	f. a. r. t. l	N. W.	f. a. r.	S. E.
31st	f.	N. W.	c. a. r.	N. E.

1 The following remarks are those included in the table given above. — ED.
2 The following table is for Clark's separate itinerary, and is found in his Codex M,
p. 149. — ED.

[Clark:]   *Remarks for July, 1806.*[1]

1ˢᵗ a species of wild clover in blume.

2ⁿᵈ Musquetors very troublesom.

3ᵈ Capᵗ L. & myself part at Travellers rest.

4ᵗʰ a worm [warm] day. I saw a species of Honey suckle with a redish brown flower in blume.

5ᵗʰ cool night. Some dew this morning. the nights are cool. the musquetors are troublesom untill a little after dark when the air become cool and Musquetoes disappear.

6ᵗʰ cold night with frost. I slept cold under 2 blankets on head of Clarks river. I arived in an open plain in the middle of which a violent Wind from the N. W. accompanied with hard rain which lasted from 4 untill half past 5 P.M. quawmash in those plains at the head of wisdom River is just begining to blume and the grass is about 6 inches high.

7ᵗʰ a small Shower of rain at 4 this morning accompanied with wind from the S.S.W. saw a blowing snake.

8ᵗʰ a heavy Shower of rain accompanied with rain from the S.W from 4 to 5 P M. passed the boiling hot Springs emerced 2 peces of raw meat in the Spring and in 25 Minits the Smallest pece was sufficiently cooked and in 32 the larger was also sufficently cooked. A small shower of rain a little after dark.

9ᵗʰ Hard frost. Some ice this morning. last night was very cold and wind hard from the N. E. all night. The river is 12 inches higher than it was last summer when we made the deposit here and portage from this place. More Snow on the adjacent mountains than was at that time.

10ᵗʰ a large white frost last night. the air extreemly cold. Ice ¾ of an inch thick on Standing water. grass killed by the frost. river falling proceviable.

11ᵗʰ a Slight frost last night. the air cool. the Musquetors retired a little after dark, and did not return untill about an hour after Sun-rise. goslins nearly grown fishing hawks have their young. The yellow current nearly ripe.

12ᵗʰ Wisdom river is high but falling. Prickly pears in blume.

14ᵗʰ Saw a Tobaco worm shown me by *York.*

15ᵗʰ Struck the river Rochejhone 120 yᵈˢ wide water falling a little.

16ᵗʰ Saw the wild indigo & common sunflower.

---

[1] The following remarks are compiled from the column of remarks in the table, and the notes following in Codex M, pp. 147–149. — ED.

17th a heavy Shower of rain accompanied with hail Thunder and Lightning at 2 a.m. with hard wind from the S.W. after the Shower was over it cleared away and became fair.

18th yellow, purple, & black currents ripe and abundant.

19th Saw the 1st Grape vine of the dark purple kind the grape nearly grown.

20th The River Rochejhone falls about ½ an inch in 24 hours and becoms much clearer than above. The Grass hoppers are emencely noumerous and have distroyed every Species of grass from one to 10 Miles above on the river & a great distance back.

21st river falls a little and the water is nearly clear.

22nd a fiew drops of rain last night at dark, the cloud app.d to hang to the S W, wind blew hard from different points from 5 to 8 P M which time it thundered and Lightened. The river by 11 a. m. to day had risen 15 inches, and the water of a milky white colour.

23rd The river has fallen within the last 24 hours 7 inches. the wind was violent from the S W for about 3 hours last night from the hours of 1 to 3. A.M.

24th river falling a little it is 6 feet lower than the highest appearance of it's rise. since the last rise it has fallen 13 inches. Rained from 3 to 4 P M but Slightly. the wind violent from the S. W.

25th Several Showers of rain with hard winds from the S and S W the fore part of the day. the brooks on each Side are high and water Muddye.

26th a slight shower this morning with hard wind from the S. W. The river falling, but very slowly 1 inch in 24 hs

27th Saw a flight of gulls, a small rattle snake, Several flocks of crows & black burds.

28th a fiew drops of rain this morning a little before day light. river still falling a little Bratten coet [caught] a beaver. Labeech shot 2 last evening. I saw a wild cat lying on a log over the water.

29th a fiew drops of rain accompanied with hard claps of Thunder and Sharp lightning last night wind hard from the N.E.

30th a slight Shower of rain accompanied with thunder and lightning. Several Showers in the course of this day. it cleared away in the evening and became fair river falling a little. Great quantities of coal appear in the bluffs on either Side. Some appearance of Burnt hills at a distance from the river. Great

number of swallows, they have their young. Killed black tail
deer. young gees beginning to fly.

31st. rained only a few drops last night. The wind blew hard and it
was Showery all day tho' not much rain. the clouds came up
from the W. and N W frequently in course of the day.

[Clark:] *Diary of the Weather for the Month of August, 1806.*[1]

day of the month	State of the weather at sun rise	State of wind at Sunrise	State of the weather at 4 P M	wind at 4 P M	State of river		
					rise or fall	Inches &c	part of Inches
1st	c. a. r.	N. W.	r.	N.	ris.	5	½
2nd	c. a. r.	N.	f. a. r.	N.	r	3	..
3rd	f.	S. W.	f.	S. W.	rise	2	¼
4th	f.	N. W.	f.	N. E.	fal.	6	½
5th	f.	N. E.	f.	N. E.	fal.	7	..
6th	c. a. r. t. & l.	S. W.	f.	N. E.	fall	2	¼
7th	r.	N. E.	c. a. r.	N.	fall	2	½
8th	f.	N.	f.	N. W.	fall	2	..
9th	f.	N. E.	f.	N. E.	fall	1	¼
10th	f.	E.	c.	E.	fall	..	¾
11th	f.	N. W.	f.	N. W.	fall	2	..
12th	f.	S. W.	c.	S. W.	fall	2	¼
13th	f. a. r.	S. W.	f.	S. W.	fall	2	½
14th	f.	N. E.	f.	S. W.	fall	3	½
15th	f.	N. W.	f.	N. W.	f.	2	..
16th	f.	N. W.	f	N. W.	f.	3	½
17th	c.	S. E.	c.	S. E.	..	..	..
18th	c. a. r.	S. E.	f.	S. E.	f.	1	½
19th	t. l. & r.	S. E.	c.	S. E.	f.	..	¾
20th	c. a. t l. & r.	S. W.	f.	N. W.	f.	1	¼
21st	f.	S. E.	f.	N. W.	f.	2	½
22d	c. a. r.	S. W.	f.	S. E.	f.	4	..
23rd	c.	S. E.	r.	N. W.	f.	1	½
24th	f.	N. E.	f.	N. W.	f.	2	..
25th	f.	S. W.	f.	N. W.	f.	1	¼
26th	f.	S. E.	f.	S. E.	f.	..	¾
27th	f.	S. E.	f.	S. E.	f.	1	¼
28th	f.	S. E.	f.	N. W.	..	..	..
29th	c.	N. W.	f. a. r.	S. E.	f.	..	½
30th	c. a. r.	S. E.	f.	S. E.	..	..	..
31st	c. a. l. t & l. & w.	S. E.	c. a. l.	S. E.	..	..	..

[1] The following table is found in Clark's Codex M, p. 146. As Clark reached
the Missouri River, August 3, the references thereafter apply to that river. — ED.

METEOROLOGY

Remarks for August, 1806.[1]

1st. rained last night and all day today at intervales.

2nd. rained a little last night and several showers this morn[in]g.

3d. Musquetors troublesom. heavy dew.

4th. Rochejhone falling much faster than the Missouri.

5th. Musquetors excessively troublesom   both rivers falling.

6th. rained hard last night with Thunder Lightning & hard wind from S. W.   killed a white Bear & Bighorn.

7th. commenced raining at daylight and continued at intervals all day. air cool.

8th. air cool.

9th. a heavy dew. air cool and clear   found red goose berries and a dark purple current & Service's.

10th. found a Species of Cherry resembling the read Heart cherry of our country.

11th. sarvis berries in abundance & ripe.

13th. a fiew drops of rain last night at 8 P.M. with hard S.W. wind

14th. Mandan corn now full and beginning to harden

16th. Northern lights seen last night which was in streaks

18th. rained moderately last night in forpart of the night.

19th. comenced raining at 5 A.M. and continued with a hard wind untill [blank space in MS.].

21st. rained a little in the course of the night.   at day a violent hard Shower for ½ an hour.

22nd. rained the greater part of last night. Grape and plums ripe. The rains which have fallen in this month is most commonly from flying clouds which pass in different directions, those clouds are always accompanied with hard winds, and sometimes accompanied with thunder and lightning   The river has been falling moderately Since the third of the month. the rains which has fallen has [made] no impression on the river [other] than causing it to be more muddy and probably prevents its falling fast.

23d. rained at 10 A.M. & 4 P.M.   hard wind.

24th. wind blew hard all day   grapes in abundance.

26th. Heavy dew this morning.   Saw a pilecan.

27th. first Turkeys at Tylor River above the big bend

29th. Some rain this morning only a fiew drops. and at 10 A.M.

---

1 The following remarks are found in Clark's Codex M, pp. 146, 147. References to events described in text of journals are here omitted. — ED.

30th   a fiew drops of rain last night.

31st   rained most of last night with T. Li. & a hard wind from the
S.W.   some rain to day.

Diary for the Month of September, 1806 [1]

Day of the month	State of the weather at Sun rise	Course of the wind at Sun rise	State of the weather at 4 Clock	Course of the wind at 4 P M
1st	fog	S. E.	f.a.r.	S. E.
2nd	f.	S. E.	f.	S. E.
3rd	f.	S. W.	f.	S. W.
4th	f.a.r.t. & l.	S. E.	f.	S. E.
5th	f.	S. E.	c.	S. W.
6th	c.	S. E.	f.	S. E.
7th	f.	S. E.	f.	S. E.
8th	f.	S. E.	f.	S. E.
9th	f.	S. E.	f.	S. E.
10th	f.	S. E.	f.	S. E.
11th	c.a.r.	S. E.	f.a.r.	S. E.
12th	f.	S. E.	c.a.r.	S. E.
13th	f.	S. E.	f.	S. E.
14th	f.	S. E.	c.	S. E.
15th	f.	S. E.	f.	S. E.
16th	f.	S. E.	f.	S. E.
17th	f.	S. E.	f.	S. E.
18th	f.	S. E.	c.	S. E.
19th	f.	S. E.	f.	S. E
20th	f.	N. E.	f.	S. E.
21st	c.a.r.	S. E.	c.	S. E.
22	r.a.t.l. & r.	S.	c.a.r.	S.
23	c. & r.	N. E.	c.a.r.	N. E.
24	r	. .	c.a.r.	. .
25th	c.	N. E.	f.	. .
26th	f.	S. E.	f.	S. E.
27th	f.	N. E.	f.	S. E.
28th	f.	S. E.	f.	S. E.
29th	f.	S.	f.	S. E.
30th	f.	S. E.	f.	E.

Remarks for September, 1806. [2]

1st   a thick fog untill 8 A.M.   a fiew drops of rain about 1 P. M.

2nd   Hard wind all day.   Saw the prarie fowl common in the Illinois
plains.   Saw Linn and Slipery elm.

3d   a stiff breeze from S.E. untill 12 at night when it changed to S. W.
and blew hard all night.

---

[1] The following table is found in Clark's Codex N, p. 152. — ED.

[2] The following remarks are found in Clark's Codex N, pp. 151, 152.   References to events mentioned in text of journal are here omitted. — ED.

4th at 6 P. M. a violent Storm of Thunder Lightn'g and rain untill 10 P. M. when it ceased to rain and blew hard from N. W. untill 3 A. M.

6th Heard the whipperwill common to the U. States at Soldier's river.

7th Saw the whiperwill and heard the common hooting owl Musquetors very troublesom. killed 3 Elk.

8th warmest day we have experienced in this year.

11th a fiew drops. of rain only a little before day. and some rain at 2 P. M.

12th Heavy dew this morning and fog. Some rain from 12 to 4 P.M.

15th day very worm Smokey and worm.

16th this day very Sultry and much the hotest which we have experienced.

17th day worm, but fiew Musquitors.

19th saw a green Snake as high up as Salt Rivr on the Missouri. the limestone bluffs commence below Salt river on S. side

21st a slight shower of rain a little before day light this morning.

22nd at St Charles the raine commencd about 9 P. M. and was moderate untill 4 A. M when it increased and rained without intermition untill 10 A.M: Some Thunder and lightning about daylight. it continued cloudy with small showers of rain all day.

23rd at St Louis Several light Showers in the course of this day.

24th rained moderately this morning and continued Cloudy with moderate rain at intervales all day.

26th fair and worm.

27th emencely worm.

28th   do

29th   do

30th   do

VII. ASTRONOMY

THE following description of the astronomical instruments employed by Lewis and Clark is found in Codex O, pp. 1–6, in Lewis's handwriting. Codex O was used wholly for Astronomical Observations and Geographical Notes (including Lewis's Summary Statement, pp. 29–55, *ante*). — ED.]

Camp 10 miles above the mouth of the river Platte. July 22ᶜᵈ 1804.

A summary discription of the apparatus employed in the following observations; containing also some remarks on the manner in which they have been employed, and the method observed in recording the observations made with them.

1ˢᵗ — a brass Sextant of 10 Inches radius, graduated to 15′. which by the assistance of the nonius was devisible to 15″, and half of this sum by means of the micrometer could readily be distinguished, therefore 7″.5 of an angle was perceptible with this instrument: she was also furnished with three eye-pieces, consisting of a hollow tube and two telescopes one of which last reversed the images of observed objects. finding on experiment that the reversing telescope when employed as the eye-piece gave me a more full and perfect image than either of the others, I have most generally imployed it in all the observations made with this instrument; when thus prepared I found from a series of observations that the quantity of her *index error* was 8′.45. — ; this sum is therefore to be considered as the standing error of the instrument unless otherwise expressly mentioned. *the altitudes* of all objects, observed as well with this instrument as with the Octant were by means of a reflecting surface; and those stated to have been taken with the sextant are the degrees, minutes, &c. shewn by the graduated limb of the instrument at the time of observation and are of course the double altitudes of the objects observed.

2ᵉᵈ — A common Octant of 14 Inches radius, graduated to 20′, which by means of the nonius was devisible to one 1′, half of this sum, or 30″ was perceptible by means of a micrometer. this instrument was prepared for both the *fore* and *back* observation; her *error* in the fore observation is $2°+$, &. and in the *back observation* $2°. II' 40'' .3.+$

at the time of our departure from the River Dubois untill the present moment, the sun's altitude at noon has been too great to be reached with my sextant, for this purpose I have therefore employed the Octant by the *back* observation. the degrees ' & ''., recorded for the sun's altitude by the back observation express only the angle given by the graduated limb of the instrument at the time of observation, and are the compliment of the *double Altitude* of the sun's observed limb; if therefore the angle recorded be taken from 180° the remainder will be the *double altitude* of the observed object, or that which would be given by the fore observation with a reflecting surface.

3rd — An Artificial Horizon on the construction recommended and practiced by Mr. Andrw. Ellicott of Lancaster, Pensylia, in which water is used as the reflecting surface; believing this artificial Horizon liable to less error than any other in my possession, I have uniformly used it when the object observed was sufficiently bright to reflect a distinct immage; but as much light is lost by reflection from water I found it inconvenient in most cases to take the altitude of the moon with this horizon, and that of a star impracticable with any degree of accuracy.

4th. — An Artificial Horizon constructed in the manner recommended by Mr. Patterson of Philadelphia; glass is here used as the reflecting surface. this horizon consists of a glass plane with a single reflecting surface, cemented to the flat side of the larger segment of a wooden ball; adjusted by means of a sperit-level and a triangular stand with a triangular mortice cut through it's center sufficiently large to admit of the wooden ball partially; the stand rests on three screws inserted near it's angles, which serve as feet for it to rest on while they assist also in the adjustment. this horizon I have employed in taking the altitude of the sun when his image has been reather too dull for a perfect reflection from water; I have used it generally in taking the altitude of the moon, and in some cases of the stars also; it gives the moon's image very perfectly, and when carefully adjusted I consider it as liable to but little error.

5th. — An Artificial Horizon formed of the index specula of a Sextant cemented to a flat board; adjusted by means of a sperit level and the triangular stand before discribed. as this glass reflects from both surfaces it gives the images of all objects much more bright than either of the other horizons; I have therefore most generally employed it in observing the altitudes of stars.

6th — A Chronometer; her ballance-wheel and scapement were on the most improved construction. she rested on her back, in a small case prepared for her, suspended by an universal joint. she was carefully wound up every day at twelve oclock. Her rate of going as asscertained by a series of observations made by myself for that purpose was found to be 15. Seconds and 5 tenths of a second too slow in twenty four howers on *Mean Solar time.* This is nearly the same result as that found by Mr Andrew Ellicott who was so obliging as to examine her rate of going for the space of fourteen days, in the summer 1803. her rate of going as ascertained by that gentleman was 15^s .6 too slow M. T. in 24. h. and that she went from 3 to 4. s. slower the last 12 h, than she did the first 12. h. after being wound up. at 12. OC^k on the 14th day of May 1804. (being the day on which the detatchment left the mouth of the River Dubois) the Chronometer was too fast M. T. 6 m. 32. s. & $^2/_{10}$ This time piece was regulated on *mean time*, and the time entered in the following observations is that shewn by her at the place of observation. the day is recconed on Civil time, (i e) commencing at midnight.

7th — A Circumferentor, circle 6 Inches diameter, on the common construction; by means of this instrument adjusted with the sperit level, I have taken the magnetic azimuth of the sun and pole Star. It has also been employed in taking the traverse of the river: — from the courses thus obtained, together with the distances estimated from point to point, the chart of the Missouri has been formed which now accompanys these observations. the several points of observation are marked with a cross of red ink, and numbered in such manner as to correspond with the celestial observations made at those points respectively.

RECORDS OF OBSERVATIONS

[The following records of observations from the beginning of the expedition to the close of the winter of 1804–05 were entered by Lewis in Codex O, pp. 6–52. Many of them were copied into the text of the journals proper; where thus entered, the entry here is omitted, reference being made to the given date. Occasionally, in the text of the journals, results are given which are not presented here; they have, in such cases, been transferred, and are marked [*]. An occasional difference in copying a series of figures has not been editorially noted. — ED.]

The mouth of the River Dubois opposite to the mouth of the Missouri River is situated in

Longitude West from Grenw.ʰ   89°. 57′. 45″
Latitude N. . . . . . .   38°. 55′. 19″. 6

Note — The *Longitude* of the mouth of the River Dubois was calculated from four sets of observations of the ☉ & ☽, in which the ☉ was twice West, and twice East; two sets with Aldebaran, ✳ East in one, and W. in the other; and one set with Spica, ♍., ✳ East. the Long.ᵗᵈ above stated is the mean result of those observations, and I think may with safety be depended on to two or three minutes of a degree. The Chronometer's error on M. T. was found at the mouth of the Ohio by 3 sets of Equal Altitudes, and the Long.ᵗᵈ of the mouth of the River Dubois as given by this instrument from Equal altitudes of the ☉ on the 17ᵗʰ of December 1803, was 90°. 00′. 20″. West from Gren.ʷʰ making a difference from the Longitude calculated from observation of 2′.35″.

The *Latitude* is deduced from a number of Meridian altitudes of the ☉ taken with the sextant and artificial horizon, the results of which observations seldom differed more than from 15 to 20″; I therefore believe that the Latitude above stated may be depended on as true to 100 hundred paces.

The mouth of the River Dubois is to be considered as the point of *departure*.

St. Charles. May 18ᵗʰ 1804

(*Point of Observation N°. 1.*)   Observed equal Altitudes of the ☉ with Sextant.[1]

	h	m	s			h	m	s
A. M.	9.	9.	51	. . . . . .	P. M.	2.	49.	24.
	".	10.	16.	. . . .		".	50.	50.
	".	11.	34.	. . . .		".	51.	10.

Alt.ᵈ by Sex.ᵗ at the time of this observ.ᵗⁿ 97°. 42. 37

Result.   Chronometer too fast M. T . . . . 4— 18ᵐ. 7ˢ.
Long.ᵗᵈ by Chro.ᵗ W. from Gren.ʰ   90°. 15′. 7″
Lat.ᵈ by Hor. ∠ P. M. Obs.ᵗⁿ of ☉ Cen.ᵗ. 38°. 54′. 39″

---

1 Part of this observation was entered in Codex A, p. 9, under date as here given. — ED.

Poi[*n*]*t Obs*[n] *N*[o]. *2.* On a small Island opposite to the mouth of the *Gasconade* made the following obsert[ns]

Equal Al[ds] **of ⊙ with Sextant.**[1]

Note. — The ⊙ was so much obscured during the A. M. observation, that I cannot be positive as to it's accuracy, nor could I obtain the A. M. obs[tn] at an earlier hour from the same cause.

Latitude of place of observation . . N. 38°. 44′ .35″ .3.

Poi[*n*]*t Obs*[tn] *N*[o] *3.* On the point of land formed by the confluence of the *Great Osage* River and the Missouri made the following observations.[2]

Pole *'s magnetic Azimuth by Circumf[tr]		N.	7°.	W.
Time by Chronometer at place of Obs[tn]	P. M.	10.	29.	20.
Pole *'s magnetic Azimuth by Circumfer[tr]		N.	6°. 10′.	E.
Time by Chronometer, June 2[ed]	A. M.	0.	1	20.
Latitude of place of observation		38°. 31′. 6″.9.		

(Time by Chronometer at place of Obs[tn] P. M. 10h. 29m. 20s.)

(Time by Chronometer, June 2ed A. M. 0h. 1m. 20s.)

Observed time and distance of ⊙'s and ☽'s nearest Limbs, ⊙ East. with Sextant.[2]

	Time	*Distance*
	h m s	
A. M.	7. 18. 32. 5	74°. 47′. 23″. 7.

Note — this is the mean of a set of 8.

	h m s	
A. M.	8. 13. 45.	74°. 23′. 30″.
"	". 16. 42.	". 21 . 00.
"	". 22. 27.	". 20 . 30.
"	". 24. 56.	". 19 . 20.
"	". 26. 21.	". 17 . 15.
"	". 27. 10.	". 17 . 30.

---

[1] For figures see text of journal, May 29, 1804. — Ed.

[2] Not found in text of journal. — Ed.

	Time			*Distance*		
	h	m	s			
A. M.	7.	42.	12.	74°.	36'.	00".
".		43.	52.	".	35.	00.
".		45.	39.	".	34.	45.
".		47.	22.	".	32.	00.
".		49.	34.	".	32.	45.
".		51.	12.	".	32.	00.

Note — this set is probably a little inaccurate in consequence of the moon's being obscured *in some measure by the clouds*

	h	m	s			
A. M.	7.	53.	38.	74°.	32'.	00".
".		56.	19.	".	29.	15.
".		58.	32.	".	29.	00.
	8.	0.	10.	".	28.	45.
".		2.	12.	".	26.	30.
".		4.	26.	".	26.	20.
".		6.	00.	".	25.	45.
".		7.	38.	".	24.	00.

	h	m	s			
A. M.	8.	35.	58.	74°.	14'.	7".5
".		38.	28.	".	14.	00.
".		40.	2.	".	13.	20.
".		43.	9.	".	13.	00.
".		44.	47.	".	12.	45.
".		46.	4.	".	12.	00.

Equal altitudes of the ☉ with Sextant

	h	m	s					
A. M.	8.	58.	9.	P. M.	3°.	3'.	49".	
".		59.	27.		".	5.	8.	
	9.	00.	53.		".	6.	37.	

Altitude by Sextant at time of Obs.ⁿ 95°. 50'. 45".

Meridian Alt.ᵈ of ☉'s L. L. by Back } 37°. 28'. —"
observation with Octant —
Latitude deduced from this observation 38°. 31'. 6". 9.
☉'s magnetic azimuth by Circumferenter.   Due West
Time by Chronometer . . P.M.   4. 59. 14.

Altitude by Sextant of ☉'s L. L. 52. 21. 00

☉'s magnetic azimuth by Circumfeᵗʳ N. 88°. W.
Time by Chronometer P. M. . . 5. 11. 30

[235]

Altitude of ☉'s L.L. by Sextant   47°. 16'. —".

☉'s magnetic azimuth by Circumf.ᵗʳ   N.   86°.   W.

Time by Chronometer P. M. . .   5ʰ.   23ᵐ.   14ˢ

Altitude by Sextant of ☉'s L. L.   42°.   52.'   —".

Sunday June 3ʳ.ᵈ [1]

Observed time and distance of ☉'s and ☽'s nearest limbs, the ☉ East :

	Time				Distance		
	h	m	s				
A. M.	6.	22.	21.	. . . .	61 °.	40'.	—".
	".	24.	5.	. . . .	" .	40.	—.
	".	25.	36.	. . . .	" .	39.	45.
	".	26.	44.	. . . .	" .	39.	30.
	".	28.	18.	. . . .	" .	37.	—.
	".	29.	51.	. . . .	" .	37.	30.

A. M.	6.	36.	25.	. . . .	61 .	35.	—
	".	41.	27.	. . . .	" .	34.	45.
	".	49.	6.	. . . .	" .	33.	—.
	".	54.	36.	. . . .	" .	30.	15.
	".	55.	41.	. . . .	" .	30.	7.5
	".	57.	—.	. . . .	" .	30.	—.

	Time				Distance.		
	h	m	s				
A. M.	7.	—.	7.	. . . .	61°.	27'.	30".
	".	3.	57.	. . . .	" .	27.	30.
	".	6.	1.	. . . .	" .	27.	15.
	".	7.	53.	. . . .	" .	26.	52.
	".	9.	55.	. . . .	" .	26.	—.
	".	11.	5.	. . . .	" .	25.	15.

	h	m	s				
A. M.	7.	14.	6.	. . . .	61°.	23'.	30"
	".	16.	2.	. . . .	" .	24.	—.
	".	17.	53.	. . . .	" .	23.	15.
	".	19.	33.	. . . .	" .	22.	—.
	".	23.	28.	. . . .	" .	20.	45.
	".	25.	7.	. . . .	" .	20.	45.

[1] The result only of the observation for this date is entered in the text of the journal. — ED.

	h	m	s				
A. M.	7.	29.	16.	61°.	19′.	—″
	“.	31.	17.	“ .	16.	15.
	“.	32.	56.	“ .	17.	—.
	“.	33.	56.	“ .	15.	30.
	“.	34.	50.	“ .	15.	—.
	“.	35.	59.	“ .	15.	—.

	h	m	s				
A. M.	7.	39.	55.	61°.	14′.	—″.
	“.	40.	55.	“ .	13.	45.
	“.	42.	39.	“ .	13.	15.
	“.	45.	16.	“ .	12.	45.
	“.	46.	38.	“ .	11.	30.
	“.	47.	41.	“ .	11.	—.

Equal altitudes of the ☉, with Sextant.

A M.   8. 26. 1.   P. M.   The ☉ was obscured by
      “. 27. 19.   clouds and the observation con-
      “. 28. 41.   sequently lost

Meridian alt.ᵈ of ☉'s L. L. by back ⎰ 38°. 2′. —″.
observation with Octant   ⎱

The ☉'s disk was much obscured by clouds during this observation, not much confidence is therefore due it's accuracy.

Point of observation N.° 4. On the Starbord shore one & ½ miles above the mouth of the *split rock* creek.[1]

Saturday June 9ᵗʰ

Point of Observation N.° 5 On the N. W. side of a small island, two miles above the *prarie* of the *Arrows*.[2]

Observed meridian alt.ᵈ of ☉'s L. L. with Octant by the back observaᵗⁿ 37°. —′ . —″.

Point of observation N.° 6. On the Larbord shore ¾ of a mile below the mouth of the lesser Charetton river.[3] 37°. 12′. —″.

Point of observation N.° 7. On the S side of an Island near it's upper point two miles below the mouth of the *Grand river*.[4]

Wednesday June 13ᵗʰ

Point of observation N.° 8 At the mouth of the *Grand River*.[4]
Observed time and distance of ☽ from Spica ♏. ✳ East. —

---

1 Entered in text of the journal, June 6, 1804. — ED.
2 Not found in text of journal. — ED.
3 Entered in text of journal, June 10, 1804. — ED.
4 Entered in text of journal, June 13, 1804. — ED.

	Time			Distance		
	h	m	s			
P. M.	9.	17.	49.5.	39°.	36′.	—″
	".	22.	38.	".	28.	—
	".	32.	40.	".	24.	—
	".	41.	39.	".	20.	45.
	".	47.	8.	".	17.	32.
	".	59.	48.5	".	11.	45

	h	m	s			
P. M.	10.	14.	19.	39°.	1′.	30″
	".	18.	27.	".	—.	30.
	".	21.	51.	38.	58.	15.
	".	27.	12.	".	56.	30.
	".	39.	34.	".	53.	00.
	".	45.	41.	".	48.	—

	h	m	s			
P. M.	10.	54.	38.	38°.	41′.	45″
	".	59.	49.	".	39.	—
	11.	3.	8.	".	37.	30
	".	6.	44.	".	36.	45.
	".	10.	40.	".	34.	00.
	".	16.	—	".	31.	45.

Friday June 15th

Point of Observation Nº. 9. — On the Starboard shore two miles below the Island of the Old village of the little Osages.[1]

Observed Meridian Alt.d of ☉'s L. L. with Octant by the back observation 36°. 42′. —″.

Wednesday June 20th

Point of Observation Nº. 10. — On a small Island about one mile & ¾ below Euebaux's Creek. — [1]

Observed time and distance of ☽ . from Spica ♍ . ✳ . West. —

	Time			Distance.
	h	m	s	
P. M.	10.	59.	40.3	46°. 17′. 25″.

This is the mean of a set of six observations.

Magnetic azimuth of Pole star by Circumferenter well adjusted with sper.t lev.l N. 7°. 55′. W

Time by Chronometer P. M. 12. 49. 46.6

T[h]is is the mean of a set of six observations suffering several minutes to elaps betwen each.

---

[1] Not found in text of journal. — ED.

Point of Observation N° 11. On the upper point of a large island about four miles above the Fire prarie.[1] Observed Meridian alt⁴ of ☉'s L. L. with the octant by the back obstⁿ. 36°. —'. —"

[Clark:] [2]   *Kansas River June 23rd 1804*

Equal altitudes with Sexton / Er. 8'. 45"—

	H	M	S
A. M.	8 .. 9	.. 42
"	" .. 10	.. 59
"	" 12	.. 26

Point of observation N°. 12. On the Starboard shore, about ¼ a mile above the mouth of *hay-cabbin creek*.[3] Observed meridian alt⁴ of ☉'s L. L. with octant by the back obser⁴ 36°. 13'. —"

Lattitude 38° 37' 5" N.

Point of observation N°. 13. On the Larboard shore about four mˡˢ above the mouth of the *blue water* river.[3] Observed meridian alt⁴ of ☉'s L. L. with octant by the back observ⁴ 36°. 10'. —"

Lattitude 38° 32' 15" North.

Point of observation N°. 14. On the point formed by the confluence of the Kancez River and the Missouri [3] made the following observations.

Equal altitude of the Sun, with *Sextant*

	h	m	s			h	m	s
A. M.	8.	22.	23.	. . . . P. M.	3.	49.	19.
"		23.	53.	. . . . . .	"		50.	39.
"		25.	17.	. . . . . .	"		52.	3.

Alt⁴ by Sextant at the time of this observ⁴ 81°. 15'. 15".

Lattitude 38° 31' 13"

---

1 Not found in text of journal. — ED.
2 Unfinished observation of Clark, found on last flyleaf of Codex A. — ED.
3 Only latitude deduced given in text of journal. — ED.

⊙'s magnetic azimuth by Circumfer.   .   .   S. 81°. E.

Time by Chronometer   .   .   A. M.   8^h . 22^m . 33^s.

Alt^d of ⊙'s U. L. by Sextan^t .   .   .   81°. 15'. 15''

Latitude of place of observation.   .   .   .   39°. 5'. 25''.7

Variation of the nedle   .   .   .   [blank space in MS.]

Observed Meridian Alt^d of ⊙'s L. L. with Octant by the back observation.   36°. 25'. —''

Latitude deduced from this obser^{tn} .   .   39°. 5'. 38''.5.

⊙'s magnetic azimuth by Circumferen^{tr}.   S. 88°. W

Time by Chronometer at p^l Obs^t P. M.   4^h. 52^m. 33^s.

Alt^d of ⊙'s L. L. by Sextan^t .   .   .   56°. 51'. —''.

⊙'s magnetic azimuth by Circumf^{tr} .   S. 89°. W.

Time by Chronometer.   P. M.   .   .   .   5^h. 2^m. 6^s

Alt^d of ⊙'s L. L. by Sextant.   .   .   .   53. 10. 15.

Observed magnetic azimuth of pole ✳. with my Circumferenter, taking time by Chronot.

Time by Chronom^{tr} .— ✳'s mag^t Azimuth

P. M.   9^h. 54^m. —^{s} .   .   .   .   N. 8°. W.

9. 58. 4   .   .   .   .   N. 8°. W.

10. —. 40   .   .   .   .   .   .   N. 7. 45 . W.

Thursday June 28th

Observed Equal Altitudes of ⊙, with Sextant [1]

A. M.   8^h. 9^m. 42^s.   .   .   .   .   .   P .M   4^h. 1^m. 50^s

''. 10. 59.   .   .   .   .   .   ''.   3. 9.5

''. 12. 26.   .   .   .   .   .   ''.   4. 35.5

Alt^d by Sextant at the time of Observ^{tn} 76°. 16'. 52''.

Meridian alt^d of ⊙'s L. L. with Octant by
the back observation   .   .   .   .   .   36°. 31'. —''.

Latitude deduced from this obs^t .   .   39°. 5'. 25''.7.

Friday June 29th

Observed Equal altitudes of ⊙, with Sextant.[1]

A. M.   9^h. 6^m. 46^s.   .   .   .   .   .   .   P. M.   3^h. 4^m. 29^s.

''. 8. 3.   .   .   .   .   .   .   ''. 5. 51.

''. 9. 29.   .   .   .   .   .   .   ''. 7. 15.

Alt^d by Sextant at the time of Obser^t .   .   .   .   .   .   98°. 18'. 45''.

---

[1] Not found in text of journal. — Ed.

Observed time and distance of ☉'s and ☽'s nearest Limbs, with Chronometer and Sextant, the ☉ East. —

	Time				*Distance.*
	h	m	s		
A. M.	7.	6.	2.	. . . .	104°. 13'. 30''.
".		9.	7.	. . . .	" . 12. 15.
".		11.	23.	. . . .	" . 11. 30.
".		15.	38.	. . . .	" . 10. —
".		17.	5.	. . . .	" . 9. 45.
".		18.	33.	. . . .	" . 8. 15.
".		20.	2.	. . . .	" . 8. 00.
".		22.	—.	. . . .	" . 7. 30.

	h	m	s		
A. M.	7.	33.	57.	. . . .	104°. 3'. 15''
".		35.	11.	. . . .	" . 3. —.
".		36.	33.	. . . .	" . 3. —.
".		37.	37.	. . . .	" . 2. —.
".		39.	18.	. . . .	" . 1. 15.
".		40.	26.	. . . .	" . 1. —.
".		41.	23.	. . . .	" . 1. —.
".		43.	1.	. . . .	103°. 59. 53.

	h	m	s		
A. M.	7.	51.	21.	. . . .	103°. 56'. 15''.
".		56.	49.	. . . .	" . 55. 15.
".		58.	47.	. . . .	" . 54. 52.
	8.	—	45.	. . . .	" . 54. —.
".		3.	49.	. . . .	" . 51. 45.
".		6.	57.	. . . .	" . 51. —.
".		8.	53.	. . . .	" . 50. 15.
".		10.	44.	. . . .	" . 49. 30.

	h	m	s		
A. M.	8.	16.	3.	. . . .	103°. 48'. —''.
".		17.	51.	. . . .	" . 46. 30.
".		20.	6.	. . . .	" . 45. —.
".		21.	42.	. . . .	" . 45. —.
".		23.	5.	. . . .	" . 44. —.
".		25.	40.	. . . .	" . 43. 15.
".		28.	3.	. . . .	" . 42. 45.
".		30.	36.	. . . .	" . 41. 52.

A. M. 8. 37. 25. . . . . 103 . 37. 15.

" . 39. 15. . . . . " . 37. —.

" . 40. 10. . . . . " . 36. —.

" . 43. 3. . . . . " . 35. —.

" . 44. 36. . . . . " . 34. 45.

" . 46. 7. . . . . " . 33. 30.

" . 47. 34. . . . . " . 33. 00.

" . 48. 35. . . . . " . 32. 15.

	h	m	s				

A. M. 8. 49. 55. . . . . 103°. 32'. —".

" . 51. 54. . . . . " . 31. 45.

" . 52. 57. . . . . " . 31. 15.

" . 53. 31. . . . . " . 31. —.

" . 54. 16. . . . . " . 30. 45.

" . 55. 11. . . . . " . 29. —.

" . 56. 45. . . . . " . 28. 45.

" . 57. 41. . . . . " . 28. 15.

Meridian Alt^d of ⊙'s L. L. with Octant by the back observation 36°. 36'. — ".

Latitude deduced from this obs^t.   39°. 5'. 21".2

Saturday June 30th

P^t *Obst^n. N°. 15.* On the Larboard Shore ¾ of a mile below the *Little river Platte.*[1] Observed time and distance of ⊙'s and ☽'s nearest limbs; the ⊙ East. *with Sex^t. & Chron^{tr}.*

	Time.									*Distance.*
	h	m	s							

A. M. 7. 55. 36. . . . . 90°. 58'. —".

" . 57. 16. . . . . " . 57. 45.

" . 58. 49. . . . . " . 57. 45.

8. 1. 20. . . . . " . 56. 15.

" . 2. 52. . . . . " . 55. —.

" . 4. 16. . . . . " . 55. —.

" . 5. 26. . . . . " . 54. 45.

6. 11. . . . . " . 54. 45.

" . 7. 10. . . . . " . 54. 30.

" . 8. 9. . . . . " . 54. 30.

	h	m	s				

A. M. 8. 11. 11. . . . . 90°. 50'. 30".

" . 12. 39. . . . . " . 50. 15.

" . 13. 57. . . . . " . 50. —.

" . 14. 57. . . . . " . 49. 45.

" . 15. 54. . . . . " . 49. 15.

---

[1] Not found in text of journal. — ED.

Time.				Distance.		
	h	m	s			
A. M.	8.	16.	53.	90°.	49'.	—".
	".	17.	30.	" .	48.	45.
	".	18.	53.	" .	48.	—.
	".	19.	45.	" .	48.	—.
	".	20.	24.	" .	47.	45.

Sunday July 1ˢᵗ

Point Obstⁿ. Nᵒ. 16. On the Larboard shore one ½ miles above the upper point of the dimond Island.[1]
Observed Meridian Altᵈ. of ☉'s L. L. with Octant by the back obstⁿ. 36°. 59'. 30".

Latitude deduced from this obstⁿ   39°. 9'. 38".6

Wednesday July 4ᵗʰ

Point Obstⁿ. Nᵒ. 17. On the Larboard Shore three miles below a high Prarie hill on same shore, near the 2ᵉᵈ old vilage of the Kancez.[1]
Observed Meridian Altᵈ. of ☉'s L. L. with Octant by the back obserⁿ 38° —'. —".

Latitude deduced from this obserⁿ   39°. 25'. 42".5.

Sunday July the 8ᵗʰ 1804.

Point of Observation Nᵒ. 18. On the Starboard shore immediately below an high bluff situated ¼ of a mile below the lower point of Nadawa Island.[1]
Observed Meridian altᵈ. of ○'s L. L. with Octant by the back observⁿ 39°. 18'. —".

Latitude by this observation   . . .   39°. 39'. 22".7

Wednesday July 11ᵗʰ

Point of observation Nᵒ. 19. On *New-found Island* opposite to the mouth of the great Ne-mi-Haw. made the following observations. *with Sextant and Chronometer.*

Altᵈ by Sextant of				Time of observation		
				h	m	s
☉'s L. L.	88°. 26'. 15". . . .	P. M.	3.	26.	38.
☉'s Center	" " "		".	27.	59.
☉'s U. L.	" " "		".	29.	27.
			h	m	s
☉'s L. L.	39°. 3'. —". . . .	P. M.	5.	36.	35.
☉'s U. L.	" "		".	39.	31.
☉'s magnetic azimuth by Circumfeᵗʳ		N. 89°. W.			
Altᵈ of ☉'s L. L. by Sextant		39°. 3'. —"			

[1] Not found in text of journal — Eᴅ.

	h	m	s
Time by Chronometer	5.	36.	35
Latitude of place of observation	39°.	55′.	56″

Observed time and distance of ☽ from Spica ♍. ✳, East, with Cronom^tr & Sextant.

	Time			*Distance.*		
P. M.	8. 41. 42.	31. 35. —
	". 46. 26.	". 30. 45.
	". 50. 18.	". 30. 45.
	". 54. 44.	". 27. 30.
	". 58. 48.	". 26. —
	9. 2. —.	". 24. —.
	". 7. 15.	". 21. —.
	". 10. 17.	". 20. 30.
	". 12. 15.	". 19. —.
	". 14. 3.	". 17. 30.
	". 16. 15.	". 16. 30.
	". 18. 22.	". 15. 45.
	". 22. 50.	". 13. —
	". 30. 33.	". 6. 15.

Thursday July 12th

Observed Equal Altitudes of the ☉ with Sextant.[1]

A M.	7. 58. 59.	P. M.	4. 12. 29.
	8. —. 19.		". 13. 48.
	". 1. 45.		". 15. 14.

Altitude by Sextant at the time of this Obs^t 70°. 42′. 45″.

Observed meridian alt^d of ☉'s L. L. with Octant by the back observa^tn 40°. 53′. —″.

Latitude deduced from this observa^tn 39°. 55′. 56″.

Observed time and distance of ☉'s and ☽'s nearest limbs the ☉.West, with Sextant.

	Time			*Distance.*		
	h m s					
P. M.	4. 51. 11.	70°. 31′. 30″.
	5. 5. 48.	". 35 . 30 .
	". 11. 52.	". 37 . 30 .
	". 12. 47.	". 38 . —″
	". 16. 30.	". 39 . —″
	". 18. 8.	". 39 . 15 .
	". 19. 51.	". 39 . 30 .
	". 21. 9.	". 39 . 30 .
	". 24. 50.	". 41 . 30 .
	". 26. 14.	". 42 . 30 .

[1] Latitude only given in text of journal. — ED.

P. M.
h m s		
5. 32. 40.	. . . .	70°. 42′. —″
". 33. 53.	. . . .	". 44 . 45 .
". 38. 55.	. . . .	". 45 . 45 .
". 42. 11.	. . . .	". 46 . 30 .
". 43. 42.	. . . .	". 47 . 30 .
". 45. 25.	. . . .	". 47 . 30 .

☉'s Magnetic azimuth by Circumf.^r   N.   86°.   W.

                                    h   m   s

Time by Chronometer . . P. M.   5.   59 .   20.

Alt^d of ☉'s L. L. by Sextant . .   31°.   26′.   30″.

☉'s Magnetic azimuth by Circumf.^t   N.   85°.   W.

                                    h   m   s

Time by Chronometer. . P. M.   6.   5 .   10.

Alt^d of ☉'s L. L. by Sextant . .   29°.   19′.   30″

Observed time and distance of ☽, and Spica ♍. *, East, with Sextant.

             Time   *Distance.*

          h   m   s

P. M.   8.   26.   58 . . . . . .   19°.   18′.   15″

Note — this is a mean of four observations which were not so perfect as I could have wished them, in consequence of the moon being obscured in some measure by the clouds, which soon became so general as to put an end to my observations during this evening.

Sunday July 15th

Point of observation N°. 20. On the upper point of an Island mentioned in the 2^ed & 3rd course of this day.[1]

Observed meridian Alt^d of ☉ L. L.

   with Octant by back observa^n   42°. 11′. —″.

        Latitude deduced from this observat^n 40°.   8′.   31″.8 —

This evening I discovered that my Chronometer had stoped, nor can I assign any cause for this accedent; she had been wound up the preceding noon as usual. This is the third instance in which this instrument has stopt in a similar manner since she has been in my possession, tho' the fi[r]st only since our departure from the River Dubois. in the two preceding cases when she was again set in motion, and her rate of going determined by a series of equal altitudes of the ☉ taken for that purpose, it was found to be the same precisely as that mentioned in the preliminary remarks to these observations, or 15. s. & 5 tenths too slow in 24.h. — as her *rate of going* after stoping, and being again set in mo-

---

1 Not found in text of journal. — ED.

tion has in two instances proved to be the same, I have concluded, that whatever this impediment may proceed from, it is not caused by any material injury which her works have sustained, and that when she is in motion, her error on *mean time* above stated, may be depended on as accurate. In consequence of the chronometer's having thus accidentally stoped, I determined to come too at the first convenient place and make such observations as were necessary to ascertain her error, establish the Latitude & Longitude, and determine the variation of the nedle, in order to fix a *second point of departure.* accordingly on

Monday 16ᵗʰ we set out at an early hour; the morning was cloudy; could find no convenient situation for observation; proceeded untill a little before noon when we came too

Point of observation Nᵒ 21. On the Larᵈ Shore opposite to the center of good Island¹ where I observed the meridian altitude of ☉'s L. L. with Octant by the back observation, which gave me for Latitude 40°. 20'. 12''. N. I now set the Chronometer as near noon as this observation would enable me, and proceeded untill evening, when we came too on the Starᵈ shore opposite the *lower point* of the *Island of the Bald prarie* where we encamped.

Tuesday July 17ᵗʰ

Point of Observation Nᵒ 22, & of departure Nᵒ 2. Camp at the lower point of the Island of the bald Prarie²

Observed Meridian altᵈ of ☉'s L. L. with Octant by back observation 43°. 27'. — ''.

Latitude deduced from this observᵗⁿ 40°. 27'. 6''.4

From Equal Altitudes of ☉'s center found that ☉'s Center was truly on the Meridian

M. T. Pʳ Chronometer at $\quad$ 11ʰ. 58ᵐ. 51ˢ.

Chronometer too slow M. T. $\quad$ 6ᵐ. 51.6ˢ.

Observed Altitude of pole Star with Sextant $\quad$ 81°. 9'. 15''

Time by Chronometer P. M. $\quad$ 10ʰ. 23ᵐ. 18ˢ.

¹ Not found in text of journal. — ED.

² Most of the observations at this point are entered in text of journal, July 17, 1804. Those thus entered are omitted here. — ED.

ASTRONOMY

Thursday July 19th

Point of observation N°. 23. Under a bold bluff on Lar^d Shore, opposite to the Star^d point terminateing the 4th course of this day.[1]

Observed Meridian Alt^d of ☉'s L. L. with Octant by back observation 44°. 15'. —

   Latitude deduced from this obsev^t 40°. 29'. 50"

Sunday July 22^{ed}

Point of Observation N°. 24. on the Starboard shore above the River Platte, the mouth of which bore S. 15° E. distant 10 miles. —

Observed Equal Altitudes of the ☉ with Sext^t[2]

	h	m	s								h	m	s
A. M.	8.	53.	53.	.	.	.	.	.	P. M.	2.	58.	37.
	".	55.	20.	.	.	.	.	.		3.	—.	—
	".	56.	48.	.	.	.	.	.		".	1.	28.

Alt^d by Sextant at the time of observation. 92°. 37'. —"

Observed Meridian alt^d of ☉'s L. L. with Octant by the back Obset^n 46°. 31'. —"

   Latitude deduced from this obsev^{tn} 41°. 3'. 19".4.

Observed time and distance of ☽ and Antares. ✳. West, with Sextant. —

		Time											Distance.		
		h	m	s											
P. M.	10.	23.	20.		.	.	.	.	.	.	.	.	58.	42.	—
	".	28.	3.		.	.	.	.	.	.	.	.	".	43.	30.
	".	32.	7.		.	.	.	.	.	.	.	.	".	44.	—.
	".	35.	4.		.	.	.	.	.	.	.	.	".	45.	7.
	".	38.	15.		.	.	.	.	.	.	.	.	".	47.	—.
	".	41.	34.		.	.	.	.	.	.	.	.	".	48.	15.

Monday July 23rd

Observed Equal Altitudes of the ☉ with Sext.[2]

		h	m	s							h	m
A. M.	8.	—	49.		.	.	.	.	P. M.	3.	51.	56.
	".	2.	9.		.	.	.	.		".	52.	14.
	".	3.	38.		.	.	.	.		".	53.	45.

   Altitude by Sextant at the time of Obs^{tn} 72°. 49' —"

Observed Meridian Alt^d of ☉'s L. L. with Octant by the back observ^t 46°. 55' —"

   Latitude deduced from this Obs^{tn} [blank space in MS.]

---

[1] Not found in text of journal. — ED

[2] This observation is omitted from text of journal for July 23, 1804. — ED

Tuesday July 24th

⊙.'s Magnetic Azimuth by Circumft^r [1] . . . S. 85°. E.

Time by Chronometer . . . . . . A. M. 8^h. 8^m. 8^s.

Alt^d of ⊙'s U. L. by Sextant. . . . . 75°. 5'. 15".

Wednesday July 25th

Observed Equal Alt^{ds} of the ⊙ with Sextant.[2]

A. M. 8^h. 5^m. 20^s. . . . P. M. 3^h. 44^m. 38^s.

" . 6. 42. . . . ⊙. Obscured by cloud

" . 8. 7·5 . . . 3. 47. 27.

Alt^d by Sextant at the time of Observ^{tn}. . . . . . 74°. 19'. 30"

Thursday July 26th

Observed Equal Altitudes of ⊙ with Sextant.[2]

A. M. 7^h. 33^m. 32^s. . . . . . . P. M. 4^h. 15^m. 24^s.

" . 34. 55. . . . . . " . 16. 51.

" . 36. 22. . . . . . " . 18. 14.

Altitude by Sextant at the time of Obs^t . . . . . . 62°. 18'. 15"

Friday July 27th

Observed time and distance of ☽ and *a*. Aquilæ, ✶. West. *with Sextant*.[2]

	Time.				Distance	
	h	m	s			
A. M.	2.	47.	6.		64°. 48'. 15".	
	" .	55.	9.		" . 50 . 30 .	
	" .	59.	39.		" . 51 . 30 .	
	3.	2.	12.		" . 52 . — .	
	" .	4.	42.		" . 52 . 45 .	
	" .	6.	31.		" . 53 . — .	

I wished to have taken one or two sets more with moon and Aquilæ, but the clouds obscured the star. I was also anxious to have taken some sets with Aldeberan, then in reach of observation and East of the moon, but was prevented by the intervention of the clouds, which soon became so general as to obscure the whole horizon. —

Observed meridian Altitude of ⊙'s L. L. with Octant by the back ob^s. 48°. 44'

Latitude deduced from this obs^{tn} . . . . 41°. 5'. 35".2

---

[1] Not found in text of journal. — ED.

[2] This observation was in part entered in text of journal for July 23, 1804, but has been omitted therefrom and all placed here. — ED.

Tuesday July 31st

Point of observation N°. 25.   Camp at Council Bluffs, Larboard shore.[1]
Observed Meridian Alt^d of ⊙'s L. L. with Octant by the back observtn.
51°. 4'. 30''
Latitude deduced from this obser^tn   .   .   .   .   41°. 18'. 1''. 5

Wednesday August 1st

Observed meridian Alt^d of ⊙'s L. L. with Octant by the back observ^tn.
51°. 29'. 30''
Observed Equal Altitudes of the ⊙, with Sextant.[2]
⊙'s Magnetic azimuth by Circumferenter   N. 86°. E.

h   m   s
Time by Chronometer.   .   .   .   .   A. M. 7 . 52 . 55 .
Altitude by Sextant of ⊙'s U. L.   .   .   .   .   .   68°. 47'. 15''.
Latitude of place deduced from two observt^ns of ⊙'s
Mer^dn alt^d being as mean of the same .   .   .   .   .   41°. 17'. 0''.2

Saturday August 4th 1804

Point of observation N°. 26.   On the Starboard shore, opposite to the
mouth of *pond inlet.*[3]
Observed meridian alt^d of ⊙'s L. L. with Octant by the back observat^n.
53°. 20'. 30'.
Latitude deduced from this obser^tn   .   .   .   .   .   41°. 25'. 3''.8

note — the ⊙'s disk was frequently obscured in the course of this
observation, it is therefore probable that it is not accurate by 2 or 3
minutes of Latitude, and I believe it too much by that sum.

Sunday August 5th

Point of Observation N°. 27.   On the Larboard shore of main channel,
and on the starboard side of the Sand Island. —[3]
Observed meridian Alt^d of ⊙'s L. L. with Octant by the back observ^tn.
54°. 3'. —''
Latitude deduced from this observation .   .   .   .   41°. 30'. 6''.7

Wednesday August 8th

Point of observation N°. 28.   On the Starboard shore, the mouth of the
river E-ā-nearh war,-da-pon or Stone river bearing Due N. distant
one ½ miles, made the following observations with Sextant.[1]

---

[1] Latitude given in text of journal, July 31, 1804. — ED.
[2] Figures given in text of journal, August 1, 1804. — ED.
[3] Not found in text of journal. — ED.

Altitude of					Time by Chronometer.		
					h	m	s
⊙'s U. L. 80°. 14'. 15".	.	.	.	A. M.	8.	26.	59.
⊙'s Center " " "	.	.	.		".	28.	29.
⊙'s L. L. " " "	.	.	.		".	30.	3.

Point of observation N.º 29. On the Larboard Shore, the mouth of Stone river bearing due E. one mile dist.ⁿ [1]

Observed meridian Altitude of ⊙'s L. L. with Octant by the back observatⁿ 56°. 9'. — "

Latitude deduced from this observ.ᵗ 41°. 42'. 34".3.

Saterday August 11ᵗʰ.

Point of observation N.º 30. On the Starboard shore one mile above the mouth of the *Creek of Evil Sperits*.[2]

Sunday August 12ᵗʰ

Point of Observation N.º 31. On the Larboard shore in the center of a bend, being North, and by measurement 974 yards from the Lard. shore opposite to the point of observation of yesterday.[3]

Observed Meridian altitude of ⊙'s L. L. with Octant by the back obsᵗⁿ 59°. 8'. — "

Latitude deduced from this observat.ⁿ 42°. 1'. 47". 6.

Monday August 13ᵗʰ

Point of observation N.º 32. On the Larboard shore about three miles East of the Maha vilage.[4]

Observed time and distance of ⊙'s & ☽'s nearest limbs. *with Sextant.* —

	Time.													Distance.		
	h	m	s													
P. M.	3.	57.	9.	.	.	.	.	.	.	.	.		95°.	56'.	15"
	4.	1.	32.	.	.	.	.	.	.	.	.		".	58.	—.
	".	4.	45.	.	.	.	.	.	.	.	.		".	59.	30.
	".	6.	51.	.	.	.	.	.	.	.	.		96.	—.	—
	".	7.	57.	.	.	.	.	.	.	.	.		".	—.	30.
	".	9.	17.	.	.	.	.	.	.	.	.		".	—.	45.
	".	11.	52.	.	.	.	.	.	.	.	.		".	1.	7.5
	".	13.	—.	.	.	.	.	.	.	.	.		".	2.	—

¹ Results given in text of journal, August 8, 1804. — ED.
² For figures, see text of journal, August 11, 1804. — ED.
³ Not found in text of journal. — ED.
⁴ Clark entered this series of observations on the last flyleaf of Codex A, in their proper chronological sequence ; otherwise that entry is identical with this. Not included in text of journal. — ED.

	h	m	s				
P. M.	4.	51.	9.	. . . .	96°.	12′.	30″
	".	52.	33.	. . . .	".	13.	—
	".	54.	5.	. . . .	".	13.	30
	".	55.	26.	. . . .	".	14.	—
	".	56.	22.	. . . .	".	14.	15.
	".	57.	36.	. . . .	".	14.	30.

	h	m	s				
P. M.	4.	33.	18.	. . . .	96°.	7′.	45″
	".	34.	44.	. . . .	".	8.	30.
	".	35.	7.	. . . .	".	8.	37.5.
	".	37.	22.	. . . .	".	9.	15.
	".	38.	24.	. . . .	".	9.	45.
	".	39.	22.	. . . .	".	9.	45.

	h	m	s				
P. M.	5.	7.	59.	. . . .	96°.	17′.	45″
	".	10.	56.	. . . .	".	18.	30.
	".	12.	23.	. . . .	".	19.	45.
	".	15.	5.	. . . .	".	20.	15.
	".	16.	6.	. . . .	".	20.	15.
	".	17.	1.	. . . .	".	20.	45.
	".	18.	5.	. . . .	".	21.	—
	".	19.	1.	. . . .	".	21.	22.5.

Tuesday August 14ᵗʰ [1]

☉'s magnetic azimuth by Circumferenter   N. 87. E.

                                                    h   m   s

Time by Chronometer A. M. . . . .   7.   3.   4.

Altitude by Sextant of ☉'s U. L.   59°. 19′. 15″

☉'s magnetic azimuth by Circumferenter   N. 88. E.

                                                    h   m   s

Time by Chronometer. . . .   A. M. 7. 41. 19.

Alt^d of ☉'s U. L. by Sextant. . . . . 62°. —′. —″

Observed Equal Altitudes of the ☉, with Sextant.

	h	m	s				h	m	s
A. M.	7.	45.	16.	. . . . . .	P. M.	3.	45.	15.
	".	46.	43.	. . . . . .		".	46.	47. not certain
	".	48.	12.	. . . . . .		".	Lost by clouds	

Alt^d given by Sextant at the time of obs^tn   63°. 26′. 45″.

---

1 Entered in part by Clark on the last flyleaf of Codex A ; not included in text of journal. — ED.

observed Meridian altitude of ☉'s L. L. with Octant by the back observat.ⁿ 60°. 45′. 30″.

Latitude deduced from this observatⁿ   42°. 12′. 10″.9

Wednesday August 15ᵗʰ

Observed Equal Altitudes of the ☉, with Sextant.[1]

	h	m	s			h	m	s
A. M.	8.	0.	29.	. . . .	P. M.	3.	28.	42.
".	1.	52.		. . . . . .		".	30.	11.
".	3.	28.		. . . . . .		".	31.	38.

Alt.ᵈ by Sextant at the time of this observ.ᵗ   68°. 45′. 45″.

Observed meridian Alt.ᵈ of ☉'s L. L. with Octant by the back observ.ᵗ 61°. 27′. —″

Latitude deduced from this observ.ᵗ   42° 15′. 13″.4

Saturday, August 18ᵗʰ

Observed meridian alt.ᵈ [1] of ☉'s L. L. with Octant by the back observ.ᵗ 63°. 23′. —″

Latitude deduced from this obse.ᵗ   [blank space in MS.]

Observed Equal Altitudes of the ☉ with Sextant.

	h	m	s			h	m	s
A. M.	7.	38.	1.	. . . . . .	P. M.	3.	46.	48.
".	39.	28.		. . . . . .		".	48.	13.
".	40.	58.		. . . . . .		".	49.	42.

Alt.ᵈ by Sextant at the time of Obs.ᵗⁿ   60°. 8′. —″

Tuesday, August 21ˢᵗ

Point of observation Nº 33. On a large sand bar Star.ᵈ, 4 miles above the mouth of the river Souix.[1]

Observed meri.ᵈⁿ Alt.ᵈ of ☉'s L. L. with Octant by the back observation 65°. 47′. —″

Latitude deduced from this observatⁿ   42°. 28′. 29″.

Friday, August 24ᵗʰ

This day the Chronometer stoped again just after being wound up; I know not the cause, but fear it procedes from some defect which it is not in my power to remedy.[1]

Monday August 27ᵗʰ

Point of Observation Nº 34. On the Star.ᵈ shore, opposite to the lower point, or commencement of the white C[h]alk Bluff.[1]

---

[1] Not found in text of journal. — ED.

Observed Magnetic azim.th of ☉ by Circumf.^{r} S. 85°. E.

		h	m	s
Time by Chronometer A. M.	. . . . .	7.	41.	52.
Alt.^{d} of ☉'s U. L. by Sextant.	. . .	60°.	4'.	—''
☉ magnetic Azimuth by circumferent.^{r}	.	S.	84°.	E.
		h	m	s
Time by Chronometer A. M.	. . .	7.	46.	13.
Alt.^{d} of ☉' U. L. by Sextant .	. . .	61 .	57'.	—''

Observed time and altitudes of ☉ with Sextant

	Time.					Altitude of		
	h	m	s					
A. M.	7.	49.	37.	. .	☉'s U. Limb.	. .	63°. 8.' 15''	
".	51.	3.		. .	☉'s Center.	. .	" " "	
".	52.	40.		. .	☉'s L. Limb.	. .	" " "	

Point of observation N.º 35. On the Star.^{d} shore opposite to the upper point of the white Chalk Bluffs.[1]

Observed Meridian Alt.^{d} U. L. with Sextant by the fore observation 115°. —'. 45''

Latitude deduced from the observt.^{n} 42. 53. 13

Thursday August 30th

Point of Observation N.º 36. On the Lar.^{d} Shore at the lower point of Calumet Bluff.[1]

Observed equal Alt.^{d} of the ☉, with Sextant

	h	m	s						h	m	s
A. M.	8.	14.	51.	. . . . .	P. M.	2.	49.	24.
	".	16.	22.	. . . . .		".	50.	59.
	".	18.	3.	. . . . .		".	52.	38.

Alt.^{d} given by Sextant at time of obst.^{n} 70°. 42'. —''

Friday August 31st

Observed time and distance of ☉'s and ☽'s nearest limbs, with Sextant. the ☽ West.[1]

	Time.				Distance.	
	h	m	s			
A. M.	11.	12.	18.	. . . .	41°. 51'.	—''
	".	14.	23	. . . .	". 48 .	—
	".	15.	49	. . . .	". 47 . 45	
	".	16.	42.	. . . .	". 46 . 30	
	".	17.	52.	. . . .	". 46 . 30	
	".	19.	32.	. . . .	". 45 . 45	

---

[1] Not found in text of journal. — ED.

Saturday September 8th

Point of observation N.º 37. On the Lard. Shore $3\frac{1}{2}$ miles below M.ʳ Trudeau's House,[1]

Observed ☉'s Magnetic azimuth with Circumfert.ʳ S. 85.º E.

Time by Chronometer A. M. . . . . $7 \cdot 27 \cdot 59$ (h m s)
Alt.ᵈ of ☉'s U. L. by Sextant. . . . . 51°. 4′. 30″
☉'s Magnetic Azimuth by Circumferent.ʳ   S. 84. E.

Time by Chronometer A. M. . . . . $7 \cdot 33 \cdot 30$ (h m s) .
Alt. by Sextant of ☉'s U. L. . . . . 53°. 2′. —″.

Observed time and Altitude of ☉, with Sextant

	Time. h m s		Altitude of
A. M.	7. 33. 30	☉'s U.S.	53°. 2′. —″
".	35. 5.	☉'s Center	". ". —.
".	36. 41.	☉'s L.L.	". ". —.

I could not obtain the meridian altitude of sun this day in consequence of not being able to come too in time, without infinite danger of injuring the boat. the evening was cloudy, which prevented my taking the altitude of any fixed star.

September 9th Sunday

Point of Observation N.º 38. On the Lar.ᵈ Shore opposite to the upper point of boat Island.[1]

observed. ☉'s Magnetic azimuth by Circumferent.ʳ S. 89° E.

Time by Chronometer A.M. $7 \cdot 6 \cdot 3$ (h m s)
Alt.ᵈ of ☉'s U.L. by Sextant   43°. —′. —″

☉'s Magnetic azimuth by Circumfet.ʳ S. 88.º E.

Time by Chronometer A.M. . . . . $7 \cdot 12 \cdot 3$ (h m s) .
Alt.ᵈ of ☉'s U.L. by Sextant . . . . . . 44 · 57 · 15 .

Observed time; and Alt.ᵈ of ☉, with Sextant.

	Time h m s		Altitude of
A.M.	7. 12. 3.	☉'s U.L.	44°. 57′. 15″.
".	13. 31.	☉'s Center	". ". ".
".	15. 4.	☉'s L.L.	". ". ".

Point of Observation N.º 39. On the Star.ᵈ shore, near a point of woodland, being the extremity of the third course of this day.[1]

Observed Meridian alt.ᵈ of ☉'s U. L. with Sextant fore observation—
— 104°. 51′. 30″.

Latitude deduced from this Observat.ⁿ 43°. 11′. 56″.1,

---

[1] Not found in text of journal. — Ed.

Point of observation Nᵒ. 40. On the Larᵈ shore, under a high bluff, 2 miles below Ceder Island. — [1]

Observed Meridian Altᵈ of ☉'s U. L. with Sextant by the fore Observtⁿ.
103 . 53 . 15

Latitude deduced from this observtⁿ [blank space in MS.]

Point of Observation Nᵒ 41. On the Starᵈ Shore 4 miles above the point of observation at noon — Observed time and distance of ☉'s & ☽'s nearest limbs, the ☽ East.

	Time.				Distance.		
	h	m	s		°	′	″
P. M.	4.	31.	15	. . . .	76.	55.	15
	".	34.	5	. . . .	".	56.	—.
	".	35.	7	. . . .	".	56.	30.
	".	36.	14	. . . .	".	57.	15.
	".	37.	50.	. . . .	".	57.	—.
	".	38.	54.	. . . .	".	57.	30.
	h	m	s		°	′	″
P. M.	5.	25.	26.	. . . .	77.	9.	15.

Point of Obsⁿ Nᵒ. 42. On the Larᵈ shore, one mile and a haf above the mouth of Corvus Creek[1] observed equal altitudes of ☉ with Sextant.

	h	m	s			h	m	s
A. M.	7.	46.	49.	. . . . . .	A. M.	2.	59.	50.
	".	47.	25.	. . . .		3.	1.	30.
	".	49.	12.	. . . .		".	3.	3.

Altᵈ by sextant at the time of Observatⁿ. 53°. 17′. 45″.

Observed meridian Altitude of ☉'s L. L. with Octant by the back Observation 87°. 31′. 00″.

Point of Observation Nᵒ. 43. On the Larᵈ shore opposite to the mouth of the lower of the two rivers of the Siouxs pass.[1] Observed Meridian Altᵈ of ☉'s U. L. with Sextant by the fore observation 95°. 30′. 15.

---

1 Not found in text of journal. — ED.

Saturday Septr. 22^{ed} 1804.

Point of observation N°. 44. On the Star^d. shore, about one mile below the lower Island of the three sisters.[1]

Sunday September 23rd 1804.

Point of observation N°. 45. On the Lar^d. Shore 3 miles below Elk Island. observed meridian alt^d. of ☉'s U. L. with Sextant by the fore observation   91°. 48'. 45"

Tuesday October 2^{ed} 1804.

Point of observation N°. 46. On a large sand bar Lar^d. shore, opposite to the gorge of the bend *look-out*.[2] Observed the meridian alt^d. of ☉'s U. L. with Sextant by the fore observation   84°. 45'. 15".

Latitude deduced from this observation.   N. 44°. 19'. 36". 3

Monday October 8th 1804.

Point of observation N°. 47. On the Lar^d. shore, in the point fromed [formed] by the junction of the Weterhoo river with the Missouri.[3] Observed meridian alt^d. of ☉'s U. L. with Sextant by the fore observation   77°. 35'. —".

Latitude deduced from this observation   N. 45°. 39'. 5".

Thursday October 11th 1804.

Point of observation N° 48. at our camp on the Lar^d shore a small distance above the upper point of an Island on which the lower village of the Ricaras is situated.[3]

Observed Equal Altitude of the ☉ with Sextant.

		h	m	s				h	m	s
A. M.		9.	8.	7.	. . . . . .	P. M.		3.	41.	49.
.	".	10.	1.		. . . .		".		42.	36.
	".	11.	57.		. . . .		".		44.	40.

Altitude by Sextant at the time of observ^{tn}   42°. 16'. 45."

Wednesday October 17th 1804.

Point of observation N°. 49. On the Star^d shore, opposite to a high projecting Bluff; which from the great number of rattlesnakes found near it, we called the *rattlesnake Bluff*.[4]

Observed meridian alt^d. of ☉'s U. L. with Sextant by the fore observation   69°. 17'. —.

Latitude deduced from this observation   N. 46 . 23'. 57"

---

[1] Figures given in text of journal, Sept. 22, 1804. — ED.

[2] Latitude only given in text of journal, for respective dates. — ED.

[3] Not found in text of journal. — ED.

[4] Latitude given in text of journal, Oct. 17, 1804. — ED.

Point of Observation Nᵒ. 50. On the starᵈ shore at council camp, about half a mile above the upper Mandan Village.[1]

Observed meridian Altᵈ of ⊙'s U. L. with Sextant by the fore observation   58°. 55'. 15".

Latitude deduced from this observation   N. 47°. 22'. 56". 7

☞ The Chronometer ran down today.   I was so much engaged with the Indians, that I omited winding her up.

Tuesday October 30ᵗʰ 1804.

at the same place   Wound up the Chronometer, and observed equal Altitudes of the ⊙ with Sextant.[1]

A. M. 8. 4. 44.	P. M. ⎫	lost in consequence
".. 7. 31.	⎬	of the sun's being
".. 10. 31.	⎭	obscured by clouds.

Altitude given by Sextant at the time of Obsᵗⁿ   44°. 53'. 15".

Wednesday October 31ˢᵗ 1804.

The river being very low and the season so far advanced that it frequently shuts up with ice in this climate we determined to spend the Winter in this neighbourhood, accordingly Capᵗ Clark with a party of men reconnoitred the country for some miles above our encampment; he returned in the evening without having succeed[ed] in finding an eligible situation for our purpose.

Thursday November 1ˢᵗ 1804.

The wind blew so violently during the greater part of this day that we were unable to quit our encampment; in the evening it abated; we droped down about seven miles and land on N. E. side of the river at a large point of Woodland.

Friday November 2ᵈ 1804.

This morning early we fixed on the site for our fortification which we immediately set about.   This place we have named Fort Mandan in honour of our Neighbours.

Fort Mandan, Sunday November 11ᵗʰ 1804.

Point of Obsⁿ Nᵒ. 51.   Observed Meridian altitude of ⊙'s U. L. with Sextant by the fore observation[1]   51°. 4'. 52."

Latitude deduced from this observation   N. 47°. 21'. 32". 8

---

[1] Not found in text of journal. — Eᴅ.

Saturday December 22ᵈ 1804.

Observed Equal altitudes of ☉. with Sextant.[1]

	h	m	s			h	m	s
A. M.	9.	6.	43.	. . . .	P. M.	1.	25.	39.
"		9.	52.	. . . . . .		"	28.	57.
"	13.	9.	. . . . . .			"	32.	10.

Chronometer too slow on Mean time   0. 39. 37.6 (h m s)

Monday January 7ᵗʰ 1805.

Observed time and distance of ☉'s and ☽'s nearest limbs, with Sextant.[1]
☉. West.

	Time									*Distance.*		
	h	m	s									
A. M.	2.	21.	—.	. . . .	79°.	25'.	45".
"		23.	55.	. . . .	"	26.	15.
"		25.	3.	. . . .	"	26.	30.
"		26.	3.	. . . .	"	27.	—.
"		27.	47.	. . . .	"	27.	15.
"		29.	29.	. . . .	"	28.	—.
	h	m	s				
P. M.	2.	38.	12.	. . . .	79°.	30'.	15".
"		39.	22.	. . . .	"	31.	—.
"		40.	19.	. . . .	"	31.	45.
"		41.	36.	. . . .	"	32.	15.
"		42.	33.	. . . .	"	32.	45.
"		43.	25.	. . . .	"	33.	—.

Sunday January 13ᵗʰ 1805.

Observed Meridian altitude of ☉. U. L. with Sextant and glass artificial Horizon.[1] 43°. 18'. 30"

Latitude deduced from this observation. N. 47°. 20'. 52".6

Monday January 14ᵗʰ astronomical 1805.

Observed an Eclips of the Moon. I had no other glass to assist me in this observation but a small refracting telescope belonging to my sextant, which however was of considerable service, as it enabled me to define the edge of the moon's immage with much more precision than I could have done with the natural eye. The commencement of the eclips was obscured by clouds, which continued to interrupt me throughout the whole observation; to this cause is also attributable the inacuracy of the observation of the *commencement of total darkness.*

---

[1] Not found in text of journal. — ED.

I do not put much confidence in the observation of the middle of the Eclips, as it is the wo[r]st point of the eclips to distinguish with accuracy. The two last observations (i.e.) the *end of total darkness*, and the *end of the eclips*, were more satisfactory ; they are as accurate as the circumstances under which I laboured would permit me to make them. —

	h	m	s
Commencement of total darkness . .	12.	28.	5.
Middle of the Eclips	12.	57.	24.
End of total darkness	13.	41.	30.
End of the eclips	14.	39.	10. [1]

Tuesday January 15th 1805.

Observed equal Altitudes of the ⊙ with sextant and Glass artificial horizon adjusted with a sperit level [2]

A. M.	h 8.	m 26.	s 32.	. . . . . P. M.	h —	m —	s —
".		29.	14.	. . . .	—	—	—
".		32.	1.	. . . .	1.	49.	46

Altitude given by the sextant at the time of obᵗⁿ 26°. 6′ 15″.

Chronometer too slow on mean time . . . 1. h 1. m 57.7 s

Chronometer's daily rate of going, as deduced from this observation, and that of the 22ᵉᵈ of December 1804 is too slow on mean time 55. 8. s

☞ I do not place much confidence in this observation in consequence of loosing the observation of the Altitude of the ⊙'s L. L. and center P. M. and that [of] his U. L. was somewhat obscured by a cloud. the weather was so could [cold] that I could not use water as the reflecting surface, and I was obliged to remove my glass horizon from it's first adjustment lest the savages should pilfer it.

Sunday January 20th 1805.

Observed Equal altitudes of the ⊙, with Sextant & glass horizon. [2]

A. M.	h 8.	m 40.	s 20.	. . . . . . P. M.	h 1.	m 21.	s 55.
".		47.	15.	. . . . .	".	24.	47.
".		50.	10.	. . . . .		lost by a cloud	

Altitude given by Sextant at the time of obˢᵗ 31°. 40′. 15″.

Chronometer too slow on mean time 1. h 15. m 20.3 s

☞ the horizon was removed from it's first adjustment.

---

[1] Clark gives the figures in their ordinary foim, with one variant. See text of journal, January 15, 1805. — ED.

[2] Not found in text of journal. — ED.

Saturday January 26th 1805.

Observed Meridian Altitude of ⊙'s U. L. with sextant and artific. Horz[n] of water [1]   48°.   50'.   —''

Latitude deduced from this observat[n] N.   47.   21.   47.

Monday January 28th 1805.

Observed Equal altitudes with Sextant and artificial Horizon on the construction recommended by M[r] Andrew Ellicott, in which sperits were substituted for water, it being to could to use the latter.[1]

A. M.	8.	7.	29.	. . . .	P. M.	1.	52.	34.
".	9.	51.		. . . .		".	54.	58.
".	12.	20.		. . . .		".	57.	26.

Alt[d] by Sextant at the time of observation   33°.   25'.   —''

$$\begin{array}{ccc} h & m & s \end{array}$$

Chronometer too slow on mean time . .   1.   11.   12.2

—   —   51[s].2

☞ the accuracy of this observation may be depended on.

Longitude of Fort Mandan as deduced from the observation of the end of total darkness when the eclips of the moon tok place the 14th of January Astrono[cl] 1805

W. from Greenwich 6. 37. 31.2 or 99°. 22'. 45''.3

$$\begin{array}{ccc} h & m & s \end{array}$$

Longitude of Fort Mandan as deduced from the *end* of the

same eclips   6. 37. 47. or 99°. 26'. 45''.

$$\begin{array}{ccc} h & m & s \end{array}$$

Wednesday February 6th 1805.

Observed equal altitude of the ⊙ with Sextant artificial horizon with water [1]

	h	m	s			h	m	s
A. M.	7.	59.	31	. . . . . .	P. M.	1.	49.	31
	8.	1.	36	. . . . . .		".	51.	24
	".	3.	5.	. . . . . .		".	53.	41.

Altitude given by Sextant at the time of Obs[t] 32°. 11'. 15.''

---

[1] Not found in text of journal. — ED.

Observed time and distance of ☉' and ☽'s nearest limbs with Sextant the ☉ West.

Time				Distance.
P. M.	2.	8. 32	. . . .	87. 28. 15
	".	12. 16	. . . .	". 30. —
	".	15. 58	. . . .	". 30. 45.
	".	18. 48	. . . .	". 32. —
	".	20. —	. . . .	". 33. —
	".	22. 25	. . . .	". 34. —

Time.				Distance.
	h	m	s	
P. M.	2.	26.	15	. . . . 87°. 35'. 15".
	".	29.	40.	. . . . ". 35 . 45 .
	".	31.	37.	. . . . ". 36 . 30 .
	".	33.	27.	. . . . ". 36 . 45 .
	".	35.	3.	. . . . ". 37 . 30 .
	".	36.	38.	. . . . ". 38 . — .

I do not place great confidence in these observations, as the person who took the time was not much accustomed to the business. Cap! Clark was absent.

Saturday February 23ʳᵈ 1805.

Observed time and distance of ☉'s and ☽'s nearest limbs with Sextant, ☉ East.[1]

Time				Distance
	h	m	s	
A. M.	6.	12.	15	. . . . 66°. 24'. 15".
	".	14.	17.	. . . . " . 23 . 45 .
	".	16.	14.	. . . . " . 22. 45 .
	".	17.	51.	. . . . " . 22. — .
	".	20.	23.	. . . . " . 21 . 25 .
	".	22.	18.	. . . . " . 21 . — .

	h	m	s	
A. M.	6.	25.	56.	. . . . 66°. 20'. —".
	".	28.	5.	. . . . " . 19. 15 .
	".	29.	6.	. . . . " . 19. — .
	".	30.	58.	. . . . " . 18 . — .
	".	32.	38.	. . . . " . 17 . 45 .
	".	34.	59.	. . . . " . 17 . 15 .

---

[1] Not found in text of journal —ED.

Immediately after the Lunar observations observed Equal altitudes of the ☉ with Sextant and artificial Horizon with water.

	h	m	s			h	m	s
A. M.	6.	41.	5	. . . .	P.M.	—.	46.	20
".	43.	9	. . . .		".	48.	30.
".	45.	19.	. . . .		".	50.	35.

Altitude given by Sextant at the time of observation   40°. 15′. 45″

	h	m	s
Chronometer too slow Mean Time	2.	28.	14.9

Monday March 25ᵗʰ 1805.

Observed ☉'s magnetic Azimuth with Circumferenter[1] S. 60°. W.

		h	m	s
Time by Chronometer . . . . . . P. M.		5.	7.	49.
Altitude of ☉'s L. L. by Sextant		32°	2.′	0″.
☉'s Magnetic Azimuth by Circumferenter	S.	61°.	W.	
Time by Chronometer P. M.		5.	11.	31.
Altitude of ☉'s L. L. by Sextand.		30°.	49′.	15″
☉'s Magnetic Azimuth by Circumferenᵗ.	S.	63°.	W.	
Time by Chronometer P. M.		5.	19.	30
Altᵈ by Sextant of ☉'s L. L.		28°.	13′.	30″.

Thursday March 28ᵗʰ 1805.

Observed Equal altitudes of the ☉ with Sextant & water artifc. Horizon.

	h	m	s			h	m	s
A. M.	8.	45.	28.5	. . . . . .	P. M.	4.	17.	4.
".	47.	9.	. . . .		".	18.	15.5
".	48.	57.	. . . .		".	20.	43.

Altitude by Sextᵗ at time of Observation   48°. 50′. —″.

Saturday March 30ᵗʰ 1805.

Observed Equal Altitudes of the ☉, with Sextant and artificial Horzⁿ of Water.[1]

	h	m	s			h	m	s
A. M.	8.	42.	46.	. . . . . .	P. M.	4.	17.	33.
".	44.	27.	. . . .		".	19.	15.
".	46.	10.	. . . .		".	20.	59.

Altᵈ by Sextant at the time of observᵗ   49°. 45′. 00″.

[1] Not found in text of journal. — Ed.

[Here ends the series of observations entered in Codex O, which was sent down to St. Louis with the boat that left the Mandans, April 7, 1805. From this time on, Lewis entered his observations in the text of the journal, taking a new point of departure. On April 12, 1805, at the mouth of the Little Missouri, he begins "*Point of Observation N°. 1*," and continues to "*Point of Observation N° 46.*," at Traveller's Rest Creek. Until September 30, 1805, Clark does not enter anything but the latitude deduced from observations; from that time, however, until November 24, 1805, on the Pacific coast, he enters a number of observations — among them are the following, found in Codex H, pp. 23, 24, transferred hither from the text of the journal. — ED.]

Celestial observations taken in the junction of the Columbia & Lewis's Rivers.

Thursday October 17ᵗʰ 1805

Altitude taken with Sextant the error of which is 8′ — 45″ Subtraitive.

A. M. 7 — 40 — 13 ⎫
"   " — 42 — 58 ⎬ Altitude produced   22° — 25′ — 15″.
"   " — 43 — 44 ⎭

Observed time and Distance of Sun and Moon's nearest limbs, Sun East

Time	Distance		Time	Distance
A. M. 7. 51. 43	60°. 47′. 15″	A. M. 8. 00. 26	60°. 43′. 45″
". 53. 33	". 46. 30	". 1. 22	". 43. 15
". 54. 35	". 45. 45	". 3. 8	". 43. 0
". 55. 55	". 45. 0	". 4. 43	". 42. 30
". 57. 37	". 45. "	". 6. 5	". 43. 0
". 58. 29	". 44. "	". 7. 52	". 41. 30

Magnetic Azmoth of the Sun, time and distance

Azmᵗ	Time	Distance
A. M. S. 75° East	8 — 15 — 45	33°. 4′. 30″
" S. 74° East	8 — 19 — 43	34. 13. 0

[263]

Equal Altitudes with Sextant.

	h	m	s		h	m	s
A. M.	8.	23.	0.	P. M.	3.	21.	53.
".		24.	25.	".		23.	50.
".		26.	49.	".		25.	42.

Altitude produced from the observation is 35°. 9′. 30″. —

Friday October 18ᵗʰ. 1805

Took one altitude of the Sun's upper limb

Alt 28°. 22′. 15″. at 8. 1. 24 A. M.
(h m s)

Observed time and distance of Sun and Moon's nearest limbs Sun East. —

	Time										*Distance*		
	h	m	s										
AM	9.	37.	46	.	.	.	.	.	.	.	47°.	15′.	30″.
".		40.	32	.	.	.	.	.	.	.	".	14.	15
".		41.	47	.	.	.	.	.	.	.	".	14.	"
".		42.	55	.	.	.	.	.	.	.	".	13.	30
".		43.	44	.	.	.	.	.	.	.	".	12.	45
".		46.	2	.	.	.	.	.	.	.	".	12.	30
".		47.	18	.	.	.	.	.	.	.	".	12.	0
".		48.	35	.	.	.	.	.	.	.	".	11.	45
".		49.	45	.	.	.	.	.	.	.	".	11.	15
".		50.	53	.	.	.	.	.	.	.	".	11.	"
".		52.	0	.	.	.	.	.	.	.	".	9.	30
".		53.	46	.	.	.	.	.	.	.	".	9.	30

Took an altitude of the Suns upper Limb

58°. 34′. 45″ at 10. 3. 59 A. M.
(h m s)

Took a *Meridian* Altitude Suns upper Limb which gave 68°. 57′. 30″.—
The Latitude produced is 46°. 15′. 13.″ 9 North

I measured the wedth of each river by angles as follows i. e.

The *Columbia River* is 960 yards wide
The Lewis's River is 575   do   do

Imedeately below the junction the Columbia River is from one to three miles wide including the Islands.

[Lewis apparently took fewer observations during the winter at Fort Clatsop than while at Fort Mandan. For such as are recorded, see text of the journals proper, January 1 to March 23, 1806. On the return journey he marks " *Point of Observation N? 55,*" on April 1, 1806. After a few observations (embodied in the text of the journals), to correct his instruments, the next point of observation is dated May 25, 1806, and situated on the Kooskooskee (see text of journals). At the Quamash Flats, he made observations, all embodied in text of the journals, save the following, which is found on the first flyleaf of Codex L. — ED.]

by octant ⊙*'s L. L. 51? 20' June 9ᵗʰ 1806.*

June 9ᵗʰ 1806.

Error of the Sextant 6'. 15 — or Subtractive
Error of Octant by the back observation
   on the *distant fragment* of the broken limb } 2°. 30'. 4".5 +

additive.

[The final observation was that made on Maria River, by Lewis, July 23, 1806, and entered both by him and Clark in the text of the journals.—ED.]

VIII. Miscellaneous Memoranda

IN the last book of the journals proper, Codex N, were a number of blank pages on which Clark jotted down the following notes obtained by him from traders and Indians. The context shows that much of this material was obtained at dates subsequent to the expedition. — ED.]

Notes of Information I believe Correct

an establishment was made by a Hunting and trading Company from S! Louis at the Enterance of the Big horn River into the Rochejhone 437 miles up that river in the fall 1807. from which they Traded with Sundery bands of Crow Indians, and took the Beaver in their neighbour-hood, in the fall 1809 a Company formed of S! Louis, The S! Louis Missouri Fur Company with 150 men went into the Rocky Mountains about the Missouri & Clarks River, for the purpose of takeing the Fur and made establishments on the River Rochejhone where it enters the Rocky Mountains one other at the 3 forks of the Missouri and [blank space in MS.]

The Company which first formed and established at the Bighorn Joined the S! L M. Fur Compy [1]

" about 100 Miles on a direct line from the enterance of Big horn River it passes th[r]o one range of the Rocky Mountains, — at this place on the East Side of the River and imediately below a fork of the R —, and from the Mount! there Issues Such a quantity of hot water that the river is not frozen in the extreem of Winter for maney miles below, a good Canoe navigation to this Mountain and the river about 40 yds. wide, it is here contracted to 10 yds. wide only " [2]

a remarkable Lake of about 440 yds. in diameter situated at the foot of the Rocky Mountains on a west branch of Tongu river (a branch of Rochejhone) on the side next to the Mn! the rocks rise from the waters edge about 30 feet and occupies about half the circumfrance

---

[1] See Chittenden's account of the various associations known under the name of Missouri Fur Company (1794–1830), in his *Amer. Fur Trade*, i, pp. 137–158. — ED.

[2] These are the notes referred to by Clark in Codex M, p. 98, as a description "of the country South of the Rochejhone." — ED.

of the lake which is Circular, the other Side is a butifull plain. This river is called by the Indians Min-na-e-sa (or big water).

At the head of this river the nativs give an account that there is frequently herd a loud noise, like Thunder, which makes the earth Tremble, they State that they seldom go there because their children Cannot sleep — and Conceive it possessed of spirits, who were averse that men Should be near them

Ship tâh-cha a band of Crow Indians of 150 Lodges and about 1500 soles rove on Big horn River & Rochejhone.

Ap-shâ-roo-kee [Absaroka] a band of Crow Indians of 200 Lodges and about 2000 soles rove on the Tonge River, big horn & River Rochejhone.

(*omit this band*) a Band of Crow Indians of 50 Lodges rove in the Same Cty

E-cup-scup-pe-âh a Band of Tushapaws Speak their language and Sometimes rove on the waters of the Rojhone, of about 80 Lodges 800 soles

On the Tonge & Bighorn and Clarks fork of the Rojhone there is an abundance of dry Grass of which the Indian horses live dureing the winter.

from the Fort or enterance of Big horn River the Indians Say a man on horseback can travel to the Spanish Settlements in 14 days on the head of *Del Norte*.

Misselanious Notes Given by a Trader.

This Saline he visited last Winter, when he observed its Situation Particularly as also eve[r]y Circumstance in relation to its Peculiarities. It is Situated on the east Side of the first of what are usually called the three forks of the Arcansas river[1] within a quarter of a league of that Stream. This Junction called the three forks of the Arcansas is estimated is at two hundred and forty leagues from its Junction of the Mississippi.

At the mouth of the small stream which discharges itself from this saline their is a thick Wood which Continues on both Sides of the Same Within a small distance of the Saline   Near this place are several remarkable Salines One of Which in Particular contains about 4 acres it contains a Variety of Springs which boil from the ground and hence they have obtained amoung the Indians [the name of] *the Pots*   so strong is the water that the Salt concretes as it comes from the ground and forms a kind of rim around the edges

---

[1] East of the Neosho River, which with the Verdigris falls into the Arkansas near Fort Gibson, Indian Territory. — ED.

Great Saline to the westward of the main branch of the Arkansaw. From the Osage Town on the Osage River 11 days travel to the Great saline From St Louis to the Osage Village thence West 120 leagues to the great saline Situated on a Southern branch of the river Arkansas called niscud [Ne-ne-scah] and by the French the River of the grand Saline which after pursuing a course of about 40 leagues discharges itself into the Arkansas about 30 leagues due West, from the great Saline and Situated on the S W Side of a considerable Southern branch of the Arkansas Islands [is] the Saline which Produces the Purest rock Salt. it is of white a clear colour, this Stream is called by the Osages the *Na chu richin gar*. 30 leagues below this Saline and on the same side of that stream is Situated the red Saline so named from the Colour of the Salt it lies S. W. 20 leagues from the great Saline this stream discharges itself into the Arcansaw about 20 leagues of [up] that river, after travrseing the country for about 60 leagues, after it passes the red Saline.

The Pot Saline Situated on the Eastern bank of the most Easterlye of the three forks of the Arcansaw River about 10 leagues from its mouth this stream is navigable to the Saline and maney miles above it for Peroagues or light boats.

Two other Salines of inferior note are found West from the Osage Village. The first 55 leagues W. near the head of the Middle fork of the Arkansas call^d *Vai ce ton hand hos* The other bearing a little South of West from the same & distant from it about 30 leagues the last is near the Main river Arkansas On its North Side I II & denotes the Villages of the snake lizzard and squirrel

In the Parris (Prarie) County at the head of the river Cansies [Kansas] is a large Saline of the same nature of the great Saline of th[e] Osages The narrowest part of the Osage country is 300 Miles bordering on the Mississippi

The names of the Forts or British Trading Establishments on the Ossiniboine

		L S		
1st Que[e]ns Fort[1] (La prairie) . . .		20		from red river
2. Mouse River fort	58	d^o	38
3. Hump Mountain fort	83	d^o	25
4. Catapie River (the rout to the Missouri 150 miles)	99	d^o	16
5. Swan River	114	d^o	15
6. Coude de l'homme (or Mans Elbow) .	129	d^o	15
7. Sourse at Lake Manitou	149	d^o	20

[1] A translation of its earlier French name, Fort de la Reine. This post was established by La Vérendrye in October, 1738, at the place now known as Portage la

red river of Lake Osnepegui[1] 285 Leagues long (Hay) Wooded & low on both Sides

The streams of the Missouri near and within those mountains abound in beaver & Otter.

The muddyness of the Missoury is caused by the washing in of its banks — within the rocky mountains the water is Clear.

The pumies stone which is found as low as the Illinois Country is form^d by the banks or stratums of Coal taking fire and burning the earth imediately above it into either pumies stone or Lavia, this Coal Country is principally above the Mandans.

The Country from the Mississippi to the River platt — 630 miles furnishes a sufficient qt^y of wood for Settlements — above that River the Country becomes more open, and wood principally confined to river & Creek bottoms. the uplands furtile and open, with some exceptions on the Rockejhone R. Capt. Clark saw some Pine Country. and the ranges of low Black Mountains are covered with wood. most of the large Rivers fall in on the south side of the Missouri.

[Financial memoranda, by Lewis, found on the back of a flyleaf of Codex P. — Ed.]

Decr 4th

this day drew in favour of William Morrison on the secretary of War draught dated Jany 1st 1804 payable 3 days after sight for $136.

No. 2 on the Set^y of War for 33$ forwarded Gover Morrison in favor of it being for flagg stuf sent me by the gov^r. and was drawn payable 3 days after sight. dated 25th Feb^r

N^o. *3. 4. & 5* for 500 $ each and left blank as to the name of the person in whose favour they were drawn, and sent to Mr Pike for negociation were dated on the 28th of March 1804 *these draughts were not negociated but* were returned me and destroyed.

Prairie; in 1796 the Hudson Bay Co. built a fort near its site. At the mouth of Souris (Mouse) River was Assiniboin House, erected by the Northwest Company in 1795; and not far from it was Brandon House, built by the Hudson's Bay Company in the preceding year, about 17 miles below the present city of Brandon, Man. "Catapie" is probably a blunder for Qu'Appelle River. Farther up the Assiniboin River, not far from a bend in Swan River, was the noted Fort Pelly, a post of the Hudson's Bay Co. It is impossible to identify all the localities here named, or Clark's distances. — Ed.

[1] Apparently a misnomer for Quinipigou, the Algonkin name of Lake Winnipeg (this name a corruption of the former). — Ed.

N° 6 drawn in favour of Mr. John Hay dated March 29ᵗʰ 1804 Cahokia, for the sum of 159 $ 81½ Cents. On Sect⁷ of war.
N° 3 of which duplicates were signed for 1500$ fifteen hundred dollars on the War Department, in favour of Charles Gregoire or order, dated S⁺ Louis *March 28ᵗʰ 1804.*

[Note by Lewis, in Codex P, p. 133.]

Memorandoms Misscellanious.

Mʳ Labaum informs that a Mʳ Tebaux who is at present with Louasell up the Missouri can give us much infomation in relation to that country.

[Memoranda by Clark, in Codex C, pp. 256–274. — ED.]¹

Baling Invoice of

Sundries for Indians Presents

N°. 30 a Bag Contᵍ
  2 Chief's Coats
  2 hats & plumes
  2 White Shirts
  2 Medals 2ᵈ Size
  2 hair pipes   for first Chiefs of Ottos or Panis
  2 wrist Bands
  2 Arm Bands
  2 Bundles Gartᵍ
  2 pr Leggins
  2 Britch Clouts
  3 Medals 3ᵈ Size
  3 Blue Blankets
  3 prs Scarlet Leggins   2ᵈ Chief
  3 Britch Clouts
  3 Bundles Gartᵍ
  3 Medals 3ᵈ Size
  3 Scarlet Leggins
  3 white Shirts   3ᵈ Chief
  3 Britch Clouts
  3 Bundles Gartᵍ

---

¹ See in vol. vii, Appendix, documents connected with the outfitting of the expedition. — ED.

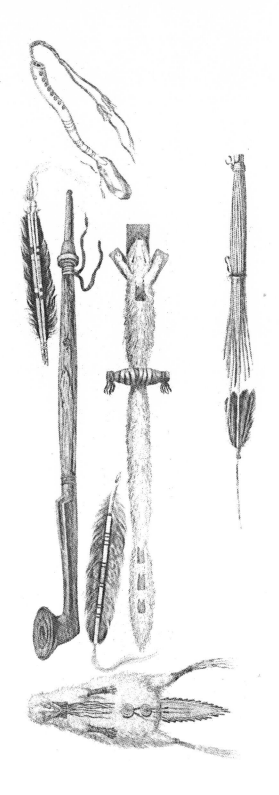

INDIAN UTENSILS AND ARMS

N° 13 a Bag,
  1 Medal 2^d Size
  1 Chiefs Coat
  1 White Shirt
  1 Hat & Plume
  1 Hairpipe
  1 Wrist Band
  1 Arm Band
  1 p^r Scarlet Leggins
  1 Blue Britch Clout
  1 Flag of 2^d sise

} 1st Cheef of Ponkas or any other that may be met this Side of Mahas.

  2 p^r Scarlet Leggins
  4 Blue Britch Clouts
  4 p^r Leggins
14 Silk Handkfs.
26 pocket Ditto
  4 Rolls Ribbon
  4 Callico Shirts
  4 hair pipes
  4 Rolls Gart^g small Bundles
  5 looking Glasses
14 Small Bundles Ribbon
  1 large Roll Gart^g
  1 Blue Blanket

1^{lb} Col^d thread
1^{lb} White do
10 pieces Nonsoprettys

} this part intended for foreign nations. Should any of the three above Nations be met ; the presents of Small articles may be taken from the Bags n°. 33, 15, 42, 9, 36, 16, 45 or 26

N° 33 a bag Cont^g
  1 Chiefs Coat
  1 hat & circle feather
  1 White Shirt
  1 p^r Scarlet Leggins
  1 Britch Clout Scarlet
  1 Large Medal
  1 Small Bundle Gart^g
  1 Silver Moon
  1 Wrist Band
  1 Arm Band
  1 Flag

} for the Maha Chief

1 Medal 2ᵈ Size	⎫
1 Blue Blanket	⎪
1 pʳ Leggin & Britch Clout	⎪
1 Callico Shirt	⎬ for 2ᵈ Dᵒ
1 Wampum hair pipe	⎪
1 Small Bundle tape	⎭
1 Medal 3ᵈ Size	⎫
1 Britch Clout & Shirt	⎬ for 3ᵈ Dᵒ
1 pʳ Leggins, 1 Bundle Gartᵍ	⎭
1 Scarlet Blanket	⎫
1 Roll Ribbon	⎬ for 1ˢᵗ Chief's wife
1 Silk handkf	⎭

1 Callico Shirt	Some Great man
1 tomyhawk	Some Considered man
5 handkfs	1 to each young men
1 Ivory Comb	Some woman of consideration
2 Bunches of thread	1 Skaine to Sundry women
2 Bundles Gartᵍ	to Some young women
1 Doz. Knives 5 Lookᵍ Glasses	1 to Sundry men
2 Bead Neck Laces	for young women
3 Burnᵍ Glasses	to young men
1 Small Bundle Gartᵍ (say Ribbon)	to some Girl
3 pieces Dutch Tape	by ½ pᶜᵉ to young women
10 Maces[1] White Rᵈ Beads	to Girls
2 Maces Sky blue Rᵈ dᵒ	"
3 do Yellow dᵒ	"
3 do Red Dᵒ	"
14 do Yellow Seed Dᵒ	"
5 do Mock Garnets	"
1 Doz Small Hawk Bells	young men
5 large dᵒ	"
6 tinsel hat Bands	"
1 needle case	woman
3 pʳ Glass Ear Bobs	dᵒ
100 Broaches	by 10 to young warriors
6 Silver Rings	to women
9 pʳ Scissars	"
2 Collars of Quill wire	men of Consequence
3 Rolls Snare dᵒ	young men by 1 fathom

[1] Probably a phonetic spelling of "mease," a provincial English word meaning "measure." — Ed.

1 Bunch Knitting pins	by 3, to men ab^t 35 or 40
412 needles	by 10, to women
61 fish hooks	by 4 or 5 to men
½ doz. Iron Combs	to Women
14 thimbles (Steel)	by 1 to women
1^{lb} vermillion in 10 papers	to young warriors
50 Awls	1 at a time to men
½ doz. Jews harps	to young men
3 Razors	to men
1 large flat file	to some elderly man
1 smaller d^o	"
1 Doz fire Steels	to young men
5 Skaines Silk	to women
1 Roll Gartering	by 1 fathom to women
3 pewter look^g glasses	young girls
18 Curtain Rings	young women
1 piece Nonsopretty	by 2 fathoms to women
1 paper Verdigrease	by 1 oz. : to young men

N° 15 The Same (Chiefs dress for Rickaras)
      & one Flag

42 The Same Ditto for Mandanes
      & a Flag of 2^d size

45 The Same, except no Scarlet Britch Clouts blue ones in lieu, and
      no large medals for 1st Chiefs, But Medals of 2^d size & no
      Scarlet Blanket, but 1 Shirt in lieu
      & a Flag 2^d Size

36 The Same as no 45
      & a Flag of 2^d Size
16 The Same as No 45
      & a Flag of 3^d size

26 The Same D^o & N° 9
      (and flag of 3 size) these two Bales haves artillery
      Coats
Two Carrots of Tobacco will be Added to every 1st Chief
      Dress, and 1 Carrot to the 2^{nds} & 3^{ds}
      and 6 Carrots to be given to the Nation
    The follow. Bales intended for foreign Nations: that is those
beyond the mandanes

N° 18, a Bag Containing

1 Chiefs Coat
1 Medal 2ᵈ Size
1 pʳ Leggins
1 Britch Clout } 1ˢᵗ Chief
1 White Shirt
1 Small Bundle Gartˢ
1 lookˢ Glass
1 Burnˢ Glass

1 Callico Shirt
1 Medal 4ᵗʰ & 5ᵗʰ Size
1 Small bundle gartˢ
1 pʳ Leggins } 2ᵈ Chief
1 Britch Clout
1 Wampum hair pipe

1 Medal 5 Size
1 Britch Clout } 3 Chief
1 Shirt
1 Small Bundle Gartˢ

3 Rolls Ear Wire
3 dᵒ Snare Wire
1 " Knitting pins
½ lb. Vermillion in 5 papers
18 Knives
1 Doz: fire Steels
3 pewter lookˢ glasses
24 Curtain Rings
1 piece Nonsopretty
1 Tomyhawk
2 pieces Dutch Tape
3 Bead Necklaces
2 Rolls Ribbon — by fathoms to Girls
4 lookˢ Glasses
4 Burnˢ Dᵒ
10 Maces White Rᵈ Beads
2 do Blue Dᵒ
2 do Yellow Dᵒ
3 do Mock garnets
1 Doz hawk Bells
5 large dᵒ

1 Needle Case
6 Cotton handkᶠˢ
3 Silk Dᵒ to women of Consideration
½ Doz: Iron Combs
10 Skaines thread
3 Doz: Brass thimbles (by 4 or 5 to children
6 pʳ Scissars
1 fine Necklace
2 Romall hkf
6 Silver Rings women of considration
100 Needles
50 Broaches
2 pʳ Bracelets to Some Young Chiefs or Chiefs Sons
3 pʳ Glass Ear Bobs
4 fathoms Red flannel in 2 pieces
1 Gro Awls
2 Wampum Shells

1 Extra Chiefs Coat
1 Medal 3 Size
1 White Shirt
1 Britch Clout
1 look.ᵍ Glass
1 Burn.ᵍ Glass
1 piece fancy handkf
1ᵉᵇ Col.ᵈ thread

} for a 1ˢᵗ Chief

No 14 The Same

No 24 5 Callico Shirts
8 fathoms Red flannel in 4 pieces
2 Bunches Blue Beads
2 d° — Red — d°
10 Small bunches white Seed d°
14 Rolls Wire diff.ᵗ Sizes
7 Bunches White R.ᵈ Beads
17 Maces Mock Garnets
6½ doz : pewter look.ᵍ Glasses
18 p.ʳ of Scissars diff.ᵗ Sizes
1 Extra Bunch of Beads
9 Doz thimbles
6 Medals Dom : Animals
20 d° Sowing
5ᵉᵇ Vermillion in 10 papers Ea.
12ᵉᵇ Silver Rings
2 doz : Small hawk Bells & 2
     Gro : d°
5 Bunches large D°
10/12 Gro Rings
6 Doz : Jews harps
3 Rolls Binding
200 Needles

12 p.ʳ Glass Ear Bobs
2 p.ʳ Braslets
1 Card of Beads
20 Single p.ˢ Narrow Ribbon
1 Needle Case
7 White Metal Earrings
1ᵉᵇ Nuns thread
1ᵉᵇ Col.ᵈ thread
1 pce Bandano Hkf:
3 Britch Clouts
4 Bunches Yellow Beads
4 Silk Handkfs
50 Broaches
4 pce dutch tape
2 pce Nonsopretty
20 fancy handkfs
2 hair pipes
1 Silver Arm Band
1 Wrist Band
1 Tomyhawk
3¾ doz : paper look.ᵍ Glasses
2⅓ Doz : Burn.ᵍ Glasses

N° 3. The Same, Except the followg. articles more — v.ᵗ[1] 1 Gorget,
1 Medal, 1° vermillion, 1 Bunch Bells, 3 hair pipes, 1 Burn.ᵍ glass, 1
Necklace & 1 remnant of Scarlet. and the follow.ᵍ articles, less v.ᵗ
1 Arm & Wrist Band, 1 Bunch Yellow Beads & 1 Callico Shirt

N° 4 a Case
15   Doz : Butchers Knives
5 10/12 " Bone handle D°

3⅓ " Staghandle D°
6 half round files
12 tomyhawks

---

[1] Here and elsewhere apparently an abbreviation for *videlicet.* — ED.

2 Doz: fire Steels   1¾ Doz: large   Dᵒ
7 Doz: Iron Combs   8ˡᵇ Red Lead
1 Gro: Awls   24 Squaw axes
8 Bundles Knitting Pins   2 Bundles of Pieces of Brass & Iron
48 Collar needles   28 fish Spears
2⅓ Doz: Small Scissars   5 large Canoe awls

In a Box of necessary Stores Nᵒ 8 are the follˢ belongˢ to Indian Department 27 fish Spears 5 large Canoe Awls

RECAPITULATION *of the Above fourteen Bags & 1 Box of Indian Presents.* Vɪzᵗ

15 Chief Coats (of which 9 are Artillery Coats)
11 hats & 6 Circle feathers, & 5 Soldier's plumes
18 White Shirts

20 Scarlet   Leggins
 1 Remnant Scarlet
 3 Britch Clouts dᵒ   } equal to 1 pce Scarlet
 3 Blankets   . dᵒ

 3 large Medals
13 2ᵈ Size dᵒ   } Likenesses

71 Medals 3ᵈ & 4ᵗʰ Size   12 Silver Arm Bands
 8 Silver   Moons   12 Wrist Do — Dᵒ
12 Wampum Dᵒ   72 Rings   Silver
24 hairpipes   Dᵒ   1500 Broaches Dᵒ

12 Blue Blankets
20 prs. Leggins   } equal to 3 pces Strouds [1]
45 Britch Clouts

44 Callico Shirts   ½ pce Romall handkf
12 Rolls Gartˢ   10lb threads
 2 doz: Dutch tape   35 Doz: Knives, of which 22 doz.
 2 doz: Nonsoprettys   Butchers Knives
12 Rolls Narrow Ribbon   12 doz. Dutch paper lookˢ glasses
24 Tomyhawks   2 Cards of Bead Necklaces
 8 Ivory Combs   3 fine   Dɪtto
 7 pces fancy handkf: 7¾ doz. Burning Glasses
 5 pce, Bandano Dᵒ   120 Small Maces white Rᵈ Beads

---

[1] "Stroud, Gloucestershire, was noted for its woollen manufactures. The fur companies bought largely of its coloured blankets, and its name became a trade-mark for those of the best quality." — BAIN (*Henry's Travels*, p. 116).

7	Bunches Sky Blue	Beads
17	D° Yellow . .	D°
20	d° White Seed .	D°
4	d° Red . . .	D°
1	D° Green . .	D°
10	D° Yellow Seed .	D°
8	D° Mock Garnets or 80 Maces	

8 ⅓ Doz : large Size hawk Bells
6 Gro : Small   D°
3 Doz : Tinsel hat Bands
48 pr Glass Ear Bobs
8 pr Do Braslets
12½ Doz : Scissars large & Small
30 Collars Brass Wire, quill Size
16 D° " Ear Wire
34 Bunches Snare D°
18 Bunches Knitting Pins
3900 Needles Assorted
12 Needle Cases
about 500 fish hooks
12 Doz : Iron Combs

9 ⅓ Doz : taylors Steel thimbles
19lb Vermillion
5¾ Gro : Awls
3 Doz : Razors
22 files
12 Doz : fire Steels
40 Skaines Silk
18 Doz : Pewter look^g Glasses
3 Gro : Curtain Rings
10lb Verdigrease or near ab^t
24 fathoms of Red flannel in 12
   pieces = to a piece of flannel
48 Collar Needles
8lb Red Lead
24 Squaw axes
2 Bundles of pieces of Brass & Iron
55 fish Spears
5 large Canoe Awls
130 Pigtail Tobacco w^t 63^{lb}
176 Carrots tobacco ab^t 500 [lbs. ?
   — ED.] in 9 Bales.
26 Silver Ear Rings

BAILING INVOICE *of Sundries, being necessary Stores Viz.*

N° 1. a Bale Cont^g
4 Blankets
3 fine Cloth Jackets
6 flannel Shirts
3 pr Russia Over Alls
5 frocks
4 White Shirts
200 flints
2 Spike Gimblets
2 Small D°

12 pr Socks
2 tin Boxes, with 2 me^m Books
   in Ea.
½ lb Col^d thread
1 Romall Handkf
1 Paper Ink Powder
1 pce Catgut
3 Setts Rifle Locks
1 Screw Driver

No. 2. The Same

" 3 The Same

" 4 The Same, except 1 p. trowsers less and 1 flannel Shirt in lieu

No. 5 a Bale
4 Blankets
1 Cloth Jacket
4 flannel Shirts
2 frocks
2 Watch Coats
50 flints
1 White Shirt
1 Spike Gimblet
6 pr Socks
½ lb Nuns thread
1 pce Catgut
1 pce Silk Handkf
4 Quire Comn fool's Cap
9 half quires post paper
4 Sticks Sealing wax
1 Romall Handkf:
1 Vice
1 Sett of Gunlocks
1 Nipper

" 6 The Same, except 1 watch Coat less & 3 Cloth overalls, 2 pr ox hide Shoes, ½ m fish hooks, & 1 Gro: awls more.

" 7 a Bale
6 Blankets
1 Watch Coat
2 pr ox hide Shoes
4 papers of fish hooks
1 Gro Awls
1 Vice Smallest Size
1 Screw Driver
1 quire paper fools Cap
5 Romall Handkfs
1 fancy Do
1 Drawing Knife
3 pr Socks
3 pr Cloth overalls
2 flannel Shirts
2 frocks
1 pr English Shoes
1 fine Cloth Jacket
11 Cartridge Box Belts
¼ lb Nuns thread
25 flints

" 8 a Box
27 fish Spears
the Glue
Sundry Iron Works for Guns
3 Screw Augurs
62 files difft Sizes
1 Dradle [treadle — Ed.]
1 Brace
5 Chizels
5 large Canoe Awls
2 Gimblets
Primg wires & Brushes
Capt: Lewis Gunlock
1 Bundle Iron Wire
18 Axes
2 howels
1 Adze
Iron Weights

RECAPITULATION *of Seven Bales & 1 Box of necessary Stores Viz:*

30 Blankets
15 fine Cloth Jackets
35 flannel Shirts
11 pr Russia Overalls
7 pr Cloth Ditto
26 frocks
18 White Shirts
925 flints
11 Spike Gimblets
8 Small Do

63 pr Socks
8 tin Boxes with mem.ᵐ Books
2 ˡᵇ Colᵈ thread
¼ lb Nuns thread
11 Romall Handkf
4 papers Ink powder
6 pces Catgut
14 Setts Gunlocks
5 Screw Drivers
2 pᶜˢ Silk Handkf
9 quires fools Cap Paper
18 half quires post
8 Sticks sealing Wax
3 vices
2 Nippers

4 Watch Coats
4 pr. ox hide Shoes
1 pr English Do
2 Gro Awls
1000 fish hooks
1 fancy handkf.
1 Drawᵍ Knife
11 Cartridge Box Belts
the Glue
3 screw Augurs
62 files diffᵗ Sizes
5 Chizels
18 Axes
2 howels
1 adze

[Memoranda by Clark, in Codex N, pp. 1, 2. — Eᴅ.]

From Sᵗ Louis 1806   Memorandum of articles fo[r]warded to Louis-
ville by Capᵗ Clark in care of Mr. Wolpards 1 s.

one large Box Containing

4 large Horns of the Bighorn
    animal
2 Sceletens dᵒ   dᵒ   dᵒ
2 Skins horns & bon[e]s of dᵒ
4 Mandan Robes of Buffalow
1 Indian Blanket of the Sheep
1 Sheep Skin of the rocky
    mountains
1 Brarow Skin
3 Bear Skins of the White
    Speces

3 barking Squir[e]ls
2 Skins of the big horn
1 Mule or black tail Deer Skin
1 Hat made by the Clatsops
    Indians
2 Indian Baskets
4 buffalow horns
1 Tigor Cat Skin Coat
1 long box of sundery articles
1 Tin box containing Medicine
    &c. &c. &c. &c.

a Small Box of papers

Books and Sundery Small articles

a Hat Box

containing the 4 vol⁵ of the Deckinsery [Dictionary] of arts an[d] ciences   two Indian wallets   a tale of the black taile Deer of the Ocean & a Vulters quill with a buffalow Coat.

Cap⁴ Lewis forward to Washington by Lieu⁴ Peters in Box N⁰ 1
6 Skins and Sceletens complete of the mountain ram, three male and 3 female

    1 Blacktail Deer Skin   3 Bear Skins
    1 Sheep Skin   1 White Wolf
    4 Barking Squirels   3 beaver tales

N° 2

2 Boxes Containing Various articles
1 Tin Case   d°   d°
1 air gun
4 Robins
1 Clatsop hat

END OF LEWIS AND CLARK JOURNALS

The Original Journals of the Lewis and Clark Expedition

8 Volume Set: Tradepaper ISBN: 158218-651-0   Hardcover ISBN: 1-58218-660-X

Individual Titles:

Volume I Parts 1 & 2
Tradepaper ISBN: 1-58218-652-9   Hardcover ISBN: 1-58218-661-8
Part 1 - Journals and Orderly Book of Lewis and Clark, from River Dubois to the Vermilion River Jan. 30, 1804 - Aug. 24, 1804.
Part 2 - Journals and Order Book of Lewis and Clark, from the Vermilion River to Two-Thousand-Mile Creek Aug. 25, 1804 - May 5, 1805.

Volume II Parts 1 & 2
Tradepaper ISBN: 1-58218-653-7   Hardcover ISBN: 1-58218-662-6
Part 1 - Journals and Orderly Book of Lewis and Clark, from Two -Thousand-Mile Creek to the Great Falls of the Missouri May 6 - June 20, 1805.
Part 2 - Journals and Orderly Book of Lewis and Clark, from the Great Falls of the Missouri to the Shoshoni Camp on Lembi River June 21 - August 20, 1805.

Volume III Parts 1 & 2
Tradepaper ISBN: 1-58218-654-5   Hardcover ISBN: 1-58218-663-4
Part 1 - Journals and Orderly Book of Lewis and Clark, from the Shoshoni Camp on Lembi River to the Encampment on the Columbia River near the Mouth of the Umatilla River.
August 21, 1805 - October 20, 1805.
Part 2 - Journals and Orderly Book of Lewis and Clark, from the Encampment on the Columbia River near the Mouth of the Umatilla River to Fort Clatsop October 21, 1805 - January 20, 1806.

Volume IV Parts 1 & 2
Tradepaper ISBN: 1-58218-655-3   Hardcover ISBN: 1-58218-664-2
Part 1 - Journals and Orderly Book of Lewis and Clark, from Fort Clatsop (preparation for the start home) to Fort Clatsop, January 21 - May 17, 1806.
Part 2 - Journals and Orderly Book of Lewis and Clark, from Fort Clatsop (preparation for the start home) to Musquetoe Creek March 18 - May 7, 1806.

Volume V Parts 1 & 2
Tradepaper ISBN 1-58218-656-1   Hardcover ISBN: 1-58218-665-0
Part 1 - Journals of Lewis and Clark, from Musquetoe Creek to Travellers Rest.
May 8 - July 2, 1806.
Part 2 - Journals of Lewis and Clark, from Travellers Rest to St. Louis.
July 3 - September 26, 1806.

Volume VI Parts 1 & 2
Tradepaper ISBN: 1-58218-657-X   Hardcover ISBN: 1-58218-666-9
Part 1 - Scientific Data accompanying the Journals of Lewis and Clark; Geography, Ethnology, Zoology.
Part 2 - Botany, Mineralogy, Meteorology, Astronomy, and Miscellaneous Memoranda.

Volume VII Parts 1 & 2
Tradepaper ISBN: 1-58218-658-8   Hardcover ISBN: 1-58218-667-7
Part 1 - Journals of Charles Floyd and Joseph Whitehouse; Appendix.
Part 2 - Appendix; Index.

Atlas -Tradepaper ISBN: 1-58218-659-6   Hardcover ISBN: 1-58218-668-5

Printed in the United States
31015LVS00004B/76-84